Liberty and Equality

American Political Thought

Wilson Carey McWilliams and Lance Banning
Founding Editors

Liberty and Equality

The American Conversation

Edited by

S. Adam Seagrave

University Press of Kansas

Published by the University Press of Kansas (Lawrence, Kansas 66045), which was organized by the Kansas Board of Regents and is operated and funded by Emporia State University, Fort Hays State University, Kansas State University, Pittsburg State University, the University of Kansas, and Wichita State University

Library of Congress Cataloging-in-Publication Data

Liberty and equality: the American conversation / edited by S. Adam Seagrave
pages cm – (American political thought)
Includes index.
ISBN 978-0-7006-2126-2 (hardback)
ISBN 978-0-7006-2174-3 (paperback)
ISBN 978-0-7006-2162-0 (ebook)
1. Liberty—United States. 2. Equality—United States. 3. Democracy—United States.
4. United States—History. 5. United States—Politics and government. I. Seagrave, S. Adam.
JC599.U5L474 2015
320.973.01—dc23 2015013778

British Library Cataloguing-in-Publication Data is available.

Printed in the United States of America

10 9 8 7 6 5 4 3 2 1

The paper used in this publication is recycled and contains 30 percent postconsumer waste. It is acid free and meets the minimum requirements of the American National Standard for Permanence of Paper for Printed Library Materials Z39.48-1992.

To Olivia
You are my sunshine

Contents

Acknowledgments

A book like this one does not come into being without the coordinated work of many expert hands. I must first thank Fred Woodward, without whose early and consistent support and advice the idea for this book would never have been realized. Each of the contributors is a model of what is best in academic scholarship, having agreed to lend their formidable learning and talent to this project purely for the sake of furthering our understanding of important subjects. Michael Zuckert was particularly instrumental, providing invaluable assistance and counsel on many points in addition to contributing his essay.

Lewis Hoss provided meticulous and efficient assistance at various stages of development, as did Stephen Clouse. Generous funding for the completion of this book was provided by the Earhart Foundation as well as a Northern Illinois University Research and Artistry grant. All translations of Tocqueville's *Democracy in America* are from the Liberty Fund edition, four volumes, edited by Eduardo Nolla, translated by James T. Schleifer (Indianapolis, IN: Liberty Fund, 2010) and are reprinted here with the publisher's permission.

Liberty and Equality

Introduction

Nearly everyone admits the profound effect of ideas on society and politics, even if the effect of this or that set of ideas on a given society or particular political situation is often a matter of debate. As one prominent scholar recently put it, political development over time is like an ongoing "spiral" in which politics both drives and is driven by the formation and re-formation of ideas.[1] Although this interaction would seem common to all human societies—because all or nearly all human beings regularly act under the influence of their ideas about the context within which they act—the American case may indeed present an "exceptional" example of this phenomenon.

This is, at any rate, what Alexander Hamilton claimed in his first words as Publius in *The Federalist*. According to Hamilton, it appeared to have been "reserved" to the American people to determine "whether societies of men are really capable or not of establishing good government from reflection and choice, or whether they are forever destined to depend for their political constitutions on accident and force." As Alexis de Tocqueville would later comment in his introduction to *Democracy in America*, the circumstances surrounding the early development of American political society were in point of fact unique, even to a great extent unprecedented in recorded history, and it was as a direct result of this uniqueness that Tocqueville found the study of America so instructive for the Europeans of his time. The "societies of men" on the European continent—and, for that matter, nearly every society one could point to in human history—simply could not escape the intermixture of "accident and force" in the development of their political constitutions. Political societies tend, as political philosophers from Aristotle to John Locke generally agreed, to grow organically out of extended families and to be governed automatically by a patriarchal figure; after this unreflective and unchosen path is begun, "accident and force" appear inescapable realities of the future development of such societies.

To use an analogy suggested by Tocqueville, European political societies were like individual plants in a crowded rain forest; although some measure of "reflection and choice" might inform the politics of such societies in the same way sunlight fights its way through the canopy to reach plants below, these plants are necessarily limited by the presence of their towering neighbors just as political societies are limited by the presence of entrenched structures of social and political influence. Such plants can only hope to grow unimpeded by the uprooting of their surrounding predecessors; and this is precisely what was attempted with disastrous results in the French Revolution.

American society, on the other hand, was like a plant in a greenhouse; having been "transplanted" from its native and inherently constraining surroundings, it was free to pursue a course of growth nourished to an unprecedented extent by "reflection and choice." American society had no history at all during the time of its development in the seventeenth and eighteenth centuries and therefore no competing or constraining impediments in the form of long-entrenched centers of social and political power to uproot before pursuing its desired course of growth.[2] According to Tocqueville, America's more significant "revolution" occurred, as Peter S. Onuf explains, peacefully and in slow motion.[3]

If there is any truth to the various claims of "American exceptionalism" that ring throughout American history up to the present time, it would seem to lie first and foremost in this account of our origins, constructed jointly by Publius and Tocqueville at the beginnings of their respective great works.[4] The relatively free reign given to "reflection and choice" in the development of the American constitution[5] throughout our history has, moreover, had the effect of blending and intertwining philosophy and politics, the abstract and the practical, political thought and development, to an extent truly unique among the nations of the world. As a result of this intertwining, one might very well argue that American political thought possesses both unity and distinctiveness to an extent rarely, if ever, seen in human history.

There have certainly been other momentous flowerings of philosophical inquiry clearly associated with particular political societies or nations, such as Confucianism in China, the Scottish Enlightenment, or German idealism, to name only a few. In these and other comparable cases, however, the practical political dimension was more of a consequence or corollary than a primary focus; such intellectual movements never served as recognized public doctrines informing the construction and maintenance of a political society throughout its entire history. Politics and philosophy almost invariably grow up separately from each other and proceed along parallel tracks; although they undoubtedly exert a mutual influence on each other over time, their direct and short-term interactions are much more often antagonistic than cooperative. One need only recall the famous example of Socrates, regularly repeated in various ways throughout the world since, for a conspicuous reminder of this point.

In America, however, the Socratic equivalents were not executed—they were, instead, lauded as almost godlike founders and elected to the highest political positions. Of course, this is partly explained by the fact that the early American intellectual giants were not really Socratic equivalents at all; they shared Socrates's concern for the pursuit of wisdom, to be sure, but they bent this pursuit to the service of practical political concerns and tethered their philosophical inquiry tightly to the concrete situations in which they found themselves. They went much further in this direction even than Cicero, who managed to compose ambitious philosophical treatises to stand alongside his illustrious political career. Cicero emulated Plato in writing philosophical dialogues such as the *Republic* and the *Laws*; the American founders' crowning literary achievement, by contrast, was *The Federalist*, a work directed to an immediate political context.[6]

To a remarkable extent, American politics has always been thoughtful, and American thought has always been political. Our greatest minds tend to concern themselves with politics, and our greatest political moments are driven by and immortalized through philosophically inflected rhetoric and discourse. This is why the growing academic field of American political thought is equally at home in political science and history departments. One simply cannot understand American history without engaging the abstract, philosophical dimension informing American political discourse and inspiring American social movements; similarly, one cannot understand American political philosophical principles and the writings of their greatest exponents without paying attention to the political historical context with which they were themselves closely concerned.[7] The very continuity of time and of the American national identity over time has, in this way, produced in some measure the unity of American political thought; to the extent American history is unique, so too is the political thought inextricably linked to it.

There is, moreover, even more to this story. As Tocqueville also argued in his introduction, the development of American society had occurred more or less in step with a larger, worldwide social progression toward increasing equality or "democracy." The "democratic revolution" occurring throughout the West had progressed to its furthest point in America because of the unique, greenhouse-like conditions of American society. America was, for Tocqueville, a sort of prototype of an emergent democratic age, situated on the cutting edge of the new, modern world. America would be an important guide through this modern world, enlightening the inevitable historical trend toward democracy with the "reflection and choice" enabled by its unique circumstances and given political efficacy through the vitality of its political traditions. America, unlike his native France, could enter the new democratic age uninhibited by the negative consequences of entirely rejecting the old.

This American opportunity to build a modern political society without having to destroy a premodern one is reflected—unsurprisingly, given the unique linkages described above—in the manner in which American political thought, though recognizably and undeniably modern, has appropriated and incorporated certain elements of premodern political thought. In terms of Benjamin Constant's famous essay, for example, Americans from the time of the founding have always understood the concept of liberty to include versions of both the "liberty of the ancients" and the "liberty of the moderns": both the liberty to engage in collective self-government and the liberty to engage in a private "pursuit of happiness."[8] Interpreters of the American founding have found influences of classical republicanism extending all the way back to Cicero and Aristotle alongside the more prominent influences of modern political philosophers such as Locke and Montesquieu. The famously realist James Madison asserted in *Federalist* 57 that "the aim of every political constitution is, or ought to be, first, to obtain for rulers men who possess most wisdom to discern, and most virtue to pursue, the common good of the society," a statement that could have readily been said by Aristotle or St. Thomas Aquinas. Just as American society found a way to enter Tocqueville's democratic age without having to violently overturn the preceding one, so American political thought characteristically strives to secure modern insights without ignoring or blindly denigrating medieval or ancient ones.

Precisely this sort of measured, balanced approach—an approach uniquely enabled both by the circumstances surrounding the development of American society and the timing of this development at the dawn of a new age—is reflected in the unifying theme of this book. As the standard-bearer for what Tocqueville identified as the irresistible march of democracy throughout the world, American political thought has always been centrally concerned with equality. This equality was originally and primarily understood in rather precise terms, following Locke, as the equal possession of natural rights to life, liberty, and the pursuit of happiness.[9] In this way the idea of liberty enters into the definition of equality, and the two are, as Tocqueville eloquently explains in *Democracy in America*, inextricably conjoined: equality means equal natural liberty.

This simple equation involving liberty and equality has served as a sort of mathematical function according to which American political institutions have been built and American political discourse has been guided from the beginning until the present. The simplicity of the equation belies, however, the extreme complexity involved in actually plotting out the corresponding curve. Even American history, after all, has not been able to escape the influence of "accident and force," and no amount of collective "reflection" on the abstract ideas of liberty and equality has been able to permanently clarify or settle the meaning and proper application of either.

The conjunction of liberty and equality in American political thought is recognizable and distinctive, but it is also fluid and dynamic: it is, as the subtitle of this book affirms, the unifying inspiration for an ongoing conversation rather than a static assertion. The existence and vitality of this conversation throughout American history is a testament to the truth of Publius's assertion; we have largely been able, thus far, to direct our political course according to "reflection and choice" rather than being at the mercy of "accident and force." Even the moments in our history that would seem to be prime examples of "accident and force"—the institution of slavery and the resulting Civil War—were turned at the hands of Frederick Douglass, Abraham Lincoln, and many others into golden opportunities to move this conversation forward toward a truer understanding of liberty and equality. As Tocqueville remarkably and insightfully said, "I find that they establish the advantages of equality much less by democracy than by slavery," and it was by finally defeating slavery and race-based inequality on the battlefield of ideas that the American conversation secured its most important advance to date.[10]

As the case of slavery and racism shows, the American conversation about liberty and equality is not an aimless or empty one; the participants in this conversation typically think their understanding is truer than that of their opponents, and the balance of arguments in debate can lead to real progress in our understanding of these difficult concepts and their proper application. The possibility of real progress does not, however, amount to an inevitability, and its foremost contributors have always acknowledged that the American conversation about liberty and equality should not occur in isolation from related conversations persisting throughout the history of ideas. Our own, distinctive conversation about liberty and equality itself has a place amid wider, transhistorical conversations regarding our status within, and relationship to, the world in which we live.

This book may be viewed as a summary of American history told through ideas rather than events; or, alternatively, as an inquiry into the abstract ideas of liberty and equality through the concrete lens of American history. Each chapter contains some of the most illuminating and influential contributions to the American conversation about liberty and equality organized according to the most important themes to which these contributions have historically been addressed: constitutional principles (democracy and representation, federalism, and separation of powers), religion, and race. These primary sources have been selected on the basis of the quality of their impact upon understandings of liberty and equality as these concepts relate to the theme of the chapter. They are intended to be a representative, but not exhaustive, sampling of the best American political thought sources on each topic. These sources are paired with extended reflections written by a few of the very best living scholars and practitioners of American political thought.

Peter S. Onuf's essay in Chapter 1 lays important conceptual groundwork for what follows, showing how the conversation between Tocqueville and Jefferson on the ideas of liberty and equality provides an extraordinarily illuminating basis for understanding the origins and trajectory of the American experiment in liberal democracy. The conversation Onuf relates contains the seeds of many of the most important insights and controversies of American political thought: the nature and meaning of American "exceptionalism," the place of assertions of transhistorical truth in the context of ongoing historical development, the relationship between "positive" or active liberty and "negative" or defensive liberty, and the meaning of human equality both as it relates to the abstract idea of liberty and as it is applied to the practical problems of aristocracy and, especially, slavery.

In the first section of Chapter 2, Ralph Ketcham highlights the significance of the "bottom-up" approach to democratic politics that both Tocqueville and Jefferson enthusiastically embraced. Ketcham focuses upon a crucial perennial problem for democracies: namely, how they can provide the sort of "good government" that historically has seemed to require some amount of political inequality. Ketcham's answer draws on certain strands of antifederalist thought, as well as that of Benjamin Franklin and Thomas Jefferson, in arguing a certain amount of "virtue and public spirit" is indeed necessary to sustain the elusive compound of "good democratic government" at which the American founders aimed.

In the next section of Chapter 2, Alan Gibson and James H. Read provide an illuminating explanation of how the "Father of the Constitution," James Madison, approached one of the most intractable difficulties of American constitutionalism: federalism, or the balance between the state and national governments. Gibson and Read insightfully connect Madison's extremely subtle and "complex balancing act" on the issue of federalism with his "broader belief that liberty was endangered by both too much and too little government power." The close connection between federalism and liberty as well as the incredible fragility of both were clearly demonstrated, Gibson and Read point out, by our struggle with slavery before, during, and after the Civil War.

Michael P. Zuckert's essay in the final section of Chapter 2 continues the focus on Madison begun in Gibson and Read's essay on federalism and complements Ketcham's analysis of representation and democracy in the first section of the chapter. Zuckert persuasively corrects the long-standing "textbook" account of separation of powers, arguing that the purpose of separation of powers is not to create checks and balances that will thwart the functioning of government but rather to ensure the rule of law as well as the production of the "qualities necessary to good governance" in the different parts of the government itself. Zuckert elaborates an "institutional republicanism" embraced by Madison and the other constitutional framers in which the "institution makes the man" and therefore in which good government "does not depend on preformed individuals of any particular sort." The apparent tension between this "institutional republicanism" and Ketcham's emphasis upon the importance of personal and social prerequisites for good democratic government echoes one of the central debates of American political thought, including both the Federalist/Anti-Federalist debate as well as the prior tension Onuf relates between Jefferson's Declaration of Independence and Tocqueville's *Democracy in America*.

Wilfred M. McClay's essay on religious liberty in Chapter 3 resonates with Tocqueville's treatment of religion in *Democracy in America* as the single most important social prerequisite for good democratic government, placing this point within the context of the controversy over the proper relationship between religion and politics that has animated American history from its beginning to the present. McClay provides five different arguments in support of the special status of religion as well as of the deferential attention it has traditionally been granted in the United States, and concludes by intriguingly highlighting the connection between religious liberty and the issue of American slavery and racism through the famous words of the notoriously skeptical Thomas Jefferson.

In the final chapter, Peter Myers provides a sweeping and profound account of the history of slavery and its legacy of racism extending from the founding to the present. Myers's concluding essay mirrors and complements Onuf's introductory one by reflecting upon the juxtaposition of the "uniquely propitious opportunity" presented by the American situation with the "unique challenge race has posed" to the American fulfillment of this opportunity. As Tocqueville had suggested and as Lincoln famously affirmed in his Gettysburg Address, it would be through our struggle with slavery and racism that the exceptional and world-historical significance of the American experiment in liberal democracy would be either secured or lost—and, according to Myers's cautiously optimistic conclusion, we have solid grounds for hope that it will indeed be secured.

Taken together, these reflective essays and primary sources are intended to contribute to the important task of revealing and assessing the character, content, and significance of American political thought taken as a whole. American political thought is not a collection of doctrines but a living conversation; it is a conversation that is fundamentally about the ideas of liberty and equality; and it is itself one voice in a larger conversation embracing all nations and peoples throughout intellectual history. Armed with this broad view of our political tradition as Americans, we will be better equipped as citizens and scholars to contribute meaningfully to it.

1 • Liberty and Equality: The American Ideas

DECLARATION OF INDEPENDENCE

When, in the course of human events, it becomes necessary for one people to dissolve the political bonds which have connected them with another, and to assume among the powers of the earth, the separate and equal station to which the laws of nature and of nature's God entitle them, a decent respect to the opinions of mankind requires that they should declare the causes which impel them to the separation.

We hold these truths to be self-evident, that all men are created equal, that they are endowed by their Creator with certain unalienable rights, that among these are life, liberty and the pursuit of happiness. That to secure these rights, governments are instituted among men, deriving their just powers from the consent of the governed. That whenever any form of government becomes destructive of these ends, it is the right of the people to alter or to abolish it, and to institute new government, laying its foundation on such principles and organizing its powers in such form, as to them shall seem most likely to effect their safety and happiness. Prudence, indeed, will dictate that governments long established should not be changed for light and transient causes; and accordingly all experience hath shown that mankind are more disposed to suffer, while evils are sufferable, than to right themselves by abolishing the forms to which they are accustomed. But when a long train of abuses and usurpations, pursuing invariably the same object evinces a design to reduce them under absolute despotism, it is their right, it is their duty, to throw off such government, and to provide new guards for their future security.

Such has been the patient sufferance of these colonies; and such is now the necessity which constrains them to alter their former systems of government. The history of the present King of Great Britain is a history of repeated injuries and usurpations, all having in direct object the establishment of an absolute tyranny over these states. To prove this, let facts be submitted to a candid world.

He has refused his assent to laws, the most wholesome and necessary for the public good.

He has forbidden his governors to pass laws of immediate and pressing importance, unless suspended in their operation till his assent should be obtained; and when so suspended, he has utterly neglected to attend to them.

He has refused to pass other laws for the accommodation of large districts of people, unless those people would relinquish the right of representation in the legislature, a right inestimable to them and formidable to tyrants only.

He has called together legislative bodies at places unusual, uncomfortable, and distant from the depository of their public records, for the sole purpose of fatiguing them into compliance with his measures.

He has dissolved representative houses repeatedly, for opposing with manly firmness his invasions on the rights of the people.

He has refused for a long time, after such dissolutions, to cause others to be elected; whereby the legislative powers, incapable of annihilation, have returned to the people at large for their exercise; the state remaining in the meantime exposed to all the dangers of invasion from without, and convulsions within.

He has endeavored to prevent the population of these states; for that purpose obstructing the laws for naturalization of foreigners; refusing to pass others to encourage their migration hither, and raising the conditions of new appropriations of lands.

He has obstructed the administration of justice, by refusing his assent to laws for establishing judiciary powers.

He has made judges dependent on his will alone, for the tenure of their offices, and the amount and payment of their salaries.

He has erected a multitude of new offices, and sent hither swarms of officers to harass our people, and eat out their substance.

He has kept among us, in times of peace, standing armies without the consent of our legislature.

He has affected to render the military independent of and superior to civil power.

He has combined with others to subject us to a jurisdiction foreign to our constitution, and unacknowledged by our laws; giving his assent to their acts of pretended legislation:

- For quartering large bodies of armed troops among us:
- For protecting them, by mock trial, from punishment for any murders which they should commit on the inhabitants of these states:
- For cutting off our trade with all parts of the world:
- For imposing taxes on us without our consent:
- For depriving us in many cases, of the benefits of trial by jury:

- For transporting us beyond seas to be tried for pretended offenses:
- For abolishing the free system of English laws in a neighboring province, establishing therein an arbitrary government, and enlarging its boundaries so as to render it at once an example and fit instrument for introducing the same absolute rule in these colonies:
- For taking away our charters, abolishing our most valuable laws, and altering fundamentally the forms of our governments:
- For suspending our own legislatures, and declaring themselves invested with power to legislate for us in all cases whatsoever.

He has abdicated government here, by declaring us out of his protection and waging war against us.

He has plundered our seas, ravaged our coasts, burned our towns, and destroyed the lives of our people.

He is at this time transporting large armies of foreign mercenaries to complete the works of death, desolation and tyranny, already begun with circumstances of cruelty and perfidy scarcely paralleled in the most barbarous ages, and totally unworthy the head of a civilized nation.

He has constrained our fellow-citizens taken captive on the high seas to bear arms against their country, to become the executioners of their friends and brethren, or to fall themselves by their hands.

He has excited domestic insurrections amongst us, and has endeavored to bring on the inhabitants of our frontiers, the merciless Indian savages, whose known rule of warfare, is undistinguished destruction of all ages, sexes and conditions.

In every stage of these oppressions we have petitioned for redress in the most humble terms: our repeated petitions have been answered only by repeated injury. A prince, whose character is thus marked by every act which may define a tyrant, is unfit to be the ruler of a free people.

Nor have we been wanting in attention to our British brethren. We have warned them from time to time of attempts by their legislature to extend an unwarrantable jurisdiction over us. We have reminded them of the circumstances of our emigration and settlement here. We have appealed to their native justice and magnanimity, and we have conjured them by the ties of our common kindred to disavow these usurpations, which would inevitably interrupt our connections and correspondence. We must, therefore, acquiesce in the necessity, which denounces our separation, and hold them, as we hold the rest of mankind, enemies in war, in peace friends.

We, therefore, the representatives of the United States of America, in General Congress assembled, appealing to the Supreme Judge of the world for the rectitude of our intentions, do, in the name, and by the authority of the good people of these colonies, solemnly publish and declare, that these united colonies are, and of right ought to be free and independent states; that they are absolved from all allegiance to the British Crown, and that all political connection between them and the state of Great Britain, is and ought to be totally dissolved; and that as free and independent states, they have full power to levy war, conclude peace, contract alliances, establish commerce, and to do all other acts and things which independent states may of right do. And for the support of this declaration, with a firm reliance on the protection of Divine Providence, we mutually pledge to each other our lives, our fortunes and our sacred honor.

SLAVERY PARAGRAPH FROM THOMAS JEFFERSON'S DRAFT OF THE DECLARATION OF INDEPENDENCE

He has waged cruel war against human nature itself, violating its most sacred rights of life and liberty in the persons of a distant people who never offended him, captivating & carrying them into slavery in another hemisphere, or to incur miserable death in their transportation thither. This piratical warfare, the opprobrium of INFIDEL Powers, is the warfare of the CHRISTIAN king of Great Britain. Determined to keep open a market where MEN should be bought & sold, he has prostituted his negative for suppressing every legislative attempt to prohibit or to restrain this execrable commerce. And that this assemblage of horrors might want no fact of distinguished die, he is now exciting those very people to rise in arms among us, and to purchase that liberty of which he has deprived them, by murdering the people on whom he also obtruded them: thus paying off former crimes committed against the LIBERTIES of one people, with crimes which he urges them to commit against the LIVES of another.

THOMAS JEFFERSON TO ROGER WEIGHTMAN

June 24, 1826

The kind invitation I received from you on the part of the citizens of the city of Washington, to be present with them at their celebration of the 50th anniversary of American independence; as one of the surviving signers of an instrument pregnant with our own, and the fate of the world, is most flattering to myself, and heightened by the honorable accompaniment proposed for the comfort of such a journey. It adds sensibly to the sufferings of sickness, to be deprived by it of a personal participation in the rejoicings of that day. But acquiescence is a duty, under circumstances not placed among those we are permitted to controul. I should, indeed, with peculiar delight, have met and exchanged there congratulations personally with the small band, the remnant of that host of worthies, who joined with us on that day, in the bold and doubtful election we were to make for our country, between submission or the sword; and to have enjoyed with them the consolatory fact, that our fellow-citizens, after half a century of experience and prosperity, continue to approve the choice we made. May it be to the world, what I believe it will be, (to some parts sooner, to others later, but finally to all,) the Signal of arousing men to burst the chains, under which monkish ignorance and superstition had persuaded them to bind themselves, and to assume the blessings & security of self-government. That form which we have substituted, restores the free right to the unbounded exercise of reason and freedom of opinion. All eyes are opened, or opening, to the rights of man. The general spread of the light of science has already laid open to every view, the palpable truth, that the mass of mankind has not been born with saddles on their backs, nor a favored few booted and spurred, ready to ride them legitimately, by the grace of god. These are grounds of hope for others. For ourselves, let the annual return of this day forever refresh our recollections of these rights, and an undiminished devotion to them.

DEMOCRACY IN AMERICA, AUTHOR'S INTRODUCTION TO VOLUME I, PART 1

Among the new objects that attracted my attention during my stay in the United States, none struck me more vividly than the equality of conditions. I discovered without difficulty the prodigious influence that this primary fact exercises on the march of society; it gives a certain direction to the public mind, a certain turn to the laws; to those governing, new maxims, and particular habits to the governed.

Soon I recognized that this same fact extends its influence far beyond political mores and laws, and that it has no less dominion over civil society, than over government: it creates opinions, gives birth to sentiments, suggests customs and modifies all that it does not produce.

Therefore, as I studied American society, I saw more and more, in equality of conditions, the generating fact from which each particular fact seemed to derive, and I rediscovered it constantly before me as a central point where all of my observations came together.

Then I turned my thought back toward our hemisphere, and it seemed to me that I perceived something analogous to the spectacle that the New World offered me. I saw equality of conditions that, without having reached its extreme limits as in the United States, approached those limits more each day; and this same democracy that reigned in American societies, appeared to me to advance rapidly toward power in Europe.

From that moment, I conceived the idea of the book you are about to read.

A great democratic revolution is taking place among us; everyone sees it, but not everyone judges it in the same way. Some consider it as something new and, taking it for an accident, they hope still to be able to stop it; while others judge it irresistible, because it seems to them the most continuous, oldest and most permanent fact known in history.

I look back for a moment to what France was seven hundred years ago: I find it divided up among a small number of families who own the land and govern the inhabitants; at that time, the right to command is passed down with inheritances from generation to generation; men have only a single way to act on one another, force; you discover only a single source of power, landed property.

But then the political power of the clergy becomes established and is soon expanding. The clergy opens its ranks to all, to the poor and to the rich, to the commoner and to the lord; equality begins to penetrate through the Church into the government, and someone who would have vegetated as a serf in eternal slavery takes his place as a priest among nobles and often goes to take a seat above kings.

As society becomes more civilized and more stable with time, the different relationships among men become more complicated and more numerous. The need for civil laws is intensely felt. Then jurists arise; they emerge from the dark precinct of the courts and from the dusty recess of the clerks' offices, and they go to sit in the court of the prince, alongside feudal barons covered with ermine and iron.

Kings ruin themselves in great enterprises; nobles exhaust themselves in private wars; commoners enrich themselves in commerce. The influence of money begins to make itself felt in affairs of State. Trade is a new source of power, and financiers become a political power that is scorned and flattered.

Little by little, enlightenment spreads; the taste for literature and the arts reawakens; then the mind becomes an element of success; knowledge is a means of government; intelligence, a social force; men of letters reach public affairs.

As new roads to achieve power are found, however, we see the value of birth fall. In the 11th century, nobility had an inestimable value; it is purchased in the 13th; the first granting of nobility takes place in 1270, and equality is finally introduced into government by aristocracy itself.

During the seven hundred years that have just passed, it sometimes happened that, in order to struggle against royal authority, or to take power away from their rivals, the nobles gave political power to the people.

Even more often, you saw kings make the lower classes of the State participate in government in order to humble the aristocracy.

In France, kings showed themselves to be the most active and most constant of levelers. When they were ambitious and strong, they worked to raise the people to the level of the nobles, and when they were moderate and weak, they allowed the people to put themselves above kings. The former helped democracy by their talents, the latter by their vices. Louis XI and Louis XIV took care to equalize everything below the throne, and Louis XV himself finally descended into the dust with his court.

As soon as citizens began to own the land in ways other than by feudal tenure, and as soon as personal wealth, once known, could in turn create influence and confer power, no discoveries were made in the arts, no further improvements were introduced into commerce and industry, without also creating as many new elements of equality among men. From this moment, all processes that are found, all needs that are born, all desires that demand to be satisfied, are progress toward universal leveling. The taste for luxury, the love of war, the sway of fashion, the most superficial passions of the human heart as well as the most profound, seem to work in concert to impoverish the rich and to enrich the poor.

From the time when works of the mind became sources of strength and wealth, each development of science, each new element of knowledge, each new idea had to be considered as a germ of power put within reach of the people. Poetry, eloquence, memory, mental graces, fires of the imagination, depth of thought, all these gifts that heaven distributes at random, profited democracy, and even when they were in the possession of democracy's adversaries, they still served its cause by putting into relief the natural grandeur of man; so democracy's conquests spread with those of civilization and enlightenment, and literature was an arsenal open to all, where the weak and the poor came each day to find arms.

When you skim the pages of our history you do not find so to speak any great events that for seven hundred years have not turned to the profit of equality.

The Crusades and the English wars decimate the nobles and divide their lands; the institution of the towns introduces democratic liberty into the feudal monarchy; the discovery of firearms equalizes the villain and the noble on the field of battle; printing offers equal resources to their minds; the post comes to deposit enlightenment at the threshold of the hut of the poor as at the gate of palaces; Protestantism maintains that all men are equally able to find the way to heaven. America, which comes into sight, presents a thousand new paths to fortune and delivers the wealth and power reserved to kings to obscure adventurers.

If you examine what is happening in France from the 11th century every fifty years, at the end of each one of these periods, you will not fail to notice that a double revolution has taken place in the state of society. The noble will have slipped on the social ladder, the commoner will have risen; the one descends, the other ascends. Each half-century brings them closer together, and soon they are going to touch.

And this is not only particular to France. In whatever direction we cast our eyes, we notice the same revolution continuing in all of the Christian universe. Let someone cite to me a republic or a kingdom in which the nobles of today can be compared, I would not say to the nobles of feudal times, but only to their fathers of the last century.

For seven hundred years, there is not a single event among Christians that has not turned to the profit of democracy, not a man who has not served its triumph. The clergy by spreading enlightenment and by applying within its bosom the principle of Christian equality, kings by opposing the people to nobles, nobles by opposing the people to kings; writers and the learned by creating intellectual riches for democracy's use; tradesmen by providing unknown resources for democracy's activity; the navigator by finding democracy new worlds.

Everywhere you saw the various incidents in the lives of peoples turn to the profit of democracy; all men aided it by their efforts: those who had in view contributing to its success and those who did not think of serving it; those who fought for it and even those who declared themselves its enemies; all were pushed pell-mell along the same path, and all worked in common, some despite themselves, others without their knowledge, blind instruments in the hands of God.

So the gradual development of equality of conditions is a providential fact; it has the principal characteristics of one: it is universal, it is lasting, it escapes every day from human power; all events, like all men, serve its development.

Would it be wise to believe that a social movement that comes from so far could be suspended by the efforts of a generation? Do you think that after having destroyed feudalism and vanquished kings, democracy will retreat before the bourgeois and the rich? Will it stop now that it has become so strong and its adversaries so weak?

So where are we going? No one can say; for we are already lacking terms of comparison; conditions are more equal today among Christians than they have ever been in any time or in any country in the world; thus we are prevented by the magnitude of what is already done from foreseeing what can still be done.

The entire book that you are about to read has been written under the impression of a sort of religious terror produced in the soul of the author by the sight of this irresistible revolution that has marched for so many centuries over all obstacles, and that we still see today advancing amid the ruins that it has made.

It isn't necessary for God himself to speak in order for us to discover sure signs of his will; it is enough to examine the regular march of nature and the continuous tendency of events; I know, without the Creator raising his voice, that the stars in space follow the curves traced by his fingers.

If long observations and sincere meditations led men of today to recognize that the gradual and progressive development of equality is at once the past and the future of their history, this discovery alone would give this development the sacred character of the will of God. To want to stop democracy would then seem to be struggling against God himself, and it would only remain for nations to accommodate themselves to the social state that Providence imposes on them.

Christian peoples seem to me to offer today a frightening spectacle. The movement that sweeps them along is already so strong that it cannot be suspended, and it is not yet so rapid as to despair of directing it. Their fate is in their hands; but soon it escapes them.

To instruct democracy, to revive its beliefs if possible, to purify its mores, to regulate its movements, to substitute little by little the science of public affairs for its inexperience, knowledge of its true interests for its blind instincts; to adapt its government to times and places; to modify it according to circumstances and men; such is the first of duties imposed today on those who lead society.

A new political science is needed for a world entirely new.

But that is what we scarcely consider; placed in the middle of a rapid river, we obstinately fix our eyes on some debris that we still see on the bank, while the current carries us away and pushes us backwards toward the abyss.

There is no people of Europe among whom the great social revolution that I have just described has made more rapid progress than among us; but here it has always marched haphazardly.

The heads of State never thought to prepare anything in advance for it; it came about despite them or without their knowledge. The most powerful, most intelligent and most moral classes of the nation did not try to take hold of it in order to direct it. So democracy has been abandoned to its wild instincts; it has grown up like those children, deprived of paternal care, who raise themselves in the streets of our cities, and who know society only by its vices and miseries. We still seemed unaware of its existence, when it took hold of power without warning. Then each person submitted with servility to its slightest desires; it was adored as the image of strength; when later it was weakened by its own excesses, legislators conceived the imprudent plan of destroying it instead of trying to instruct and correct it, and not wanting to teach it to govern, they thought only about pushing it away from government.

The result was that the democratic revolution took place in the material aspect of society without happening in the laws, ideas, habits and mores, the change that would have been necessary to make this revolution useful. We therefore have democracy, minus what must attenuate its vices and bring out its natural advantages; and seeing already the evils that it brings, we are still unaware of the good that it can give.

When royal power, supported by the aristocracy, peacefully governed the peoples of Europe, society, amid its miseries, enjoyed several kinds of happiness, which are difficult to imagine and appreciate today.

The power of some subjects raised insurmountable barriers to the tyranny of the prince; and kings, feeling vested in the eyes of the crowd with a nearly divine character, drew, from the very respect that they caused, the will not to abuse their power.

Placed an immense distance from the people, the nobles nonetheless took the type of benevolent and tranquil interest in the fate of the people that the shepherd gives to his flock; and without seeing the poor man as their equal, they watched over his lot as a trust put in their hands by Providence.

Not having conceived the idea of a social state other than their own, not imagining that they could ever be equal to their rulers, the people accepted the benefits and did not question the rights of their rulers. They loved them when they were lenient and just and submitted without difficulty and without servility to their rigors as to inevitable evils sent to them by the hand of God. Custom and mores had, moreover, established limits to tyranny and founded a kind of right in the very midst of force.

Since the noble did not think that someone would want to wrest from him the privileges that he believed legitimate, and the serf regarded his inferiority as a result of the immutable order of nature, it is conceivable that a kind of reciprocal benevolence could be established between these two classes sharing so different a fate. You then saw in society inequality, miseries, but souls were not degraded.

It is not the use of power or the habit of obedience that depraves men; it is the use of a power that they consider as illegitimate and obedience to a power that they regard as usurped and oppressive.

On one side were wealth, force, leisure and with them the pursuit of luxury, refinements of taste, pleasures of the mind, devotion to the arts; on the other, work, coarseness and ignorance.

But within this ignorant and coarse crowd, you met energetic passions, generous sentiments, profound beliefs and untamed virtues.

The social body organized in this way could have stability, power, and above all glory.

But ranks are merging; barriers raised between men are falling; estates are being divided; power is being shared, enlightenment is spreading, intellects are becoming equal; the social state is becoming democratic, and the dominion of democracy is finally being established peacefully in institutions and in mores.

Then I imagine a society where all, seeing the law as their work, would love it and would submit to it without difficulty; where since the authority of the government is respected as necessary and not as divine, the love that is felt for the head of State would be not a passion, but a reasoned and calm sentiment. Since each person has rights and is assured of preserving his rights, a manly confidence and a kind of reciprocal condescension, as far from pride as from servility, would be established among all classes.

Instructed in their true interests, the people would understand that, in order to take advantage of the good things of society, you must submit to its burdens. The free association of citizens would then be able to replace the individual power of the nobles, and the State would be sheltered from tyranny and from license.

I understand that in a democratic State, constituted in this manner, society will not be immobile; but the movements of the social body will be able to be regulated and progressive; if you meet less brilliance there than within an aristocracy, you will find less misery; pleasures will be less extreme and well-being more general; knowledge not as great and ignorance more rare; sentiments less energetic and habits more mild; there you will notice more vices and fewer crimes.

If there is no enthusiasm and fervor of beliefs, enlightenment and experience will sometimes obtain great sacrifices from citizens; each man, equally weak, will feel an equal need for his fellows; and knowing that he can gain their support only on condition of lending them his help, he will discover without difficulty that for him particular interest merges with the general interest.

The nation taken as a body will be less brilliant, less glorious, less strong perhaps; but the majority of citizens there will enjoy a more prosperous lot, and the people will appear untroubled, not because they despair of being better, but because they know they are well-off.

If everything was not good and useful in such an order of things, society at least would have appropriated everything useful and good that such an order can present; and men, while abandoning forever the social advantages that aristocracy can provide, would have taken from democracy all the good that the latter can offer to them.

But we, while giving up the social state of our ancestors, while throwing pell-mell their institutions, their ideas, and their mores behind us, what have we put in their place?

The prestige of royal power has vanished, without being replaced by the majesty of laws; today the people scorn authority, but they fear it, and fear extracts more from them than respect and love formerly yielded.

I notice that we have destroyed the individual existences that could struggle separately against tyranny, but I see the government that alone inherits all the prerogatives wrenched from families, from corporations or from men; so, to the sometimes oppressive but often conservative strength of a small number of citizens, the weakness of all has succeeded.

The division of fortunes has reduced the distance that separated the poor from the rich; but by coming closer together, they seem to have found new reasons to hate each other, and, eyeing one another with looks full of terror and envy, they mutually push each other away from power; for the one as for the other, the idea of rights does not exist, and force appears to them both as the only reason for the present and the sole guarantee of the future.

The poor man has kept most of the prejudices of his fathers, without their beliefs; their ignorance, without their virtues; he has accepted, as the rule for his actions, the doctrine of interest, without knowing the science of interest, and his egoism is as wanting in enlightenment as his devotion formerly was.

Society is tranquil, not because it is conscious of its strength and its well-being, but on the contrary because it believes itself weak and frail; it is afraid of dying by making an effort. Everyone feels that things are going badly, but no one has the necessary courage and energy to seek something better; we have desires, regrets, sorrows and joys that produce nothing visible or lasting, similar to the passions of old men that end in impotence.

Thus we have abandoned what the old state could present of the good, without acquiring what the current state would be able to offer of the useful; we have destroyed an aristocratic society, and we do not think about organizing on its ruins a moral and tranquil democracy; and, stopping out of complacency amid the debris of the former edifice, we seem to want to settle there forever.

What is happening in the intellectual world is no less deplorable.

Hindered in its march or abandoned without support to its disorderly passions, democracy in France has overturned everything that it met on its way, weakening what it did not destroy. You did not see it take hold of society little by little in order to establish its dominion peacefully; it has not ceased to march amid the disorders and the agitation of battle. Animated by the heat of the struggle, pushed beyond the natural limits of his opinion by the opinions and excesses of his adversaries, each person loses sight of the very object of his pursuits and uses a language that corresponds badly to his true sentiments and to his secret instincts.

From that results the strange confusion that we are forced to witness.

I search my memory in vain; I find nothing that deserves to excite more distress and more pity than what is happening before our eyes; it seems that today we have broken the natural bond that unites opinions to tastes and actions to beliefs; the sympathy that has been observed in all times between the sentiments and the ideas of men seems to be destroyed, and you would say that all the laws of moral analogy are abolished.

You still meet among us Christians full of zeal, whose religious souls love to be nourished by the truths of the other life; they are undoubtedly going to become active in favor of human liberty, source of all moral grandeur. Christianity, which has made all men equal before God, will not be loath to see all citizens equal before the law. But, by a combination of strange events, religion is at the moment involved amid the powers that democracy is overturning, and it often happens that religion rejects the equality that it loves and curses liberty as an adversary, while, by taking liberty by the hand, religion could be able to sanctify its efforts.

Next to these religious men, I find others whose sights are turned toward the earth rather than toward heaven; partisans of liberty, not only because they see in it the origin of the most noble virtues, but above all because they consider it as the source of the greatest advantages, they sincerely desire to secure its dominion and to have men taste its benefits. I understand that the latter are going to hasten to call religion to their aid, for they must know that you cannot establish the reign of liberty without that of mores, nor found mores without beliefs; but they have seen religion in the ranks of their adversaries; that is enough for them; some attack religion and the others dare not defend it.

Past centuries saw base and venal souls advocate slavery, while independent spirits and generous hearts struggled without hope to save human liberty. But today you often meet men naturally noble and proud whose opinions are in direct opposition to their tastes, and who speak in praise of the servility and baseness that they have never known for themselves. There are others, in contrast, who speak of liberty as if they could feel what is holy and great in it and who loudly claim on behalf of humanity rights that they have always disregarded.

I notice virtuous and peaceful men placed naturally by their pure morals, tranquil habits, prosperity and enlightenment at the head of the populations that surround them. Full of a sincere love of country, they are ready to make great sacrifices for it. Civilization, however, often finds them to be adversaries; they confuse its abuses with its benefits, and in their minds the idea of evil is indissolubly united with the idea of the new.

Nearby I see other men who, in the name of progress, try hard to materialize man, wanting to find the useful without attending to the just, wanting to find knowledge far from beliefs and well-being separate from virtue. These claim to be champions of modern civilization and they arrogantly put themselves at its head, usurping a place that is abandoned to them and that their unworthiness denies to them.

So where are we?

Religious men combat liberty, and the friends of liberty attack religion; noble and generous spirits speak in praise of slavery, and base and servile souls advocate independence; honest and enlightened citizens are enemies of all progress, while men without patriotism and without mores become the apostles of civilization and enlightenment!

Have all centuries resembled ours then? Has man always had before his eyes, as today, a world where nothing is connected, where virtue is without genius, and genius without honor; where love of order merges with the taste for tyrants and the holy cult of liberty with scorn for human laws; where conscience throws only a doubtful light upon human actions; where nothing any longer seems either forbidden, or permitted, or honest, or shameful, or true, or false?

Will I think that the Creator made man in order to leave him to struggle endlessly amid the intellectual miseries that surround us? I cannot believe it; God is preparing for European societies a future more settled and more calm; I do not know his plans, but I will not cease to believe in them because I cannot fathom them, and I will prefer to doubt my knowledge than his justice.

There is a country in the world where the great social revolution that I am speaking about seems more or less to have reached its natural limits; it came about there in a simple and easy way, or rather it can be said that this country sees the results of the democratic revolution that is taking place among us, without having had the revolution itself.

The emigrants who came to settle in America at the beginning of the 17th century in a way freed the principle of democracy from all those principles that it struggled against within the old societies of Europe, and they transplanted it alone to the shores of the New World. There it was able to grow in liberty and, moving ahead with mores, to develop peacefully in the laws.

It seems to me beyond doubt that sooner or later, we will arrive, like the Americans, at a nearly complete equality of conditions. From that, I do not conclude that one day we are necessarily called to draw from such a social state the political consequences that the Americans have drawn from it. I am very far from believing that they have found the only form of government that democracy may take; but in the two countries the generating cause of laws and mores is the same; that is enough for us to have an immense interest in knowing what that generating cause has produced in each of them.

So it is not only to satisfy a curiosity, legitimate for that matter, that I examined America; I wanted to find lessons there from which we would be able to profit. You would be strangely mistaken if you thought that I wanted to do a panegyric; whoever reads this book will be clearly convinced that such was not my purpose; nor was my goal to advocate any particular form of government in general; for I am among those who believe that there is hardly ever absolute good in laws; I did not even claim to judge if the social revolution, whose march seems irresistible to me, was advantageous or harmful to humanity. I have acknowledged this revolution as an accomplished or nearly accomplished fact, and, from among the peoples who have seen it taking place among them, I sought the people among whom it has reached the most complete and most peaceful development, in order to discern clearly its natural consequences and, if possible, to see the means to make it profitable to men. I admit that in America I saw more than America; I sought there an image of democracy itself, its tendencies, its character, its prejudices, its passions; I wanted to know democracy, if only to know at least what we must hope or fear from it.

In the first part of this work, I tried to show the direction that democracy, delivered in America to its tendencies and abandoned almost without constraint to its instincts, gave naturally to laws, the course that it imparted to government, and in general the power that it gained over public affairs. I wanted to know what good and bad it produced. I sought out what precautions the Americans have used to direct it and what others they have omitted, and I undertook to discern the causes that allow it to govern society.

My goal was to portray in a second part the influence that equality of conditions and the government of democracy exercise in America on civil society, on habits, ideas and mores; but I begin to feel less enthusiasm about accomplishing this plan. Before I can complete in this way the task that I proposed for myself, my work will have become nearly useless. Someone else will soon show readers the principal features of the American character and, hiding the seriousness of the descriptions behind a light veil, will lend truth charms with which I would not be able to adorn it.

I do not know if I have succeeded in making known what I saw in America, but I am sure that I sincerely desired to do so, and that I never yielded, except unknowingly, to the need to adapt facts to ideas, instead of subjecting ideas to facts.

When a point could be established with the help of written documents, I have taken care to turn to original texts and to the most authentic and most respected works. I have indicated my sources in notes, and everyone will be able to verify them. When it was a matter of opinions, of political customs, of observations of mores, I sought to consult the most enlightened men. If something happened to be important or doubtful, I was not content with one witness, but decided only on the basis of the body of testimonies.

Here the reader must necessarily take me at my word. I would often have been able to cite in support of what I advance the authority of names that are known to him, or that at least are worthy to be; but I have refrained from doing so. The stranger often learns by the hearth of his host important truths, that the latter would perhaps conceal from a friend; with the stranger you ease the burden of a forced silence; you are not afraid of his indiscretion because he is passing through. Each one of these confidences was recorded by me as soon as received, but they will never emerge from my manuscripts; I prefer to detract from the success of my accounts than to add my name to the list of those travelers who send sorrows and troubles in return for the generous hospitality that they received.

I know that, despite my care, nothing will be easier than to criticize this book, if anyone ever thinks to examine it critically.

Those who will want to look closely at it will find, I think, in the entire work, a generative thought that links so to speak all its parts. But the diversity of the subjects that I had to treat is very great, and whoever will undertake to contrast an isolated fact to the whole of the facts that I cite, a detached idea to the whole of the ideas, will succeed without difficulty. So I would like you to grant me the favor of reading me with the same spirit that presided over my work, and would like you to judge this book by the general impression that it leaves, as I myself came to a decision, not due to a particular reason, but due to the mass of reasons.

Nor must it be forgotten that the author who wants to make himself understood is obliged to push each of his ideas to all of their theoretical consequences, and often to the limits of what is false and impractical; for if it is sometimes necessary to step back from the rules of logic in actions, you cannot do the same in discourses, and man finds it almost as difficult to be inconsistent in his words as he normally finds it to be consistent in his actions. This, to say in passing, brings out one of the great advantages of free governments, an advantage about which you scarcely think. In these governments, it is necessary to talk a great deal. The need to talk forces men of State to reason, and from speeches a bit of logic is introduced into public affairs.

I finish by pointing out myself what a great number of readers will consider as the capital defect of the work. This book follows in no one's train exactly; by writing it I did not mean either to serve or to combat any party; I set about to see, not differently, but farther than parties; and while they are concerned with the next day, I wanted to think about the future.

DEMOCRACY IN AMERICA, VOLUME I, PART I, CHAPTER 3: "SOCIAL STATE OF THE ANGLO-AMERICANS"

The social state is ordinarily the result of a fact, sometimes of laws, most often of these two causes together. But once it exists, it can itself be considered the first cause of most of the laws, customs and ideas that regulate the conduct of nations; what it does not produce, it modifies.

So to know the legislation and the mores of a people, it is necessary to begin by studying its social state.

That the Salient Point of the Social State of the Anglo-Americans Is to Be Essentially Democratic

Several important remarks about the social state of the Anglo-Americans could be made, but one dominates all the others.

The social state of the Americans is eminently democratic. It has had this character since the birth of the colonies; it has it even more today.

As soon as you look at the civil and political society of the United States, you discover two great facts that dominate all the others and from which the others are derived. Democracy constitutes the social state; the dogma of the sovereignty of the people, the political law.

These two things are not analogous. Democracy is society's way of being. Sovereignty of the people, a form of government. Nor are they inseparable, because democracy is even more compatible with despotism than with liberty.

But they are correlative. Sovereignty of the people is always more or less a fiction wherever democracy is not established.

I said in the preceding chapter that a very great equality reigned among the emigrants who came to settle on the shores of New England. Not even the germ of aristocracy was ever deposited in that part of the Union. No influences except intellectual ones could ever be established there. The people got used to revering certain names, as symbols of learning and virtue. The voice of certain citizens gained a power over the people that perhaps could have been correctly called aristocratic, if it could have been passed down invariably from father to son.

This happened east of the Hudson; southwest of this river, and as far down as Florida, things were otherwise.

In most of the States situated southwest of the Hudson, great English landholders had come to settle. Aristocratic principles, and with them English laws of inheritance, had been imported. I have shown the reasons that prevented a powerful aristocracy from ever being established in America. But these reasons, though existing southwest of the Hudson, had less power there than east of this river. To the south, one man alone could, with the help of slaves, cultivate a large expanse of land. So in this part of the continent wealthy landed proprietors were seen; but their influence was not precisely aristocratic, as understood in Europe, because they had no privileges at all, and cultivation by slaves gave them no tenants and therefore no patronage. Nonetheless, south of the Hudson, the great landholders formed a superior class, with its own ideas and tastes and generally concentrating political activity within its ranks. It was a kind of aristocracy not much different from the mass of the people whose passions and interests it easily embraced, exciting neither love nor hate; in sum, weak and not very hardy. It was this class that, in the South, put itself at the head of the insurrection; the American Revolution owed its greatest men to it.

In this period, the entire society was shaken. The people, in whose name the struggle was waged, the people—now a power—conceived the desire to act by themselves; democratic instincts awoke. By breaking the yoke of the home country, the people acquired a taste for all kinds of independence. Little by little, individual influences ceased to make themselves felt; habits as well as laws began to march in unison toward the same end.

But it was the law of inheritance that pushed equality to its last stage.

I am astonished that ancient and modern political writers have not attributed a greater influence on the course of human affairs to the laws of landed inheritance. These laws belong, it is true, to the civil order; but they should be placed at the head of all political institutions, for they have an incredible influence on the social state of peoples, political laws being just the expression of the social state. In addition, the laws of inheritance have a sure and uniform way of operating on society; in a sense they lay hold of generations before their birth. Through them, man is armed with an almost divine power over the future of his fellows. The law-maker regulates the inheritance of citizens once, and he remains at rest for centuries: his work put in motion, he can keep his hands off; the machine acts on its own power, and moves as if self-directed toward an end set in advance.

Constituted in a certain way, the law of inheritance reunites, concentrates, gathers property and, soon after, power, around some head; in a way it makes aristocracy spring from the soil. Driven by other principles and set along another path, its action is even more rapid; it divides, shares, disseminates property and power. Sometimes people are then frightened by the rapidity of its march. Despairing of stopping its movement, they seek at least to create difficulties and obstacles before it; they want to counterbalance its action with opposing efforts; useless exertions! It crushes or sends flying into pieces all that gets in its way; it constantly rises and falls on the earth until nothing is left in sight but a shifting and intangible dust on which democracy takes its seat.

When the law of inheritance allows and, even more, requires the equal division of the father's property among all the children, its effects are of two sorts; they should be carefully distinguished, even though they lead to the same end.

Due to the law of inheritance, the death of each owner leads to a revolution in property; not only do the holdings change masters, but so to speak, they change nature; they are constantly split into smaller portions.

That is the direct and, in a sense, the material effect of the law. So in countries where legislation establishes equal division, property and particularly territorial fortunes necessarily have a permanent tendency to grow smaller. Nonetheless, if the law were left to itself, the effects of this legislation would make themselves felt only over time. Because as long as the family includes not more than two children (and the average for families in a populated country like France, we are told, is only three), these children, sharing the wealth of their father and their mother, will be no less wealthy than each parent individually.

But the law of equal division exerts its influence not on the fate of property alone; it acts on the very soul of the proprietors, and calls their passions to its aid. These indirect effects rapidly destroy great fortunes and, above all, great estates.

Among peoples for whom the inheritance law is based on the right of primogeniture, landed estates most often pass from generation to generation without being divided. That causes family spirit to be, in a way, embodied in the land. The family represents the land; the land represents the family; the land perpetuates its name, origin, glory, power and virtues. It is an undying witness to the past and a precious guarantee of life to come.

When the inheritance law establishes equal division, it destroys the intimate connection that existed between family spirit and keeping the land; the land ceases to represent the family, for the land, inescapably divided after one or two generations, clearly must shrink continually and disappear entirely in the end. The sons of a great landed proprietor, if they are few, or if fortune favors them, can maintain the hope of not being poorer than their progenitor, but not of owning the same lands as he; their wealth will necessarily consist of other elements than his.

Now, from the moment you take away from landed proprietors any great interest—arising from sentiment, memory, pride, or ambition—in keeping the land, you can be sure that sooner or later they will sell it. They have a great pecuniary interest in selling, since movable assets produce more income than other assets and lend themselves much more easily to satisfying the passions of the moment.

Once divided, great landed estates are never reassembled; for the small landholder gains proportionately more revenue from his field than the large landholder; so he sells it at a much higher price than the large landholder. Thus the economic calculations that brought a rich man to sell vast properties, will prevent him, with all the more reason, from buying small properties in order to reassemble large estates.

What is called family spirit is often based on an illusion of individual egoism.

A person seeks to perpetuate and, in a way, to immortalize himself in his great-nephews. Where family spirit ends, individual egoism reverts to its true inclinations. Since the family no longer enters the mind except as something vague, indeterminate, and uncertain, each man concentrates on present convenience; he considers the establishment of the generation immediately following, and nothing more.

So a person does not try to perpetuate his family, or at least he tries to perpetuate it by means other than landed property.

Thus, not only does the inheritance law make it difficult for families to keep the same estates intact, but also it removes the desire to try and leads families, in a way, to cooperate in their own ruin.

The law of equal division proceeds in two ways: by acting on the thing, it acts on the man; by acting on the man, it affects the thing.

In these two ways it succeeds in profoundly attacking landed property and in making families as well as fortunes rapidly disappear.

Surely it is not up to us, the French of the nineteenth century, daily witnesses to the political and social changes that the inheritance law brings about, to question its power. Each day we see it constantly move back and forth over our soil, toppling in its path the walls of our dwellings and destroying the hedges of our fields. But if the inheritance law has already accomplished much among us, much still remains for it to do. Our memories, opinions, and habits present it with powerful obstacles.

In the United States, its work of destruction is nearly finished. That is where its principal results can be studied.

English legislation on the transmission of property was abolished in nearly all the states at the time of the Revolution.

The law of entail was modified so as to interfere only imperceptibly with the free circulation of property.

The first generation disappeared; landed estates began to divide. As time went by, the movement became more and more rapid, as a stone thrown from the top of a tower accelerates as it moves through space. Today, when hardly sixty years have gone by, the appearance of society is already unrecognizable; the families of the great landed proprietors are almost entirely engulfed by the common mass. In the state of New York, which had a very large number of such families, two barely stay afloat above the abyss ready to swallow them. Today, the sons of these opulent citizens are businessmen, lawyers, doctors. Most have fallen into the most profound obscurity. The last trace of hereditary rank and distinction is destroyed; the law of inheritance has done its leveling everywhere.

It is not that there are no rich in the United States as there are elsewhere; I do not even know of a country where the love of money holds a greater place in the human heart and where a deeper contempt is professed for the theory of the permanent equality of property. But wealth circulates there with incredible rapidity, and experience teaches that it is rare to see two generations reap the rewards of wealth.

This picture, however colored you think it is, still gives only an incomplete idea of what is happening in the new states of the West and Southwest.

At the end of the last century, hardy adventurers began to penetrate the valleys of the Mississippi. This was like a new discovery of America: soon the bulk of emigration went there; you saw unknown societies suddenly emerge from the wilderness. States, whose names did not even exist a few years before, took a place within the American Union. In the West democracy can be observed carried to its extreme limit. In these states, in a way improvised by chance, the inhabitants arrived but yesterday on the soil they occupy. They scarcely know each other, and each one is unaware of the history of his closest neighbor. So in this part of the American continent, the population escapes not only from the influence of great names and great wealth, but also from the natural aristocracy that arises from enlightenment and virtue. There, no one exercises the power that men grant out of respect for an entire life spent in doing good before their eyes. The new states of the West already have inhabitants; society still does not exist.

But not only fortunes are equal in America; to a certain degree, equality extends to minds themselves.

I do not think there is any country in the world where, in proportion to the population, there exist so small a number of ignorant and fewer learned men than in America.

There primary education is available to everyone; higher education is hardly available to anyone.

This is easily understood and is, so to speak, the necessary result of what we advanced above.

Nearly all Americans live comfortably; so they can easily gain the primary elements of human knowledge.

In America, there are few rich; nearly all Americans need to have an occupation. Now, every occupation requires an apprenticeship. So Americans can devote only the first years of life to general cultivation of the mind; at age fifteen, they begin a career; most often, therefore, their education concludes when ours begins. If pursued further, it is directed only toward a specialized and lucrative field; they study a field of knowledge in the way they prepare for a trade; and they take only the applications recognized to have immediate utility.

In America, most of the rich began by being poor; nearly all the men of leisure were busy men in their youth. The result is that when they could have the taste for study, they do not have the time to devote themselves to it; and when they have gained the time, they no longer have the taste.

So in America no class exists that honors intellectual work and in which the penchant for intellectual pleasures is handed down with affluence and hereditary leisure.

Both the will and the power to devote oneself to this work are therefore missing.

In America a certain middling level of human knowledge is established. All minds have approached it; some by rising, others by falling.

So you meet a great multitude of individuals who have about the same number of notions in matters of religion, history, the sciences, political economy, legislation, and government.

Intellectual inequality comes directly from God, and man cannot prevent it from always reappearing.

But it follows, at least from what we have just said, that minds, while still remaining unequal as the Creator intended, find equal means at their disposal. Thus, today in America, the aristocratic element, always feeble since its birth, is, if not destroyed, at least weakened further; so it is difficult to assign it any influence whatsoever in the course of public affairs.

Time, events, and the laws have, on the contrary, made the democratic element not only preponderant but also, so to speak, unique. No family or group influence can be seen; often not even an individual influence, no matter how ephemeral, can be found.

For a people that has reached such a social state, mixed governments are more or less impractical; hardly any choice exists for them other than absolute power or a sovereignty of the people.

America found itself in circumstances fortunate for escaping despotism and favorable for adopting a republic.

So America presents, in its social state, the strangest phenomenon. There, men appear more equal in fortune and in mind or, in other words, more equal in strength than they are in any other country in the world and have been in any century that history remembers.

Political Consequences of the Social State of the Anglo-Americans

The political consequences of such a social state are easy to deduce.

It is impossible to think that, in the end, equality would not penetrate the political world as it does elsewhere. You cannot imagine men, equal in all other ways, forever unequal to each other on a single point; so in time they will become equal in all ways.

Now I know only two ways to have equality rule in the political world: rights must either be given to each citizen or given to no one.

For peoples who have arrived at the same social state as the Anglo-Americans, it is therefore very difficult to see a middle course between the sovereignty of all and the absolute power of one man.

We must not hide from the fact that the social state I have just described lends itself almost as easily to the one as to the other of these two consequences.

There is in fact a manly and legitimate passion for equality that incites men to want to be strong and esteemed. This passion tends to elevate the small to the rank of the great. But in the human heart a depraved taste for equality is also found that leads the weak to want to bring the strong down to their level and that reduces men to preferring equality in servitude to inequality in liberty. Not that peoples whose social state is democratic naturally scorn liberty; on the contrary, they have an instinctive taste for it. But liberty is not the principal and constant object of their desire; what they love with undying love is equality; they rush toward liberty by rapid impulses and sudden efforts, and if they miss the goal, they resign themselves; but without equality nothing can satisfy them, and rather than lose it, they would agree to perish.

On the other hand, when citizens are all more or less equal, it becomes difficult for them to defend their independence against the aggressions of power. Since none among them is then strong enough to struggle alone with any advantage, it is only the combination of the strength of all that can guarantee liberty. Now, such a combination is not always found.

Peoples can therefore draw two great political consequences from the same social state; these consequences differ prodigiously, but they both arise from the same fact.

The first to be subjected to this fearful alternative that I have just described, the Anglo-Americans have been fortunate enough to escape absolute power. Circumstances, origin, enlightenment, and above all, mores have allowed them to establish and to maintain the sovereignty of the people.

DEMOCRACY IN AMERICA, VOLUME II, PART 2, CHAPTER 1: "WHY DEMOCRATIC PEOPLES SHOW A MORE ARDENT AND MORE ENDURING LOVE FOR EQUALITY THAN FOR LIBERTY"

The first and most intense of the passions given birth by equality of conditions, I do not need to say, is the love of this very equality. So no one will be surprised that I talk about it before all the others.

Everyone has noted that in our time, and especially in France, this passion for equality has a greater place in the human heart every day. It has been said a hundred times that our contemporaries have a much more ardent and much more tenacious love for equality than for liberty; but I do not find that we have yet adequately gone back to the causes of this fact. I am going to try.

You can imagine an extreme point where liberty and equality meet and merge.

Suppose that all citizens participate in the government and that each one has an equal right to take part in it.

Since no one then differs from his fellows, no one will be able to exercise a tyrannical power; men will be perfectly free, because they will all be entirely equal;

and they will all be perfectly equal, because they will be entirely free. Democratic peoples tend toward this ideal.

That is the most complete form that equality can take on earth; but there are a thousand other forms that, without being as perfect, are scarcely less dear to these peoples.

Equality can become established in civil society and not reign in the political world. Everyone can have the right to pursue the same pleasures, to enter the same professions, to meet in the same places; in a word, to live in the same way and to pursue wealth by the same means, without all taking the same part in government.

A kind of equality can even become established in the political world, even if political liberty does not exist. Everyone is equal to all his fellows, except one, who is, without distinction, the master of all, and who takes the agents of his power equally from among all.

It would be easy to form several other hypotheses according to which a very great equality could easily be combined with institutions more or less free, or even with institutions that would not be free at all.

So although men cannot become absolutely equal without being entirely free, and consequently equality at its most extreme level merges with liberty, you are justified in distinguishing the one from the other.

The taste that men have for liberty and the one that they feel for equality are, in fact, two distinct things, and I am not afraid to add that, among democratic peoples, they are two unequal things.

If you want to pay attention, you will see that in each century, a singular and dominant fact is found to which the other facts are related; this fact almost always gives birth to a generative thought, or to a principal passion that then ends by drawing to itself and carrying along in its course all sentiments and all ideas. It is like the great river toward which all of the surrounding streams seem to flow.

Liberty has shown itself to men in different times and in different forms; it has not been linked exclusively to one social state, and you find it elsewhere than in democracies. So it cannot form the distinctive characteristic of democratic centuries.

The particular and dominant fact that singles out these centuries is equality of conditions; the principal passion that agitates men in those times is love of this equality.

Do not ask what singular charm the men of democratic ages find in living equal; or the particular reasons that they can have to be so stubbornly attached to equality rather than to the other advantages that society presents to them. Equality forms the distinctive characteristic of the period in which they live; that alone is enough to explain why they prefer it to everything else.

But, apart from this reason, there are several others that, in all times, will habitually lead men to prefer equality to liberty.

If a people could ever succeed in destroying by itself or only in decreasing the equality that reigns within it, it would do so only by long and difficult efforts. It would have to modify its social state, abolish its laws, replace its ideas, change its habits, alter its mores. But, to lose political liberty, it is enough not to hold on to it, and liberty escapes.

So men do not hold on to equality only because it is dear to them; they are also attached to it because they believe it must last forever.

You do not find men so limited and so superficial that they do not discover that political liberty may, by its excesses, compromise tranquility, patrimony, and the life of individuals. But only attentive and clear-sighted men see the dangers with which equality threatens us, and ordinarily they avoid pointing these dangers out. They know that the miseries that they fear are remote, and they imagine that those miseries affect only the generations to come, about whom the present generation scarcely worries. The evils that liberty sometimes brings are immediate; they are visible to all, and more or less everyone feels them. The evils that extreme equality can produce appear only little by little; they gradually insinuate themselves into the social body; they are seen only now and then, and, at the moment when they become most violent, habit has already made it so that they are no longer felt.

The good things that liberty brings show themselves only over time, and it is always easy to fail to recognize the cause that gives them birth.

The advantages of equality make themselves felt immediately, and every day you see them flow from their source.

Political liberty, from time to time, gives sublime pleasures to a certain number of citizens.

Equality provides a multitude of small enjoyments to each man every day. The charms of equality are felt at every moment, and they are within reach of all; the most noble hearts are not insensitive to them, and they are the delight of the most common souls. So the passion to which equality gives birth has to be at the very same time forceful and general.

Men cannot enjoy political liberty without purchasing it at the cost of some sacrifices, and they never secure it except by a great deal of effort. But the pleasures provided by equality are there for the taking. Each one of the small incidents of private life seems to give birth to them, and to enjoy them, you only have to be alive.

Democratic peoples love equality at all times, but there are certain periods when they push the passion that they feel for it to the point of delirium. This happens at the moment when the old social hierarchy, threatened for a long time, is finally destroyed, after a final internal struggle, when the barriers that separated citizens are at last overturned. Men then rush toward equality as toward a conquest, and they cling to it as to a precious good that someone wants to take away from them. The passion for equality penetrates the human heart from all directions, it spreads and fills it entirely. Do not tell men that by giving themselves so blindly to one exclusive passion, they compromise their dearest interests; they are deaf. Do not show them that liberty is escaping from their hands while they are looking elsewhere; they are blind, or rather they see in the whole universe only one single good worthy of desire.

What precedes applies to all democratic nations. What follows concerns only ourselves.

Among most modern nations, and in particular among all the peoples of the continent of Europe, the taste and the idea of liberty only began to arise and to develop at the moment when conditions began to become equal, and as a consequence of this very equality. It was absolute kings who worked hardest to level ranks among their subjects. Among these peoples, equality preceded liberty; so equality was an ancient fact, when liberty was still something new; the one had already created opinions, customs, laws that were its own, when the other appeared alone, and for the first time, in full view. Thus, the second was still only in ideas and in tastes, while the first had already penetrated habits, had taken hold of mores, and had given a particular turn to the least actions of life. Why be surprised if men today prefer the one to the other?

I think that democratic peoples have a natural taste for liberty; left to themselves, they seek it, they love it, and it is only with pain that they see themselves separated from it. But they have an ardent, insatiable, eternal, invincible passion for equality; they want equality in liberty, and if they cannot obtain that, they still want equality in slavery. They will suffer poverty, enslavement, barbarism, but they will not suffer aristocracy.

This is true in all times, and above all in our own. All men and all powers that would like to fight against this irresistible power will be overturned and destroyed by it. In our day, liberty cannot be established without its support, and despotism itself cannot reign without it.

DEMOCRACY IN AMERICA, VOLUME II, PART 2, CHAPTER 4: "HOW THE AMERICANS COMBAT INDIVIDUALISM WITH FREE INSTITUTIONS"

Despotism, which, by its nature, is fearful, sees in the isolation of men the most certain guarantee of its own duration, and it ordinarily puts all its efforts into isolating them. There is no vice of the human heart that pleases it as much as egoism: a despot easily pardons the governed for not loving him, provided that they do not love each other. He does not ask them to help him lead the State; it is enough that they do not claim to run it themselves. Those who claim to unite their efforts in order to create common prosperity, he calls unruly and restless spirits; and, changing the natural meaning of words, he calls good citizens those who withdraw narrowly into themselves.

Thus, the vices given birth by despotism are precisely those that equality favors. The two things complement each other and help one another in a fatal way.

Equality places men side by side, without a common bond to hold them. Despotism raises barriers between them and separates them. It disposes them not to think about their fellows and makes indifference into a kind of public virtue.

So despotism, which is dangerous in all times, is to be particularly feared in democratic centuries.

It is easy to see that in these same centuries men have a particular need for liberty.

When citizens are forced to occupy themselves with public affairs, they are necessarily drawn away from the middle of their individual interests and are, from time to time, dragged away from looking at themselves.

From the moment when common affairs are treated together, each man notices that he is not as independent of his fellows as he first imagined, and that, to gain their support, he must often lend them his help.

When the public governs, there is no man who does not feel the value of the public's regard and who does not seek to win it by gaining the esteem and affection of those among whom he must live.

Several of the passions that chill and divide hearts are then forced to withdraw deep into the soul and hide there. Pride conceals itself; scorn dares not to show itself. Egoism is afraid of itself. You dread to offend and you love to serve.

Under a free government, since most public functions are elective, the men who feel cramped in private life because of the loftiness of their souls or the restlessness of their desires, sense every day that they cannot do without the population that surrounds them.

It then happens that you think about your fellows out of ambition, and that often, in a way, you find it in your interest to forget yourself. This finally produces within democratic nations something analogous to what was seen in aristocracies.

In aristocratic countries men are bound tightly together by their very inequalities. In democratic countries where the various representatives of public power are elected, men attach themselves to each other by the exertion of their own will, and it is in this sense then that you can say that in those countries election replaces hierarchy to a certain degree. I know that you can raise the objection here of all the intrigues given birth by an election, the shameful means that the candidates often use and the slanders that their enemies spread. Those are occasions of hatred, and they present themselves all the more often as elections become more frequent.

These evils are no doubt great, but they are temporary, while the good things that arise with them endure.

The desire to be elected can, for a short while, lead certain men to make war on each other; but this same desire leads all men in the long run to lend each other natural support; and, if it happens that an election accidentally divides two friends, the electoral system draws closer together in a permanent way a multitude of citizens who would always have remained strangers to each other. Liberty creates particular hatreds, but despotism gives birth to general indifference.

The Americans fought, by means of liberty, against the individualism given birth by equality, and they defeated it.

The law-makers of America did not believe that to cure an illness so natural and so fatal to the social body in democratic times, it was sufficient to grant the nation a single way of representing itself as a whole; they thought, as well, that it was appropriate to give political life to each portion of the territory, in order infinitely to multiply for citizens the occasions to act together, and to make the citizens feel every day that they depend on each other.

This was to behave with wisdom.

The general affairs of a country occupy only the principal citizens. The latter gather together in the same places only from time to time; and, as it often happens that afterward they lose sight of each other, no lasting bonds are established among them. But, when it is a matter of having the particular affairs of a district regulated by the men who live there, the same individuals are always in contact, and they are in a way forced to know each other and to please each other.

You draw a man out of himself with difficulty in order to interest him in the destiny of the entire State, because he poorly understands the influence that the destiny of the State can exercise on his fate. But if it is necessary to have a road pass by the end of his property, he will see at first glance that there is a connection between this small public affair and his greatest private affairs, and he will discover, without anyone showing him, the close bond that here unites particular interest to general interest.

So it is by charging citizens with the administration of small affairs, much more than by giving them the government of great ones, that you interest them in the public good and make them see the need that they constantly have for each other in order to produce that good.

You can, by a dazzling action, suddenly capture the favor of a people; but, to win the love and respect of the population that surrounds you, there must be a long succession of small services provided, humble good offices, a constant habit of benevolence and a well-established reputation of disinterestedness.

So local liberties, which make a great number of citizens put value on the affection of their neighbors and of those nearby, constantly bring men back toward each other despite the instincts that separate them, and force them to help each other.

In the United States, the most opulent citizens are very careful not to isolate themselves from the people; on the contrary, they constantly draw closer to them, they readily listen to them and speak with them every day. They know that in democracies the rich always need the poor and that, in democratic times, the poor are attached by manners more than by benefits. The very grandeur of these benefits, which brings out the difference of conditions, causes a secret irritation to those who profit from them; but simplicity of manners has nearly irresistible charms; familiarity of manners seduces and even their coarseness does not always displease.

This truth does not at first sight penetrate the mind of the rich. Usually, they resist it as long as the democratic revolution lasts, and they do not even admit it immediately after the revolution is accomplished. They willingly agree to do good for the people; but they want to continue to hold them carefully at a distance. They believe that is enough; they are wrong. They would ruin themselves in this way without rekindling the heart of the population that surrounds them. It is not the sacrifice of their money that is demanded of them; it is the sacrifice of their pride.

You would say that in the United States there is no imagination that does not exhaust itself inventing means to increase wealth and to satisfy the needs of the public. The most enlightened inhabitants of each district are constantly using their knowledge to discover new secrets appropriate for increasing common prosperity; and, when they have found some, they hasten to give them to the crowd.

While closely examining the vices and weaknesses often shown by those who govern in America, you are astonished by the growing prosperity of the people, and you are mistaken. It is not the elected magistrate who makes the American democracy prosper; but it prospers because the magistrate is elective.

It would be unjust to believe that the patriotism of the Americans and the zeal that each of them shows for the well-being of his fellow-citizens has nothing real about it. Although private interest directs most human actions in the United States as well as elsewhere, it does not determine all of them.

I must say that I have often seen Americans make great and true sacrifices for public affairs, and I have observed a hundred times that they hardly ever fail to lend faithful support to each other as needed.

The free institutions that the inhabitants of the United States possess, and the political rights that they use so much, recall constantly, and in a thousand ways, to each citizen that he lives in society. They lead his mind at every moment toward this idea, that the duty as well as the interest of men is to make themselves useful to their fellows; and, as he sees no particular cause to hate them, since he is never either their slave or their master, his heart inclines easily in the direction of benevolence. You first get involved in the general interest by necessity, and then by choice; what was calculation becomes instinct; and by working for the good of your fellow-citizens, you finally acquire the habit and taste of serving them.

When men, unequal to each other, put all their political powers in the hands of one man, that is not enough for them to become indifferent and cold toward each other, because they continue to need each other constantly in civil life.

But when equal men do not take part in government, they almost entirely lack the occasion to harm each other or to make use of each other. Each one forgets his fellows to think only of the prince and himself.

So political liberty, which is useful when conditions are unequal, becomes necessary in proportion as they become equal.

Many people in France consider equality of conditions as a first evil, and political liberty as a second. When they are forced to submit to the one, they try hard at least to escape the other. As for me, I say that, to combat the evils that equality can produce, there is only one effective remedy: political liberty.

DEMOCRACY IN AMERICA, VOLUME II, PART 4, CHAPTER 1: "EQUALITY NATURALLY GIVES MEN THE TASTE FOR FREE INSTITUTIONS"

Equality, which makes men independent of each other, makes them contract the habit and the taste to follow only their will in their personal actions. This complete independence, which they enjoy continually vis-à-vis their equals and in the practice of private life, disposes them to consider all authority with a discontented eye, and soon suggests to them the idea and the love of political liberty. So men who live in these times march on a natural slope that leads them toward free institutions. Take one of them at random; go back, if possible, to his primitive instincts; you will discover that, among the different governments, the one that he conceives first and that he prizes most, is the government whose leader he has elected and whose actions he controls.

Of all the political effects that equality of conditions produces, it is this love of independence that first strikes our attention and that timid spirits fear even more; and we cannot say that they are absolutely wrong to be afraid, for anarchy has more frightening features in democratic countries than elsewhere. Since citizens have no effect on each other, at the instant when the national power that keeps them all in their place becomes absent, it seems that disorder must immediately be at its height and that, with each citizen on his own, the social body is suddenly going to find itself reduced to dust.

I am convinced nevertheless that anarchy is not the principal evil that democratic centuries must fear, but the least.

Equality produces, in fact, two tendencies: one leads men directly to independence and can push them suddenly as far as anarchy; the other leads them by a longer, more secret, but surer road toward servitude.

Peoples easily see the first and resist it; they allow themselves to be carried along by the other without seeing it; it is particularly important to show it.

As for me, far from reproaching equality for the unruliness that it inspires, I praise it principally for that. I admire equality when I see it deposit deep within the mind and heart of each man this obscure notion of and this instinctive propensity for political independence. In this way equality prepares the remedy for the evil to which it gives birth. It is from this side that I am attached to it.

JEFFERSON AND TOCQUEVILLE ON LIBERTY AND EQUALITY

Peter S. Onuf

Thomas Jefferson believed the American Declaration of Independence, adopted by Congress on July 4, 1776, changed everything. Disclaiming any "originality" as the Declaration's draftsman, Jefferson predicted that on the eve of its fiftieth anniversary—and of his own death—the Declaration would arouse men everywhere to "burst the chains under which monkish ignorance and superstition had persuaded them to bind themselves, and to assume the blessings and security of self-government." As one of the few "surviving signers of an instrument pregnant with our own, and the fate of the world," Jefferson regretted that age and illness prevented him from attending the Independence Day celebration in Washington, DC.

However, it was gratifying for him to reflect that "our fellow-citizens, after half a century of experience and prosperity, continue to approve" the "bold and doubtful election" Jefferson and his fellow patriots had made "for our country, between submission or the sword." By proclaiming the right to govern themselves, Americans restored the "free right to the unbounded exercise of reason and freedom of opinion."[1]

The United States set an example for the benighted and oppressed nations of the world, enabling them to grasp the "self-evident" truths that inspired revolutionary patriots to overthrow Britain's tyrannical rule. The new nation was "exceptional" only because it was precocious. "All eyes are opened, or opening, to the rights of man," Jefferson wrote Roger Weightman, one of the organizers of the July 4 celebration. Though democratic revolutions had been suppressed and "rivers of blood" had flowed across battle-scarred Europe, the old regime was nonetheless in its death throes. "The general spread of the light of science has already laid open to every view the palpable truth, that the mass of mankind has not been born with saddles on their backs, nor a favored few booted and spurred, ready to ride them legitimately, by the grace of God." The misguided faith in divinely sanctioned hierarchy that had sustained monarchy and aristocracy through centuries of darkness and ignorance had been irrevocably shattered. "These are grounds of hope for others," Jefferson concluded.

Defenders of the old regime would exact enormous sacrifices from freedom-loving peoples who sought to vindicate their rights. During the French Revolution a younger Jefferson had written that "the liberty of the whole earth was depending on the issue of the contest," and "rather than it should have failed, I would have seen half the earth desolated." "Were there but an Adam and an Eve left in every country, and left free, it would be better than as it now is."[2] The fundamental principles of equal rights Jefferson articulated on behalf of his fellow Americans in the Declaration would ultimately lead to the "liberty of the whole earth." The democratic revolution was irreversible.

Alexis de Tocqueville reached a similar conclusion in *Democracy in America*.[3] "A great democratic revolution is taking place among us," he wrote, long after the French Revolutionary War had "devastated" Europe. This "irresistible revolution" was a "providential fact," the inevitable culmination of the "gradual development of equality of conditions" in "all of the Christian universe." The role of "nature's God" in Jefferson's Declaration anticipated the God in Tocqueville's *Democracy*, whose will was reflected "in the regular march of nature and the continuous tendency of events"; in similar fashion, Jefferson's invocation of the American people's recognition of fundamental natural rights principles previewed the recognition of the emergence of a democratic "social state" that preoccupied Tocqueville.[4] Yet if both thinkers can be described as democratic determinists, their understandings of historical change and the role of "political science" or philosophy in discerning and possibly directing the course of history diverged profoundly.

The optimism Jefferson expressed to Weightman about the progress of enlightenment and the coming worldwide republican millennium stands in stark contrast to Tocqueville's prophetic warnings about democratic despotism. Jefferson argued that recognition of equal rights, grounded in nature, would lead to the "liberty of the whole earth": equality and liberty are inextricably and unproblematically linked. But Tocqueville insisted that "the taste that men have for liberty and the one that they feel for equality are, in fact, two distinct things, and I am not afraid to add that, among democratic peoples, they are two unequal things." Indeed, "a depraved taste for equality . . . leads the weak to want to bring the strong down to their level and that reduces men to preferring equality in servitude to inequality in liberty."[5]

My goal in this essay will be to put Jefferson and Tocqueville into conversation with each other, beginning with a discussion of their different perspectives on the course of history and the importance of the Declaration of Independence. A closer look at their understandings of the relationship between liberty and equality will reveal more fundamental agreements.

Tocqueville's great discovery in *Democracy in America* was that the two great "passions" coexisted and reinforced each other in the extraordinary circumstances he observed on his travels in America. For his part, Jefferson's legendary optimism was shadowed by anxieties about the future of republicanism, both in the larger world, where peoples could still only "hope" to overthrow despotic regimes, and in the United States itself, where counterrevolutionary tendencies to concentrate power and assault liberty were all too conspicuous. The two philosophical statesmen were equally unwilling to observe history take its irresistible course. Both sought to develop an enlightened political science that would sustain liberty in a democratic world, both looked to constitutional design and the law of inheritance to promote civic participation and rights consciousness, and both could "imagine," in Tocqueville's words, "an extreme point where liberty and equality meet and merge."[6]

Seeing Things Differently

Though Tocqueville called Jefferson the "greatest democrat who has yet emerged from within the American democracy," he never discussed the Declaration of Independence. Nor, in Tocqueville's view, did the American Revolution make America democratic: "This country sees the results of the democratic revolution that is taking place among us, without having had the revolution itself." "The principle of democracy" was "transplanted . . . to the shores of the New World" without the countervailing, hierarchical principles against which it struggled in Europe and was then "able to grow in liberty and, moving ahead with mores, to develop peacefully in the laws." Aristocracy never took root in British America, notwithstanding the social aspirations of great slaveholding planters. Provincial grandees lacked the privileges and patronage that enabled their European counterparts to command the deference of their humble neighbors. Because they were "not much different from the mass of the people whose passions and interests" they "easily embraced," patriots such as Jefferson put themselves "at the head of the insurrection." Ordinary people, "in whose name" the Revolution was fought, "acquired a taste for all kinds of independence," but this mobilization of popular political energy reinforced broadly shared commitments to liberty and the rule of law. There was no social revolution in America.[7]

Cross-class social solidarity in the American colonies made it possible for Jefferson and his fellow patriots to invoke the language of equality and natural rights. Confident in the capacity of the "mass of the people" to grasp the "self-evident" axioms of republican government, revolutionary leaders looked forward to the progress of enlightenment. The civic health of the new American republic depended on the transparency that enabled vigilant citizens to monitor the exercise of power by public "servants." The defense of liberty in America was predicated on clear-sighted vision, exposing the secret machinations of the privileged and powerful to the light of day: "All eyes are opened, or opening, to the rights of man," as Jefferson put it, and they must be kept open.

Tocqueville's France presented a much different and more confusing spectacle. If American revolutionaries recognized and sought to preserve an "eminently democratic . . . social state," "democracy in France has overturned everything that it met on its way, weakening what it did not destroy." When French revolutionaries invoked natural rights principles, they unleashed a powerful counterrevolutionary reaction. "We have destroyed an aristocratic society," abandoning "what the old state could present of the good" without acquiring the benefits of a "moral and tranquil democracy." The popular rage for equality unleashed destructive forces that subverted liberty, property, and privilege, sundering the social bonds that sustained national solidarity. The democratic revolution brought mutually suspicious and hostile groups "closer together," giving them all "new reasons to hate each other." The pervasive loss of trust and social capital led French citizens to eye "one another with looks full of terror and envy" and "mutually push each other away from power." Turning to an all-powerful state, fearful citizens resigned themselves to the loss of liberty. "Society is tranquil, not because it is conscious of its strength and its well-being, but on the contrary because it believes itself weak and frail; it is afraid of dying by making an effort." The sorry result, Tocqueville concluded, was that the "idea of rights does not exist."[8]

If for Jefferson the recognition of natural rights and the ultimate triumph of republicanism defined the progressively enlightened modern age, Tocqueville bore witness to the "strange confusion" of a world turned upside down when a person's "language" no longer corresponded to "his true sentiments and to his secret instincts."[9] "Religious men combat liberty, and the friends of liberty attack religion; noble and generous spirits speak in praise of slavery, and base and servile souls advocate independence; honest and enlightened citizens are enemies of all progress, while men without patriotism and without mores become the apostles of civilization and enlightenment!"[10]

The ordinary men whose "devotion" to their social superiors sustained the old regime were the leading victims of this epistemological confusion. "By giving themselves so blindly" to the "exclusive passion" for equality, "they compromise their dearest interests." The people cannot see clearly, "or rather they see in the whole universe only one single good worthy of desire." "The passion for equality penetrates the human heart from all directions, it spreads and fills it entirely."[11]

Tocqueville's great insight was that the survival of liberty in the democratic future depended on the social trust fostered by the customs or mores that defined a people and made them recognizable to each other. In the wake of violent regime change, the French seemingly ceased to be a "people." The progress of equality divided and isolated fearful and distrustful French citizens, subverting the traditional society of ranks and orders but offering no coherent substitute. "So where are we going?" Tocqueville asked his countrymen in the introduction to *Democracy in America*. The invocation of collective identity in his question—the "we" that included Tocqueville and his readers—suggested the possibility of a hopeful answer. If there was no turning back from the great social fact of equality, "we" might nonetheless discern a different destination, a France where liberty could flourish.

"Have all centuries resembled ours?" Tocqueville asked. Survivors of the French revolutionary rupture had known a different world. "Has man always had before his eyes, as today, a world where nothing is connected," a world where man was at war with himself and alienated from his neighbors and "where virtue is without genius, and genius without honor; where love of order merges with the taste for tyrants and the holy cult of liberty with scorn for human laws?"[12] Tocqueville did not want to restore a lost world of inequality and privilege. As Jefferson had told a "candid world," "all men are created equal," and there was no turning back. The democratic "movement . . . is already so strong that it cannot be suspended," for no one could now pretend that rulers had a God-given right to rule over others. "To want to stop democracy," Tocqueville wrote, "would then seem to be struggling against God himself." Yet much that was good had been lost with the demystification and collapse of the old regime, including the very idea of liberty itself. The great challenge to modern political leaders therefore was to develop a "new political science" before it was too late, for the progress of democracy was "not yet so rapid as to despair of directing it." It was incumbent on them to "instruct democracy, to revive its beliefs if possible, to purify its mores, to regulate its movements, to substitute little by little the science of public affairs for its inexperience, knowledge of its true interests for its blind instincts."[13]

What could the political scientist see that was not apparent to a people "blinded" by its passion for equality? *Democracy in America* was Tocqueville's answer. Combining a long view of the progress of the equality principle across the centuries with a cross-national comparison of distinctive pathways to the future, Tocqueville sought to identify the specific historical and cultural circumstances that fostered a love of liberty under the old regime and that might enable it to survive in a democratic age. "When royal power, supported by the aristocracy, peacefully governed the peoples of Europe," Tocqueville wrote, "society, amid its miseries, enjoyed several kinds of happiness, which are difficult to imagine and appreciate today."[14] A hierarchical social order seemed natural and legitimate before the principle of equality was abstracted from the social reality of increasingly equal conditions in the modern era.

When philosophers asserted and revolutionary leaders acted on the premise that all men were equal by nature, the legitimacy of the old regime was shattered and the fabric of social relations was torn asunder. Before equality became a rallying cry, the "people accepted the benefits and did not question the rights of their rulers." For their part, monarchs, "feeling vested in the eyes of the crowd with a nearly divine character, drew, from the very respect that they caused, the will not to abuse their power," thus buttressing their authority against powerful nobles who aspired to royal authority; these nobles in turn did not fear challenges from below, for serfs saw their "inferiority as a result of the immutable order of nature," making possible a "kind of reciprocal" (if highly asymmetrical) "benevolence." A rough balance of power among the privileged ruling classes thus gave rise to "customs and mores" that "established limits to tyranny and founded *a kind of right* in the very midst of force."[15] Liberty coexisted with inequality; indeed the "kind of right" that the most miserable and oppressed subjects of the old regime enjoyed depended on universal belief in hierarchy. "You then saw in society inequality, miseries, but souls were not degraded."

The customs and mores of the old regime buffered social relations and mitigated the miseries of a hierarchical social order. When French revolutionaries embraced the idea of equality, they demolished the web of reciprocal relationships that protected vulnerable individuals against despotic force in an anarchic "state of nature." The goal of Tocqueville's "political science" was not to turn back the clock but rather to sustain and promote social attachments in a democratic world in which "all men are created equal" and hierarchical distinctions are seen as unnatural and illegitimate. The great question was whether the "ardent, insatiable, eternal, invincible passion for equality" that the French Revolution unleashed would destroy liberty. The people may "want equality in liberty," Tocqueville warned, but "if they cannot obtain that, they still want equality in slavery. They will suffer poverty, enslavement, barbarism, but they will not suffer aristocracy."[16]

Spared the indiscriminate destructiveness of the French Revolution, American democracy showed that the social order and political regime could evolve progressively toward the "equality of conditions" that Tocqueville saw as history's endpoint. His travels in America enabled him

> to imagine a society where all, seeing the law as their work, would love it and would submit to it without difficulty; where since the authority of the government is respected as necessary and not as divine, the love that is felt for the head of State would be not a passion, but a reasoned and calm sentiment. Since each person has rights and is assured of preserving his rights, a manly confidence and a kind of reciprocal condescension, as far from pride as from servility, would be established among all classes.[17]

Seeing democracy at work in the United States, Tocqueville could imagine a different and better future for his own country in the wake of the "strange confusion" and "intellectual miseries" of the French Revolution. France's redemption and its prospects as a modern, democratic nation depended on the reconstruction of civil society on a horizontal plane, through the "free association of citizens" who were "instructed in their true interests" and who recognized that they could only "take advantage of the good things of society" if they submitted to its "burdens."[18] Liberty for Tocqueville was contingent on citizens' recognition of their dependence on each other in specific historical circumstances.

Tocqueville ignored the Declaration of Independence in *Democracy in America* because the distinctive social and cultural settings that made Jefferson's natural rights claims seem commonsensical and self-evident to his original auditors were more significant to him than the claims themselves. Developing in tandem with liberty in America, equality described an emerging social state. Jefferson said as much when he wrote that the Declaration was intended "to be an expression of the American mind" and disclaimed any "originality of principle or sentiment" as the document's author.[19] As Americans mobilized to preserve their liberty against British tyranny, they became conscious of their equality with each other. "By breaking the yoke of the home country," Tocqueville wrote, Americans preserved their "eminently democratic . . . social state."[20] In France, by contrast, equality was a powerful and destructive abstraction. Appeals to natural rights accelerated progress toward equality of conditions but left individuals isolated, disconnected, and powerless.

Tocqueville and Jefferson saw the democratic revolution in radically different terms. For Tocqueville, the "irresistible" progress of equality was the "most continuous, oldest and most permanent fact known in history," the result of increasingly complicated social relationships, the division of great estates, the rising influence of commerce, and the spread of enlightenment. "As new roads to achieve power are found," Tocqueville concluded, "we see the value of birth fall." If you reviewed French history at half-century intervals from the eleventh century forward, "you will not fail to have noticed" that the "noble will have slipped on the social ladder, the commoner will have risen; the one descends, the other ascends." For Tocqueville equality therefore was an emerging social fact, immanent in long-term historical developments.[21]

Jefferson and his revolutionary colleagues looked beyond history to people's inherent capacity to shape their own destiny in accord with the "laws of nature & of nature's god."[22] Only by demystifying and demolishing the old regime could colonial subjects of King George III recognize themselves as citizens capable of self-government. Declaring independence constituted a sudden moment of collective enlightenment, when the people saw through the unnatural and illegitimate pretensions of arbitrary power. Recognizing themselves as human beings with rights grounded in nature rather than in property titles descending through history from godlike kings with sovereign authority over their vast dominions, Americans claimed an "equal and independent station . . . among the powers of the earth."[23] As they inaugurated their "new order of the ages," forward-looking American patriots rejected history, articulating universal natural rights claims for all.

Origins of American Democracy

Tocqueville's dark forebodings about the potential loss of liberty in the modern world and the "equality in servitude" that might be the ultimate result of the "great democratic revolution . . . taking place among us"[24] contrast starkly with Jefferson's optimistic vision of the spread of natural rights thinking and republican self-government in a progressively enlightened world. Jefferson and his fellow revolutionaries invoked timeless, universal, and abstract principles in order to establish their self-created nation's claims to legitimacy. As Congressmen contemplated the "bold and doubtful election we were to make for our country," the vindication of those principles and the new nation's very existence seemed to hang in the balance.

Taking the existence of the democratic nation for granted, Tocqueville paid little attention to the American Revolution: the *real* "democratic revolution" was immanent in the distinctive circumstances of the colonies' original settlement and their subsequent development; it was not, as Jefferson claimed, the product of a seminal moment, "pregnant with our own, and the fate of the world."[25]

Yet it would be a mistake to exaggerate differences between the two thinkers. Jefferson, the visionary nation maker, looked forward. The exigencies of the revolutionary moment led him to deny historical continuities and thus suppress the mother country's critical contributions to the history of American democracy. The Anglophobic patriot framed the decision for independence in black and white terms, as a fateful choice between British slavery and American freedom. The British threat continued to loom large in subsequent decades as the former mother country spearheaded the "conspiracy of kings" against revolutionary France. Epitomizing everything wrong with the old European regime, monarchical Britain provided the negative referent for American national identity.[26]

Tocqueville's brilliant analysis of the "social state of the *Anglo*-Americans" minimized the significance of the break with Britain.[27] Looking back from the Jacksonian era, *Democracy in America* reflected an emerging understanding of the history of liberty, widely shared among the French visitor's Whig informants, that obscured the contingencies Jeffersonian Democrats emphasized. In retrospect, the claim that July 4, 1776, changed everything seemed absurdly overblown, but Jefferson and his fellow revolutionaries recognized the fateful consequences of failure for themselves, their families, and future generations. Their most momentous challenge was to sustain patriotic commitments to the "common cause"; only by establishing and perfecting union among the new state-republics—or what George Washington later called "wretched fragments of Empire"—could the American experiment in republican government succeed.[28] Without union there could be no American nation and therefore no democracy for Tocqueville to analyze.

Jefferson's Declaration offered "Americans" a compelling narrative of recent events that enabled them to recognize each other as countrymen. By articulating and embracing natural rights principles set forth in the Declaration's opening paragraphs, patriots could transcend their provincial, *Anglo-American* identities and imagine themselves a single people. Jefferson appealed to rights-conscious individuals, urging them to choose freedom over slavery. His recital of the king's crimes in the body of the Declaration demolished the legitimacy of monarchical rule and thus converted rebellious traitors into self-governing republicans, but the significance of these choices was to give the people collectively a legitimating pedigree. As Jefferson put it late in his life, the Declaration created one people out of many: it was the "fundamental act of union of these States."[29] It gave Americans a nation-making script for declaring and performing independence. Turning away from the Anglo-American constitutional tradition—and the claims to the "rights of

Englishmen" that had inspired resistance to British authority in the first place—the Declaration relentlessly focused on the misguided policies that alienated Americans from their "British brethren." Translating recent events into a "*long* train of abuses & usurpations" that revealed the king's abiding intention to establish an "absolute tyranny over these states," the Declaration cast the longer arc of Anglo-American history into the shadows.[30]

The American Revolution produced a new nation, but, unlike the French Revolution, it did not (pretend to) produce new people. Tocqueville and Jefferson agreed on the character of the Americans but diverged on their national destiny. In *Democracy* Tocqueville explained how "Anglo-Americans" were drawn to each other by deep-seated cultural predispositions: "The thirteen colonies that simultaneously threw off the yoke of England . . . [had] the same religion, the same language, the same mores, nearly the same laws; they struggled against a common enemy. So they must have had strong reasons to unite closely together, and to be absorbed into one and the same nation." The popular mobilization that culminated in the American Revolution testified to their common heritage and culture. Yet, as Tocqueville's passive construction suggests, Americans were swept along by history, "absorbed" into a single nation: "the United States owed their victory" more to their isolated "position" on the far shores of the Atlantic "than to the merit of their armies or to the patriotism of their citizens."[31]

Jefferson's self-declared American "people" was precociously (we might say, exceptionally) enlightened. He would have endorsed Tocqueville's later argument that popular enlightenment reflected the distinctive laws, customs, culture, and historical experiences of provincial Anglo-Americans. All peoples were not equally capable of governing themselves, Jefferson understood, even if they were "created equal." Yet the political capacity of the Americans, grounded in their long history of self-government, did not necessarily translate into peace, prosperity, and enduring union. Many British commentators predicted—and American patriots feared—that the collapse of the empire would exacerbate long-simmering conflicts within and among the former British provinces. Disunion and a state of war would make citizens of the new state-republics into potentially hostile peoples, as Publius so brilliantly demonstrated in the early numbers of *The Federalist*. America would then become the image of Europe, "a DISUNITED PEOPLE . . . divided and subdivided into little Common-wealths, or Principalities," and the singular character of "Americans," which so fascinated Tocqueville, would fade from view.[32]

Jefferson's invocation of natural rights expressed deeply conservative fears of British reform measures that would reduce liberty-loving Americans to dependence and servility. The body of the Declaration chronicled the "long train of abuses" that subverted the allegiance of George III's faithful subjects, alienating them from their "British brethren" and forcing them to claim independence. "We might have been a free & a great people together," Jefferson exclaimed in a passage Congress excised from the adopted Declaration, "but a communication of grandeur & of freedom it seems is below their dignity."[33] Jefferson's sentimental language illuminates a critical dimension of American nation making—and of the history of democracy—that was obscure to Tocqueville. Before the imperial crisis Anglo-Americans did *not* think of themselves as a distinct people. Colonists instead aspired to equality within the empire and recognition of their standing as part of a single, great British nation. The declaration that Americans constituted a separate people thus negated everything they had argued for during the escalating crisis and obliterated the hybrid identity Tocqueville imputed to them. Independent Americans suppressed their British origins, insisting that they had made their own history.

Jefferson offered the most radical reimagining of the American past in his *Summary View of the Rights of British America* (1774). Before emigrating, he claimed, the first settlers had been the "free inhabitants of the British dominions in Europe." They possessed the right, "which nature has given to all men, of departing from the country in which chance, not choice has placed them, of going in quest of new habitations, and of there establishing new societies, under such laws and regulations as to them shall seem most likely to promote public happiness."[34] Jefferson elaborated on this right of expatriation in his draft of the Declaration. Colonial settlements "were effected at the expence of our own blood & treasure" without any assistance from Great Britain; as they constituted their own governments, settlers "adopted one common king, thereby laying a foundation for perpetual league & amity with them."[35] Jefferson's revisionist account made "our ancestors" the founders not only of their own colonies but of the empire as a whole: by voluntarily "adopting" the king as their own and incorporating him into their constitutions, they established a "perpetual league" or union of British peoples.

When revolutionary Americans declared their independence, Jefferson suggested, they were simply recognizing—and reenacting—what their ancestor-founders had long since accomplished. "Their own blood was spilt in acquiring lands for their settlement, their own fortunes expended in making that settlement effectual," he concluded in his *Summary View*: "For themselves they fought, for themselves they conquered, and for themselves alone they have right to hold."[36] Jefferson's conception of popular sovereignty and national identity thus came into clear focus in his imaginative rewriting of colonial and imperial history. Revolutionaries sought to preserve the precious legacy of liberty bequeathed to them by their ancestors; recognizing themselves as fellow legatees of liberty, they turned against the "tyrant" who had shown himself "unfit to be the ruler of a free people." However, this did not mean Americans rejected the union symbolized by allegiance to the same sovereign. Nation-making patriots instead followed the glorious example of their ancestors as they forged a more perfect union and pledged to "each other our Lives, our Fortunes and our sacred Honor." Congress filled the vacuum of legitimate authority created by George III's abdication.[37]

Natural rights and revisionist history offered complementary justifications for American independence. Every people or nation had the sovereign right to determine its own political destiny; Americans constituted a people because of what Congress ambiguously described as the peculiar "circumstances of our emigration and settlement" in the final version of the Declaration. (Jefferson's explication of those "circumstances" did not survive the editing process, perhaps because of the unsettling implications of his expatriation theory for the European imperial powers from which the new nation sought recognition.) Geopolitical imperatives led Congress to frame its bid for independence in the universal terms of what eminent jurist Emerich de Vattel called *The Law of Nations or the Principles of Natural Law* (1758). The historical claims colonists had made to the "rights of Englishmen" could not be sustained in the international arena after they renounced the sovereign authority of their king. Foreign powers could not intervene in a British civil war without encouraging challenges to their own legitimacy. Anglo-American constitutional claims thus had to be universalized and so abstracted from their original contexts. Only by invoking their natural rights could Americans make a plausible claim to recognition as a separate, independent people.

Jefferson's invocation of natural rights in the Declaration exaggerates his differences with Tocqueville. When nation-making Americans made their "bold and doubtful" choice for independence, they appealed to the higher law of "nature's God." It was incumbent on reluctant revolutionaries to persuade themselves and a "candid world" that George III had abdicated his authority and that Congress spoke for a united people forced by a "history of unremitting injuries and usurpations" to exercise sovereignty in his place.[38] Yet if the "yoke" of metropolitan rule was galling, Americans—including Jefferson—had no intention of demolishing their own old regimes when they metaphorically killed the British king. As Jefferson later wrote Edmund Randolph, the peoples of Virginia and the American province-states sustained their legal regimes across the break with Britain: "When by the declaration of Independance [*sic*] they chose to abolish their former organs for declaring their will, the acts of will already formally & constitutionally declared, remained untouched." The "nation" was reconstituted and re-formed, "not dissolved."[39]

State-making patriots sought to consolidate the authority of their new republican governments by emphasizing and institutionalizing continuity across regime change. They drew deeply on the Anglo-American constitutional tradition as they mobilized voters to authorize new state constitutions that recognized their sovereignty and purged references to the king. Mobilization widened the ambit of popular, democratic politics, as patriot leaders called on their countrymen to pledge their "lives" and "fortunes" to the common cause. But a politicized "people" conscious of its rights had no more interest in turning the world upside down than its leaders. The history-minded, culturally distinctive rights discourse that inspired resistance to British imperial reform efforts thus continued to shape legal and constitutional developments in the states. It was this legal continuity that so impressed Tocqueville, and it was no coincidence that he accorded lawyers such a crucial role in sustaining the balance between equality and liberty in the new American republic. Jefferson was one of these lawyer-statesmen, and his prescriptions for Virginia and the new United States anticipated Tocqueville's major themes.

Aristocracy

The natural rights language of the Declaration performed a vital function in buttressing the legitimacy of the new United States in its quest for recognition. It also pointed toward a glorious future for the first great modern republic, liberated from the despotic rule of a distant and unresponsive metropolis. Yet American revolutionaries knew their republican experiment could fail: counterrevolutionary forces at home and abroad threatened to destroy the union. Despite his faith in the capacity of the people to grasp the fundamental principles of self-government, Jefferson suspected that the human urge to exercise power over others could not be easily suppressed. The aristocratic impulse to perpetuate the rule of privileged families—or what Tocqueville called "family spirit"—was in some sense "natural" and could take myriad forms.[40] Fear of resurgent aristocracy thus animated the Jeffersonian crusade against the high Federalists who infested the Washington and Adams administrations and continued to haunt the American political imagination in subsequent decades.

The aristocratic Tocqueville did not share Jefferson's anxieties about resurgent aristocracy, focusing instead on the powerful tendency immanent in democracy itself to destroy liberty and reduce the masses to a condition of "equality in slavery." What was remarkable about democratic America was the historic linkage of equality and liberty through widespread political participation and civic association. "Democratic liberty" was a legacy of the autonomous corporate governance of English towns that was replicated in the first colonial settlements.[41] In effect, feudal institutions and the liberties they fostered survived in democratic America, emerging unscathed from a revolution that confirmed the "equality of conditions" Americans had so long enjoyed.

Drawing a sharp distinction between the future of democracy in Old World and New, Tocqueville offered a more optimistic assessment of democracy's prospects in America than Jefferson, the iconic optimist, could sustain in his darker moments. Articulating an inspiring vision of the progress of enlightenment and the coming worldwide republican millennium, the author of the Declaration of Independence could not suppress anxieties about the seemingly irrepressible aristocratic and "monocratic" (monarchical) tendencies that threatened to reverse the outcome of the American Revolution. The conception of history that emerges from Jefferson's state papers and correspondence differs fundamentally from the one Tocqueville elaborated so brilliantly in *Democracy*, making it seem that they were talking about different "Americas." However, a closer look at Tocqueville's "political science" and Jefferson's prescriptions for democratic reform reveal their common ground.

Tocqueville's political science was designed to enable European nations to "accommodate themselves to the social state that Providence imposes on them." There was no turning back from democracy: "The movement that sweeps them along is already so strong that it cannot be suspended," but "it is not yet so rapid as to despair of directing it."[42] Jefferson feared that Americans would lose sight of the new nation's founding ideals, and democracy would fail. As he sought to prevent that calamitous outcome, Jefferson emphasized the same bulwarks of liberty Tocqueville identified on his travels of America: broad distribution of landed property, robust institutions of local self-government, widespread political participation and civic association, and deep-seated commitment to the rule of law. Tocqueville took these mitigating characteristics of American democracy for granted, imputing them to the serendipitous combination of the laws, customs, and mores settlers brought with them and a bountiful New World environment. Jefferson was much less sanguine about that colonial legacy.

Anglicizing provincial elites aspired to replicate the society and culture of the metropolis, monopolizing land and labor to distance themselves from their supposed social inferiors. If Tocqueville consigned aristocracy to the predemocratic past, assuming it had never taken root in America, Jefferson was acutely conscious that his own gentry-planter class was all too eager to exploit its domination of provincial politics to establish family dynasties. Tocqueville's discussion of the "laws of landed inheritance" in *Democracy* echoed Jefferson's indictment of the "dead hand of the past" in his famous letter to James Madison in 1789 on generational sovereignty.[43] "The laws of inheritance have a sure and uniform way of operating on society," Tocqueville wrote, laying hold of future "generations before their birth." "Constituted in a certain way," they concentrate "property and, soon after, power, around some head," making aristocracy seem to "spring from the soil" as if naturally or by divine decree.[44] Jefferson feared that this seemingly natural process was already unfolding in provincial Virginia.

As a lawyer steeped in the common law, Jefferson could see how provisions for primogeniture and entail were already leading to the concentration of land ownership in the province's leading families. Land law reform thus constituted a crucial part of the republican law giver's systematic effort to eradicate "every fibre . . . of antient [*sic*] or *future* aristocracy" and lay the "foundation" for a "truly republican" government. In his *Autobiography*, written late in life for family consumption, Jefferson proudly recalled his role in shaping his country's future. "The abolition of primogeniture, and equal partition of inheritances" secured domestic harmony in Virginia by removing the "feudal and unnatural distinctions which made one member of every family rich, and all the rest poor."[45] Repeal of entail meant that the laws would no longer artificially support the "accumulation and perpetuation of wealth in select families." Divisions within and among families that prevented Virginians from recognizing each other as equals would be eliminated. The "family spirit" that dynastic privilege and power fostered and that came to be "embodied in the land" would give way to a genuine and inclusive patriotism.[46] A "truly republican" people then would be devoted to each other and to their "country," the great estate they held in common.

Jefferson may have exaggerated the threat of an "aristocratic revival," but recent scholarship on late provincial Anglo-America suggests a growing concentration of wealth and power in governing elites who did not lack privileges or patronage. Democracy may not have been the irreversible "social fact" Tocqueville imagined. Virginians' traditional reverence for property rights and the rule of law could lead them to submit to growing inequality and an increasingly hierarchical social order. The customs, mores, and laws that Tocqueville believed would perpetuate the democratic social state in America could instead provide fertile ground for aristocracy's emergence and democracy's demise.

For Tocqueville there was no turning back from equality and a democratic future—for better or worse. The demolition of the old regime was absolute and irreversible: equality "crushes or sends flying into pieces all that gets in its way; it constantly rises and falls on the earth until nothing is left in sight but a shifting and intangible dust on which democracy takes its seat."[47] Jefferson was much less certain about the direction of historical change. His faith in the progress of enlightenment and the ultimate triumph of democracy was belied by anxieties about aristocratic and monarchical tendencies in postcolonial America. There was no guarantee that the "equality of conditions" that sustained democracy in America would persist or that the people would be able to preserve their liberties against self-aggrandizing ruling elites. George III and his corrupt ministers had threatened to reduce the colonists to slavery, setting an ominous precedent for the future. The future of republicanism thus depended on the virtuous, public-spirited character of the people. If republicans did not vigilantly keep the "sacred fire of liberty" burning, the American experiment in republican government would fail.

Liberty and Equality

Tocqueville's great fear was that the inevitable triumph of democracy would demolish liberty by leaving equal individuals isolated and alienated from each other and therefore lacking the civic capacity—or what we might call social capital—to resist encroachments on their liberties. Jefferson feared that Americans' love of liberty would prove evanescent. If their civic capacity was embedded in a culture of liberty, as Tocqueville suggested, it also depended on the determination of enlightened and vigilant citizens to defend their rights. The Declaration of Independence would thus be Jefferson's "touchstone" throughout his political career. As the new president told his countrymen in his 1801 Inaugural Address, the principles patriots lived and died for "should be the creed of our political faith [and] the text of civic instruction."[48] Jefferson's prescriptions for preserving the republic previewed Tocqueville's descriptions of the political culture he encountered in democratic America. The challenge to Jefferson's revolutionary generation was to demolish the traditional assumption that all men, in a properly ordered society, were "created unequal." The equality of conditions in provincial Anglo-America may have made it possible to conceive of a republic organized on the premise of equal rights, but what would keep a society of equals from flying apart and descending into anarchy? Tocqueville addressed this fundamental question when he contemplated the future of democracy in Europe. "Anarchy has more frightening features in democratic countries than elsewhere," he acknowledged, and it was hardly surprising that reactionary defenders of traditional order should seek to stem the democratic tide. "Since citizens have no effect on each other, at the instant when the national power that keeps them all in their place becomes absent, it seems that disorder must immediately be at its height and that, with each citizen on his own, the social body is suddenly going to find itself reduced to dust."[49] But the American experience demonstrated that the irrepressible impulse toward equality could be contained and directed in a democratic culture of political participation. Political liberty, Tocqueville and Jefferson agreed, was equality's antidote. The alternative was slavery, whether by submission to a royal tyrant or a democratic despot. The urge to escape the turbulence of democratic politics "would lead by a longer, more secret, but surer road toward servitude."[50]

Jefferson and Tocqueville both thought of liberty in social and civic terms. The political or "positive" liberty Ralph Ketcham discusses in his contribution to this volume was predicated on the isolated individual's incapacity to defend his or her rights or pursue his or her own interests. "Each man, equally weak, will feel an equal need for his fellows," Tocqueville wrote; "knowing that he can gain their support only on condition of lending them his help, he will discover without difficulty that for him particular interest merges with the general interest." The "science of interest" depended on the "enlightenment" that social interaction generated; in free governments, "it is necessary to talk a great deal," and the "need to talk forces men of State to reason, and from speeches a bit of logic is introduced into public affairs."[51] Enlightenment was a virtuous circle, leading citizens both to be vigilant in defense of their rights and conscious of the need to discover and pursue common interests in collaboration with others.

Jefferson did not assume that a talking, deliberative, civic-minded citizenry would emerge spontaneously from the demolition of the provincial old regime. Popular enlightenment depended on the institution of free governments and the republican reformation of the laws. According to an unsuccessful bill Jefferson proposed to the Virginia General Assembly in 1779, a free people must be educated so that it "may be enabled to know ambition under all its shapes"; republican political leaders, "those persons, whom nature hath endowed with genius and virtue, should be rendered by liberal education worthy to receive, and able to guard the sacred deposit of the rights and liberties of their fellow-citizens."[52] Jefferson's famous Bill for Religious Freedom, proposed at the same time and finally adopted in 1786, was designed to protect freedom of mind and speech from clerical domination: "Almighty God hath created the mind free, and manifested his supreme will that free it shall remain by making it altogether insusceptible of restraint."[53] Free speech would sustain free government.

Hierarchical regimes rested on the coercive force that kept people in their places and prevented them from freely associating. Aristocracy fostered what Tocqueville called "family spirit," enabling the favored few to monopolize power and resources and perpetuate their domination across generations. However, the "dead have no rights," Jefferson insisted, for the dead "are nothing; and nothing cannot own something."[54] With the destruction of aristocracy, families could assume their natural form. Family members would be bound to each other by affectionate ties that expressed and fulfilled their true natures; families would in turn recognize the natural affinities and common interests that made them into a "generation." As they did so, they would define themselves against preceding generations even as they acknowledged responsibility for their successors, for "*the earth belongs in usufruct* [or stewardship] *to the living.*" Republican self-government depended on the autonomy and agency—or sovereignty—of each living generation. "By the law of nature," he concluded, "one generation is to another as one independant [*sic*] nation to another."[55]

Jefferson provocatively conflated the most powerful natural tie that bound humans to one another—between one generation and the next, parents and children—to the conventionally antagonistic and often belligerent relationship between "independant [*sic*] nations." Of course, the idealistic republican reformer believed that truly self-governing nations would not make war on each other but would instead recognize their common interests. Jefferson's more fundamental insight was that liberty was the predicate of consent: the sociable impulses that according to Enlightenment moral philosophers defined human nature could only be fully expressed when the rights of consenting citizens were fully secured.

For Jefferson the idea of equality was only meaningful in conjunction with rights: "All men are created equal & independant [*sic*], that from that equal creation they derive rights."[56] Tocqueville's equality was contingently linked with liberty: "nature's God" did not decree their conjunction, nor would it result from history's providential logic. Yet if the two philosophers apparently diverged on fundamental questions, they agreed on the importance of preserving liberty—or equal rights—in the dawning democratic age. For all his faith in the future, Jefferson recognized the need to constitute republican regimes that would safeguard rights and thus enable consenting citizens to forge ever more perfect unions. He enjoined vigilant citizens to defend their rights *as individuals* so that they might freely associate and fulfill their human potential *in society*. "To lose political liberty," Tocqueville later warned, "it is enough not to hold on to it, and liberty escapes"; liberty could only survive under exceptional circumstances such as those he encountered in democratic America, where a free people, secure in their rights, recognized their dependence on one another.[57]

Jefferson's paradoxical injunction was that a free, self-governing people must divide in order to unite. There must be limits to the political will of evanescent majorities if the rights of individual citizens on which the legitimacy of the republic was grounded were to be secured. His conception of generational sovereignty expressed those limits in temporal terms: dividing generation from generation—banishing aristocracy and its perversion of family values—would give rise to new, more natural, cross-generational solidarities. When "family spirit" and dynastic impulses were suppressed, and the "people" subsumed and leveled the ranks and orders of the old regime, enlightened attachments to the nation as a whole would flourish.

Federalism, the division and subdivision of territorial jurisdictions, would have the same benign effect. "It is by dividing and subdividing these republics from the great national one down through all its subordinations," Jefferson wrote Joseph Cabell in 1816, "until it ends in the administration of every man's farm by himself; by placing under every one what his own eye may superintend, that all will be done for the best." The paradoxical effect of this regression from whole to part, Jefferson believed, would be to reverse the centrifugal tendencies that threatened to tear an expanding union apart. Secure in their rights and politically active in their local communities, Americans would identify with each other across the far reaches of their continental empire. "Where every man is a sharer in the direction of his ward-republic," Jefferson told Cabell, "or of some of the higher ones, and feels that he is a participator in the government of affairs, not merely at an election one day in the year, but every day; when there shall not be a man in the State who will not be a member of some one of its councils, great or small, he will let the heart be torn out of his body sooner than his power be wrested from him by a Caesar or a Bonaparte."[58] Civic participation, Tocqueville agreed, fostered patriotic sentiments and strengthened the bonds of union in a culture of liberty.

Slavery and Union

Jefferson's democratic constitutionalism departed from the more familiar Anglo-American tradition associated with his colleague Madison, a difference Madison made clear in his hostile response to Jefferson's conception of generational sovereignty.[59] Madison drew on the Anglo-American constitutional tradition to construct a federal republican superstructure that would balance contending forces and curb democratic excesses: for Madison, as Michael Zuckert shows, the preservation of liberty depended on a constitutional separation of powers. Working from the bottom up, Jefferson's answer to the problems of democratic government was *more* democracy. He sought to create and sustain the culture of liberty Tocqueville so admired in *Democracy in America* by dividing and subdividing the "people"—through time and across space—and fostering political participation and constitutional renewal. Though he took America's democratic culture for granted, reading its origins back to the distinctive circumstances of colonial development and minimizing the importance of the Revolution, Tocqueville's emphasis on a broad distribution of property, robust civic participation, and the American genius for free association echoed Jefferson's main preoccupations. Tocqueville's conception of democracy's inexorable ascent made him oblivious to the protean shapes "aristocracy" might take, but he shared Jefferson's anxieties about the future. Whether a revival of the monarchical old regime or an insensible slide into democratic despotism subverted the American culture of liberty, the ultimate result was the same: slavery.

Of course, slavery was already well established in Jefferson's time. Far from being an awful, distant prospect, the "peculiar institution" was an existing "social fact" that would become more deeply entrenched over the antebellum decades. Divisions over slavery, as Peter Myers argues, constituted a fundamental threat to the union's survival—and therefore to the success of the American experiment in republican government.[60] During the dark days of the Missouri Crisis of 1819–1821, Jefferson looked into the abyss of disunion. "I regret that I am now to die in the belief," he wrote ally John Holmes in the Maine District of Massachusetts, "that the useless sacrifice of themselves by the generation of 1776, to acquire self-government and happiness to their country, is to be thrown away by the unwise and unworthy passions of their sons, and that my only consolation is to be, that I live not to weep over it. If they would but dispassionately weigh the blessings they will throw away, against an abstract principle more likely to be effected by union than by scission, they would pause before they would perpetrate this act of suicide on themselves, and of treason against the hopes of the world."[61] That "abstract principle" was the radical injustice of racial slavery, an institution Jefferson had so eloquently condemned; the "treason" in question was the restrictionist campaign to limit the spread of slavery into the new State of Missouri.

A democratic culture of liberty was the cause and consequence of the remarkable efflorescence of popular political activity that Tocqueville witnessed in the decades after the Missouri Crisis. His genius was to discern deep sources of stability beneath the tumultuous surface of partisan conflict. In the land of liberty, equality did not necessarily lead to slavery, but Tocqueville could not yet see that the reverse might be true: that the very existence of racial slavery jeopardized the federal union and therefore the exceptional circumstances in which the American democratic synthesis of liberty and equality flourished. The Frenchman devoted an extraordinary chapter to the "three races" in America—white, red, and black—and agreed with Jefferson on the impossibility of their becoming a single people through integration and assimilation. When he wrote *Democracy in America*, however, Tocqueville assumed that racial solidarity among whites would lead to the removal, extinction, or permanent subordination of the other "nations."

Profoundly shaken by the Missouri Crisis, Jefferson recognized the fragility of the union. The divisions and subdivisions he hoped would promote and sustain liberty by securing the rights of citizens, wards, counties, and states might instead become defensive barriers and belligerent frontiers. Southerners would demolish the union in order to vindicate their property rights in slaves: he knew this because he knew he would join his neighbors in defending their "peculiar," "domestic institution" even as he continued to acknowledge its fundamental injustice. "A geographical line, coinciding with a marked principle, moral and political, once conceived and held up to the angry passions of men," Jefferson wrote Holmes, "will never be obliterated."[62] Federalism would then unleash the "angry passions" that he hoped and prayed the republican regime would contain and ameliorate. Tocqueville offered a brilliant analysis of the surprising ways in which American democracy resolved the inherent tension between liberty and equality, but his penetrating analysis of the exceptional character of Anglo-American political culture blinded him to the fragility of the federal union. He could not anticipate the collapse of the union and the democracy's defining crisis in the Civil War. A despairing Jefferson proved to be a better prophet of the coming cataclysm, but the principles Jefferson articulated so eloquently in the Declaration and reiterated in his letter to Roger Weightman offered an enduring inspiration to American democrats. American democracy may have failed in the great sectional conflagration, but its promise could be renewed and redeemed by future generations. After all, as Jefferson told Madison, "*the earth belongs in usufruct to the living.*"

2 • Liberty, Equality, and Constitutional Principles

Representation and Democracy

FEDERALIST 10

Among the numerous advantages promised by a well constructed Union, none deserves to be more accurately developed than its tendency to break and control the violence of faction. The friend of popular governments never finds himself so much alarmed for their character and fate, as when he contemplates their propensity to this dangerous vice. He will not fail, therefore, to set a due value on any plan which, without violating the principles to which he is attached, provides a proper cure for it. The instability, injustice, and confusion introduced into the public councils, have, in truth, been the mortal diseases under which popular governments have everywhere perished; as they continue to be the favorite and fruitful topics from which the adversaries to liberty derive their most specious declamations. The valuable improvements made by the American constitutions on the popular models, both ancient and modern, cannot certainly be too much admired; but it would be an unwarrantable partiality, to contend that they have as effectually obviated the danger on this side, as was wished and expected. Complaints are everywhere heard from our most considerate and virtuous citizens, equally the friends of public and private faith, and of public and personal liberty, that our governments are too unstable, that the public good is disregarded in the conflicts of rival parties, and that measures are too often decided, not according to the rules of justice and the rights of the minor party, but by the superior force of an interested and overbearing majority. However anxiously we may wish that these complaints had no foundation, the evidence, of known facts will not permit us to deny that they are in some degree true. It will be found, indeed, on a candid review of our situation, that some of the distresses under which we labor have been erroneously charged on the operation of our governments; but it will be found, at the same time, that other causes will not alone account for many of our heaviest misfortunes; and, particularly, for that prevailing and increasing distrust of public engagements, and alarm for private rights, which are echoed from one end of the continent to the other. These must be chiefly, if not wholly, effects of the unsteadiness and injustice with which a factious spirit has tainted our public administrations.

By a faction, I understand a number of citizens, whether amounting to a majority or a minority of the whole, who are united and actuated by some common impulse of passion, or of interest, adverse to the rights of other citizens, or to the permanent and aggregate interests of the community.

There are two methods of curing the mischiefs of faction: the one, by removing its causes; the other, by controlling its effects.

There are again two methods of removing the causes of faction: the one, by destroying the liberty which is essential to its existence; the other, by giving to every citizen the same opinions, the same passions, and the same interests.

It could never be more truly said then of the first remedy, that it was worse than the disease. Liberty is to faction what air is to fire, an aliment without which it instantly expires. But it could not be less folly to abolish liberty, which is essential to political life, because it nourishes faction, than it would be to wish the annihilation of air, which is essential to animal life, because it imparts to fire its destructive agency.

The second expedient is as impracticable as the first would be unwise. As long as the reason of man continues fallible, and he is at liberty to exercise it, different opinions will be formed. As long as the connection subsists between his reason and his self-love, his opinions and his passions will have a reciprocal influence on each other; and the former will be objects to which the latter will attach themselves. The diversity in the faculties of men, from which the rights of property originate, is not less an insuperable obstacle to a uniformity of interests. The protection of these faculties is the first object of government. From the protection of different and unequal faculties of acquiring property, the possession of different degrees and kinds of property immediately results; and from the influence of these on the sentiments and views of the respective proprietors, ensues a division of the society into different interests and parties.

The latent causes of faction are thus sown in the nature of man; and we see them everywhere brought into different degrees of activity, according to the different circumstances of civil society. A zeal for different opinions concerning religion, concerning government, and many other points, as well of speculation as of practice; an attachment to different leaders ambitiously contending for pre-eminence and power; or to persons of other descriptions whose fortunes have been interesting to the human passions, have, in turn, divided mankind into parties, inflamed them with mutual animosity, and rendered them much more disposed to vex and oppress each other than to co-operate for their common good. So strong is this propensity of mankind to fall into mutual animosities, that where no substantial occasion presents itself, the most frivolous and fanciful distinctions have been sufficient to kindle their unfriendly passions and excite their most violent conflicts. But the most common and durable source of factions has been the various and unequal distribution of property. Those who hold and those who are without property have ever formed distinct interests in society. Those who are creditors, and those who are debtors, fall under a like discrimination. A landed interest, a manufacturing interest, a mercantile interest, a moneyed interest, with many lesser interests, grow up of necessity in civilized nations, and divide them into different classes, actuated by different sentiments and views. The regulation of these various and interfering interests forms the principal task of modern legislation, and involves the spirit of party and faction in the necessary and ordinary operations of the government.

No man is allowed to be a judge in his own cause, because his interest would certainly bias his judgment, and, not improbably, corrupt his integrity. With equal, nay with greater reason, a body of men are unfit to be both judges and parties at the same time; yet what are many of the most important acts of legislation, but so many judicial determinations, not indeed concerning the rights of single persons, but concerning the rights of large bodies of citizens? And what are the different classes of legislators but advocates and parties to the causes which they determine? Is a law proposed concerning private debts? It is a question to which the creditors are parties on one side and the debtors on the other. Justice ought to hold the balance between them. Yet the parties are, and must be, themselves the judges; and the most numerous party, or, in other words, the most powerful faction must be expected to prevail. Shall domestic manufactures be encouraged, and in what degree, by restrictions on foreign manufactures? are questions which would be differently decided by the landed and the manufacturing classes, and probably by neither with a sole regard to justice and the public good. The apportionment of taxes on the various descriptions of property is an act which seems to require the most exact impartiality; yet there is, perhaps, no legislative act in which greater opportunity and temptation are given to a predominant party to trample on the rules of justice. Every shilling with which they overburden the inferior number, is a shilling saved to their own pockets.

It is in vain to say that enlightened statesmen will be able to adjust these clashing interests, and render them all subservient to the public good. Enlightened statesmen will not always be at the helm. Nor, in many cases, can such an adjustment be made at all without taking into view indirect and remote considerations, which will rarely prevail over the immediate interest which one party may find in disregarding the rights of another or the good of the whole.

The inference to which we are brought is, that the *causes* of faction cannot be removed, and that relief is only to be sought in the means of controlling its *effects*.

If a faction consists of less than a majority, relief is supplied by the republican principle, which enables the majority to defeat its sinister views by regular vote. It may clog the administration, it may convulse the society; but it will be unable to execute and mask its violence under the forms of the Constitution. When a majority is included in a faction, the form of popular government, on the other hand, enables it to sacrifice to its ruling passion or interest both the public good and the rights of other citizens. To secure the public good and private rights against the danger of such a faction, and at the same time to preserve the spirit and the form of popular government, is then the great object to which our inquiries are directed. Let me add that it is the great desideratum by which this form of government can be rescued from the opprobrium under which it has so long labored, and be recommended to the esteem and adoption of mankind.

By what means is this object attainable? Evidently by one of two only. Either the existence of the same passion or interest in a majority at the same time must be prevented, or the majority, having such coexistent passion or interest, must be rendered, by their number and local situation, unable to concert and carry into effect schemes of oppression. If the impulse and the opportunity be suffered to coincide, we well know that neither moral nor religious motives can be relied on as an adequate control. They are not found to be such on the injustice and violence of individuals, and lose their efficacy in proportion to the number combined together, that is, in proportion as their efficacy becomes needful.

From this view of the subject it may be concluded that a pure democracy, by which I mean a society consisting of a small number of citizens, who assemble and administer the government in person, can admit of no cure for the mischiefs of faction. A common passion or interest will, in almost every case, be felt by a majority of the whole; a communication and concert result from the form of government itself; and there is nothing to check the inducements to sacrifice the weaker party or an obnoxious individual. Hence it is that such democracies have ever been spectacles of turbulence and contention; have ever been found incompatible with personal security or the rights of property; and have in general been as short in their lives as they have been violent in their deaths. Theoretic politicians, who have patronized this species of government, have erroneously supposed that by reducing mankind to a perfect equality in their political rights, they would, at the same time, be perfectly equalized and assimilated in their possessions, their opinions, and their passions.

A republic, by which I mean a government in which the scheme of representation takes place, opens a different prospect, and promises the cure for which we are seeking. Let us examine the points in which it varies from pure democracy, and we shall comprehend both the nature of the cure and the efficacy which it must derive from the Union.

The two great points of difference between a democracy and a republic are: first, the delegation of the government, in the latter, to a small number of citizens elected by the rest; secondly, the greater number of citizens, and greater sphere of country, over which the latter may be extended.

The effect of the first difference is, on the one hand, to refine and enlarge the public views, by passing them through the medium of a chosen body of citizens, whose wisdom may best discern the true interest of their country, and whose patriotism and love of justice will be least likely to sacrifice it to temporary or partial considerations. Under such a regulation, it may well happen that the public voice, pronounced by the representatives of the people, will be more consonant to the public good than if pronounced by the people themselves, convened for the purpose. On the other hand, the effect may be inverted. Men of factious tempers, of local prejudices, or of sinister designs, may, by intrigue, by corruption, or by other means, first obtain the suffrages, and then betray the interests, of the people. The question resulting is, whether small or extensive republics are more favorable to the election of proper guardians of the public weal; and it is clearly decided in favor of the latter by two obvious considerations:

In the first place, it is to be remarked that, however small the republic may be, the representatives must be raised to a certain number, in order to guard against the cabals of a few; and that, however large it may be, they must be limited to a certain number, in order to guard against the confusion of a multitude. Hence, the number of representatives in the two cases not being in proportion to that of the two constituents, and being proportionally greater in the small republic, it follows that, if the proportion of fit characters be not less in the large than in the small republic, the former will present a greater option, and consequently a greater probability of a fit choice.

In the next place, as each representative will be chosen by a greater number of citizens in the large than in the small republic, it will be more difficult for unworthy candidates to practice with success the vicious arts by which elections are too often carried; and the suffrages of the people being more free, will be more likely to centre in men who possess the most attractive merit and the most diffusive and established characters.

It must be confessed that in this, as in most other cases, there is a mean, on both sides of which inconveniences will be found to lie. By enlarging too much the number of electors, you render the representatives too little acquainted with all their local circumstances and lesser interests; as by reducing it too much, you render him unduly attached to these, and too little fit to comprehend and pursue great and national objects. The federal Constitution forms a happy combination in this respect; the great and aggregate interests being referred to the national, the local and particular to the State legislatures.

The other point of difference is, the greater number of citizens and extent of territory which may be brought within the compass of republican than of democratic government; and it is this circumstance principally which renders factious combinations less to be dreaded in the former than in the latter. The smaller the society, the fewer probably will be the distinct parties and interests composing it;

the fewer the distinct parties and interests, the more frequently will a majority be found of the same party; and the smaller the number of individuals composing a majority, and the smaller the compass within which they are placed, the more easily will they concert and execute their plans of oppression. Extend the sphere, and you take in a greater variety of parties and interests; you make it less probable that a majority of the whole will have a common motive to invade the rights of other citizens; or if such a common motive exists, it will be more difficult for all who feel it to discover their own strength, and to act in unison with each other. Besides other impediments, it may be remarked that, where there is a consciousness of unjust or dishonorable purposes, communication is always checked by distrust in proportion to the number whose concurrence is necessary.

Hence, it clearly appears, that the same advantage which a republic has over a democracy, in controlling the effects of faction, is enjoyed by a large over a small republic—is enjoyed by the Union over the States composing it. Does the advantage consist in the substitution of representatives whose enlightened views and virtuous sentiments render them superior to local prejudices and schemes of injustice? It will not be denied that the representation of the Union will be most likely to possess these requisite endowments. Does it consist in the greater security afforded by a greater variety of parties, against the event of any one party being able to outnumber and oppress the rest? In an equal degree does the increased variety of parties comprised within the Union, increase this security. Does it, in fine, consist in the greater obstacles opposed to the concert and accomplishment of the secret wishes of an unjust and interested majority? Here, again, the extent of the Union gives it the most palpable advantage.

The influence of factious leaders may kindle a flame within their particular States, but will be unable to spread a general conflagration through the other States. A religious sect may degenerate into a political faction in a part of the Confederacy; but the variety of sects dispersed over the entire face of it must secure the national councils against any danger from that source. A rage for paper money, for an abolition of debts, for an equal division of property, or for any other improper or wicked project, will be less apt to pervade the whole body of the Union than a particular member of it; in the same proportion as such a malady is more likely to taint a particular county or district, than an entire State.

In the extent and proper structure of the Union, therefore, we behold a republican remedy for the diseases most incident to republican government. And according to the degree of pleasure and pride we feel in being republicans, ought to be our zeal in cherishing the spirit and supporting the character of Federalists.

FEDERALIST 39 (First Half)

The last paper having concluded the observations which were meant to introduce a candid survey of the plan of government reported by the convention, we now proceed to the execution of that part of our undertaking.

The first question that offers itself is, whether the general form and aspect of the government be strictly republican. It is evident that no other form would be reconcilable with the genius of the people of America; with the fundamental principles of the Revolution; or with that honorable determination which animates every votary of freedom, to rest all our political experiments on the capacity of mankind for self-government. If the plan of the convention, therefore, be found to depart from the republican character, its advocates must abandon it as no longer defensible.

What, then, are the distinctive characters of the republican form? Were an answer to this question to be sought, not by recurring to principles, but in the application of the term by political writers, to the constitution of different States, no satisfactory one would ever be found. Holland, in which no particle of the supreme authority is derived from the people, has passed almost universally under the denomination of a republic. The same title has been bestowed on Venice, where absolute power over the great body of the people is exercised, in the most absolute manner, by a small body of hereditary nobles. Poland, which is a mixture of aristocracy and of monarchy in their worst forms, has been dignified with the same appellation. The government of England, which has one republican branch only, combined with an hereditary aristocracy and monarchy, has, with equal impropriety, been frequently placed on the list of republics. These examples, which are nearly as dissimilar to each other as to a genuine republic, show the extreme inaccuracy with which the term has been used in political disquisitions.

If we resort for a criterion to the different principles on which different forms of government are established, we may define a republic to be, or at least may bestow that name on, a government which derives all its powers directly or indirectly from the great body of the people, and is administered by persons holding their offices during pleasure, for a limited period, or during good behavior. It is *essential* to such a government that it be derived from the great body of the society, not from an inconsiderable proportion, or a favored class of it; otherwise a handful of tyrannical nobles, exercising their oppressions by a delegation of their powers, might aspire to the rank of republicans, and claim for their government the honorable title of republic. It is *sufficient* for such a government that the persons administering it be appointed, either directly or indirectly, by the people; and that they hold their appointments by either of the tenures just specified; otherwise every government in the United States, as well as every other popular government that has been or can be well organized or well executed, would be degraded from the republican character. According to the constitution of every State in the Union, some or other of the officers of government are appointed indirectly only by the people. According to most of them, the chief magistrate himself is so appointed. And according to one, this mode of appointment is extended to one of the co-ordinate branches of the legislature. According to all the constitutions, also, the tenure of the highest offices is extended to a definite period, and in many instances, both within the legislative and executive departments, to a period of years. According to the provisions of most of the constitutions, again, as well as according to the most respectable and received opinions on the subject, the members of the judiciary department are to retain their offices by the firm tenure of good behavior.

On comparing the Constitution planned by the convention with the standard here fixed, we perceive at once that it is, in the most rigid sense, conformable to it. The House of Representatives, like that of one branch at least of all the State legislatures, is elected immediately by the great body of the people. The Senate, like the present Congress, and the Senate of Maryland, derives its appointment indirectly from the people. The President is indirectly derived from the choice of the people, according to the example in most of the States. Even the judges, with all other officers of the Union, will, as in the several States, be the choice, though a remote choice, of the people themselves, the duration of the appointments is equally conformable to the republican standard, and to the model of State constitutions. The House of Representatives is periodically elective, as in all the States; and for the period of two years, as in the State of South Carolina. The Senate is elective, for the period of six years; which is but one year more than the period of the Senate of Maryland, and but two more than that of the Senates of New York and Virginia. The President is to continue in office for the period of four years; as in New York and Delaware, the chief magistrate is elected for three years, and in South Carolina for two years. In the other States the election is annual. In several of the States, however, no constitutional provision is made for the impeachment of the chief magistrate. And in Delaware and Virginia he is not impeachable till out of office. The President of the United States is impeachable at any time during his continuance in office. The tenure by which the judges are to hold their places, is, as it unquestionably ought to be, that of good behavior. The tenure of the ministerial offices generally, will be a subject of legal regulation, conformably to the reason of the case and the example of the State constitutions.

Could any further proof be required of the republican complexion of this system, the most decisive one might be found in its absolute prohibition of titles of nobility, both under the federal and the State governments; and in its express guaranty of the republican form to each of the latter.

FEDERALIST 57

The *third* charge against the House of Representatives is, that it will be taken from that class of citizens which will have least sympathy with the mass of the people, and be most likely to aim at an ambitious sacrifice of the many to the aggrandizement of the few.

Of all the objections which have been framed against the federal Constitution, this is perhaps the most extraordinary. Whilst the objection itself is leveled against a pretended oligarchy, the principle of it strikes at the very root of republican government.

The aim of every political constitution is, or ought to be, first to obtain for rulers men who possess most wisdom to discern, and most virtue to pursue, the common good of the society; and in the next place, to take the most effectual precautions for keeping them virtuous whilst they continue to hold their public trust. The elective mode of obtaining rulers is the characteristic policy of republican government. The means relied on in this form of government for preventing their degeneracy are numerous and various. The most effectual one, is such a limitation of the term of appointments, as will maintain a proper responsibility to the people.

Let me now ask what circumstance there is in the constitution of the House of Representatives that violates the principles of republican government, or favors the elevation of the few on the ruins of the many? Let me ask whether every circumstance is not, on the contrary, strictly conformable to these principles, and scrupulously impartial to the rights and pretensions of every class and description of citizens?

Who are to be the electors of the federal representatives? Not the rich, more than the poor; not the learned, more than the ignorant; not the haughty heirs of distinguished names, more than the humble sons of obscurity and unpropitious fortune. The electors are to be the great body of the people of the United States. They are to be the same who exercise the right in every State of electing the corresponding branch of the legislature of the State.

Who are to be the objects of popular choice? Every citizen whose merit may recommend him to the esteem and confidence of his country. No qualification of wealth, of birth, of religious faith, or of civil profession is permitted to fetter the judgment or disappoint the inclination of the people.

If we consider the situation of the men on whom the free suffrages of their fellow-citizens may confer the representative trust, we shall find it involving every security which can be devised or desired for their fidelity to their constituents.

In the first place, as they will have been distinguished by the preference of their fellow-citizens, we are to presume that in general they will be somewhat distinguished also by those qualities which entitle them to it, and which promise a sincere and scrupulous regard to the nature of their engagements.

In the second place, they will enter into the public service under circumstances which cannot fail to produce a temporary affection at least to their constituents. There is in every breast a sensibility to marks of honor, of favor, of esteem, and of confidence, which, apart from all considerations of interest, is some pledge for grateful and benevolent returns. Ingratitude is a common topic of declamation against human nature; and it must be confessed that instances of it are but too frequent and flagrant, both in public and in private life. But the universal and extreme indignation which it inspires is itself a proof of the energy and prevalence of the contrary sentiment.

In the third place, those ties which bind the representative to his constituents are strengthened by motives of a more selfish nature. His pride and vanity attach him to a form of government which favors his pretensions and gives him a share in its honors and distinctions. Whatever hopes or projects might be entertained by a few aspiring characters, it must generally happen that a great proportion of the men deriving their advancement from their influence with the people, would have more to hope from a preservation of the favor, than from innovations in the government subversive of the authority of the people.

All these securities, however, would be found very insufficient without the restraint of frequent elections. Hence, in the fourth place, the House of Representatives is so constituted as to support in the members an habitual recollection of their dependence on the people. Before the sentiments impressed on their minds by the mode of their elevation can be effaced by the exercise of power, they will be compelled to anticipate the moment when their power is to cease, when their exercise of it is to be reviewed, and when they must descend to the level from which they were raised; there forever to remain unless a faithful discharge of their trust shall have established their title to a renewal of it.

I will add, as a fifth circumstance in the situation of the House of Representatives, restraining them from oppressive measures, that they can make no law which will not have its full operation on themselves and their friends, as well as on the great mass of the society. This has always been deemed one of the strongest bonds by which human policy can connect the rulers and the people together. It creates between them that communion of interests and sympathy of sentiments, of which few governments have furnished examples; but without which every government degenerates into tyranny. If it be asked, what is to restrain the House of Representatives from making legal discriminations in favor of themselves and a particular class of the society? I answer: the genius of the whole system; the nature of just and constitutional laws; and above all, the vigilant and manly spirit which actuates the people of America, a spirit which nourishes freedom, and in return is nourished by it.

If this spirit shall ever be so far debased as to tolerate a law not obligatory on the legislature, as well as on the people, the people will be prepared to tolerate anything but liberty.

Such will be the relation between the House of Representatives and their constituents. Duty, gratitude, interest, ambition itself, are the chords by which they will be bound to fidelity and sympathy with the great mass of the people. It is possible that these may all be insufficient to control the caprice and wickedness of man. But are they not all that government will admit, and that human prudence can devise? Are they not the genuine and the characteristic means by which republican government provides for the liberty and happiness of the people? Are they not the identical means on which every State government in the Union relies for the attainment of these important ends? What then are we to understand by the objection which this paper has combated? What are we to say to the men who profess the most flaming zeal for republican government, yet boldly impeach the fundamental principle of it; who pretend to be champions for the right and the capacity of the people to choose their own rulers, yet maintain that they will prefer those only who will immediately and infallibly betray the trust committed to them?

Were the objection to be read by one who had not seen the mode prescribed by the Constitution for the choice of representatives, he could suppose nothing less than that some unreasonable qualification of property was annexed to the right of suffrage; or that the right of eligibility was limited to persons of particular families or fortunes; or at least that the mode prescribed by the State constitutions was in some respect or other, very grossly departed from. We have seen how far such a supposition would err, as to the two first points. Nor would it, in fact, be less erroneous as to the last. The only difference discoverable between the two cases is, that each representative of the United States will be elected by five or six thousand citizens; whilst in the individual States, the election of a representative is left to about as many hundreds. Will it be pretended that this difference is sufficient to justify an attachment to the State governments, and an abhorrence to the federal government? If this be the point on which the objection turns, it deserves to be examined.

Is it supported by *reason*? This cannot be said, without maintaining that five or six thousand citizens are less capable of choosing a fit representative, or more liable to be corrupted by an unfit one, than five or six hundred. Reason, on the contrary, assures us, that as in so great a number a fit representative would be most likely to be found, so the choice would be less likely to be diverted from him by the intrigues of the ambitious or the bribes of the rich.

Is the *consequence* from this doctrine admissible? If we say that five or six hundred citizens are as many as can jointly exercise their right of suffrage, must we not deprive the people of the immediate choice of their public servants, in every instance where the administration of the government does not require as many of them as will amount to one for that number of citizens?

Is the doctrine warranted by *facts*? It was shown in the last paper, that the real representation in the British House of Commons very little exceeds the proportion of one for every thirty thousand inhabitants. Besides a variety of powerful causes not existing here, and which favor in that country the pretensions of rank and wealth, no person is eligible as a representative of a county, unless he possess real estate of the clear value of six hundred pounds sterling per year; nor of a city or borough, unless he possess a like estate of half that annual value. To this qualification on the part of the county representatives is added another on the part of the county electors, which restrains the right of suffrage to persons having a freehold estate of the annual value of more than twenty pounds sterling, according to the present rate of money. Notwithstanding these unfavorable circumstances, and notwithstanding some very unequal laws in the British code, it cannot be said that the representatives of the nation have elevated the few on the ruins of the many.

But we need not resort to foreign experience on this subject. Our own is explicit and decisive. The districts in New Hampshire in which the senators are chosen immediately by the people, are nearly as large as will be necessary for her representatives in the Congress. Those of Massachusetts are larger than will be necessary for that purpose; and those of New York still more so. In the last State the members of Assembly for the cities and counties of New York and Albany are elected by very nearly as many voters as will be entitled to a representative in the Congress, calculating on the number of sixty-five representatives only. It makes no difference that in these senatorial districts and counties a number of representatives are voted for by each elector at the same time. If the same electors at the same time are capable of choosing four or five representatives, they cannot be incapable of choosing one. Pennsylvania is an additional example. Some of her counties, which elect her State representatives, are almost as large as her districts will be by which her federal representatives will be elected. The city of Philadelphia is supposed to contain between fifty and sixty thousand souls. It will therefore form nearly two districts for the choice of federal representatives. It forms, however, but one county, in which every elector votes for each of its representatives in the State legislature. And what may appear to be still more directly to our purpose, the whole city actually elects a *single member* for the executive council. This is the case in all the other counties of the State.

Are not these facts the most satisfactory proofs of the fallacy which has been employed against the branch of the federal government under consideration? Has it appeared on trial that the senators of New Hampshire, Massachusetts, and New York, or the executive council of Pennsylvania, or the members of the Assembly in the two last States, have betrayed any peculiar disposition to sacrifice the many to the few, or are in any respect less worthy of their places than the representatives and magistrates appointed in other States by very small divisions of the people? But there are cases of a stronger complexion than any which I have yet quoted. One branch of the legislature of Connecticut is so constituted that each member of it is elected by the whole State. So is the governor of that State, of Massachusetts, and of this State, and the president of New Hampshire. I leave every man to decide whether the result of any one of these experiments can be said to countenance a suspicion, that a diffusive mode of choosing representatives of the people tends to elevate traitors and to undermine the public liberty.

THOMAS JEFFERSON TO JAMES MADISON

September 6, 1789
Paris

The question Whether one generation of men has a right to bind another, seems never to have been started either on this or our side of the water. Yet it is a question of such consequences as not only to merit decision, but place also, among the fundamental principles of every government. The course of reflection in which we are immersed here on the elementary principles of society has presented this question to my mind; and that no such obligation can be so transmitted I think very capable of proof. I set out on this ground, which I suppose to be self-evident, "*that the earth belongs in usufruct to the living*"; that the dead have neither powers nor rights over it. The portion occupied by an individual ceases to be his when himself ceases to be, and reverts to the society. If the society has formed no rules for the appropriation of its lands in severalty, it will be taken by the first occupants. These will generally be the wife and children of the decedent. If they have formed rules of appropriation, those rules may give it to the wife and children, or to some one of them, or to the legatee of the deceased. So they may give it to his creditor. But the child, the legatee, or creditor takes it, not by any natural right, but by a law of the society of which they are members, and to which they are subject. Then no man can, by *natural right*, oblige the lands he occupied, or the persons who succeed him in that occupation, to the payment of debts contracted by him. For if he could, he might, during his own life, eat up the usufruct of the lands for several generations to come, and then the lands would belong to the dead, and not to the living, which would be the reverse of our principle.

What is true of every member of the society individually, is true of them all collectively, since the rights of the whole can be no more than the sum of the rights of the individuals. To keep our ideas clear when applying them to a multitude, let us suppose a whole generation of men to be born on the same day, to attain mature age on the same day, and to die on the same day, leaving a succeeding generation in the moment of attaining their mature age all together. Let the ripe age be supposed of 21 years, and their period of life 34 years more, that being the average term given by the bills of mortality to persons who have already attained 21 years of age. Each successive generation would, in this way, come on, and go off the stage at a fixed moment, as individuals do now. Then I say the earth belongs to each of these generations, during its course, fully, and in their own right. The 2nd generation receives it clear of the debts and encumbrances of the 1st, the 3rd of the 2nd and so on.

For if the 1st could charge it with a debt, then the earth would belong to the dead and not the living generation. Then no generation can contract debts greater than may be paid during the course of its own existence. At 21 years of age they may bind themselves and their lands for 34 years to come: at 22 for 33: at 23 for 32 and at 54 for one year only; because these are the terms of life which remain to them at those respective epochs. But a material difference must be noted between the succession of an individual, and that of a whole generation. Individuals are parts only of a society, subject to the laws of the whole. These laws may appropriate the portion of land occupied by a decedent to his creditor rather than to any other, or to his child on condition he satisfies the creditor. But when a whole generation, that is, the whole society dies, as in the case we have supposed, and another generation or society succeeds, this forms a whole, and there is no superior who can give their territory to a third society, who may have lent money to their predecessors beyond their faculties of paying.

What is true of a generation all arriving to self-government on the same day, and dying all on the same day, is true of those in a constant course of decay and renewal, with this only difference. A generation coming in and going out entire, as in the first case, would have a right in the 1st year of their self-dominion to contract a debt for 33 years, in the 10th for 24, in the 20th for 14, in the 30th for 4 whereas generations, changing daily by daily deaths and births, have one constant term, beginning at the date of their contract, and ending when a majority of those of full age at that date shall be dead. The length of that term may be estimated from the tables of mortality, corrected by the circumstances of climate, occupation etc. peculiar to the country of the contractors. Take, for instance, the table of M. de Buffon wherein he states 23,994 deaths, and the ages at which they happened. Suppose a society in which 23,994 persons are born every year, and live to the ages stated in this table. The conditions of that society will be as follows. 1st. It will consist constantly of 617,703 persons of all ages. 2dly. Of those living at any one instant of time, one half will be dead in 24 years 8 months. 3dly. 10,675 will arrive every year at the age of 21 years complete. 4thly. It will constantly have 348,417 persons of all ages above 21 years. 5ly. And the half of those of 21 years and upwards living at any one instant of time will be dead in 18 years 8 months, or say 19 years as the nearest integral number. Then 19 years is the term beyond which neither the representatives of a nation, nor even the whole nation itself assembled, can validly extend a debt.

To render this conclusion palpable by example, suppose that Louis XIV and XV had contracted debts in the name of the French nation to the amount of 10,000 milliards of livres, and that the whole had been contracted in Genoa. The interest of this sum would be 500 milliards, which is said to be the whole rent roll or net proceeds of the territory of France. Must the present generation of men have retired from the territory in which nature produced them, and ceded it to the Genoese creditors? No. They have the same rights over the soil on which they were produced, as the preceding generations had. They derive these rights not from their predecessors, but from nature. They then and their soil are by nature clear of the debts of their predecessors.

Again suppose Louis XV and his contemporary generation had said to the money-lenders of Genoa, give us money that we may eat, drink, and be merry in our day; and on condition you will demand no interest till the end of 19 years you shall then forever after receive an annual interest of 125/8 per cent. The money is lent on these conditions, is divided among the living, eaten, drank, and squandered. Would the present generation be obliged to apply the produce of the earth and of their labor to replace their dissipations? Not at all.

I suppose that the received opinion, that the public debts of one generation devolve on the next, has been suggested by our seeing habitually in private life that he who succeeds to lands is required to pay the debts of his ancestor or testator: without considering that this requisition is municipal only, not moral; flowing from the will of the society, which has found it convenient to appropriate lands, become vacant by the death of their occupant, on the condition of a payment of his debts: but that between society and society, or generation and generation, there is no municipal obligation, no umpire but the law of nature. We seem not to have perceived that, by the law of nature, one generation is to another as one independent nation to another.

The interest of the national debt of France being in fact but a two thousandth part of its rent roll, the payment of it is practicable enough: and so becomes a question merely of honor, or of expediency. But with respect to future debts, would it not be wise and just for that nation to declare, in the constitution they are forming, that neither the legislature, nor the nation itself, can validly contract more debt than they may pay within their own age, or within the term of 19 years? And that all future contracts will be deemed void as to what shall remain unpaid at the end of 19 years from their date? This would put the lenders, and the borrowers also, on their guard. By reducing too the faculty of borrowing within its natural limits, it would bridle the spirit of war, to which too free a course has been procured by the inattention of money-lenders to this law of nature, that succeeding generations are not responsible for the preceding.

On similar ground it may be proved that no society can make a perpetual constitution, or even a perpetual law. The earth belongs always to the living generation. They may manage it then, and what proceeds from it, as they please, during their usufruct. They are masters too of their own persons, and consequently may govern them as they please. But persons and property make the sum of the objects of government. The constitution and the laws of their predecessors extinguished then in their natural course with those who gave them being. This could preserve that being till it ceased to be itself, and no longer. Every constitution then, and every law, naturally expires at the end of 19 years. If it be enforced longer, it is an act of force, and not of right. It may be said that the succeeding generation exercising in fact the power of repeal, this leaves them as free as if the constitution or law has been expressly limited to 19 years only. In the first place, this objection admits the right, in proposing an equivalent. But the power of repeal is not an equivalent. It might be indeed if every form of government were so perfectly contrived that the will of the majority could always be obtained fairly and without impediment. But this is true of no form. The people cannot assemble themselves. Their representation is unequal and vicious. Various checks are opposed to every legislative proposition. Factions get possession of the public councils. Bribery corrupts them. Personal interests lead them astray from the general interests of their constituents: and other impediments arise so as to prove to every practical man that a law of limited duration is much more manageable than one which needs a repeal.

This principle that the earth belongs to the living, and not to the dead, is of very extensive application and consequences, in every country, and most especially in France. It enters into the resolution of the questions Whether the nation may change the descent of lands holden in tail? Whether they may change the appropriation of lands given anciently to the church, to hospitals, colleges, orders of chivalry, and otherwise in perpetuity? Whether they may abolish the charges and privileges attached on lands, including the whole catalogue ecclesiastical and feudal? It goes to hereditary offices, authorities and jurisdictions; to hereditary orders, distinctions and appellations; to perpetual monopolies in commerce, the arts and sciences; with a long train of etceteras: and it renders the question of reimbursement a question of generosity and not of right. In all these cases, the legislature of the day could authorize such appropriations and establishments for their own time, but no longer; and the present holders, even where they, or their ancestors, have purchased, are in the case of bona fide purchasers of what the seller had no right to convey.

Turn this subject in your mind, my dear Sir, and particularly as to the power of contracting debts; and develop it with that perspicuity and cogent logic so peculiarly yours. Your station in the councils of our country gives you an opportunity of producing it to public consideration, of forcing it into discussion. At first blush it may be rallied, as a theoretical speculation: but examination will prove it to be solid and salutary. It would furnish matter for a fine preamble to our first law for appropriating the public revenue; and it will exclude at the threshold of our new government the contagious and ruinous errors of this quarter of the globe, which have armed despots with means, not sanctioned by nature, for binding in chains their fellow men. We have already given in example one effectual check to the Dog of war by transferring the power of letting him loose from the Executive to the Legislative body, from those who are to spend to those who are to pay. I should be pleased to see this second obstacle held out by us also in the first instance. No nation can make a declaration against the validity of long-contracted debts so disinterestedly as we, since we do not owe a shilling which may not be paid with ease, principal and interest, within the time of our own lives. Establish the principle also in the new law to be passed for protecting copyrights and new inventions, by securing the exclusive right for 19 instead of 14 years. Besides familiarizing us to this term, it will be an instance the more of our taking reason for our guide, instead of English precedent, the habit of which fetters us with all the political heresies of a nation equally remarkable for its early excitement from some errors, and long slumbering under others.

THOMAS JEFFERSON TO SAMUEL KERCHEVAL

June 12, 1816

I duly received your favor of June the 13th, with the copy of the letters on the calling a convention, on which you are pleased to ask my opinion. I have not been in the habit of mysterious reserve on any subject, nor of buttoning up my opinions within my own doublet. On the contrary, while in public service especially, I thought the public entitled to frankness, and intimately to know whom they employed. But I am now retired: I resign myself, as a passenger, with confidence to those at present at the helm, and ask but for rest, peace and good will. The question you propose, on equal representation, has become a party one, in which I wish to take no public share. Yet, if it be asked for your own satisfaction only, and not to be quoted before the public, I have no motive to withhold it, and the less from you, as it coincides with your own. At the birth of our republic, I committed that opinion to the world, in the draught of a constitution annexed to the "Notes on Virginia," in which a provision was inserted for a representation permanently equal. The infancy of the subject at that moment, and our inexperience of self-government, occasioned gross departures in that draught from genuine republican canons. In truth, the abuses of monarchy had so much filled all the space of political contemplation, that we imagined everything republican which was not monarchy. We had not yet penetrated to the mother principle, that "governments are republican only in proportion as they embody the will of their people, and execute it." Hence, our first constitutions had really no leading principles in them. But experience and reflection have but more and more confirmed me in the particular importance of the equal representation then proposed. On that point, then, I am entirely in sentiment with your letters; and only lament that a copyright of your pamphlet prevents their appearance in the newspapers, where alone they would be generally read, and produce general effect. The present vacancy too, of other matter, would give them place in every paper, and bring the question home to every man's conscience.

But inequality of representation in both Houses of our legislature, is not the only republican heresy in this first essay of our revolutionary patriots at forming a constitution. For let it be agreed that a government is republican in proportion as every member composing it has his equal voice in the direction of its concerns (not indeed in person, which would be impracticable beyond the limits of a city, or small township, but) by representatives chosen by himself, and responsible to him at short periods, and let us bring to the test of this canon every branch of our constitution.

In the legislature, the House of Representatives is chosen by less than half the people, and not at all in proportion to those who do choose. The Senate are still more disproportionate, and for long terms of irresponsibility. In the Executive, the Governor is entirely independent of the choice of the people, and of their control; his Council equally so, and at best but a fifth wheel to a wagon. In the Judiciary, the judges of the highest courts are dependent on none but themselves. In England, where judges were named and removable at the will of an hereditary executive, from which branch most misrule was feared, and has flowed, it was a great point gained, by fixing them for life, to make them independent of that executive. But in a government founded on the public will, this principle operates in an opposite direction, and against that will. There, too, they were still removable on a concurrence of the executive and legislative branches. But we have made them independent of the nation itself. They are irremovable, but by their own body, for any depravities of conduct, and even by their own body for the imbecilities of dotage. The justices of the inferior courts are self-chosen, are for life, and perpetuate their own body in succession forever, so that a faction once possessing themselves of the bench of a county, can never be broken up, but hold their county in chains, forever indissoluble. Yet these justices are the real executive as well as judiciary, in all our minor and most ordinary concerns. They tax us at will; fill the office of sheriff, the most important of all the executive officers of the county; name nearly all our military leaders, which leaders, once named, are removable but by themselves. The juries, our judges of all fact, and of law when they choose it, are not selected by the people, nor amenable to them. They are chosen by an officer named by the court and executive. Chosen, did I say? Picked up by the sheriff from the loungings of the court yard, after everything respectable has retired from it. Where then is our republicanism to be found? Not in our constitution certainly, but merely in the spirit of our people. That would oblige even a despot to govern us republicanly. Owing to this spirit, and to nothing in the form of our constitution, all things have gone well. But this fact, so triumphantly misquoted by the enemies of reformation, is not the fruit of our constitution, but has prevailed in spite of it. Our functionaries have done well, because generally honest men. If any were not so, they feared to show it.

But it will be said, it is easier to find faults than to amend them. I do not think their amendment so difficult as is pretended. Only lay down true principles, and adhere to them inflexibly. Do not be frightened into their surrender by the alarms of the timid, or the croakings of wealth against the ascendency of the people. If experience be called for, appeal to that of our fifteen or twenty governments for forty years, and show me where the people have done half the mischief in these forty years, that a single despot would have done in a single year; or show half the riots and rebellions, the crimes and the punishments, which have taken place in any single nation, under kingly government, during the same period. The true foundation of republican government is the equal right of every citizen, in his person and property, and in their management. Try by this, as a tally, every provision of our constitution, and see if it hangs directly on the will of the people. Reduce your legislature to a convenient number for full, but orderly discussion. Let every man who fights or pays, exercise his just and equal right in their election. Submit them to approbation or rejection at short intervals. Let the executive be chosen in the same way, and for the same term, by those whose agent he is to be; and leave no screen of a council behind which to skulk from responsibility. It has been thought that the people are not competent electors of judges *learned in the law*. But I do not know that this is true, and, if doubtful, we should follow principle. In this, as in many other elections, they would be guided by reputation, which would not err oftener, perhaps, than the present mode of appointment. In one State of the Union, at least, it has long been tried, and with the most satisfactory success. The judges of Connecticut have been chosen by the people every six months, for nearly two centuries, and I believe there has hardly ever been an instance of change; so powerful is the curb of incessant responsibility. If prejudice, however, derived from a monarchical institution, is still to prevail against the vital elective principle of our own, and if the existing example among ourselves of periodical election of judges by the people be still mistrusted, let us at least not adopt the evil, and reject the good, of the English precedent; let us retain immovability on the concurrence of the executive and legislative branches, and nomination by the executive alone. Nomination to office is an executive function. To give it to the legislature, as we do, is a violation of the principle of the separation of powers. It swerves the members from correctness, by temptations to intrigue for office themselves, and to a corrupt barter of votes; and destroys responsibility by dividing it among a multitude. By leaving nomination in its proper place, among executive functions, the principle of the distribution of power is preserved, and responsibility weighs with its heaviest force on a single head.

The organization of our county administrations may be thought more difficult. But follow principle, and the knot unties itself. Divide the counties into wards of such size as that every citizen can attend, when called on, and act in person. Ascribe to them the government of their wards in all things relating to themselves exclusively. A justice, chosen by themselves, in each, a constable, a military company, a patrol, a school, the care of their own poor, their own portion of the public roads, the choice of one or more jurors to serve in some court, and the delivery, within their own wards, of their own votes for all elective officers of higher sphere, will relieve the county administration of nearly all its business, will have it better done, and by making every citizen an acting member of the government, and in the offices nearest and most interesting to him, will attach him by his strongest feelings to the independence of his country, and its republican constitution. The justices thus chosen by every ward, would constitute the county court, would do its judiciary business, direct roads and bridges, levy county and poor rates, and administer all the matters of common interest to the whole country. These wards, called townships in New England, are the vital principle of their governments, and have proved themselves the wisest invention ever devised by the wit of man for the perfect exercise of self-government, and for its preservation. We should thus marshal our government into, 1, the general federal republic, for all concerns foreign and federal; 2, that of the State, for what relates to our own citizens exclusively; 3, the county republics, for the duties and concerns of the county; and 4, the ward republics, for the small, and yet numerous and interesting concerns of the neighborhood; and in government, as well as in every other business of life, it is by division and subdivision of duties alone, that all matters, great and small, can be managed to perfection. And the whole is cemented by giving to every citizen, personally, a part in the administration of the public affairs.

The sum of these amendments is, 1. General Suffrage. 2. Equal representation in the legislature. 3. An executive chosen by the people. 4. Judges elective or immovable. 5. Justices, jurors, and sheriffs elective. 6. Ward divisions. And 7. Periodical amendments of the constitution.

I have thrown out these as loose heads of amendment, for consideration and correction; and their object is to secure self-government by the republicanism of our constitution, as well as by the spirit of the people; and to nourish and perpetuate that spirit. I am not among those who fear the people. They, and not the rich, are our dependence for continued freedom. And to preserve their independence, we must not let our rulers load us with perpetual debt. We must make our election between *economy and liberty*, or *profusion and servitude*. If we run into such debts, as that we must be taxed in our meat and in our drink, in our necessaries and our comforts, in our labors and our amusements, for our callings and our creeds, as the people of England are, our people, like them, must come to labor sixteen hours in the twenty-four, give the earnings of fifteen of these to the government for their debts and daily expenses; and the sixteenth being insufficient to afford us bread, we must live, as they now do, on oatmeal and potatoes; have no time to think, no means of calling the mismanagers to account; but be glad to obtain subsistence by hiring ourselves to rivet their chains on the necks of our fellow-sufferers. Our landholders, too, like theirs, retaining indeed the title and stewardship of estates called theirs, but held really in trust for the treasury, must wander, like theirs, in foreign countries, and be contented with penury, obscurity, exile, and the glory of the nation. This example reads to us the salutary lesson, that private fortunes are destroyed by public as well as by private extravagance. And this is the tendency of all human governments. A departure from principle in one instance becomes a precedent for a second; that second for a third; and so on, till the bulk of the society is reduced to be mere automatons of misery, and to have no sensibilities left but for sinning and suffering. Then begins, indeed, the *bellum omnium in omnia*, which some philosophers observing to be so general in this world, have mistaken it for the natural, instead of the abusive state of man. And the fore horse of this frightful team is public debt. Taxation follows that, and in its train wretchedness and oppression.

Some men look at constitutions with sanctimonious reverence, and deem them like the arc of the covenant, too sacred to be touched. They ascribe to the men of the preceding age a wisdom more than human, and suppose what they did to be beyond amendment. I knew that age well; I belonged to it, and labored with it. It deserved well of its country. It was very like the present, but without the experience of the present; and forty years of experience in government is worth a century of book-reading; and this they would say themselves, were they to rise from the dead. I am certainly not an advocate for frequent and untried changes in laws and constitutions. I think moderate imperfections had better be borne with; because, when once known, we accommodate ourselves to them, and find practical means of correcting their ill effects. But I know also, that laws and institutions must go hand in hand with the progress of the human mind. As that becomes more developed, more enlightened, as new discoveries are made, new truths disclosed, and manners and opinions change with the change of circumstances, institutions must advance also, and keep pace with the times. We might as well require a man to wear still the coat which fitted him when a boy, as civilized society to remain ever under the regimen of their barbarous ancestors. It is this preposterous idea which has lately deluged Europe in blood. Their monarchs, instead of wisely yielding to the gradual change of circumstances, of favoring progressive accommodation to progressive improvement, have clung to old abuses, entrenched themselves behind steady habits, and obliged their subjects to seek through blood and violence rash and ruinous innovations, which, had they been referred to the peaceful deliberations and collected wisdom of the nation, would have been put into acceptable and salutary forms. Let us follow no such examples, nor weakly believe that one generation is not as capable as another of taking care of itself, and of ordering its own affairs. Let us, as our sister States have done, avail ourselves of our reason and experience, to correct the crude essays of our first and unexperienced, although wise, virtuous, and well-meaning councils. And lastly, let us provide in our constitution for its revision at stated periods. What these periods should be, nature herself indicates. By the European tables of mortality, of the adults living at any one moment of time, a majority will be dead in about nineteen years. At the end of that period, then, a new majority is come into place; or, in other words, a new generation. Each generation is as independent as the one preceding, as that was of all which had gone before. It has then, like them, a right to choose for itself the form of government it believes most promotive of its own happiness; consequently, to accommodate to the circumstances in which it finds itself, that received from its predecessors; and it is for the peace and good of mankind, that a solemn opportunity of doing this every nineteen or twenty years, should be provided by the constitution; so that it may be handed on, with periodical repairs, from generation to generation, to the end of time, if anything human can so long endure. It is now forty years since the constitution of Virginia was formed. The same tables inform us, that, within that period, two-thirds of the adults then living are now dead. Have then the remaining third, even if they had the wish, the right to hold in obedience to their will, and to laws heretofore made by them, the other two-thirds, who, with themselves, compose the present mass of adults? If they have not, who has? The dead? But the dead have no rights. They are nothing; and nothing cannot own something. Where there is no substance, there can be no accident. This corporeal globe, and everything upon it, belong to its present corporeal inhabitants, during their generation. They alone have a right to direct what is the concern of themselves alone, and to declare the law of that direction; and this declaration can only be made by their majority. That majority, then, has a right to depute representatives to a convention, and to make the constitution what they think will be the best for themselves. But how collect their voice? This is the real difficulty. If invited by private authority, or county or district meetings, these divisions are so large that few will attend; and their voice will be imperfectly, or falsely pronounced. Here, then, would be one of the advantages of the ward divisions I have proposed. The mayor of every ward, on a question like the present, would call his ward together, take the simple yea or nay of its members, convey these to the county court, who would hand on those of all its wards to the proper general authority; and the voice of the whole people would be thus fairly, fully, and peaceably expressed, discussed, and decided by the common reason of the society. If this avenue be shut to the call of sufferance, it will make itself heard through that of force, and we shall go on, as other nations are doing, in the endless circle of oppression, rebellion, reformation; and oppression, rebellion, reformation, again; and so on forever.

These, Sir, are my opinions of the governments we see among men, and of the principles by which alone we may prevent our own from falling into the same dreadful track. I have given them at greater length than your letter called for. But I cannot say things by halves; and I confide them to your honor, so to use them as to preserve me from the gridiron of the public papers. If you shall approve and enforce them, as you have done that of equal representation, they may do some good. If not, keep them to yourself as the effusions of withered age and useless time. I shall, with not the less truth, assure you of my great respect and consideration.

DEMOCRACY IN AMERICA, VOLUME I, PART 1, CHAPTER 4: "OF THE PRINCIPLE OF THE SOVEREIGNTY OF THE PEOPLE IN AMERICA"

When you want to talk about the political laws of the United States, you must always begin with the dogma of the sovereignty of the people.

The principle of the sovereignty of the people, which is more or less always found at the base of nearly all human institutions, ordinarily remains there as if buried. It is obeyed without being recognized, or if sometimes it happens, for a moment, to be brought into the full light of day, people soon rush to push it back into the shadows of the sanctuary.

The national will is one of those terms abused most widely by schemers of all times and despots of all ages. Some have seen it expressed in votes bought from the brokers of power; others in the votes of an interested or fearful minority. There are even some who have discovered it fully formulated in the silence of the people and who have thought that from the *fact* of obedience came, for them, the *right* of command.

In America, the principle of the sovereignty of the people is not hidden or sterile as it is in certain nations; it is recognized by the mores, proclaimed by the laws; it spreads freely and reaches its fullest consequences without obstacles.

If there is a single country in the world where the true value of the dogma of the sovereignty of the people can hope to be appreciated, where its application to the affairs of society can be studied and where its advantages and dangers can be judged, that country is assuredly America.

I said before that, from the beginning, the principle of the sovereignty of the people had been the generative principle of most of the English colonies of America.

It then fell far short, however, of dominating the government of society as it does today.

Two obstacles, one external, one internal, slowed its invasive march.

It could not appear openly in the laws because the colonies were still forced to obey the home country; so it was reduced to hiding in the provincial assemblies and especially in the town. There it spread in secret.

American society at that time was not yet ready to adopt it in all its consequences. For a long time, learning in New England and wealth south of the Hudson, exercised, as I showed in the preceding chapter, a sort of aristocratic influence that tended to confine the exercise of social powers to a few hands. It still fell far short of electing all public officials and of making all citizens, voters. Everywhere the right to vote was restricted to certain limits and subordinated to the existence of a property qualification which was very low in the North and more considerable in the South.

The American Revolution broke out. The dogma of the sovereignty of the people emerged from the town and took over the government; all classes took risks for its cause; they fought and triumphed in its name; it became the law of laws.

A change almost as rapid was carried out within the interior of society. The law of inheritance completed the dismantling of local influences.

At the moment when this effect of the laws and of the revolution began to be evident to all, victory had already been irrevocably declared in favor of democracy. Power was in fact in its hands. Even struggling against it was no longer permitted. So the upper classes submitted without a murmur and without a fight to an evil henceforth inevitable. What usually happens to powers that are in decline happened to them: individual egoism took hold of the members of the upper classes. Since force could no longer be wrested from the hands of the people and since they did not detest the multitude enough to take pleasure in defying it, they came to think only of winning its good will at any cost. In an effort to outdo each other, the most democratic laws were then voted by the men whose interests were most damaged by them. In this way, the upper classes did not incite popular passions against themselves; but they themselves hastened the triumph of the new order. So, a strange thing! The democratic impulse showed itself that much more irresistible in the states where aristocracy had more roots.

The state of Maryland, which had been founded by great lords, was the first to proclaim universal suffrage and introduced the most democratic forms into its whole government.

When a people begins to tamper with the electoral qualification, you can foresee that, after a more or less long delay, it will make that qualification disappear completely. That is one of the most invariable rules that govern societies. As the limit of electoral rights is pushed back, the need grows to push it further; for, after each new concession, the forces of democracy increase and its demands grow with its new power. The ambition of those left below the electoral qualification is aroused in proportion to the great number of those who are found above. Finally, the exception becomes the rule; concessions follow one after the other without letup, and there is no more stopping until universal suffrage is reached.

Today in the United States the principle of the sovereignty of the people has attained all the practical developments that imagination can conceive. It has been freed from all the fictions that have been carefully placed around it elsewhere; it is seen successively clothed in all forms according to the necessity of the case. Sometimes the people as a body make the laws as at Athens; sometimes the deputies created by universal suffrage represent the people and act in their name under their almost immediate supervision.

There are countries where a power, in a way external to the social body, acts on it and forces it to follow a certain path.

There are others where force is divided, being simultaneously inside and outside the society. Nothing of the sort is seen in the United States; there society acts by itself and on itself. Power exists only inside it; hardly anyone may even be found who dares to conceive and especially to express the idea of seeking power elsewhere. The people participate in the composition of the laws by the choice of the legislators, in their application by the election of the agents of executive power. It can be said that they govern themselves, so weak and restricted is the part left to the administration, so much does the administration feel its popular origin and obey the power from which it emanates. The people rule the American political world as God rules the universe. They are the cause and the end of all things; everything arises from them and everything is absorbed by them.

DEMOCRACY IN AMERICA, VOLUME I, PART 1, CHAPTER 5: "NECESSITY OF STUDYING WHAT HAPPENS IN THE INDIVIDUAL STATES BEFORE SPEAKING ABOUT THE GOVERNMENT OF THE UNION"

Of the Town System in America

Not by chance do I first examine the town.

The town is the first element of the societies out of which peoples take form; it is the social molecule; if I can express myself in this way, it is the embryo that already represents and contains the seed of the complete being.

The town is the only association that is so much a part of nature that wherever men are gathered together, a town takes shape by itself.

Town society exists therefore among all peoples no matter what their customs and their laws; it is man who establishes kingdoms and creates republics; the town seems to come directly from the hands of God. But if the town has existed ever since there have been men, town liberty is something rare and fragile. A people can always establish great political assemblies, because it usually contains a certain number of men among whom, to a certain degree, enlightenment takes the place of the practice of public affairs. The town is made up of crude elements that often resist the action of the legislator. Instead of diminishing as nations become more enlightened, the difficulty of establishing town independence increases with their enlightenment. A highly civilized society tolerates the trial efforts of town liberty only with difficulty; it rebels at the sight of its numerous errors and despairs of success before having reached the final result of the experiment.

Of all liberties, town liberty, which is so difficult to establish, is also the most exposed to the encroachments of power. Left to themselves, town institutions could scarcely resist a strong and enterprising government; to defend themselves successfully, they must have reached their fullest development and be mingled with national ideas and habits. Thus, as long as town liberty has not become part of the mores, it is easy to destroy; and it can become part of the mores only after existing in the laws for a long time.

Town liberty therefore escapes human effort so to speak. Consequently it is rarely created; in a sense it arises by itself. It develops almost in secret within a semi-barbaric society. The continuous action of laws and of mores, circumstances, and above all time succeed in its consolidation. You can say that, of all the nations of the European continent, not a single one knows town liberty.

The strength of free peoples resides in the town, however. Town institutions are to liberty what primary schools are to knowledge; they put it within the grasp of the people; they give them a taste of its peaceful practice and accustom them to its use. Without town institutions, a nation can pretend to have a free government, but it does not possess the spirit of liberty. Temporary passions, momentary interests, the chance of circumstances can give it the external forms of independence; but despotism, driven back into the interior of the social body, reappears sooner or later at the surface.

To make the reader understand well the general principles on which the political organization of the town and the county in the United States rests, I thought that it was useful to take one state in particular as a model, to examine in detail what happens there, and then to cast a quick glance over the rest of the country.

I have chosen one of the states of New England.

The town and the county are not organized in the same way in all the parts of the Union; it is easy to recognize, however, that throughout the Union the same principles, more or less, have presided over the formation of both.

Now, it seemed to me that in New England these principles were considerably more developed and had attained further consequences than anywhere else. So they are, so to speak, more evident there and are thus more accessible to the observation of the foreigner.

The town institutions of New England form a complete and regular whole. They are old; they are strong because of the laws, stronger still because of the mores; they exercise a prodigious influence over the entire society.

In all these ways, they merit our attention.

Town District

The town in New England (*Township*) falls between the *canton* and the *commune* in France. Generally it numbers from two to three thousand inhabitants. So it is not too extensive for all its inhabitants to share nearly the same interests; and on the other hand, it is populated enough to assure that elements of a good administration are always found within it.

Town Powers in New England

In the town as everywhere else, the people are the source of social powers, but nowhere else do they exercise their power more directly. In America, the people are a master who has to be pleased to the greatest possible degree.

In New England, the majority acts through representatives when the general affairs of the state must be dealt with. This was necessary; but in the town, where legislative and governmental action is closer to the governed, the law of representation is not accepted. There is no town council; the body of voters, after naming their magistrates, directs them in everything that is not the pure and simple execution of the laws of the state.

This state of things is so contrary to our ideas, and so opposed to our habits, that it is necessary to provide a few examples here for it to be well understood.

Public offices are extremely numerous and highly divided in the town, as we will see below. The largest part of administrative powers is concentrated, however, in the hands of a small number of individuals elected annually who are called selectmen.

The general laws of the state have imposed a certain number of obligations on the selectmen. To fulfill them they do not need the authorization of those under their jurisdiction, and they cannot avoid their obligations without engaging their personal responsibility. State law charges them, for example, with drawing up the electoral lists in their town; if they fail to do so, they make themselves guilty of a misdemeanor. But in all things that are left to the direction of the town authority, the selectmen are the executors of the popular will, as with us the mayor is the executor of the deliberations of the town council. Most often they act on their private responsibility and, in actual practice, only carry out the implications of principles previously set down by the majority. But if they want to introduce any change whatsoever in the established order, if they desire to pursue a new undertaking, they must return to the source of their power. Suppose that it is a question of establishing a school: the selectmen convoke on a given day, in a place specified in advance, the whole body of voters; there, they set forth the need that is felt; they show the means to satisfy it, the money that must be spent, the location that should be chosen. The assembly, consulted on all those points, adopts the principle, determines the location, votes the tax and puts the execution of its will into the hands of the selectmen.

Only the selectmen have the right to call the town meeting, but they can be made to do so. If ten property owners conceive a new project and want to submit it for approval by the town, they call for a general convocation of the inhabitants; the selectmen are obliged to agree to the call and only retain the right to preside over the meeting.

Without a doubt, these political mores, these social customs are very far from us. At this moment I want neither to judge them nor to show the hidden causes that produce and animate them; I am limiting myself to presenting them.

The selectmen are elected annually in the month of April or May. At the same time the town meeting chooses a host of other town magistrates, appointed for certain important administrative tasks. Some, known as assessors, must determine the tax; others, known as collectors, must collect it. One officer, called the *constable,* is charged with keeping the peace, supervising public places and assuring the physical execution of the laws. Another, named the town clerk, records all deliberations; he keeps minutes of the acts of the civil registry. A treasurer keeps the town funds. Add to these officers an overseer of the poor, whose duty, very difficult to fulfill, is to enforce the laws relative to the poor; school commissioners, who direct public education; road surveyors, who are responsible for all the routine tasks relating to the roadways, large and small; and you will have the list of the principal agents of town administration. But the division of offices does not stop there. You still find, among the town officers, parish commissioners who must regulate church expenses; inspectors of various kinds, some charged with directing the efforts of citizens in case of fire; others, with overseeing the harvest; these, with temporarily relieving difficulties that can arise from fencing; those, with supervising wood allotments or with inspecting weights and measures.

In all, principal offices in the town number nineteen. Each inhabitant is obligated, under penalty of a fine, to accept these different offices; but also most of these offices are paid, so that poor citizens can devote their time to them without suffering a loss. The American system, moreover, does not give any fixed salary to officers. In general, each act of their administration has a value, and they are remunerated only in proportion to what they have done.

Of Town Life

I said previously that the principle of sovereignty of the people hovers over the entire political system of the Anglo-Americans. Each page of this book will show some new applications of this doctrine.

Among nations where the dogma of the sovereignty of the people reigns, each individual forms an equal portion of the sovereign power, and participates equally in the government of the state.

Each individual is therefore considered to be as enlightened, as virtuous, as strong as any of his fellows.

So why does he obey society, and what are the natural limits of this obedience?

He obeys society, not at all because he is inferior to those who direct it, or less capable than another man of governing himself; he obeys society because union with his fellows seems useful to him and because he knows that this union cannot exist without a regulatory power.

So in all that concerns the mutual duties of citizens, he has become a subject. In all that concerns only himself, he has remained the master; he is free and is accountable for his actions only to God. Thus this maxim, that the individual is the best as well as the only judge of his particular interest and that society has the right to direct his actions only when it feels harmed by them, or when it needs to call for his support.

This doctrine is universally accepted in the United States. Elsewhere I will examine what general influence it exercises over even the ordinary acts of life; but at this moment I am talking about the towns.

The town, taken as a whole and in relation to the central government, is only an individual like any other to whom the theory I have just indicated applies.

Town liberty in the United States follows, therefore, from the very dogma of the sovereignty of the people. All the American republics have more or less recognized this independence; but among the people of New England, circumstances have particularly favored its development.

In this part of the Union, political life was born very much within the towns; you could almost say that at its origin each of them was an independent nation. When the Kings of England later demanded their share of sovereignty, they limited themselves to taking central power. They left the town in the situation where they found it; now the towns of New England are subjects; but in the beginning they were not or were scarcely so. They did not therefore receive their powers; on the contrary, they seem to have relinquished a portion of their independence in favor of the state; an important distinction which the reader must keep in mind.

In general the towns are subject to the states only when an interest that I will call *social* is concerned, that is to say, an interest that the towns share with others.

For everything that relates only to them alone, the towns have remained independent bodies. No one among the inhabitants of New England, I think, recognizes the right of the state government to intervene in the direction of purely town interests.

So the towns of New England are seen to buy and sell, to sue and to defend themselves before the courts, to increase or reduce their budget without any administrative authority whatsoever thinking to oppose them.

As for social duties, they are required to fulfill them. Thus, if the state needs money, the town is not free to grant or to deny its cooperation. If the state wants to open a road, the town does not have the right to close its territory. If it establishes a regulation concerning public order, the town must execute it. If it wants to organize education according to a uniform plan throughout the country, the town is required to create the schools desired by the law. We will see, when we talk about administration in the United States, how and by whom the towns, in all these different cases, are forced to obey. Here I only want to establish the existence of the obligation. This obligation is strict, but the state government, while imposing it, only enacts a principle; for carrying out the principle, the town generally recovers all its rights of individuality. Thus, it is true that the tax is voted by the legislature, but it is the town that apportions and collects it; a school is prescribed, but it is the town that builds, funds and directs it.

In France the tax collector of the State levies the taxes of the town; in America the tax collector of the town raises the tax of the state.

With us, therefore, the central government lends its agents to the town; in America, the town lends its officers to the government. That alone makes clear to what degree the two societies differ.

Of Town Spirit in New England

Laws act on mores; and mores, on laws. Wherever these two things do not lend each other mutual support, there is unrest, revolution tearing apart the society.

The legislation of New England constituted the town. Habits have completed the establishment of a true town spirit there.

The town is a center around which interests and passions gather and where real and sustained activity reigns.

In America not only do town institutions exist, but also a town spirit that sustains and animates them.

The New England town brings together two advantages that, wherever they are found, strongly excite the interest of men—namely, independence and power. It acts, it is true, within a circle that it cannot leave, but within that circle its movements are free. This independence alone would already give the town real importance even if its population and size would not assure its importance.

You must realize that in general the affections of men go only where strength is found. Love of native land does not reign for long in a conquered country. The inhabitant of New England is attached to his town, not so much because he was born there as because he sees in this town a free and strong corporate body to which he belongs and which merits the trouble of trying to direct it.

In Europe the very people who govern often regret the absence of town spirit; for everyone agrees that town spirit is a great element of order and public tranquility; but they do not know how to produce it. By making the town strong and independent, they fear dividing social power and exposing the State to anarchy. Now, take strength and independence away from the town, and you will forever find there only people who are administered, not citizens.

Note, moreover, an important fact. The New England town is so constituted that it can serve as a center of strong affections, and at the same time there is nothing nearby that strongly attracts the ambitious passions of the human heart.

The officials of the county are not elected and their authority is limited. The state itself has only a secondary importance; its existence is indistinct and tranquil. To gain the right to administer it, few men agree to distance themselves from the center of their interests and to disrupt their existence.

The federal government confers power and glory on those who direct it; but the number of men who are able to influence its destiny is very small. The presidency is a high office that can hardly be attained except after reaching an advanced age. When someone reaches other high level federal offices, it is by chance in a way and after already becoming famous by pursuing another career. Ambition cannot make these high offices the permanent aim of its efforts. It is in the town, at the center of the ordinary relations of life, that the desire for esteem, the need for real interests, the taste for power and notice are focused. These passions, which so often trouble society, change character when they can operate thus near the domestic hearth and, in a way, within the family.

See with what art, in the American town, care has been taken to *scatter* power, if I can express myself in this way, in order to interest more people in public life. Apart from the voters called from time to time to perform the acts of government, how many diverse offices, how many different magistrates, who all, in the circle of their attributions, represent the powerful corporate body in whose name they act! How many men thus exploit the power of the town for their profit and are interested in it for themselves!

Nor is the American system, even as it divides municipal power among a great number of citizens, afraid to multiply town duties. In the United States people think rightly that love of country is a kind of religious cult that attaches men by observances.

In this way, town life makes itself felt at every moment as it were; it manifests itself every day by the accomplishment of a duty or by the exercise of a right. This political existence imparts a continual, but at the same time peaceful, movement to society that agitates without troubling it.

The Americans are attached to the city by a reason analogous to the one that makes mountain dwellers love their country. Among them the native land has marked and characteristic features; it has a more distinctive physiognomy than elsewhere.

In general the New England towns have a happy existence. Their government suits their taste and is their choice as well. Within the profound peace and material prosperity that reign in America, the storms of municipal life are few. Leadership of town interests is easy. The political education of the people, moreover, was done a long time ago, or rather they arrived already educated on the soil they occupy. In New England, division of ranks does not exist even in memory; so there is no portion of the town tempted to oppress the other, and injustices, which strike only isolated individuals, are lost in the general contentment. Should the government exhibit some faults, and certainly it is easy to point them out, they are not obvious to view, because the government truly derives from the governed. And it is sufficient for town government to operate, whether well or poorly, for it to be protected by a kind of paternal pride. The Americans, moreover, have no point of comparison.

England once ruled the colonies as a whole, but the people have always directed town affairs. So sovereignty of the people in the town is not only a long-standing condition, but also an original one.

The inhabitant of New England is attached to his town, because it is strong and independent; he is interested in it, because he participates in its leadership; he loves it, because he has nothing to complain about in his lot. In the town he places his ambition and his future; he joins in each of the incidents of town life; in this limited sphere, accessible to him, he tries his hand at governing society. He becomes accustomed to the forms without which liberty proceeds only by revolutions, is infused with their spirit, acquires a taste for order, understands the harmony of powers, and finally gathers clear and practical ideas about the nature of his duties as well as the extent of his rights.

DEMOCRACY IN AMERICA, VOLUME II, PART 3, CHAPTER 12: "HOW THE AMERICANS UNDERSTAND THE EQUALITY OF MAN AND OF WOMAN"

I showed how democracy destroyed or modified the various inequalities given birth by society; but is that all, and does democracy not succeed finally in acting on this great inequality of man and woman, which has seemed, until today, to have its eternal foundation in nature?

I think that the social movement that brings closer to the same level the son and the father, the servant and the master, and in general, the inferior and the superior, elevates the woman and must more and more make her the equal of the man.

But here, more than ever, I feel the need to be well understood; for there is no subject on which the coarse and disorderly imagination of our century has been given a freer rein.

There are men in Europe who, confusing the different attributes of the sexes, claim to make the man and the woman beings, not only equal, but similar. They give to the one as to the other the same functions, impose the same duties on them, and grant them the same rights; they mix them in everything, work, pleasures, public affairs. It can easily be imagined that by trying hard in this way to make one sex equal to the other, both are degraded; and that from this crude mixture of the works of nature only weak men and dishonest women can ever emerge.

This is not how the Americans understood the type of democratic equality that can be established between the woman and the man. They thought that, since nature had established such a great variation between the physical and moral constitution of the man and that of the woman, it's clearly indicated goal was to give a different use to their different faculties; and they judged that progress did not consist of making almost the same things out of dissimilar beings, but of having each of them fulfill his task to the best possible degree. The Americans applied to the two sexes the great principle of political economy that dominates industry today. They carefully divided the functions of the man and the woman, in order that the great work of society was better accomplished.

America is the country in the world where the most constant care has been taken to draw clearly separated lines of action for the two sexes, and where the desire has been that both marched with an equal step, but always along different paths. You do not see American women lead matters outside of the family, conduct business, or finally enter into the political sphere; but you also do not find any who are forced to give themselves to the hard work of plowing or to any one of the difficult exercises that require the development of physical strength. There are no families so poor that they make an exception to this rule.

If the American woman cannot escape the peaceful circle of domestic occupations, she is, on the other hand, never forced to leave it. She has been enclosed in her home, but there she rules.

The result is that American women, who often show a male reason and an entirely manly energy, conserve in general a very delicate appearance, and always remain women by manners, although they reveal themselves as men sometimes by mind and heart.

Nor have the Americans ever imagined that the consequence of democratic principles was to overturn marital authority and to introduce confusion of authority into the family. They thought that every association, to be effective, must have a head, and that the natural head of the conjugal association was the man. So they do not deny to the latter the right to direct his companion; and they believe that, in the small society of husband and wife, as in the great political society, the goal of democracy is to regulate necessary powers and to make them legitimate, and not to destroy all power. The Americans have, however, drawn the man and the woman closer than any other people, but it is only in the moral order.

This opinion is not particular to one sex and contested by the other. I did not notice that American women considered conjugal authority as a happy usurpation of their rights, or that they believed that it was degrading to submit to it. I seemed to see, on the contrary, that they took a kind of glory in the voluntary surrender of their will, and that they located their grandeur in bending to the yoke themselves and not in escaping it. That, at least, was the sentiment expressed by the most virtuous; the others kept silent, and you do not hear in the United States the adulterous wife noisily claim the rights of woman, while trampling her most holy duties under foot.

It has often been remarked that in Europe a certain disdain is found even amid the flatteries that men lavish on women; although the European man often makes himself the slave of the woman, you see that he never sincerely believes her his equal.

In the United States, women are scarcely praised; but it is seen every day that they are respected.

American men constantly exhibit a full confidence in the reason of their companion, and a profound respect for her liberty. They judge that her mind is as capable as that of man of discovering the naked truth, and her heart firm enough to follow the truth; and they have never sought to shelter the virtue of one more than that of the other from prejudices, ignorance or fear.

It seems that in Europe, where you submit so easily to the despotic rule of women, you nonetheless refuse them some of the greatest attributes of the human species, and that you consider them as seductive and incomplete beings; and, what you cannot find too astonishing, women themselves finish by seeing themselves in the same light, and they are not far from considering as a privilege the ability that is left to them to appear frivolous, weak and fearful. American women do not demand such rights.

You would say, on the other hand, that as regards morals, we have granted to the man a kind of singular immunity; so that there is as it were one virtue for him, and another one for his companion; and that, according to public opinion, the same act may be alternatively a crime or only a failing.

The Americans do not know this iniquitous division of duties and rights. Among them, purity of morals in marriage and respect for conjugal faith are imposed equally on the man and on the woman and the seducer is as dishonored as his victim.

It is true that American men rarely show to women these attentive considerations with which we enjoy surrounding them in Europe; but they always show, by their conduct, that they assume them to be virtuous and delicate; and they have such a great respect for their moral liberty that in their presence each man carefully watches his words, for fear that the women may be forced to hear language that wounds them. In America, a young girl undertakes a long journey, alone and without fear.

The legislators of the United States, who have made nearly all the provisions of the penal code milder, punish rape with death; and there is no crime that public opinion pursues with a more inexorable ardor. This can be explained: since the Americans imagine nothing more precious than the honor of the woman, or nothing so respectable as her independence, they consider that there is no punishment too severe for those who take them away from her against her will.

In France, where the same crime is struck by much milder penalties, it is often difficult to find a jury that convicts. Would it be scorn for modesty or scorn for the woman? I cannot prevent myself from believing that it is both.

Thus, the Americans do not believe that man and woman have the duty or the right to do the same things, but they show the same respect for the role of each one of them, and they consider them as beings whose value is equal, although their destinies differ. They do not give the courage of the woman the same form or the same use as that of the man; but they never doubt her courage; and if they consider that the man and his companion should not always use their intelligence and their reason in the same way, they judge, as least, that the reason of the one is as certain as that of the other, and her intelligence as clear.

So the Americans, who have allowed the inferiority of the woman to continue to exist in society, have with all their power elevated her, in the intellectual and moral world, to the level of the man; and in this they seem to me to have understood admirably the true notion of democratic progress. They have not imagined for the woman a greatness similar to that of the man, but they have imagined her as great as the man, and they have made her their equal even when they have kept the necessary right to command her.

As for me, I will not hesitate to say it: although in the United States the woman hardly leaves the domestic circle, and although she is, in certain respects, very dependent, nowhere has her position seemed higher to me; and if, now that I am approaching the end of this book, in which I have shown so many considerable things done by the Americans, you asked me to what I think the singular prosperity and growing strength of this people must be principally attributed, I would answer that it is to the superiority of their women.

SENECA FALLS DECLARATION OF SENTIMENTS

When, in the course of human events, it becomes necessary for one portion of the family of man to assume among the people of the earth a position different from that which they have hitherto occupied, but one to which the laws of nature and of nature's God entitle them, a decent respect to the opinions of mankind requires that they should declare the causes that impel them to such a course.

We hold these truths to be self-evident: that all men and women are created equal; that they are endowed by their Creator with certain inalienable rights; that among these are life, liberty, and the pursuit of happiness; that to secure these rights governments are instituted, deriving their just powers from the consent of the governed. Whenever any form of government becomes destructive of these ends, it is the right of those who suffer from it to refuse allegiance to it, and to insist upon the institution of a new government, laying its foundation on such principles, and organizing its powers in such form, as to them shall seem most likely to effect their safety and happiness. Prudence, indeed, will dictate that governments long established should not be changed for light and transient causes; and accordingly all experience hath shown that mankind are more disposed to suffer, while evils are sufferable, than to right themselves by abolishing the forms to which they were accustomed. But when a long train of abuses and usurpations, pursuing invariably the same object evinces a design to reduce them under absolute despotism, it is their duty to throw off such government, and to provide new guards for their future security. Such has been the patient sufferance of the women under this government, and such is now the necessity which constrains them to demand the equal station to which they are entitled.

The history of mankind is a history of repeated injuries and usurpations on the part of man toward woman, having in direct object the establishment of an absolute tyranny over her. To prove this, let facts be submitted to a candid world.

He has never permitted her to exercise her inalienable right to the elective franchise.

He has compelled her to submit to laws, in the formation of which she had no voice.

He has withheld from her rights which are given to the most ignorant and degraded men—both natives and foreigners.

Having deprived her of this first right of a citizen, the elective franchise, thereby leaving her without representation in the halls of legislation, he has oppressed her on all sides.

He has made her, if married, in the eye of the law, civilly dead.

He has taken from her all right in property, even to the wages she earns.

He has made her, morally, an irresponsible being, as she can commit many crimes with impunity, provided they be done in the presence of her husband. In the covenant of marriage, she is compelled to promise obedience to her husband, he becoming, to all intents and purposes, her master—the law giving him power to deprive her of her liberty, and to administer chastisement.

He has so framed the laws of divorce, as to what shall be the proper causes, and in case of separation, to whom the guardianship of the children shall be given, as to be wholly regardless of the happiness of women—the law, in all cases, going upon a false supposition of the supremacy of man, and giving all power into his hands.

After depriving her of all rights as a married woman, if single, and the owner of property, he has taxed her to support a government which recognizes her only when her property can be made profitable to it.

He has monopolized nearly all the profitable employments, and from those she is permitted to follow, she receives but a scanty remuneration. He closes against her all the avenues to wealth and distinction which he considers most honorable to himself. As a teacher of theology, medicine, or law, she is not known.

He has denied her the facilities for obtaining a thorough education, all colleges being closed against her.

He allows her in Church, as well as State, but a subordinate position, claiming Apostolic authority for her exclusion from the ministry, and, with some exceptions, from any public participation in the affairs of the Church.

He has created a false public sentiment by giving to the world a different code of morals for men and women, by which moral delinquencies which exclude women from society, are not only tolerated, but deemed of little account in man.

He has usurped the prerogative of Jehovah himself, claiming it as his right to assign for her a sphere of action, when that belongs to her conscience and to her God.

He has endeavored, in every way that he could, to destroy her confidence in her own powers, to lessen her self-respect, and to make her willing to lead a dependent and abject life.

Now, in view of this entire disfranchisement of one-half the people of this country, their social and religious degradation—in view of the unjust laws above mentioned, and because women do feel themselves aggrieved, oppressed, and fraudulently deprived of their most sacred rights, we insist that they have immediate admission to all the rights and privileges which belong to them as citizens of the United States.

In entering upon the great work before us, we anticipate no small amount of misconception, misrepresentation, and ridicule; but we shall use every instrumentality within our power to effect our object. We shall employ agents, circulate tracts, petition the State and National legislatures, and endeavor to enlist the pulpit and the press in our behalf. We hope this Convention will be followed by a series of Conventions embracing every part of the country.

FRANKLIN DELANO ROOSEVELT, "ECONOMIC BILL OF RIGHTS"

State of the Union Message to Congress

January 11, 1944

This Republic had its beginning, and grew to its present strength, under the protection of certain inalienable political rights—among them the right of free speech, free press, free worship, trial by jury, freedom from unreasonable searches and seizures. They were our rights to life and liberty.

As our Nation has grown in size and stature, however—as our industrial economy expanded—these political rights proved inadequate to assure us equality in the pursuit of happiness.

We have come to a clear realization of the fact that true individual freedom cannot exist without economic security and independence. "Necessitous men are not free men." People who are hungry and out of a job are the stuff of which dictatorships are made.

In our day these economic truths have become accepted as self-evident. We have accepted, so to speak, a second Bill of Rights under which a new basis of security and prosperity can be established for all regardless of station, race, or creed.

Among these are:

The right to a useful and remunerative job in the industries or shops or farms or mines of the Nation;

The right to earn enough to provide adequate food and clothing and recreation;

The right of every farmer to raise and sell his products at a return which will give him and his family a decent living;

The right of every businessman, large and small, to trade in an atmosphere of freedom from unfair competition and domination by monopolies at home or abroad;

The right of every family to a decent home;

The right to adequate medical care and the opportunity to achieve and enjoy good health;

The right to adequate protection from the economic fears of old age, sickness, accident, and unemployment;

The right to a good education.

All of these rights spell security. And after this war is won we must be prepared to move forward, in the implementation of these rights, to new goals of human happiness and well-being.

America's own rightful place in the world depends in large part upon how fully these and similar rights have been carried into practice for our citizens. For unless there is security here at home there cannot be lasting peace in the world.

One of the great American industrialists of our day—a man who has rendered yeoman service to his country in this crisis—recently emphasized the grave dangers of "rightist reaction" in this Nation. All clear-thinking businessmen share his concern. Indeed, if such reaction should develop—if history were to repeat itself and we were to return to the so-called "normalcy" of the 1920s—then it is certain that even though we shall have conquered our enemies on the battlefields abroad, we shall have yielded to the spirit of Fascism here at home.

I ask the Congress to explore the means for implementing this economic bill of rights—for it is definitely the responsibility of the Congress so to do. Many of these problems are already before committees of the Congress in the form of proposed legislation. I shall from time to time communicate with the Congress with respect to these and further proposals. In the event that no adequate program of progress is evolved, I am certain that the Nation will be conscious of the fact.

Our fighting men abroad—and their families at home—expect such a program and have the right to insist upon it. It is to their demands that this Government should pay heed rather than to the whining demands of selfish pressure groups who seek to feather their nests while young Americans are dying.

The foreign policy that we have been following—the policy that guided us at Moscow, Cairo, and Teheran—is based on the common sense principle which was best expressed by Benjamin Franklin on July 4, 1776: "We must all hang together, or assuredly we shall all hang separately."

I have often said that there are no two fronts for America in this war. There is only one front. There is one line of unity which extends from the hearts of the people at home to the men of our attacking forces in our farthest outposts. When we speak of our total effort, we speak of the factory and the field, and the mine as well as of the battleground—we speak of the soldier and the civilian, the citizen and his Government.

Each and every one of us has a solemn obligation under God to serve this Nation in its most critical hour—to keep this Nation great—to make this Nation greater in a better world.

SUGGESTED ADDITIONAL READINGS (Freely Available Online)

Federalist 52
Federalist 68
Jane Addams, "Why Women Should Vote" (http://www.digitalhistory.uh.edu/disp_textbook.cfm?smtid=3&psid=3609)
Theodore Roosevelt, "Two Noteworthy Books on Democracy" (http://www.theodore-roosevelt.com/images/research/treditorials/o116.pdf)
Theodore Roosevelt, "The Right of the People to Rule" (http://teachingamericanhistory.org/library/document/the-right-of-the-people-to-rule/)
Franklin D. Roosevelt, "Commonwealth Club Address" (http://www.americanrhetoric.com/speeches/fdrcommonwealth.htm)

REPRESENTATION AND DEMOCRACY

Ralph Ketcham

Jefferson explained in the fiftieth year of the Declaration of Independence the sources of its revolutionary political philosophy that "all men are created equal, that they are endowed by their Creator with certain unalienable rights, that among these are life, liberty, and the pursuit of happiness," and that "to secure these rights, governments are instituted among men, deriving their just powers from the consent of the governed." The philosophy expressed, he wrote, "the harmonizing sentiments of the day, whether in conversation, in letters, printed essays, or in the elementary books of public right, as Aristotle, Cicero, Locke, Sidney, etc."[1] The undergirding political philosophy of the new nation, that is, was to be found in a careful reading of a few simple but powerful books and in public sentiment nourished in profound debate over the nature of government as the struggle with Britain had evolved over the past decade or so. In proclaiming "life," for example, to be a universal "right" under any "just government," Jefferson meant that citizens could not be hindered unlawfully in their quest for survival and well-being, including lawful possession of property, by any government. Furthermore, *their* government would protect them from infringement by any other forces or powers in the society. Citizens had the right, that is, to live and pursue their lives lawfully and unoppressed. The restraints, prohibitions, compulsions, and Gestapo or KGB of totalitarian states represented the polar opposite. "Happiness" in the eighteenth century, furthermore, represented the moral dimension of this pursuit. Moral philosophers of the time argued vigorously whether a person had to be religious in order to be moral, but all agreed that in order to be "happy" one had to be virtuous, in pursuit of moral purposes above (but not excluding) all others. The word did not have the hedonistic or libertarian connotations of later (and in some cases earlier or distant) ages.

The word with deepest meaning as the new nation sought to understand and define itself, though, was "liberty." In Jefferson's meaning in the Declaration and in the political parlance of the day it did not mean simply "absence of restraint" but rather *liberty to participate,* the essential foundation and protection in any actual state of all other rights and privileges. Without this liberty, governments were sure to be arbitrary and abusive and render themselves harmful to people's lives; hence Patrick Henry's famous oration, "Give me liberty or give me death." Henry meant that he needed his right to take part in his own government (being denied by Great Britain, as the Declaration would explain) in order to have some voice in laws that should, as expressed in Jefferson's first complaint in the Declaration against King George III's "refusal" of colonial laws, be "most wholesome and necessary for the public good." Liberty, then, for Jefferson, and in virtually all usage in the founding era, meant primarily positive, participating freedom, not just negative, personal freedoms from government. It meant the liberty of citizens in a self-governing society to participate and act for the public good and to use their government to seek, in Aristotle's words, "not merely life alone, but the good life."[2] Without this active participation and ability to subordinate in some degree private to public perspective, one was not, as Henry insisted, truly free. Rather, one was in the bondage of self-love, narrow-mindedness, social indifference, or outside oppression, deprived of the genuine liberty and enhancement of life that comes from living in and taking part in a well-governed state. Of course the founders valued "negative freedoms," personal freedoms government was not to infringe upon (as in the First Amendment "Congress shall make no law . . ."). Such freedoms, though, were thought to be implicitly taken care of under self-government in which active, participating citizens made their own laws—the reason little thought was given at the Constitutional Convention to adding a "negative" bill of rights. Even the idea of separation of powers, as Michael P. Zuckert makes clear in his essay for this volume, was implemented not only to protect "negative freedoms" but also to ensure the effective use of these powers by the government.[3] The very connotations of the words of the Declaration of Independence itself, then, begin to articulate the political philosophy of the American founding.

After subscribing to the "unalienable rights" of "life, liberty and the pursuit of happiness," Jefferson pointed to the requisite political solution: "Governments are instituted among men, deriving their just powers from the consent of the governed." Particularly, one of the "unalienable rights" of the "created equal" members of a political society was the right to find fulfillment for their lives through the liberty to take part in their own government. Following this, the "just powers" of government could only derive from the "consent" of the governed—the measured, deliberate, participatory acceptance of the people of laws "wholesome and necessary for the public good"—which under the unjust government of George III had been vetoed.

Though Jefferson's habit of hyperbole caused him to admire the universalizing, natural law sentiments of Thomas Paine ("the cause of America is in great measure the cause of all mankind," Paine had proclaimed in "Common Sense," as he called for liberty, "haunted and driven from the Old World," to burst forth anew in America[4]), he understood in his more reflective moments that his philosophy of free self-government had more complex, even British origins.[5] Jefferson noted as the fiftieth anniversary of the Declaration of Independence approached (see Peter S. Onuf's eloquent evocation of that event in this volume[6]) that he had composed it as "an expression of the American mind, . . . harmonizing [the] sentiments of the day" and resting on "the elementary books of public right, as Aristotle, Cicero, Locke, Sidney, etc." In 1782 he had observed to a French visitor that the "specific principles" of the new American state were a "composition of the freest principles of the English constitution, with others derived from natural right and natural reason."[7]

John Adams observed late in his long life that the "American Revolution was effected before the war commenced." "The Revolution," he said, "was in the hearts and minds of the people, a change in their religious sentiments, of their duties and obligations. . . . *This radical change in the principles, opinions, sentiments, and affections of the people was the real American Revolution.*"[8] Adams was saying that in the course of the decade or so debate leading up to the final break with Britain, the colonists had paid close attention to the arguments presented in speeches, sermons, discussions, pamphlets, and newspapers as well as to "the elementary books of public right." Thus a political philosophy had "harmonized" as an essential precursor of the struggle for independence that ensued. This was the Union, "the nation brought forth conceived in liberty and dedicated to the proposition that all . . . are created equal," to which Lincoln harked back at Gettysburg in 1863. John Marshall affirmed similarly in 1831, in the midst of the fight against nullification that the "declaration of independence itself is a declaration of a previously existing union." John Quincy Adams replied his gratification at Marshall's opinion because he too viewed the

Declaration "as a Proclamation of Union already formed by *the whole People* of the United States." Marshall replied that it was "an unquestionable maxim of government that all exercise of organized power should be for the benefit of the people . . . [with] the most extensive grant of power to the government to be exercised for the common good" that was possible without abusing the rights of anyone.[9] All were in agreement that the union of sentiment and principle created before 1776, conceived in liberty and dedicated to equality, was the bedrock of the new, independent nation—a political philosophy with which it all began that needed to be the ideal of all the forms of government to follow.

Suffrage and Citizenship

When the question of suffrage came up at the federal convening of the Union at the Convention of 1787, it soon became clear that the delegates needed to look harder at how the "consent of the governed" to the "just powers" of government might work. In a question implicit in John Adams's emphasis on the "sentiments" and "principles" "harmonized," as Jefferson pointed out, in the pre-1776 discussions and debates, would the "consenters," the people taking part in the government, be likely to exercise that participation justly, wisely for the public good? In response to a motion to "restrain the right of suffrage to freeholders," Benjamin Franklin put his finger on the crucial consideration: "It is of great consequence," he said, "that we should not depress the virtue and public spirit of the common people." He noted how large numbers of common people, many not yet freeholders, had proven themselves patriotic and public-spirited during the Revolution. American seamen captured by the British Navy had generally refused to "redeem themselves from misery" by enlisting aboard the ships of their enemy, whereas captured British sailors readily transferred to American vessels with the hope of finding a better life in America. Franklin thought this resulted from the "different manner in which the common people were treated in America and Great Britain." All such persons were likely to be public-spirited citizens ready, because of the sentiments they had displayed, to take part as voters in the new republic.

Franklin made the same point in a public letter he had published in Paris in 1782, supplying "Information to Those Who Would Remove to America." In America, he said, "people do not inquire of a stranger [immigrant], *What is he?* but, *What can he do?* If he has any useful Art, he is welcome, and if he exercises it, and behaves well, he will be respected by all who know him. . . . If they are poor, they begin first as Servants or Journeymen, and if they are sober, industrious, and frugal, they soon become Masters, establish themselves in Business, marry, raise families, and become respectable citizens." However, Franklin warned, "a mere Man of Quality," or even a titled noble, expecting "to live upon the Public, by some Office or Salary, will be despis'd and disregarded." He made the point again in response to delegates who sought high property qualifications for officeholders. He noted that "though honesty was often the companion of wealth, and if poverty was exposed to peculiar temptation, it was no less true that the possession of property increased the desire for more property." Some of the greatest rogues he was ever acquainted with were "the richest rogues." Thus, he "disliked every thing that tended to debase the spirit of the common people" and that gave privilege or advantage to what John Adams would later call the "aristocracy of birth and wealth."[10]

If one were to seek "qualifications" for suffrage, holding office, or any other empowered participation in self-government—that is, citizenship—wealth, class, or social standing were, for Franklin, very poor markers. Instead, the "qualifications" that mattered, that had brought colonials to seek independence in the first place, were "sentiments, principles, opinions, and affections," habits of the heart and mind that "common people," soldiers and sailors, or poor but hardworking and ambitious artisan and farmer immigrants, were no less likely (perhaps even more likely) to have than traditionally privileged groups.[11]

To further develop their political philosophy the founding generation understood it would have to continue to look closely at the question of citizenship: if government was to be good government, according to all the Aristotelian standards well known to educated people of the founding era, and if this just government was to be derived from the consent and equal participation of all, then much attention was needed to the qualities of the participants, the citizens. Franklin had explained how the standards traditional in England and in the colonies were defective and pointed the way toward more qualitative understandings: to play their roles properly, to be the good citizen-officeholders needed in democratic self-government, they had to be public-spirited, attentive in some degree to the public good of the whole polity rather than just to selfish, partisan, special interests.

The same point was made more legalistically when people asked the meaning of their change from being *subjects* of the king of England to being *citizens* of an independent nation. David Ramsey, an ardent revolutionist and author of the first *History of the American Revolution* (1789), wrote that "the political character of the people had changed from subjects to citizens" as a result of the Revolution. "The difference is immense," he wrote. "Subject . . . means one who is under the power of another; but the citizen is a unit of a mass of free people who, collectively, possess sovereignty. Subjects look up to a master, but citizens are so far equal, that none have hereditary rights superior to others." What was the standing, the role, the opportunity of these citizens in their new government?

The ratification contest brought this question forward in many ways. Publius (Alexander Hamilton) had heralded the opportunity, afforded by the public consideration of the proposed constitution, to displace "accident and force" as the foundation of government and replace it with "reflection and choice." He also warned against demagogues who made "zeal for the firmness and efficiency of government" appear a threat to the "rights of the people." Such self-proclaimed "zealots, by paying an obsequious court to the people," Publius explained, often "commenced demagogues and ended tyrants." Publius (James Madison) explained in *Federalist* 57 the problem facing the country: "The aim of every political constitution is, or ought to be," he noted, "first to obtain for rulers men who possess most wisdom to discern, and most virtue to pursue, the common good of the society; and in the next place, to take the most effectual precautions for keeping them virtuous whilst they continue to hold their public trust." Relatively short terms in office and frequent elections would "maintain a proper responsibility to the people."

To make this process work, Publius made a hugely important judgment about the political nature of the people given this responsibility: "As there is a degree of depravity in mankind which requires a certain degree of circumspection and distrust," he asserted, "so there are other qualities in human nature which justify a certain portion of esteem and confidence. Republican government presupposes the existence of these qualities in a higher degree than any other form. Were the pictures which have been drawn by the political jealousy of some among us faithful likenesses of the human character, the inference would be that there is not sufficient virtue among men for self-government; and that nothing less than the chains of despotism can restrain them from destroying and devouring one another." Publius made the same endorsement of human capacity again when, in defending the long terms and "refined" election of senators, he hoped these would enable "reason, justice, and truth [to] regain their authority over the public mind." The equal citizens given the crucial responsibility, directly and indirectly, to choose representatives and senators with "wisdom to discern and virtue to pursue the public good," though, were, Publius believed, up to the task (*Federalist* 55 and 63).[12]

Thus the crucial questions were whether the more "energetic" government defended by Publius would in fact end in tyranny or corrupt oligarchy and whether the elected representatives would be likely to discern and seek the public good. A further question was whether the people were in fact equally empowered under the Constitution, and if they were, whether they themselves possessed the qualities necessary to select such representatives. The New York State Ratification Convention of June 1788, for example, considered a motion to lower the number of constituents in each legislative district from 30,000 to 20,000. The antifederal majority, led by Melancton Smith, asked whether such a large constituent-representative ratio in the House of Representatives and the virtue and judgment of that electorate itself were sufficient to result in good and genuinely participatory self-government.

Smith wondered how the "will of the community" might really be expressed under the new Constitution. "Something like" meaningful participation had worked in the "ancient republics," he said, which were small. In the colonies before the Revolution something "nearer to perfection" had worked to provide liberty (to take part), but protection of the "great interest and liberties of the people," it seemed, was "impractical . . . in a consolidated government" such as that proposed under the new Constitution. Would the small number of representatives there proposed (under the 30,000 per district rule) "possess the requisite information to make happy the great number of souls . . . spread over this extensive country?" Smith asked. Furthermore, he thought government entrusted "to a few men . . . would be more liable to corruption." Though Americans had "hitherto displayed great virtues," they "were but men" and thus might be exposed to corrupt temptations under a consolidated, poorly constructed government.[13]

Hamilton replied that "popular confidence depends on circumstances very distinct from considerations of number." "Public attachment is more strongly secured by a train of prosperous events, which are a result of wise deliberation and vigorous execution," to which large councils or legislatures were "much less competent than small ones." In New York State, "there are some men who are rich, men who are poor, some who are wise, and others who are not," he said, but there was no aristocracy where some are "elevated to a perpetual rank above their fellow-citizens." There was "no such qualification," Hamilton asserted, since all "is bottomed on the broad and equal principle" of the state constitution, in which all were treated alike. Because the people could "elect their most meritorious men," there would be a tendency "to elevate merit even from obscurity," he added, "their most invaluable privilege." "As riches increase and accumulate in few hands," though, "virtue . . . [is] in a greater degree considered as only a graceful appendage of wealth." Hamilton explained that though this was the "real disposition of human nature, . . . a common misfortune," it could be neither changed nor corrected.[14]

Smith then asked those attending the convention to think more deeply about genuine representation and its standing in a truly democratic government. "It was proper," he said, "to examine the qualifications which [members of the House of Representatives] ought to possess, in order to exercise their powers discreetly for the happiness of the people. The idea that naturally suggests itself to our minds, when we speak of representatives," he insisted, "is that they resemble those they represent; they should be a true picture of the people; possess the knowledge of their circumstances and their wants, sympathize in all their distresses, and be disposed to seek their true interests." Such knowledge consisted, he explained, not only of "extensive political and commercial information, such as is acquired by men of refined education, and who have leisure to attain to high degrees of improvement" but also required an "acquaintance with the common concerns and occupations of the people, which men of the middling class of life are in general much better competent to, than those of a superior class." The true commercial interests of a country required not only general knowledge but also "knowledge of the productions of your own country, and their value, what your soil is capable of producing, the nature of your manufacturers, and the capacity of the country to increase both." Levying taxes and excises, Smith added, required "more than an acquaintance with the abstruse part of the system of finance, [it required also] . . . a knowledge of circumstances of the people in general, a discernment of how the burdens imposed will bear on the different classes."

"The same passions and prejudices," Smith said, "govern all men. [But] the circumstances in which men are placed in a great measure give a cast to the human character. Those in middling circumstances have less temptation—they are inclined by habit and the company with whom they associate, to set bounds to their passions and appetites—if this is not sufficient, the want of means to gratify them will be a restraint—they are obliged to employ their time in their respective callings—hence the substantial yeomanry of the country are more temperate, of better morals, and less ambition than the great." Though Smith did not say so at this point, he meant that hardworking farmers (90 percent of the population at the time) and those of "middling" circumstances were better positioned, in general, to be the honest, public-spirited citizens required by democratic self-government—and perhaps even to hold the offices of trust in various levels of democratic government—than the wealthy and refined.

Every society, Smith pointed out, naturally divides itself into classes. "The author of nature has disposed on some greater capacities than on others—birth, education, talents, and wealth create distinctions . . . as visible and of as much influence as titles, stars, and garters." Men of this category, Smith noted, "will command a superior degree of respect" and under the proposed Constitution, with "but few" to fill legislative and other offices, will generally hold power, "living high" as was their habit. "Men in the middling class," then, less aggressively ambitious than the "highly elevated and distinguished," would seldom fill the offices.

"Frame your election laws as you please," Smith insisted, but the "influence of the great will generally enable them to succeed in elections. . . . In districts of 30 or 40,000 inhabitants, [those of] conspicuous, military, popular, civil, or legal talents . . . who easily form associations" will win elections. "The poor and middling classes [that] form them with difficulty" will lose. "It is almost certain, none but the great will be chosen—for they easily unite their interest—the common people will divide, their divisions promoted by . . . some popular demagogue, who will probably be destitute of principle. A substantial yeoman of sense and discernment will hardly ever be chosen. . . . The government will fall into the hands of the few and the great."[15]

"It is a harsh doctrine," Hamilton exclaimed, "that men grow more wicked as they improve and enlighten their minds. Experience [did not] justify that there is more virtue in one class of men than in another. Look through the rich and the poor of the community; the learned and the ignorant. Where does virtue predominate? The difference indeed consists, not in the quantity but in the kind of vices, which are incident to the various classes; and here the advantage of character belongs to the wealthy. Their vices are probably more favorable to the prosperity of the state, than those of the indigent; and partake less of moral depravity." The poor, that is, driven to theft, dishonesty, and sloth, and thus morally flawed, were likely less useful to what Hamilton called the "prosperity of the state" than were the more "enlightened" and ambitious, whose greed and self-regarding energies (their "vices") might also be directed toward the prosperity and public good of the state.

Smith responded, unconvinced: "We ought," he urged, "to guard against the government being placed in the hands of this class . . . being in the habit of profuse living, they will be profuse in the public expenses," whereas "the middling class, from their frugal habits, and feeling for themselves the public burdens, will be careful how they increase them. . . . Men of this superior class are increasing—they have influence, talents and industry—it is time to form a barrier against them. . . . We are willing to establish a government adequate to the purposes of the union," he said, but "let us be careful to establish it on the broad basis of *equal liberty*." In this way Smith probed doggedly the deepest grounds of his conviction that only representation resting on a morally grounded citizenry could, under the new proposed Constitution, provide meaningful *equal liberty*, that is, effective and equitable opportunity for all to take part in the obligations and privileges of citizenship.[16]

The Problem of Political Parties

Before the Constitution received its ultimately Jeffersonian coloration (with antifederal overtones) in the first quarter of the nineteenth century, amendments for a bill of rights were added, and a vigorous debate between Hamiltonian "big government" and Jeffersonian "small government" consumed a decade. In proposing a bill of rights for Congress to initiate in June 1789, Madison sidelined proposals to limit the powers of the federal government, as die-hard antifederalists intended, and instead sought to strengthen, under the Constitution, the power of federal and state governments to deliberate on and enact legislation conducive to the public good. Madison's initial proposals for what became the First Amendment, for example, were:

"The Civil rights of none shall be abridged on account of religious belief or worship, nor shall any national religion be established, nor shall the full rights of conscience be in any manner, or on any pretext, infringed."

"The people shall not be deprived or abridged of their right to speak, to write, or to publish their sentiments; and the freedom of the press, as one of the great bulwarks of liberty, shall be inviolable."

"The people shall not be restrained from peaceably assembling and consulting for their common good, nor from applying to the legislature by petitions or remonstrances for the redress of their grievances."[17]

The language of the First Amendment as finally enacted, that "Congress shall make no law . . . ," is present by implication in Madison's proposals, but equally present is Madison's intention to relate all the rights and privileges to the need to ensure citizens' ability to freely, conscientiously, and fully deliberate about and act in their public role as participants in government: no religious belief or worship should interfere with performance of civic duties, nor should any national religion stunt or debase the useful growth of unestablished religions, nor should the publicly important stimulation of conscientious conviction be in any way abridged or aborted.

The same emphasis pervaded the clauses on freedom of expression: the people were not to be restrained in their reading, writing, speaking, advocacy, and deliberation regarding their "sentiments" on public affairs, nor was a free press, ever the vital engine of equal liberty (to take part) in free countries and in those seeking to be free, to be fettered or censored in any way. Although Madison was fully supportive of the personal, private freedom of expression also rightfully protected, his primary concern was for the vital place freedom of expression had in the public-spirited, political life of the new republic. The last phrases about freedom to assemble peacefully to "consult for their common good" and to address the legislature (broadened to "government" in the adopted version) about their grievances (and by implication to receive response from them) also have most to do with the people's role in the deliberative process of seeking the public good. The procedural rights defined and protected in Articles II–VIII had special significance in ensuring fair and just treatment by the law to those accused of seditious offenses. Even the possible omission of powers and restraints on Congress, and thus retention of rights by the states and the people in Articles IX and X, was seen by Madison and others as protecting, even encouraging, the people and local agencies of government to exercise faithfully their roles in the quest for good government. In a way, by the thrust and modes of expression Madison incorporated in the Bill of Rights adopted in 1791, he diverted a leftover antifederal intention to impose more limits on the new federal government into propositions that had as their primary foundation bolstering and encouraging vital public deliberation in the new republic—especially equal liberty in the choice and functioning of its representative institutions.

As the new nation began to use its new processes and institutions of representative democracy, it soon faced the chasm between the public-spirited, anti-political-party assumptions of the Constitution and the Bill of Rights and the virulent existence of what President George Washington called the "baneful effects of the spirit of party generally" in the country, leading to the clash of factions and other "horrid enormities" and "frightful despotisms." What did Washington mean by "despotisms"? He meant the prevention and denial of the deliberative, reasoned, equitable liberty to take part in politics, submerged by the sway gained over the public mind by the passions, the slander, the "partialness," and the "spirit of party" Washington saw "boiling" around him as he bade his "Farewell" to public life in 1796.[18] (Barack Obama has often expressed similar dismay at the bitter, virulent, selfish partisanship he faces.) Madison had explained in *Federalist* 10, though, that the "causes of faction were sown in the nature of man" and could not be abolished without abolishing free, participatory government itself. He theorized, hopefully, that under the carefully constructed new Constitution, the factions would in their clashes contain each other, and all be defeated or neutralized, so that what Abraham Lincoln would call the "better angels of our nature" could pursue the public good.

Madison's highly critical understanding of the place of faction, party, and local special interests in the selection of legislative members, and then his pragmatic understanding of how something like party might at times become necessary in a self-governing polity, was best articulated for him by the most notable British politician and political thinker of the day, Edmund Burke. In facing his own election to Parliament, Burke had explained to his constituents in Bristol that "Parliament is not a *congress* of ambassadors from different and hostile interests; which interests each must maintain, as an agent and advocate, against other agents and advocates." Rather, he insisted, "Parliament is a *deliberative* assembly of *one* nation, with *one* interest, that of the whole; where, not local purposes, not local prejudices ought to guide, but the general good, resulting from the general reason of the whole" (just what Madison hoped for in the House of Representatives and in the Senate). Burke said he was "not a member of Bristol, but he [was] a member of *Parliament*, [intent on] the real good of the rest of the community."[19] There simply was no place for special interests, factions, or partisan bias in the legislative body or in the attitudes of election to it; public spirit was required, we might say, on both sides of the ballot box.

A few years earlier, however, Burke had faced in Parliament a problem much like that Madison faced in the House of Representatives in 1791. In 1770 Burke had found in Parliament a dominant party "combined for no public purpose, but only as a means of furthering with joint strength their private and individual advantage." In such a scene, Burke asked, could a public-spirited man merely "vote according to his conscience and . . . harangue against every [evil] design?" Such an "innocuous and ineffectual character," Burke retorted, "falls miserably short of the mark of public duty. That duty demands and requires that what is right should not only be made known, but made prevalent; that what is evil should not only be detected, but defeated." In situations of power in public life, it was a "trespass against his duty" for a politician to "sleep upon his watch . . . or go over to the enemy." The "virtuous politician" had to find out the "proper means, . . . [to] pursue every just method to put the men who hold [good] opinions [in office], . . . [to] enable them to carry their common plans into execution." The need was to form a party of righteousness that could defeat the power of evil and faction, a party that could adhere to principles of the aggregate and public welfare—and then disappear when the politics of the country was restored to pursuit of the common good.[20]

Madison and other American leaders in 1790 did not have to turn to Burke's twenty-year-old pamphlet for guidance—Burke's point was by then conventional wisdom among those who had declared independence, fought the Revolution, and established the Constitution and would remain the *ideal*, the *theory* of American party politics until the Jacksonian era; though, of course, practice was often much different. Madison explained in a series of essays addressed to the public what he understood as the realistic condition of American politics, under Hamilton's guidance and partisanship, and what his party (of Burkean righteousness) sought instead. He viewed the Hamiltonians as a Burkean "party of evil . . . combined for no public purpose . . . [and] joined only to strengthen their private and personal advantage"; a party, as Smith had put it, of "natural aristocrats . . . of birth, education, talents, and wealth, . . . [able] to win elections on conspicuous military, popular, civil, or legal talents." Madison accused the "division" gathering around and by Hamilton as consisting of "those, who from particular interest, from natural temper, or from habits of life, are more partial to the opulent than to the other classes of society, and having debauched themselves into a persuasion that mankind are incapable of governing themselves, it follows with them, of course, that the government can be carried on only by the pageantry of rank, the influence of money and emoluments, and the terror of military force."[21]

In the spirit of Burke's call for a party of righteousness in 1770 and Smith's call for a party of morality in 1788, Madison called in 1792 for a party "believing in the doctrine that mankind are capable of governing themselves, of understanding of the general interest of the community, . . . and conducive to the preservation of republican government."[22] Though Madison knew that political parties were, as the phrase went, the inevitable "fruit of freedom," he did not see them as long-lasting and formally organized aggregates of interests sufficiently gathered and accommodated to each other's concerns to win elections that would gain something for everybody, as American political parties would become. The later British conception of the political party as "His majesty's [useful] loyal opposition," ready to assume office at the next election with a publicly articulated idea of the public good, was equally distant from any validated idea of "party" for Madison. Rather, Madison, like all the other early presidents, accepted that a Burkean-style "party," intent on seeing that evil was not only "detected but defeated," might sometimes be necessary, but he never went beyond that in his thinking.

Jefferson told Congress in his first Inauguration Address in 1801 that the nation had passed through a "contest of opinion and animat[ed] discussion . . . now decided by the voice of the nation." Deftly turning political party dispute into principled agreement, he declared, "We are all republicans—we are federalists"; not quarreling, accusing Republican and Federalist Party members but rather disputers and discussants who shared basic political principles. Now, the president-elect said, "according to the rules of the constitution," the nation would "arrange [our]selves under the will of the law, and unite in common efforts for the common good." Thus the nation might "unite with one heart and one mind . . . to restore to social intercourse that harmony and affection without which liberty and even life itself are but dreary things." Jefferson's overwhelming reelection in 1804, and Monroe's two near-unanimous electoral college victories in 1816 and 1820, were regarded by all three Republican presidents as signs that the Federalists were but a transient sectional faction. Their "party" however, they hoped, was on the road to becoming "amalgamated" (Monroe's designation), a Burkean-style entity and public-spirited sentiment, informal and unorganized. This would transcend the "horrid" party disputes of the 1790s and of the coming and conduct of the War of 1812, which had blemished Madison's administrations, and might, they hoped in perhaps forlorn aspiration, head off the bitter factional disputes that in fact would turn an "era of good feelings" into an "era of bad feelings."

Jefferson on the Prerequisites for Republican Liberty

The outlook Jefferson expressed in his Inauguration Address was a kind of summation of his thoughts that would become the core expression of American political philosophy for centuries. Its foundation is in the basically Lockean philosophy of liberty and equality Jefferson expressed so eloquently in the Declaration of Independence: all were equal in the eyes of nature and nature's God as well as of the laws that governed them, created for their protection, convenience, and well-being. They had inalienable rights to life, liberty, and the pursuit of happiness and could be governed justly only with their consent. The elaboration of these concepts into the "principles, opinions, sentiments, and affections" leading to independence in 1776 was in fact the Union, the compelling set of ideas that led to the drafting and adoption of the new, self-imposed Constitution in 1787–1789.

Jefferson believed earnestly in this simple philosophy of government, but he also understood that elaborations and projections would be necessary if it was to be workable in the United States (or anywhere in the world) and thus be a useful and fully developed political philosophy. He recognized that humans had a "first nature" that was only partly suited to the demanding requirements of good democratic government. They needed occupations and relations to land and community that nourished the habits and attitudes necessary for their benign participation in their own government; without that, self-rule would be a "tragedy or a farce," as his colleague and friend Madison once put it. Thus Jefferson favored farmers whose daily round of industriousness, care of the land, support of family, and involvement in the community sustained "substantial and genuine virtue" in their character. Those whose livelihood depended on the "casualties and caprices of customers," however, or who labored in the workshops and "operations of manufacture" of others, were oppositely formed. "Such dependence," he scorned, "begets subservience and venality, suffocates the germ of virtue, and prepares fit tools for the designs of ambition."[23] Franklin and Smith had made similar arguments: equitable and effective representation in a self-governing polity required careful, critical attention to the social circumstances and moral qualities of the participants, the citizens.

Jefferson's incessant, lifelong attention to education reveals another dimension of his conviction that there was enough intelligence and virtue, properly nourished in human "second nature," to allow self-government to be good government. He was always a conditional democrat: if it rested on enough qualified (virtuous and public-spirited) citizens and leaders, it could be the best form of government; if not, it could be as bad as any government of the one, the few, or the many that was selfish, greedy, oppressive, faction-ridden, or neglectful of the public good. The keystone of all his educational endeavors was to train the qualified leaders and citizenry at all levels of government that they might enhance the "life, liberty, and pursuit of happiness" of all; that is, fulfill their role as public-spirited citizens. His plans for a universal system of elementary and secondary public education in Virginia, his steady stream of letters of advice to his children, grandchildren, and any other young people who crossed his path, and his proposals for the University of Virginia all had the same basic premise: every citizen in Virginia, and by projection in the new United States, needed to be prepared to take their proper place in the self-governing institutions of the republic. His highest purpose for the University of Virginia was to "develop the reasoning faculties of our youth, enlarge their minds, cultivate their morals, and instill in them the precepts of virtue and order," and "to form them to the habits of reflection and correct action, rendering them examples of virtue to others and happiness within themselves." Jefferson's greatest contribution to the understanding of democratic government and the grounds for representation in it, his preeminent biographer Dumas Malone once said, was "his inexhaustible faith in the human mind." If his incessant concern for benign occupational and community circumstance, for the republican convictions of immigrants, for education at all levels, and for active, public-spirited participation in state and local politics could become permanent parts of the nation's public life, then representative democracy might be a blessing for the new nation; otherwise it might well become another in the long list of corrupt, oppressive states where the "life of man" was "nasty, poor, lonely, brutish, and short."[24]

Jefferson explained to John Adams in 1813 that there is indeed a "natural aristocracy among men," but the grounds of it, he added, are not wealth and birth but "virtue and talents." Drawing a sharp distinction, Jefferson spoke of an "artificial aristocracy founded on wealth and birth, without either virtue or talents; for with these they would belong to the first class." Jefferson considered the "natural aristocracy" thus distinguished from the "artificial" one "as the most precious gift of nature for the instruction, the trusts, and government of society. And indeed it would have been inconsistent in creation to have formed man for the social state, and not have provided virtue and wisdom enough to manage the concerns of society. May we not even say that that form of government is best which provides most effectually for a pure selection of these natural aristoi into the offices of government? The artificial aristocracy is a mischievous ingredient in government, and provision should be made to prevent its ascendency."

Jefferson rejected John Adams's theory of putting the "pseudo-aristoi" (or "artificial aristocracy") to good use by removing them from the general legislature and placing them in a "separate chamber of legislation" where they could protect their interests as well as seek their inherited or acquired sense of the public good. "I think that to give them power in order to prevent them doing mischief, is arming them for it. . . . Mischief may be done negatively as well as positively," Jefferson noted. "The best remedy," he explained, "is exactly that provided by all our constitutions, to leave to the citizens the free election and separation of the aristoi from the pseudo-aristoi, of the wheat from the chaff. In general they will elect the real good and wise. In some instances, wealth may corrupt, and birth blind them; but not in sufficient degree to endanger the society."

Jefferson then went on to explain all the laws and plans he had passed or proposed in Virginia to raise the natural over the artificial aristocracy in order to make truly representative democracy effective there. A law "abolishing the privilege of Primogeniture, and dividing the lands of intestates equally among all their children, . . . laid the axe to the root of Pseudo-aristocracy," he noted.[25] Another law, proposed but not passed, provided for the "more general diffusion of learning." It proposed a "free school in every ward (township), for reading[,] writing[,] and common arithmetic," district schools at public expense for the best students, and then "select[ing] a certain number of the most promising students [for a] University where all useful sciences should be taught." "Worth and genius," he said, would "thus have been sought out from every condition of life, and completely prepared by education for defeating the competition of wealth and birth for public trusts." Such qualified citizens would then in their local governments take "care of their poor, their roads, police, elections, the nomination of jurors, administration of justice in small cases, elementary exercises of the militia, in short, to have made them little republics," prepared then to manage the "larger republics of the county and state." "It suffices for us," Jefferson concluded, "if the moral and physical condition of our own citizens qualifies them to select the able and good for the direction of their government, with a recurrence of elections at such short periods as will enable them to displace an unfaithful servant before the mischief he premeditates may be irremediable."[26]

Conclusion

Jefferson thus affirmed the basic political philosophy that he had set forth in the Declaration of Independence nearly forty years before and that had been elaborated at many stages of the founding era. It all began, in Lincoln's concise statement, with a "new nation brought forth upon this continent, conceived in liberty and dedicated to the proposition that all . . . are created equal." That is, the nation had as its foundation certain principles that would characterize its political structure and processes and would infuse the moral understanding and public participation of its citizens. The conception and dedication arose from the "sentiments and principles" John Adams had seen arise from the prerevolutionary debates as well as from the ideas of "natural right and natural reason" found in the "elementary books of public right" well known in the colonies: all people possessed "unalienable rights . . . to life, liberty, and the pursuit of happiness," and the governments instituted by them "derived their just powers from the consent of the governed."

Franklin expressed the essential starting point about the participating citizens when he told those attending the Constitutional Convention that "the virtue and public spirit of our common people . . . was of great consequence." Then they would be able to "know and judge the characters of candidates" and choose those whose virtue and public spirit matched their own. Smith and others added, though, that to accomplish this it was necessary to take into account the way of life of the people "participating," because their various "ways" had an important impact on their character and on the dynamics of public life. People in ordinary walks of life (mostly yeoman farmers), industrious, modest in their needs, knowledgeable about local affairs, and intent on raising their families and sustaining their communities, would be "of better morals" and more public-spirited than the "superior class" possessed of "extensive political and commercial information" and focused on their own power and wealth. It was necessary, then, that representatives come from the common people and be acquainted with their concerns and occupations.

It was necessary to ensure as well that representatives who "resembled those they represent" be able to gain office. Those of "conspicuous military, popular, civil, or legal talents," almost sure to win elections in large districts, had to be mixed with voters and officeholders derived from the more morally competent lower orders more likely to flourish in smaller electorates intent on common interests. If, that is, the real life, liberty, and pursuit of happiness of the people were to be secured, the tapping of the moral virtue cultivated in ordinary paths of life as well as the elective empowering of this sentiment and sense of justice were essential to good democratic government. Added to what Publius called the "portion of esteem and confidence" properly due to human nature, these aspects of the emerging political culture were the essential starting points for the political philosophy of the American founding.

Madison and others projected the valuation of public spirit in the people into scorn for any benign conflict-of-interest model for politics. To them, any notion that the "clash of factions" would itself lead to as much justice and good government as was possible in a free society was to default the whole idea of attuning public life to the common good. Though Jefferson and Madison indeed approved of the careful separation of powers Zuckert sees as a vital institutional measure to ensure that laws for the public good would be effectively passed, executed, and validated, they also paid close attention to the intellectual and social underpinnings of good self-government. To Madison, and to the political philosophy of the Founding Era, party-generated conflict, and effective party organization to sustain it, betrayed the aspiration to rest politics on public spirit, or on the "harmony and affection . . . in social intercourse," Jefferson noted, that made the conflict-of-interest model of politics "but a dreary thing."

Most basic to the completion of the founding political philosophy was the need to further prepare citizens and leaders for their roles in self-government through education. Though finding the sense of justice inherent in people and the life circumstances of the "middling sorts" conducive to the flourishing of public spirit that was foundational to all good government, for Jefferson the spread of education, extended to all and graded to suit varied life situations, was the recurring need and pattern as the new nation sought to secure its standing as a republic. "I know of no safe depository of the ultimate powers of society," he wrote forty-four years after the Declaration of Independence, "but the people themselves: and if we think them not enlightened enough to exercise their control with a wholesome discretion, the remedy is, not to take it from them, but to inform their discretion by education. This is the true corrective for abuses of constitutional power."[27]

Resting then, as every good democratic government must, on the virtue and public spirit of its citizens (as the lessons the founders drew from the Greeks and Romans, from their Christian heritage, from the experience of English government from the Magna Carta on, and from the "benign neglect" of a century and a half of rule in the colonies all attested), government was prepared to fulfill the goals set forth in the preamble of the Constitution: full religious liberty would nourish vital public-spirited convictions of conscience; equitable yet unoppressive, even "mild," laws would establish justice and ensure domestic tranquility; national guidance of the nation's commerce and infant industrial growth would promote the general welfare; and sympathy for free governments abroad while insisting on American rights on the high seas would provide for the common defense. This was the American political philosophy of free and equitable government resting on public-spirited, representative institutions.

Federalism

FEDERALIST 14

We have seen the necessity of the Union, as our bulwark against foreign danger, as the conservator of peace among ourselves, as the guardian of our commerce and other common interests, as the only substitute for those military establishments which have subverted the liberties of the Old World, and as the proper antidote for the diseases of faction, which have proved fatal to other popular governments, and of which alarming symptoms have been betrayed by our own. All that remains, within this branch of our inquiries, is to take notice of an objection that may be drawn from the great extent of country which the Union embraces. A few observations on this subject will be the more proper, as it is perceived that the adversaries of the new Constitution are availing themselves of the prevailing prejudice with regard to the practicable sphere of republican administration, in order to supply, by imaginary difficulties, the want of those solid objections which they endeavor in vain to find.

The error which limits republican government to a narrow district has been unfolded and refuted in preceding papers. I remark here only that it seems to owe its rise and prevalence chiefly to the confounding of a republic with a democracy, applying to the former reasonings drawn from the nature of the latter. The true distinction between these forms was also adverted to on a former occasion. It is, that in a democracy, the people meet and exercise the government in person; in a republic, they assemble and administer it by their representatives and agents. A democracy, consequently, will be confined to a small spot. A republic may be extended over a large region.

To this accidental source of the error may be added the artifice of some celebrated authors, whose writings have had a great share in forming the modern standard of political opinions. Being subjects either of an absolute or limited monarchy, they have endeavored to heighten the advantages, or palliate the evils of those forms, by placing in comparison the vices and defects of the republican, and by citing as specimens of the latter the turbulent democracies of ancient Greece and modern Italy. Under the confusion of names, it has been an easy task to transfer to a republic observations applicable to a democracy only; and among others, the observation that it can never be established but among a small number of people, living within a small compass of territory.

Such a fallacy may have been the less perceived, as most of the popular governments of antiquity were of the democratic species; and even in modern Europe, to which we owe the great principle of representation, no example is seen of a government wholly popular, and founded, at the same time, wholly on that principle. If Europe has the merit of discovering this great mechanical power in government, by the simple agency of which the will of the largest political body may be concentrated, and its force directed to any object which the public good requires, America can claim the merit of making the discovery the basis of unmixed and extensive republics. It is only to be lamented that any of her citizens should wish to deprive her of the additional merit of displaying its full efficacy in the establishment of the comprehensive system now under her consideration.

As the natural limit of a democracy is that distance from the central point which will just permit the most remote citizens to assemble as often as their public functions demand, and will include no greater number than can join in those functions; so the natural limit of a republic is that distance from the centre which will barely allow the representatives to meet as often as may be necessary for the administration of public affairs. Can it be said that the limits of the United States exceed this distance? It will not be said by those who recollect that the Atlantic coast is the longest side of the Union, that during the term of thirteen years, the representatives of the States have been almost continually assembled, and that the members from the most distant States are not chargeable with greater intermissions of attendance than those from the States in the neighborhood of Congress.

That we may form a juster estimate with regard to this interesting subject, let us resort to the actual dimensions of the Union. The limits, as fixed by the treaty of peace, are: on the east the Atlantic, on the south the latitude of thirty-one degrees, on the west the Mississippi, and on the north an irregular line running in some instances beyond the forty-fifth degree, in others falling as low as the forty-second. The southern shore of Lake Erie lies below that latitude. Computing the distance between the thirty-first and forty-fifth degrees, it amounts to nine hundred and seventy-three common miles; computing it from thirty-one to forty-two degrees, to seven hundred and sixty-four miles and a half. Taking the mean for the distance, the amount will be eight hundred and sixty-eight miles and three-fourths. The mean distance from the Atlantic to the Mississippi does not probably exceed seven hundred and fifty miles. On a comparison of this extent with that of several countries in Europe, the practicability of rendering our system commensurate to it appears to be demonstrable. It is not a great deal larger than Germany, where a diet representing the whole empire is continually assembled; or than Poland before the late dismemberment, where another national diet was the depositary of the supreme power. Passing by France and Spain, we find that in Great Britain, inferior as it may be in size, the representatives of the northern extremity of the island have as far to travel to the national council as will be required of those of the most remote parts of the Union.

Favorable as this view of the subject may be, some observations remain which will place it in a light still more satisfactory.

In the first place it is to be remembered that the general government is not to be charged with the whole power of making and administering laws. Its jurisdiction is limited to certain enumerated objects, which concern all the members of the republic, but which are not to be attained by the separate provisions of any. The subordinate governments, which can extend their care to all those other subjects which can be separately provided for, will retain their due authority and activity. Were it proposed by the plan of the convention to abolish the governments of the particular States, its adversaries would have some ground for their objection;

though it would not be difficult to show that if they were abolished the general government would be compelled, by the principle of self-preservation, to reinstate them in their proper jurisdiction.

A second observation to be made is that the immediate object of the federal Constitution is to secure the union of the thirteen primitive States, which we know to be practicable; and to add to them such other States as may arise in their own bosoms, or in their neighborhoods, which we cannot doubt to be equally practicable. The arrangements that may be necessary for those angles and fractions of our territory which lie on our northwestern frontier, must be left to those whom further discoveries and experience will render more equal to the task.

Let it be remarked, in the third place, that the intercourse throughout the Union will be facilitated by new improvements. Roads will everywhere be shortened, and kept in better order; accommodations for travelers will be multiplied and meliorated; an interior navigation on our eastern side will be opened throughout, or nearly throughout, the whole extent of the thirteen States. The communication between the Western and Atlantic districts, and between different parts of each, will be rendered more and more easy by those numerous canals with which the beneficence of nature has intersected our country, and which art finds it so little difficult to connect and complete.

A fourth and still more important consideration is, that as almost every State will, on one side or other, be a frontier, and will thus find, in regard to its safety, an inducement to make some sacrifices for the sake of the general protection; so the States which lie at the greatest distance from the heart of the Union, and which, of course, may partake least of the ordinary circulation of its benefits, will be at the same time immediately contiguous to foreign nations, and will consequently stand, on particular occasions, in greatest need of its strength and resources. It may be inconvenient for Georgia, or the States forming our western or northeastern borders, to send their representatives to the seat of government; but they would find it more so to struggle alone against an invading enemy, or even to support alone the whole expense of those precautions which may be dictated by the neighborhood of continual danger. If they should derive less benefit, therefore, from the Union in some respects than the less distant States, they will derive greater benefit from it in other respects, and thus the proper equilibrium will be maintained throughout.

I submit to you, my fellow-citizens, these considerations, in full confidence that the good sense which has so often marked your decisions will allow them their due weight and effect; and that you will never suffer difficulties, however formidable in appearance, or however fashionable the error on which they may be founded, to drive you into the gloomy and perilous scene into which the advocates for disunion would conduct you. Hearken not to the unnatural voice which tells you that the people of America, knit together as they are by so many cords of affection, can no longer live together as members of the same family; can no longer continue the mutual guardians of their mutual happiness; can no longer be fellow-citizens of one great, respectable, and flourishing empire. Hearken not to the voice which petulantly tells you that the form of government recommended for your adoption is a novelty in the political world; that it has never yet had a place in the theories of the wildest projectors; that it rashly attempts what it is impossible to accomplish. No, my countrymen, shut your ears against this unhallowed language. Shut your hearts against the poison which it conveys; the kindred blood which flows in the veins of American citizens, the mingled blood which they have shed in defense of their sacred rights, consecrate their Union, and excite horror at the idea of their becoming aliens, rivals, enemies. And if novelties are to be shunned, believe me, the most alarming of all novelties, the most wild of all projects, the most rash of all attempts, is that of rending us in pieces, in order to preserve our liberties and promote our happiness. But why is the experiment of an extended republic to be rejected, merely because it may comprise what is new? Is it not the glory of the people of America, that, whilst they have paid a decent regard to the opinions of former times and other nations, they have not suffered a blind veneration for antiquity, for custom, or for names, to overrule the suggestions of their own good sense, the knowledge of their own situation, and the lessons of their own experience? To this manly spirit, posterity will be indebted for the possession, and the world for the example, of the numerous innovations displayed on the American theatre, in favor of private rights and public happiness. Had no important step been taken by the leaders of the Revolution for which a precedent could not be discovered, no government established of which an exact model did not present itself, the people of the United States might, at this moment have been numbered among the melancholy victims of misguided councils, must at best have been laboring under the weight of some of those forms which have crushed the liberties of the rest of mankind. Happily for America, happily, we trust, for the whole human race, they pursued a new and more noble course. They accomplished a revolution which has no parallel in the annals of human society. They reared the fabrics of governments which have no model on the face of the globe. They formed the design of a great Confederacy, which it is incumbent on their successors to improve and perpetuate. If their works betray imperfections, we wonder at the fewness of them. If they erred most in the structure of the Union, this was the work most difficult to be executed; this is the work which has been new modeled by the act of your convention, and it is that act on which you are now to deliberate and to decide.

FEDERALIST 15

In the course of the preceding papers, I have endeavored, my fellow-citizens, to place before you, in a clear and convincing light, the importance of Union to your political safety and happiness. I have unfolded to you a complication of dangers to which you would be exposed, should you permit that sacred knot which binds the people of America together be severed or dissolved by ambition or by avarice, by jealousy or by misrepresentation. In the sequel of the inquiry through which I propose to accompany you, the truths intended to be inculcated will receive further confirmation from facts and arguments hitherto unnoticed. If the road over which you will still have to pass should in some places appear to you tedious or irksome, you will recollect that you are in quest of information on a subject the most momentous which can engage the attention of a free people, that the field through which you have to travel is in itself spacious, and that the difficulties of the journey have been unnecessarily increased by the mazes with which sophistry has beset the way. It will be my aim to remove the obstacles from your progress in as compendious a manner as it can be done, without sacrificing utility to despatch.

In pursuance of the plan which I have laid down for the discussion of the subject, the point next in order to be examined is the "insufficiency of the present Confederation to the preservation of the Union." It may perhaps be asked what need there is of reasoning or proof to illustrate a position which is not either controverted or doubted, to which the understandings and feelings of all classes of men assent, and which in substance is admitted by the opponents as well as by the friends of the new Constitution. It must in truth be acknowledged that, however these may differ in other respects, they in general appear to harmonize in this sentiment, at least, that there are material imperfections in our national system, and that something is necessary to be done to rescue us from impending anarchy. The facts that support this opinion are no longer objects of speculation. They have forced themselves upon the sensibility of the people at large, and have at length extorted from those, whose mistaken policy has had the principal share in precipitating the extremity at which we are arrived, a reluctant confession of the reality of those defects in the scheme of our federal government, which have been long pointed out and regretted by the intelligent friends of the Union.

We may indeed with propriety be said to have reached almost the last stage of national humiliation. There is scarcely anything that can wound the pride or degrade the character of an independent nation which we do not experience. Are there engagements to the performance of which we are held by every tie respectable among men? These are the subjects of constant and unblushing violation. Do we owe debts to foreigners and to our own citizens contracted in a time of imminent peril for the preservation of our political existence? These remain without any proper or satisfactory provision for their discharge. Have we valuable territories and important posts in the possession of a foreign power which, by express stipulations, ought long since to have been surrendered? These are still retained, to the prejudice of our interests, not less than of our rights. Are we in a condition to resent or to repel the aggression? We have neither troops, nor treasury, nor government. Are we even in a condition to remonstrate with dignity? The just imputations on our own faith, in respect to the same treaty, ought first to be removed. Are we entitled by nature and compact to a free participation in the navigation of the Mississippi? Spain excludes us from it. Is public credit an indispensable resource in time of public danger? We seem to have abandoned its cause as desperate and irretrievable. Is commerce of importance to national wealth? Ours is at the lowest point of declension. Is respectability in the eyes of foreign powers a safeguard against foreign encroachments? The imbecility of our government even forbids them to treat with us. Our ambassadors abroad are the mere pageants of mimic sovereignty. Is a violent and unnatural decrease in the value of land a symptom of national distress? The price of improved land in most parts of the country is much lower than can be accounted for by the quantity of waste land at market, and can only be fully explained by that want of private and public confidence, which are so alarmingly prevalent among all ranks, and which have a direct tendency to depreciate property of every kind. Is private credit the friend and patron of industry? That most useful kind which relates to borrowing and lending is reduced within the narrowest limits, and this still more from an opinion of insecurity than from the scarcity of money. To shorten an enumeration of particulars which can afford neither pleasure nor instruction, it may in general be demanded, what indication is there of national disorder, poverty, and insignificance that could befall a community so peculiarly blessed with natural advantages as we are, which does not form a part of the dark catalogue of our public misfortunes?

This is the melancholy situation to which we have been brought by those very maxims and councils which would now deter us from adopting the proposed Constitution; and which, not content with having conducted us to the brink of a precipice, seem resolved to plunge us into the abyss that awaits us below. Here, my countrymen, impelled by every motive that ought to influence an enlightened people, let us make a firm stand for our safety, our tranquility, our dignity, our reputation. Let us at last break the fatal charm which has too long seduced us from the paths of felicity and prosperity.

It is true, as has been before observed that facts, too stubborn to be resisted, have produced a species of general assent to the abstract proposition that there exist material defects in our national system; but the usefulness of the concession, on the part of the old adversaries of federal measures, is destroyed by a strenuous opposition to a remedy, upon the only principles that can give it a chance of success. While they admit that the government of the United States is destitute of energy, they contend against conferring upon it those powers which are requisite to supply that energy. They seem still to aim at things repugnant and irreconcilable; at an augmentation of federal authority, without a diminution of State authority; at sovereignty in the Union, and complete independence in the members. They still, in fine, seem to cherish with blind devotion the political monster of an imperium in imperio. This renders a full display of the principal defects of the Confederation necessary, in order to show that the evils we experience do not proceed from minute or partial imperfections, but from fundamental errors in the structure of the building, which cannot be amended otherwise than by an alteration in the first principles and main pillars of the fabric.

The great and radical vice in the construction of the existing Confederation is in the principle of *legislation* for *states* or *governments*, in their *corporate* or *collective capacities*, and as contradistinguished from the *individuals* of which they consist. Though this principle does not run through all the powers delegated to the Union, yet it pervades and governs those on which the efficacy of the rest depends. Except as to the rule of appointment, the United States has an indefinite discretion to make requisitions for men and money; but they have no authority to raise either, by regulations extending to the individual citizens of America. The consequence of this is, that though in theory their resolutions concerning those objects are laws, constitutionally binding on the members of the Union, yet in practice they are mere recommendations which the States observe or disregard at their option.

It is a singular instance of the capriciousness of the human mind, that after all the admonitions we have had from experience on this head, there should still be found men who object to the new Constitution, for deviating from a principle which has been found the bane of the old, and which is in itself evidently incompatible with the idea of *government*; a principle, in short, which, if it is to be executed at all, must substitute the violent and sanguinary agency of the sword to the mild influence of the magistracy.

There is nothing absurd or impracticable in the idea of a league or alliance between independent nations for certain defined purposes precisely stated in a treaty regulating all the details of time, place, circumstance, and quantity; leaving nothing to future discretion; and depending for its execution on the good faith of the parties. Compacts of this kind exist among all civilized nations, subject to the usual vicissitudes of peace and war, of observance and non-observance, as the interests or passions of the contracting powers dictate. In the early part of the present century there was an epidemical rage in Europe for this species of compacts, from which the politicians of the times fondly hoped for benefits which were never realized. With a view to establishing the equilibrium of power and the peace of that part of the world, all the resources of negotiation were exhausted, and triple and quadruple alliances were formed; but they were scarcely formed before they were broken, giving an instructive but afflicting lesson to mankind, how little dependence is to be placed on treaties which have no other sanction than the obligations of good faith, and which oppose general considerations of peace and justice to the impulse of any immediate interest or passion.

If the particular States in this country are disposed to stand in a similar relation to each other, and to drop the project of a general *discretionary superintendence*, the scheme would indeed be pernicious, and would entail upon us all the mischiefs which have been enumerated under the first head; but it would have the merit of being, at least, consistent and practicable. Abandoning all views towards a confederate government, this would bring us to a simple alliance offensive and defensive; and would place us in a situation to be alternate friends and enemies of each other, as our mutual jealousies and rivalships, nourished by the intrigues of foreign nations, should prescribe to us.

But if we are unwilling to be placed in this perilous situation; if we still will adhere to the design of a national government, or, which is the same thing, of a superintending power, under the direction of a common council, we must resolve to incorporate into our plan those ingredients which may be considered as forming the characteristic difference between a league and a government; we must extend the authority of the Union to the persons of the citizens—the only proper objects of government.

Government implies the power of making laws. It is essential to the idea of a law, that it be attended with a sanction; or, in other words, a penalty or punishment for disobedience. If there be no penalty annexed to disobedience, the resolutions or commands which pretend to be laws will, in fact, amount to nothing more than advice or recommendation. This penalty, whatever it may be, can only be inflicted in two ways: by the agency of the courts and ministers of justice, or by military force; by the *coercion* of the magistracy, or by the *coercion* of arms. The first kind can evidently apply only to men; the last kind must of necessity, be employed against bodies politic, or communities, or States. It is evident that there is no process of a court by which the observance of the laws can, in the last resort, be enforced. Sentences may be denounced against them for violations of their duty; but these sentences can only be carried into execution by the sword. In an association where the general authority is confined to the collective bodies of the communities, that compose it, every breach of the laws must involve a state of war; and military execution must become the only instrument of civil obedience. Such a state of things can certainly not deserve the name of government, nor would any prudent man choose to commit his happiness to it.

There was a time when we were told that breaches, by the States, of the regulations of the federal authority were not to be expected; that a sense of common interest would preside over the conduct of the respective members, and would beget a full compliance with all the constitutional requisitions of the Union. This language, at the present day, would appear as wild as a great part of what we now hear from the same quarter will be thought, when we shall have received further lessons from that best oracle of wisdom, experience. It at all times betrayed an ignorance of the true springs by which human conduct is actuated, and belied the original inducements to the establishment of civil power. Why has government been instituted at all? Because the passions of men will not conform to the dictates of reason and justice, without constraint. Has it been found that bodies of men act with more rectitude or greater disinterestedness than individuals? The contrary of this has been inferred by all accurate observers of the conduct of mankind; and the inference is founded upon obvious reasons. Regard to reputation has a less active influence, when the infamy of a bad action is to be divided among a number than when it is to fall singly upon one. A spirit of faction, which is apt to mingle its poison in the deliberations of all bodies of men, will often hurry the persons of whom they are composed into improprieties and excesses, for which they would blush in a private capacity.

In addition to all this, there is, in the nature of sovereign power, an impatience of control, that disposes those who are invested with the exercise of it, to look with an evil eye upon all external attempts to restrain or direct its operations. From this spirit it happens, that in every political association which is formed upon the principle of uniting in a common interest a number of lesser sovereignties, there will be found a kind of eccentric tendency in the subordinate or inferior orbs, by the operation of which there will be a perpetual effort in each to fly off from the common centre. This tendency is not difficult to be accounted for. It has its origin in the love of power. Power controlled or abridged is almost always the rival and enemy of that power by which it is controlled or abridged. This simple proposition will teach us how little reason there is to expect, that the persons entrusted with the administration of the affairs of the particular members of a confederacy will at all times be ready, with perfect good-humor, and an unbiased regard to the public weal, to execute the resolutions or decrees of the general authority. The reverse of this results from the constitution of human nature.

If, therefore, the measures of the Confederacy cannot be executed without the intervention of the particular administrations, there will be little prospect of their being executed at all. The rulers of the respective members, whether they have a constitutional right to do it or not, will undertake to judge of the propriety of the measures themselves. They will consider the conformity of the thing proposed or required to their immediate interests or aims; the momentary conveniences or inconveniences that would attend its adoption. All this will be done; and in a spirit of interested and suspicious scrutiny, without that knowledge of national circumstances and reasons of state, which is essential to a right judgment, and with that strong predilection in favor of local objects, which can hardly fail to mislead the decision. The same process must be repeated in every member of which the body is constituted; and the execution of the plans, framed by the councils of the whole, will always fluctuate on the discretion of the ill-informed and prejudiced opinion of every part. Those who have been conversant in the proceedings of popular assemblies; who have seen how difficult it often is, where there is no exterior pressure of circumstances, to bring them to harmonious resolutions on important points, will readily conceive how impossible it must be to induce a number of such assemblies, deliberating at a distance from each other, at different times, and under different impressions, long to co-operate in the same views and pursuits.

In our case, the concurrence of thirteen distinct sovereign wills is requisite, under the Confederation, to the complete execution of every important measure that proceeds from the Union. It has happened as was to have been foreseen. The measures of the Union have not been executed; the delinquencies of the States have, step by step, matured themselves to an extreme, which has, at length, arrested all the wheels of the national government, and brought them to an awful stand. Congress at this time scarcely possess the means of keeping up the forms of administration, till the States can have time to agree upon a more substantial substitute for the present shadow of a federal government. Things did not come to this desperate extremity at once. The causes which have been specified produced at first only unequal and disproportionate degrees of compliance with the requisitions of the Union. The greater deficiencies of some States furnished the pretext of example and the temptation of interest to the complying, or to the least delinquent States. Why should we do more in proportion than those who are embarked with us in the same political voyage? Why should we consent to bear more than our proper share of the common burden? These were suggestions which human selfishness could not withstand, and which even speculative men, who looked forward to remote consequences, could not, without hesitation, combat. Each State, yielding to the persuasive voice of immediate interest or convenience, has successively withdrawn its support, till the frail and tottering edifice seems ready to fall upon our heads, and to crush us beneath its ruins.

FEDERALIST 37

In reviewing the defects of the existing Confederation, and showing that they cannot be supplied by a government of less energy than that before the public, several of the most important principles of the latter fell of course under consideration. But as the ultimate object of these papers is to determine clearly and fully the merits of this Constitution, and the expediency of adopting it, our plan cannot be complete without taking a more critical and thorough survey of the work of the convention, without examining it on all its sides, comparing it in all its parts, and calculating its probable effects.

That this remaining task may be executed under impressions conducive to a just and fair result, some reflections must in this place be indulged, which candor previously suggests.

It is a misfortune, inseparable from human affairs, that public measures are rarely investigated with that spirit of moderation which is essential to a just estimate of their real tendency to advance or obstruct the public good; and that this spirit is more apt to be diminished than promoted, by those occasions which require an unusual exercise of it. To those who have been led by experience to attend to this consideration, it could not appear surprising, that the act of the convention, which recommends so many important changes and innovations, which may be viewed in so many lights and relations, and which touches the springs of so many passions and interests, should find or excite dispositions unfriendly, both on one side and on the other, to a fair discussion and accurate judgment of its merits. In some, it has been too evident from their own publications, that they have scanned the proposed Constitution, not only with a predisposition to censure, but with a predetermination to condemn; as the language held by others betrays an opposite predetermination or bias, which must render their opinions also of little moment in the question. In placing, however, these different characters on a level, with respect to the weight of their opinions, I wish not to insinuate that there may not be a material difference in the purity of their intentions. It is but just to remark in favor of the latter description, that as our situation is universally admitted to be peculiarly critical, and to require indispensably that something should be done for our relief, the predetermined patron of what has been actually done may have taken his bias from the weight of these considerations, as well as from considerations of a sinister nature. The predetermined adversary, on the other hand, can have been governed by no venial motive whatever. The intentions of the first may be upright, as they may on the contrary be culpable. The views of the last cannot be upright, and must be culpable. But the truth is, that these papers are not addressed to persons falling under either of these characters. They solicit the attention of those only, who add to a sincere zeal for the happiness of their country, a temper favorable to a just estimate of the means of promoting it.

Persons of this character will proceed to an examination of the plan submitted by the convention, not only without a disposition to find or to magnify faults; but will see the propriety of reflecting, that a faultless plan was not to be expected. Nor will they barely make allowances for the errors which may be chargeable on the fallibility to which the convention, as a body of men, were liable; but will keep in mind, that they themselves also are but men, and ought not to assume an infallibility in rejudging the fallible opinions of others.

With equal readiness will it be perceived, that besides these inducements to candor, many allowances ought to be made for the difficulties inherent in the very nature of the undertaking referred to the convention.

The novelty of the undertaking immediately strikes us. It has been shown in the course of these papers, that the existing Confederation is founded on principles which are fallacious; that we must consequently change this first foundation, and with it the superstructure resting upon it. It has been shown, that the other confederacies which could be consulted as precedents have been vitiated by the same erroneous principles, and can therefore furnish no other light than that of beacons, which give warning of the course to be shunned, without pointing out that which ought to be pursued. The most that the convention could do in such a situation, was to avoid the errors suggested by the past experience of other countries, as well as of our own; and to provide a convenient mode of rectifying their own errors, as future experiences may unfold them.

Among the difficulties encountered by the convention, a very important one must have lain in combining the requisite stability and energy in government, with the inviolable attention due to liberty and to the republican form. Without substantially accomplishing this part of their undertaking, they would have very imperfectly fulfilled the object of their appointment, or the expectation of the public; yet that it could not be easily accomplished, will be denied by no one who is unwilling to betray his ignorance of the subject. Energy in government is essential to that security against external and internal danger, and to that prompt and salutary execution of the laws which enter into the very definition of good government. Stability in government is essential to national character and to the advantages annexed to it, as well as to that repose and confidence in the minds of the people, which are among the chief blessings of civil society. An irregular and mutable legislation is not more an evil in itself than it is odious to the people; and it may be pronounced with assurance that the people of this country, enlightened as they are with regard to the nature, and interested, as the great body of them are, in the effects of good government, will never be satisfied till some remedy be applied to the vicissitudes and uncertainties which characterize the State administrations. On comparing, however, these valuable ingredients with the vital principles of liberty, we must perceive at once the difficulty of mingling them together in their due proportions. The genius of republican liberty seems to demand on one side, not only that all power should be derived from the people, but that those intrusted with it should be kept in dependence on the people, by a short duration of their appointments; and that even during this short period the trust should be placed not in a few, but a number of hands. Stability, on the contrary, requires that the hands in which power is lodged should continue for a length of time the same. A frequent change of men will result from a frequent return of elections; and a frequent change of measures from a frequent change of men: whilst energy in government requires not only a certain duration of power, but the execution of it by a single hand.

How far the convention may have succeeded in this part of their work, will better appear on a more accurate view of it. From the cursory view here taken, it must clearly appear to have been an arduous part.

Not less arduous must have been the task of marking the proper line of partition between the authority of the general and that of the State governments. Every man will be sensible of this difficulty, in proportion as he has been accustomed to contemplate and discriminate objects extensive and complicated in their nature. The faculties of the mind itself have never yet been distinguished and defined, with satisfactory precision, by all the efforts of the most acute and metaphysical philosophers. Sense, perception, judgment, desire, volition, memory, imagination, are found to be separated by such delicate shades and minute gradations that their boundaries have eluded the most subtle investigations, and remain a pregnant source of ingenious disquisition and controversy. The boundaries between the great kingdom of nature, and, still more, between the various provinces, and lesser portions, into which they are subdivided, afford another illustration of the same important truth. The most sagacious and laborious naturalists have never yet succeeded in tracing with certainty the line which separates the district of vegetable life from the neighboring region of unorganized matter, or which marks the termination of the former and the commencement of the animal empire. A still greater obscurity lies in the distinctive characters by which the objects in each of these great departments of nature have been arranged and assorted.

When we pass from the works of nature, in which all the delineations are perfectly accurate, and appear to be otherwise only from the imperfection of the eye which surveys them, to the institutions of man, in which the obscurity arises as well from the object itself as from the organ by which it is contemplated, we must perceive the necessity of moderating still further our expectations and hopes from the efforts of human sagacity. Experience has instructed us that no skill in the science of government has yet been able to discriminate and define, with sufficient certainty, its three great provinces the legislative, executive, and judiciary; or even the privileges and powers of the different legislative branches. Questions daily occur in the course of practice, which prove the obscurity which reins in these subjects, and which puzzle the greatest adepts in political science.

The experience of ages, with the continued and combined labors of the most enlightened legislatures and jurists, has been equally unsuccessful in delineating the several objects and limits of different codes of laws and different tribunals of justice. The precise extent of the common law, and the statute law, the maritime law, the ecclesiastical law, the law of corporations, and other local laws and customs, remains still to be clearly and finally established in Great Britain, where accuracy in such subjects has been more industriously pursued than in any other part of the world. The jurisdiction of her several courts, general and local, of law, of equity, of admiralty, etc., is not less a source of frequent and intricate discussions, sufficiently denoting the indeterminate limits by which they are respectively circumscribed. All new laws, though penned with the greatest technical skill, and passed on the fullest and most mature deliberation, are considered as more or less obscure and equivocal, until their meaning be liquidated and ascertained by a series of particular discussions and adjudications. Besides the obscurity arising from the complexity of objects, and the imperfection of the human faculties, the medium through which the conceptions of men are conveyed to each other adds a fresh embarrassment. The use of words is to express ideas. Perspicuity, therefore, requires not only that the ideas should be distinctly formed, but that they should be expressed by words distinctly and exclusively appropriate to them. But no language is so copious as to supply words and phrases for every complex idea, or so correct as not to include many equivocally denoting different ideas. Hence it must happen that however accurately objects may be discriminated in themselves, and however accurately the discrimination may be considered, the definition of them may be rendered inaccurate by the inaccuracy of the terms in which it is delivered. And this unavoidable inaccuracy must be greater or less, according to the complexity and novelty of the objects defined. When the Almighty himself condescends to address mankind in their own language, his meaning, luminous as it must be, is rendered dim and doubtful by the cloudy medium through which it is communicated.

Here, then, are three sources of vague and incorrect definitions: indistinctness of the object, imperfection of the organ of conception, inadequateness of the vehicle of ideas. Any one of these must produce a certain degree of obscurity. The convention, in delineating the boundary between the federal and State jurisdictions, must have experienced the full effect of them all.

To the difficulties already mentioned may be added the interfering pretensions of the larger and smaller States. We cannot err in supposing that the former would contend for a participation in the government, fully proportioned to their superior wealth and importance; and that the latter would not be less tenacious of the equality at present enjoyed by them. We may well suppose that neither side would entirely yield to the other, and consequently that the struggle could be terminated only by compromise. It is extremely probable, also, that after the ratio of representation had been adjusted, this very compromise must have produced a fresh struggle between the same parties, to give such a turn to the organization of the government, and to the distribution of its powers, as would increase the importance of the branches, in forming which they had respectively obtained the greatest share of influence. There are features in the Constitution which warrant each of these suppositions; and as far as either of them is well founded, it shows that the convention must have been compelled to sacrifice theoretical propriety to the force of extraneous considerations.

Nor could it have been the large and small States only, which would marshal themselves in opposition to each other on various points. Other combinations, resulting from a difference of local position and policy, must have created additional difficulties. As every State may be divided into different districts, and its citizens into different classes, which give birth to contending interests and local jealousies, so the different parts of the United States are distinguished from each other by a variety of circumstances, which produce a like effect on a larger scale. And although this variety of interests, for reasons sufficiently explained in a former paper, may have a salutary influence on the administration of the government when formed, yet every one must be sensible of the contrary influence, which must have been experienced in the task of forming it.

Would it be wonderful if, under the pressure of all these difficulties, the convention should have been forced into some deviations from that artificial structure and regular symmetry which an abstract view of the subject might lead an ingenious theorist to bestow on a Constitution planned in his closet or in his imagination? The real wonder is that so many difficulties should have been surmounted, and surmounted with a unanimity almost as unprecedented as it must have been unexpected. It is impossible for any man of candor to reflect on this circumstance without partaking of the astonishment. It is impossible for the man of pious reflection not to perceive in it a finger of that Almighty hand which has been so frequently and signally extended to our relief in the critical stages of the revolution.

We had occasion, in a former paper, to take notice of the repeated trials which have been unsuccessfully made in the United Netherlands for reforming the baneful and notorious vices of their constitution. The history of almost all the great councils and consultations held among mankind for reconciling their discordant opinions, assuaging their mutual jealousies, and adjusting their respective interests, is a history of factions, contentions, and disappointments, and may be classed among the most dark and degraded pictures which display the infirmities and depravities of the human character. If, in a few scattered instances, a brighter aspect is presented, they serve only as exceptions to admonish us of the general truth; and by their lustre to darken the gloom of the adverse prospect to which they are contrasted. In revolving the causes from which these exceptions result, and applying them to the particular instances before us, we are necessarily led to two important conclusions. The first is, that the convention must have enjoyed, in a very singular degree, an exemption from the pestilential influence of party animosities—the disease most incident to deliberative bodies, and most apt to contaminate their proceedings. The second conclusion is that all the deputations composing the convention were satisfactorily accommodated by the final act, or were induced to accede to it by a deep conviction of the necessity of sacrificing private opinions and partial interests to the public good, and by a despair of seeing this necessity diminished by delays or by new experiments.

FEDERALIST 39 (Second Half)

"But it was not sufficient," say the adversaries of the proposed Constitution, "for the convention to adhere to the republican form. They ought, with equal care, to have preserved the *federal* form, which regards the Union as a *confederacy* of sovereign states; instead of which, they have framed a *national* government, which regards the Union as a *consolidation* of the States." And it is asked by what authority this bold and radical innovation was undertaken? The handle which has been made of this objection requires that it should be examined with some precision.

Without inquiring into the accuracy of the distinction on which the objection is founded, it will be necessary to a just estimate of its force, first, to ascertain the real character of the government in question; secondly, to inquire how far the convention were authorized to propose such a government; and thirdly, how far the duty they owed to their country could supply any defect of regular authority.

First. In order to ascertain the real character of the government, it may be considered in relation to the foundation on which it is to be established; to the sources from which its ordinary powers are to be drawn; to the operation of those powers; to the extent of them; and to the authority by which future changes in the government are to be introduced.

On examining the first relation, it appears, on one hand, that the Constitution is to be founded on the assent and ratification of the people of America, given by deputies elected for the special purpose; but, on the other, that this assent and ratification is to be given by the people, not as individuals composing one entire nation, but as composing the distinct and independent States to which they respectively belong. It is to be the assent and ratification of the several States, derived from the supreme authority in each State, the authority of the people themselves. The act, therefore, establishing the Constitution, will not be a *national*, but a *federal* act.

That it will be a federal and not a national act, as these terms are understood by the objectors; the act of the people, as forming so many independent States, not as forming one aggregate nation, is obvious from this single consideration, that it is to result neither from the decision of a *majority* of the people of the Union, nor from that of a *majority* of the States. It must result from the *unanimous* assent of the several States that are parties to it, differing no otherwise from their ordinary assent than in its being expressed, not by the legislative authority, but by that of the people themselves. Were the people regarded in this transaction as forming one nation, the will of the majority of the whole people of the United States would bind the minority, in the same manner as the majority in each State must bind the minority; and the will of the majority must be determined either by a comparison of the individual votes, or by considering the will of the majority of the States as evidence of the will of a majority of the people of the United States. Neither of these rules have been adopted. Each State, in ratifying the Constitution, is considered as a sovereign body, independent of all others, and only to be bound by its own voluntary act. In this relation, then, the new Constitution will, if established, be a *federal*, and not a *national* constitution.

The next relation is, to the sources from which the ordinary powers of government are to be derived. The House of Representatives will derive its powers from the people of America; and the people will be represented in the same proportion, and on the same principle, as they are in the legislature of a particular State. So far the government is *national*, not *federal*. The Senate, on the other hand, will derive its powers from the States, as political and coequal societies; and these will be represented on the principle of equality in the Senate, as they now are in the existing Congress. So far the government is *federal*, not *national*. The executive power will be derived from a very compound source. The immediate election of the President is to be made by the States in their political characters. The votes allotted to them are in a compound ratio, which considers them partly as distinct and coequal societies, partly as unequal members of the same society. The eventual election, again, is to be made by that branch of the legislature which consists of the national representatives; but in this particular act they are to be thrown into the form of individual delegations, from so many distinct and coequal bodies politic. From this aspect of the government it appears to be of a mixed character, presenting at least as many *federal* as *national* features.

The difference between a federal and national government, as it relates to the *operation of the government*, is supposed to consist in this, that in the former the powers operate on the political bodies composing the Confederacy, in their political capacities; in the latter, on the individual citizens composing the nation, in their individual capacities. On trying the Constitution by this criterion, it falls under the *national*, not the *federal* character; though perhaps not so completely as has been understood. In several cases, and particularly in the trial of controversies to which States may be parties, they must be viewed and proceeded against in their collective and political capacities only. So far the national countenance of the government on this side seems to be disfigured by a few federal features. But this blemish is perhaps unavoidable in any plan; and the operation of the government on the people, in their individual capacities, in its ordinary and most essential proceedings, may, on the whole, designate it, in this relation, a *national* government.

But if the government be national with regard to the *operation* of its powers, it changes its aspect again when we contemplate it in relation to the *extent* of its powers. The idea of a national government involves in it, not only an authority over the individual citizens, but an indefinite supremacy over all persons and things, so far as they are objects of lawful government. Among a people consolidated into one nation, this supremacy is completely vested in the national legislature. Among communities united for particular purposes, it is vested partly in the general and partly in the municipal legislatures. In the former case, all local authorities are subordinate to the supreme; and may be controlled, directed, or abolished by it at pleasure. In the latter, the local or municipal authorities form distinct and independent portions of the supremacy, no more subject, within their respective spheres, to the general authority, than the general authority is subject to them, within its own sphere. In this relation, then, the proposed government cannot be deemed a *national* one; since its jurisdiction extends to certain enumerated objects only, and leaves to the several States a residuary and inviolable sovereignty over all other objects. It is true that in controversies relating to the boundary between the two jurisdictions, the tribunal which is ultimately to decide, is to be established under the general government. But this does not change the principle of the case. The decision is to be impartially made, according to the rules of the Constitution; and all the usual and most effectual precautions are taken to secure this impartiality. Some such tribunal is clearly essential to prevent an appeal to the sword and a dissolution of the compact; and that it ought to be established under the general rather than under the local governments, or, to speak more properly, that it could be safely established under the first alone, is a position not likely to be combated.

If we try the Constitution by its last relation to the authority by which amendments are to be made, we find it neither wholly *national* nor wholly *federal.* Were it wholly national, the supreme and ultimate authority would reside in the *majority* of the people of the Union; and this authority would be competent at all times, like that of a majority of every national society, to alter or abolish its established government. Were it wholly federal, on the other hand, the concurrence of each State in the Union would be essential to every alteration that would be binding on all. The mode provided by the plan of the convention is not founded on either of these principles. In requiring more than a majority, and particularly in computing the proportion by *states*, not by *citizens*, it departs from the *national* and advances towards the *federal* character; in rendering the concurrence of less than the whole number of States sufficient, it loses again the *federal* and partakes of the *national* character.

The proposed Constitution, therefore, is, in strictness, neither a national nor a federal Constitution, but a composition of both. In its foundation it is federal, not national; in the sources from which the ordinary powers of the government are drawn, it is partly federal and partly national; in the operation of these powers, it is national, not federal; in the extent of them, again, it is federal, not national; and, finally, in the authoritative mode of introducing amendments, it is neither wholly federal nor wholly national.

DEMOCRACY IN AMERICA, VOLUME I, PART 1, CHAPTER 8: "OF THE FEDERAL CONSTITUTION"

Legislative Powers

In the organization of the powers of the Union, the plan that was traced in advance by the particular constitution of each of the states was followed on many points.

The federal legislative body of the Union was composed of a Senate and a House of Representatives.

The spirit of conciliation caused different rules to be followed in the formation of each of these assemblies.

I brought out above that, when the Americans wanted to establish the federal constitution, two opposing interests found themselves face to face. These two interests had given birth to two opinions.

Some wanted to make the Union a league of independent states, a sort of congress where the representatives of distinct peoples would come to discuss certain points of common interest.

Others wanted to unite all the inhabitants of the old colonies into one and the same people, and give them a government that, although its sphere would be limited, would be able to act within this sphere, as the one and only representative of the nation. The practical consequences of these two theories were very different.

Thus, if it was a matter of organizing a league and not a national government, it was up to the majority of the states to make laws, and not up to the majority of the inhabitants of the Union. For each state, large or small, would then conserve its character of independent power and would enter into the Union on a perfectly equal footing.

On the contrary, from the moment when the inhabitants of the United States were considered to form one and the same people, it was natural that only the majority of the citizens of the Union made the law.

Understandably, the small states could not consent to the application of this doctrine without completely abdicating their existence in what concerned federal sovereignty; for, from co-regulating power, they would become an insignificant fraction of a great people. The first system would have granted them an unreasonable power; the second nullified them.

In this situation, what almost always happens when interests are opposed to arguments happened: the rules of logic were made to bend. The law-makers adopted a middle course that forced conciliation of two systems theoretically irreconcilable.

The principle of the independence of the states triumphed in the formation of the Senate; the dogma of national sovereignty, in the composition of the House of Representatives.

Each state had to send two senators to Congress and a certain number of representatives, in proportion to its population.

Today, as a result of this arrangement, the state of New York has forty representatives in Congress and only two senators; the state of Delaware, two senators and only one representative. So in the Senate, the state of Delaware is the equal of the state of New York, while the latter has, in the House of Representatives, forty times more influence than the first. Thus, it can happen that the minority of the nation, dominating the Senate, entirely paralyzes the desires of the majority, represented by the other chamber; this is contrary to the spirit of constitutional governments.

All this shows clearly how rare and difficult it is to link all the parts of legislation together in a logical and rational manner.

In the long run, time always gives birth to different interests and consecrates diverse rights in the same people. Then, when it is a question of establishing a general constitution, each of these interests and rights serves as so many natural obstacles that are opposed to following all of the consequences of any one political principle. So only at the birth of societies can you be perfectly logical in the laws. When you see a people enjoy this advantage, do not rush to conclude that they are wise; instead, think that they are young.

At the time when the federal Constitution was formed, only two interests positively opposed to each other existed among the Anglo-Americans: the interest of individuality for the particular states, and the interest of union for the whole people. It was necessary to come to a compromise.

You must recognize, nonetheless, that up to now this part of the Constitution has not produced the evils that could be feared.

All the states are young; they are near each other; they have homogeneous mores, ideas and needs; the difference that results from their greater or lesser size is not sufficient to give them strongly opposed interests. So the small states have never been seen to join together in the Senate against the plans of the large. There is, moreover, such an irresistible force in the legal expression of the will of an entire people that, when the majority expresses itself in the organ of the House of Representatives, the Senate, facing it, finds itself quite weak.

Beyond that, it must not be forgotten that it did not depend on the American law-makers to make one and the same nation out of the people to whom they wanted to give laws. The aim of the federal Constitution was not to destroy the existence of the states, but only to restrain it. So, from the moment when a real power was left to those secondary bodies (and it could not be taken from them), the habitual use of constraint to bend them to the will of the majority was renounced in advance. This said, the introduction of the individual strengths of the states into the mechanism of the federal government was nothing extraordinary. It only took note of an existing fact, a recognized power that had to be treated gently and not violated.

What Distinguishes the Federal Constitution of the United States of America from All Other Federal Constitutions?

The United States of America has not presented the first and only example of a confederation. Without mentioning antiquity, modern Europe has furnished several. Switzerland, the German Empire, the Dutch Republic have been or still are confederations.

When you study the constitutions of these different countries, you notice with surprise that the powers they confer on the federal government are more or less the same as those granted by the American Constitution to the government of the United States. Like the latter, they give the central power the right to make war or peace, the right to raise an army, to levy taxes, to provide for general needs and to regulate the common interests of the nation.

Among these different peoples, however, the federal government has almost always remained deficient and weak, while that of the Union conducts public affairs with vigor and ease.

Even more, the first American Union could not continue to exist because of the excessive weakness of its government. Yet this government, so weak, had received rights as extensive as the federal government of today. You can even say that in certain respects its privileges were greater.

So several new principles are found in the current Constitution of the United States that are not striking at first, but make their influence profoundly felt.

This Constitution, which at first sight you are tempted to confuse with previous federal constitutions, rests as a matter of fact on an entirely new theory that must stand out as a great discovery in the political science of today.

In all the confederations that have preceded the American confederation of 1789, peoples who combined for a common purpose agreed to obey the injunctions of a federal government; but they retained the right to command and to supervise the execution of the laws of the Union at home.

The American states that united in 1789 agreed not only that the federal government could dictate laws to them, but also that the federal government itself would execute its laws.

In the two cases, the right is the same; only the exercise of the right is different. But this single difference produces immense results.

In all the confederations that have preceded the American Union of today, the federal government, in order to provide for its needs, applied to the individual governments. In the case where the prescribed measure displeased one of them, the latter could always elude the need to obey. If it was strong it appealed to arms; if it was weak, it tolerated a resistance to the laws of the Union that had become its own, pretended weakness and resorted to the power of inertia.

Consequently, one of these two things has constantly happened: the most powerful of the united peoples, taking hold of the rights of the federal authority, has dominated all the others in its name; or the federal government has been left to its own forces. Then anarchy has become established among the confederated peoples, and the Union has fallen into impotence.

In America, the Union governs not the states, but ordinary citizens. When it wants to levy a tax, it does not apply to the government of Massachusetts, but to each inhabitant of Massachusetts. Former federal governments faced peoples; the Union faces individuals. It does not borrow its strength, but draws upon its own. It has its own administrators, courts, officers of the law, and army.

Certainly the national spirit, collective passions, provincial prejudices of each state still strongly tend to diminish the extent of federal power so constituted, and to create centers of resistance to the will of the federal power. Limited in its sovereignty, it cannot be as strong as a government that possesses complete sovereignty; but that is an evil inherent in the federal system.

In America, each state has far fewer opportunities and temptations to resist; and if the thought occurs, the state can act on it only by openly violating the laws of the Union, by interrupting the ordinary course of justice, and by raising the standard of revolt. In a word, it must suddenly take an extreme position, something men hesitate to do for a long time.

In former confederations, the rights granted to the Union were causes of war rather than of power, since these rights multiplied its demands without augmenting its means of enforcing obedience. Consequently, the real weakness of federal governments has almost always been seen to grow in direct proportion to their nominal power.

This is not so for the American Union; the federal government, like most ordinary governments, can do everything that it has the right to do.

The human mind invents things more easily than words; this is what causes the use of so many incorrect terms and incomplete expressions.

Several nations form a permanent league and establish a supreme authority that, without acting on ordinary citizens as a national government could, nonetheless acts on each of the confederated peoples, taken as a group.

This government, so different from all the others, is given the name federal.

Next, a form of society is found in which several peoples truly blend together as one for certain common interests, and remain separate and only confederated for all the others.

Here the central power acts without intermediary on the governed, administering and judging them as national governments do, but it acts this way only within a limited circle. Clearly that is no longer a federal government; it is an incomplete national government. So a form of government, neither precisely national nor federal, is found. But here things have stopped, and the new word needed to express the new thing does not yet exist.

Because this new type of confederation was unknown, all unions have arrived at civil war, or slavery, or inertia. The peoples who composed them have all lacked either the enlightenment to see the remedy to their ills, or the courage to apply them.

The first American Union had also lapsed into the same faults.

But in America, the confederated states, before achieving independence, had been part of the same empire for a long time; so they had not yet contracted the habit of complete self-government, and national prejudices had not been able to become deeply rooted. Better informed than the rest of the world, they were equal to each other in enlightenment; they only weakly felt the passions that ordinarily, among peoples, resist the extension of federal power; and these passions were fought against by the greatest citizens. The Americans, at the same time that they felt the evil, resolutely envisaged the remedy. They corrected their laws and saved the country.

SUGGESTED ADDITIONAL READINGS (Freely Available Online)

James Madison, "Vices of the Political System of the United States" (http://press-pubs.uchicago.edu/founders/documents/v1ch5s16.html)
Federalist 46
Federalist 62

MADISONIAN FEDERALISM AND THE AMERICAN CONVERSATION ON LIBERTY AND EQUALITY

Alan Gibson and James H. Read

A few years before his death in 1836, in an essay probably intended to preface his notes of debates at the Federal Convention of 1787, James Madison celebrated the American federal republic created under the Constitution as the most "interesting" federal association in the history of mankind. This association, he maintained, combined a "federal form with the forms of individual Republics" in such a way that each might remedy the "defects of the other" but obtain the advantages of both.[28]

The novel federal system Madison praised and defended throughout his life, however, was hardly the product of his thoughts and efforts alone. Key features of the constitutional reform program he developed in the spring of 1787 and fought for at Philadelphia—particularly proportional representation in both houses of Congress and a universal veto of all state laws to be lodged in Congress—were rejected at Philadelphia. After the Constitutional Convention, writing as Publius in *The Federalist*, Madison set aside his misgivings about the Constitution and began his lifelong career as its most effective exegete and apologist. Yet Madison's rejected proposals have also remained important in the history of American federalism both as inspiration for subsequent reforms and a source of criticism of our constitutional system.

This essay explores the origins, evolution, character, and complex legacies of Madisonian federalism. We begin with the problems Madison diagnosed in the federal system established under the Articles of Confederation and the constitutional reform program he took to Philadelphia. The understanding of federalism contained in this set of reform proposals might be called "imperial federalism" because, as Madison acknowledged, its signature proposal—the power for Congress to veto state legislation "*in all cases whatsoever*"—echoed the veto power the British monarch had exercised over laws passed by colonial legislatures.[29] In his preconvention writings and speeches at the Constitutional Convention, Madison also proposed national powers over commerce and taxation, the selection and pay of national officials independent of state governments, and proportional representation in a two-chamber legislative branch. These proposals were designed to prevent state encroachments on federal authority and at the same time to protect individual rights from violations by despotic majorities within the states. Madison hoped to remedy the structural defects of the Articles of Confederation, free Congress from depending on the states for the selection of its officials and the exercise of its powers, and ensure basic equity between large and small states.

The rejection of the universal veto and the "Great Compromise" providing for proportional representation only in the House of Representatives left the man later generations would call the "Father of the Constitution" initially despondent. Nevertheless, in his contributions to *The Federalist*, Madison made a good-faith effort to explain and defend the complex and tension-ridden version of federalism agreed upon at the Constitutional Convention. If Madison's preconvention reforms were designed to free the national government from dependence on the states and prevent them from encroaching on federal authority, his defense of the resolution of federalism in the Constitution attempted to make theoretical sense of a political system that combined national and federal features in a different way than he had originally favored. He also now had to respond to critics who feared that the new Constitution would create a tyrannical national government. In this changed context, Madison defended the Constitution's federal system as a means of providing "double security" for the rights of the people, meaning that each level of government (federal and state) would protect the people's rights against violation by the other.[30] Over the years, Madison came to regard this "double security" feature of the Constitution as among its most valuable qualities.

Both Madison's rejected proposals and his defense of the resolution of federalism in the Constitution have had long half-lives in American history. In 1789, as he fought for a bill of rights in Congress, Madison proposed an amendment for protecting the rights of conscience, freedom of the press, and trial by jury in criminal cases from violations by the states as well as the federal government. This amendment recalled, in modified form, one important feature of Madison's preconvention federalism: the power to strike down state laws that violate fundamental rights and liberties. This proposal was rejected, and after 1789 Madison never returned to his original vision of the national government as an impartial guardian of rights within the states. Nevertheless, as Zuckert has shown, the authors of the Fourteenth Amendment "completed," in one important sense, the Madisonian Constitution by empowering the national government to protect the rights of citizens from unjust state laws.[31]

Madison's defense of the Constitution's federalism has its own complex legacy. During the 1790s, Madison encouraged state legislatures to sound the alarm against the unconstitutional growth of the powers of the federal government, even as he rejected the proposition that states could nullify federal law. Madisonian federalism has subsequently served both as a resonant voice against excessive concentration of national power and as a check against sweeping assertions of state sovereignty and state violations of basic rights. Similarly, Madisonian federalism has been used to explain and defend the American federal system and also to offer a critical perspective on it, especially the disproportionate power of small states within the constitutional system. Most broadly, Madisonian federalism has profoundly shaped not only how we think about the relationship between states and the federal government but how we understand the fundamental principles of liberty and equality.

The Origins and Character of Madison's Preconvention Federalism

Madison's preconvention federalism followed from his diagnosis of the problems of the American confederation. That diagnosis was based upon what he learned from seven years of public service as a delegate in the Continental Congress and the Virginia House of Delegates, reinforced by his famous systematic study of ancient and modern confederacies.

Under the Articles of Confederation, each state retained "its sovereignty, freedom, and independence, and every Power, Jurisdiction and Right" not "expressly" delegated to the United States.[32] Contrary to the usual portrait of it as a weak government, the federal system created by the Articles of Confederation was neither altogether weak nor, in Madison's estimation, really a government at all because it lacked legal sanction and coercive authority.[33] It gave Congress some substantial federal powers, mostly concerning the conduct of war and foreign affairs. Nevertheless, these and other powers were exercised on the states in their corporate capacity, not directly on the citizens within them, and were not backed by coercive authority to compel obedience. The implementation of federal legislation thus depended on the uncertain cooperation of states, each of which decided for itself whether to execute or reject federal measures.

Furthermore, members of Congress were tightly leashed to the state legislatures. Delegates were appointed annually in "such a manner as the legislatures of each State shall direct."[34] All but two states chose direct appointment by the state legislatures.[35] Delegates could be recalled at any time by the legislature and were subject to rotation in office (no delegate could serve for more than three years in any term of six years). The state legislatures also paid (or sometimes failed to pay) the salaries and expenses of the delegates. There was no independent federal judiciary or executive branch, only a single-chamber Congress in which each state delegation—composed of from two to seven delegates—cast one vote regardless of its state's population. These institutional features ensured strict equality between the member states and congressmen who acted, as Akhil Reed Amar has observed, as the states' men, not statesmen.[36]

During Madison's almost four years of service from 1780 to 1783 as a Virginia delegate in the Continental Congress under the Articles of Confederation, Congress was chronically ineffective. It was unable to finance or manage the Revolutionary War effort, to meet its financial obligations to soldiers, bondholders, and foreign lenders, or to settle disputes among states over claims to western lands. It also failed to defend its few prerogatives—including conducting war and negotiating treaties—against encroachments by the states. For Madison, this period illustrated the problems of a federal system that exercised its powers on the states rather than on individual citizens and relied on the states to administer federal policies. These structural features of the Articles of Confederation, Madison believed, were the source of many of its vices, including its inability to collect taxes and requisitions and to prevent the states from encroaching on the prerogatives of the national government and violating the rights of each other.[37]

When Madison returned to Virginia politics in 1784, he was confronted with the additional threat posed by majority factions. When states passed laws favoring debtors over creditors or issued paper money of dubious value, Madison believed, they acted improperly not only because they defrauded creditors but also because they caused citizens of one state to violate the rights of citizens from another state or country, risking internal violence and foreign intervention.[38] He also witnessed, and fought against, state legislation that he believed threatened the sacred right of religious freedom.[39]

Rather than bemoaning this situation, Madison sought answers by engaging in a systematic study of ancient and modern confederacies. His research into the "science of federal government" resulted in an intellectual harvest of unprecedented importance in American constitutional history.[40] Madison produced his "Notes on Ancient and Modern Confederacies" and his private memorandum "Vices of the Political System of the United States." These essays, in turn, laid the foundation for the constitutional reforms he recommended in his preconvention correspondence and at the Constitutional Convention.

Madison's research convinced him that what separated a "political constitution" or government from a mere league or treaty between nations was a controlling sovereign that could exercise coercion to enforce its commands.[41] The absence of genuine sovereignty created the "evil of imperia in imperio" and invited the struggle between the titular head and member states that had been the perennial problem of confederate systems.[42] As he surveyed the history of ancient confederations and reflected upon the experiences of the American one, he saw parts with more weight than the whole, member states continuously encroaching upon national power, and political systems tilted (as he later put it) to suffer more from "anarchy among the members" than "tyranny in the head."[43]

Madison's proposed remedy to these problems was to create a totally reorganized national government with "positive and compleat [*sic*] authority" over all matters requiring uniformity, including the regulation of trade and the right to tax both imports and exports. These powers, Madison observed, should be exercised directly on individuals so that the national government would "operate in many essential points without the intervention of the State legislatures." He also called for independent legislative, executive, and judicial branches, proportional representation of both branches in the national government, and popular ratification of any proposed constitution to establish its legitimacy and the supremacy of federal law. Most strikingly and importantly, Madison called for a universal veto giving the national government the power to strike down state laws "in all cases whatsoever."[44]

Equal representation of states regardless of population in the Continental Congress, Madison observed, had been unfair to the larger states, but not a real threat to them because Congress could not enforce its decisions without their aid. The proposed Constitution, however, would operate without the intervention of state governments, especially in the allocation and collection of taxes, effectively ending the large states' ability to block federal measures. Basic principles of proportional fairness and equity now demanded that large states have representation commensurate with their populations and the contributions of their citizens to the federal treasury.[45]

Madison also concluded that national officials had to be selected and paid independently of the states if the integrity and effectiveness of the national system were to be preserved. This point became clear to him only after the Constitutional Convention began. In his preconvention correspondence, Madison had been unsure whether national legislators should be elected "by the [state] Legislatures or the people at large."[46] At the convention, however, Madison soon came to the firm conclusion that direct elections by the people, or at least elections independent of the state legislatures, were necessary for "avoiding too great an agency of the State Governments in the General one."[47]

Madison was most fervent, however, in his unflagging support for a universal veto of state laws. In his preconvention letters and his speeches at the convention defending the universal veto, Madison laid out two purposes for this Americanized version of the British monarch's "Kingly prerogative."[48] First, it would prevent the states from exercising the powers of the national government and thus robbing it of its essential prerogatives. For example, the federal government could use the veto to strike down state treaties with foreign nations because the power to negotiate treaties was an exclusive national prerogative. As he thought through the implications of the veto power, Madison also discovered a second "happy effect" it would have: protecting rights within the states.[49] Armed with the universal veto, the national government could reach into the states and protect individuals and minorities from debtor relief legislation and even such mischievous projects as taxes for the support of religion. Protecting rights would, in turn, diminish conflicts between the states and make it less likely that they would invite aggressions from foreign nations.

Nevertheless, Madison faced two problems in advocating a universal power to veto state laws. He first had to explain why the national government would not abuse a universal negative as the king had. Madison answered this objection by emphasizing that the veto would now be exercised by a republican legislative body that, unlike the king, would be popularly elected and accountable to the people. However, lodging the veto in Congress raised a second problem: why would the national legislature not be subject to majority tyranny just as state legislatures had been?[50] Madison's answer (most famously expressed in *Federalist* 10) was that majorities in Congress would have to form across an extended republic with its diversity of interests and religious sects. A majority faction was much less likely to take over Congress than one of the state legislatures. A Congress that was responsive and accountable, but not captured by majority factions, could exercise the veto prudently. Madison added that the republic should be neither too large nor too small but kept within a territory of "mean extent" so that a "defensive concert" could be conducted if the government became tyrannical.[51]

Unfortunately, Madison's fervent support for a national veto over state laws has been consistently misrepresented. Madison did not mean to abolish the states. He believed, on the contrary, that "a consolidation of the States into one simple republic" was both "inexpedient" and "unattainable."[52] The states were vital building blocks of the extended republic and would continue to exercise most of the functions of government under the new system he envisioned. Nor did Madison favor a massive transfer of power or functions to the national government.[53] To be sure, the new federal government would enjoy powers over commerce and taxation it had lacked before. A universal power to veto state laws would make the national government responsible for protecting individual rights against violation by majority factions acting within the state legislatures. Nevertheless, Madison was not advocating that the national government possess the power to make or dictate laws for the states. The universal negative Madison hoped to lodge in Congress was a power akin to an executive veto, not a positive power in which the national government would legislate within the states. Madison saw Congress as a neutral umpire to decisions made elsewhere, not a decision-making body for the states.[54]

Most broadly, the primary difference between the old system and the new one was not the addition of a massive complement of new powers to the national government but the ability of the national government to exercise its limited powers more effectively than before. Federal officials would no longer be selected or paid by state governments; the federal government would have its own sources of revenue, it would execute its powers directly on individuals, and it could use its veto power to prevent states from hamstringing its operations.

Federalism and the Constitution

Madison's leadership at the Constitutional Convention ensured that one of his primary goals for constitutional reform—a federal government that exercised its powers directly upon individuals, not through the medium of the states—was fully realized in the final Constitution. This was the most important transformation from the Articles of Confederation government to the new Constitution. It was also Madison's most distinctive contribution to the Constitution.

Madison was less successful in persuading his fellow delegates to accept some of his other broad goals and his preferred mechanisms for achieving them. Madison relentlessly pressed for his universal veto of state laws throughout the Constitutional Convention.[55] The other delegates, however, rejected his favorite proposal and chose instead provisions judged safer and less intrusive on the states. These provisions, which together form a skeletal remnant of Madison's universal negative, include the national supremacy clause, the enumeration of specific prohibitions against the states in Article I, Section 10, and judicial review of state laws.

At least throughout 1787, Madison found each of these alternatives to the universal veto inadequate. He believed state legislatures would artfully dodge the constitutional prohibitions targeted against them. He considered judicial review inadequate because it addressed violations only after the fact and because states that violated the Constitution were unlikely to obey judicial rulings overturning those violations.[56] For Madison, losing the universal veto meant the federal government was "materially defective" and would "neither effectually *answer* its *national object* nor prevent the local *mischiefs* which every where [*sic*] *excite disgusts* ag[ain]st the *state governments*."[57]

Madison was also relentless but unsuccessful in his demand for proportional representation in the Senate. He denied that proportional representation would threaten the rights and interests of small states. Contrary to the assertions of small-state delegates, he denied that the large states had shared interests that would lead them to form a unified voting bloc. The real danger in the Senate, he believed, was domination by a majority of (small) states who collectively represented a minority of the American population. That minority, Madison warned, might obstruct the wishes of the majority, extort measures from it, or pass malicious legislation in areas in which the Senate had exclusive constitutional authority.[58]

Madison's opposition to equal representation of all states in the Senate, like his support for the universal veto, was not easily shaken. In *Federalist* 62, Madison provided a conspicuously lukewarm defense of equal state representation in the Senate. He conceded that it might protect the residual sovereignty of the states and thus prevent their consolidation into a simple republic. Madison reiterated, however, that this provision might also promote "injurious" legislation and that small states had no reason to fear a coalition of large states. The most he could say was that compromise on representation, however flawed in principle, was better than failing to agree on the Constitution at all.[59]

The Constitutional Convention also disappointed Madison by providing that senators would be selected by the state legislatures—here contravening his effort to prevent the state governments from selecting federal officials. Madison privately criticized the Electoral College because it made selection of the American president too dependent upon the states.[60]

The absence of a universal veto, the equal state representation in the Senate, and the selection of senators by state legislatures meant that the final Constitution emerged from the Constitutional Convention containing a different combination of federal and national features than Madison had sought. To be sure, the new Constitution was a marked improvement on the old. Unlike the Articles of Confederation, the proposed Constitution did not create a "confederacy of independent states" but rather a "feudal system of republics." Nevertheless, such political systems, Madison warned in 1787, would be plagued by the same struggle between the head and member states that had always characterized simple confederations. Furthermore, without the universal veto, the new government had no means of protecting individual rights within the states.[61]

As the ratification contest proceeded, however, objections to the proposed Constitution mounted from critics who feared aristocracy and centralized power more than they did majority factions and defiant states. In defending the Constitution, Madison—writing as Publius in *The Federalist*—made a good-faith effort to understand and describe what the Constitutional Convention had wrought despite his continuing disagreement with some of its features.

One of the most important and famous of these efforts came in *Federalist* 39, in which Madison offered a complex and systematic answer to the charge that the Constitution established a "consolidated" government—that is, a system in which all important powers were concentrated in the federal government and the states were reduced to insignificance. Madison responded that in fact the government established by the Constitution was "partly national," meaning that in some respects it treated the citizens of the United States as "individuals composing one entire nation," but also "partly federal" because in other respects it treated citizens as belonging to "distinct and independent states."[62] Madison reached this conclusion by evaluating the new national government as federal, national, or a mixture of both across five distinct dimensions. The ratification of the Constitution, Madison argued, was a "federal" act because, although the people would ratify it, they would do so separately, state by state, each state acting as a "sovereign body, independent of all others" and "bound by its own voluntary act."[63] The Constitution was also "federal" because the powers assigned to the national government were enumerated and limited, not consolidated and unlimited as critics alleged.

The government established by the Constitution was "national," Madison observed, insofar as its powers operated directly on individuals. For example, it could tax individuals directly rather than relying on states to provide revenue, as under the Articles of Confederation. The House of Representatives was "national" because it was directly elected by the people and based on proportional representation; the Senate was "federal" because senators were elected by state legislatures and each state was given the same number of senators. The process by which the Constitution was amended, Madison observed, was "neither wholly *national*, nor wholly *federal.*" If it were wholly "national," then a majority of the people of the United States, regardless of states, could amend the Constitution, but in fact amendments had to be ratified by three-fourths of the states. If the process were wholly "federal," then amendments would require unanimous agreement of the states—as was the case under the Articles of Confederation. Because three-fourths of the states can amend the Constitution over the opposition of one-fourth, the Constitution treated the United States as in some sense a single, national community.[64]

Federalist 39 presents a demanding analysis that has been a lightning rod for Madison's critics.[65] Madison's treatment of the question of sovereignty is particularly ticklish. On the one hand, he sets forth a modified state compact theory of ratification and the authority of the Constitution. The people of each state in their highest capacity as sovereigns ratify the Constitution. These discrete, voluntary acts of each state give the Constitution its legitimate authority, providing the essential sanction the Articles of Confederation had lacked. That the "sovereign" people of each state ratified the Constitution was centrally important to those who later argued—against Madison's opposition—that each state was the final judge, for itself, of the meaning of the Constitution and thus had the right to nullify any federal law the state considered unconstitutional or unwise.

On the other hand, Madison explicitly announced that under the Constitution the federal government—not each state government—is the ultimate arbiter of disputes about where the boundary between federal and state power will be drawn. To allow each individual state to decide for itself where federal power ends and state power begins would, Madison warns, produce an "appeal to the sword and a dissolution of the compact." The Constitution, in other words, might be "federal" in the *extent* of its powers, but it is "national" with respect to *who decides disputes* about those powers.[66]

What remedy did the states have if Congress exceeded its enumerated powers or made this decision incorrectly? The first line of defense, Madison argued in *Federalist* 44, was that the coordinate branches of the federal government retained the power to refuse to execute unconstitutional and oppressive acts. But now, elaborating upon what he had previously called a "defensive concert," Madison observed that if separation of powers failed, then a "remedy must be obtained from the people who can, by the election of more faithful representatives, annul the acts of the usurpers."[67] In *Federalist* 46, Madison set forth in embryonic form the strategy he would unfold fully in the 1790s and crystallize in the "Virginia Resolutions of 1798":

> But ambitious encroachments of the federal government, on the authority of the State governments, would not excite the opposition of a single State, or of a few States only. They would be signals of general alarm. Every government would espouse the common cause. A correspondence would be opened. Plans of resistance would be concerted. One spirit would animate and conduct the whole. The same combinations, in short, would result from an apprehension of the federal, as was produced by the dread of a foreign yoke; and unless the projected innovations should be voluntarily renounced, the same appeal to a trial of force would be made in the one case as was made in the other.[68]

In 1788, when *Federalist* 46 was published, Madison considered "ambitious encroachments" by the federal government unlikely. However, if this occurred, the American people as a whole, animated by "one spirit," would employ the states to mount prompt and effective resistance. More broadly, in *Federalist* 51, Madison explored the idea that together the states and the federal government formed "double security" for the liberties of the people.

> In a single republic, all the power surrendered by the people is submitted to the administration of a single government; and the usurpations are guarded against by a division of the government into distinct and separate departments. In the compound republic of America, the power surrendered by the people is first divided between two distinct governments, and then the portion allotted to each subdivided among distinct and separate departments. Hence a double security arises to the rights of the people. The different governments will control each other, at the same time that each will be controlled by itself.[69]

This idea, which became one of the foundations for Madison's mature beliefs about the relationship of the federal government to the states, suggested that either level of government might threaten rights and exercise excessive power, and either level of the government might serve as a remedy for the problems caused by the other. Both levels of government, Madison hoped, would vigilantly watch over the other, while the sovereign people kept watch over both.

For Madison, then, the Constitution of 1787 established a complex, subtle, composite political system. The defense of the Constitution that Madison first fully developed writing as Publius in *The Federalist* emphasized that both the national government and the states were derived from, and accountable to, the sovereign people. The powers of the national government were enumerated or had to be directly implied from those enumerated. The states retained the lion's share of powers and duties and could not be rightfully deprived of their residual sovereignty. The federal government, not the state, was judge of where the line between federal and state authority was drawn, though it was supposed to make this judgment based upon the impartial rules of the Constitution. In 1787, Madison believed majority factions within the states and ambitious states encroaching on federal authority were the principle threats to liberty and union. Nevertheless, he was forced by the torrent of anti-Federalist hypothetical "horribles" during the ratification struggle to describe remedies for federal despotism in the unlikely event it happened. By the mid-1790s, this prospect no longer struck him as remote.

Between Consolidation and Nullification

Throughout the rest of his life, Madison consistently supported the composite interpretation of the American political system that he had set forth in *The Federalist*.[70] As Jack Rakove has observed, "Each passing decade taught Madison just how acute the analysis of *Federalist* No. 39 had been, and how hard it was to defend his original understanding of the subtleties of federalism against the simpler catechisms of national supremacy or state sovereignty."[71] Madison spent much of his postconvention career defending the Union and the Constitution against less reflective and subtle political opponents, charting a path between the Scylla of consolidation and the Charybdis of nullification. This search for the proper balance between the centripetal force of the states and gravitational pull of the federal government reflected Madison's broader belief that liberty was endangered by both too much and too little government power.[72]

Madison's commitment to protect liberty against both federal and state threats was evident in 1789 when, as a member of the First Congress, he introduced the amendments that would become the Bill of Rights. The demand for a bill of rights originally came from opponents of the proposed Constitution during the ratification contest. Madison at first considered a bill of rights unnecessary and potentially harmful because some proposed amendments—like one requiring a two-thirds vote of both houses to pass commercial regulations—would change the structure of the federal government or strip it of essential powers.[73] Any enumeration of rights, Madison also believed, would necessarily be imperfect and incomplete.[74] When the First Congress opened in 1789, Madison still thought the federal government posed little threat to liberty. Nevertheless, he concluded that a suitably framed bill of rights could strengthen the new Constitution by persuading the "doubting part of our fellow citizens" that the federal government would never "deprive them of the liberty for which they valiantly fought and honorably bled."[75]

Although he had consistently characterized bills of rights as parchment barriers during much of the ratification contest, he now found several ways in which they might be strengthened. Following Jefferson's suggestion, he argued that the courts would consider themselves "in a peculiar manner the guardians of those rights."[76] Echoing *Federalist* 44 and 46, he also emphasized that the state legislatures would closely watch the operations of the federal government and resist abuses of these rights.[77] Nevertheless, Madison believed that ultimately the rights in the Bill of Rights would be secure to the degree that they became enmeshed in the public consciousness. Where public opinion was indifferent or hostile to the rights of individuals or minorities, no "paper barriers" could protect them. But a bill of rights, Madison explained in a letter to Thomas Jefferson and his June 8 speech introducing his amendments, will "acquire by degrees the character of fundamental maxims of free Government" that, "as they become incorporated with the national sentiment, counteract the impulses of interest and passion."[78]

For the most part, Madison's amendments were designed not to impose new limits on federal power but to clarify limits he believed were already present in the original Constitution. For example, his proposed language for what ultimately became the Tenth Amendment—"The powers not delegated by this constitution, nor prohibited by it to the states, are reserved to the States respectively"—was not intended to bolster state sovereignty or to impose any new limitations on federal power. Because it was clear from the original Constitution that the federal government possessed only those powers granted to it by the Constitution, Madison admitted this amendment "may be considered as superfluous." Still, he saw no harm in restating the principle to reassure doubters.[79] Indeed, Madison successfully blocked an effort during congressional debates to turn the future Tenth Amendment into a strong affirmation of state sovereignty by limiting the federal government's powers to those "expressly" delegated. Madison feared this would straitjacket the powers of the federal government in the same way Article II of the Articles of Confederation had hampered the powers of the Continental Congress.[80]

Far from enhancing state sovereignty, Madison used his proposed Bill of Rights to make a final plea to authorize the federal government to protect individual rights within the states. The amendment he considered the "most valuable on the whole list" provided that "no state shall violate the equal right of conscience, or the freedom of the press, or the trial by jury in criminal cases."[81] This amendment, which had not appeared in any of the state recommendatory amendments, was an adumbrated version of the universal veto. Madison's experiences of the mid-1780s had taught him that majority factions more easily formed and threatened minority rights within the small sphere of the states. The logic of his theory of the extended republic suggested that private rights would be more secure under the guardianship of the federal government than that of the states.[82] In Congress, he now proposed to protect three fundamental freedoms (religion, press, and jury trial) from violation by either the states or the federal government.[83] Had it passed, this amendment would have diminished the distance between Madison's pre- and postconvention federalisms. Unfortunately for Madison, it passed the House but failed in the Senate. The Bill of Rights as enacted thus restricted only the federal government.[84]

Events of the 1790s soon persuaded Madison that he had underestimated the potential threats to liberty from the federal government. They also heightened his awareness of the link between the construction of constitutional language and the balance of power between the states and the federal government. Madison became alarmed in 1791 by Alexander Hamilton's proposed national bank—less by the bank itself than by the expansive reading of the "general welfare" and "necessary and proper" clauses of the Constitution employed to justify it. So flexible a rule of construction, Madison argued, would soon "reach every object of legislation," violating the principle that the federal government's powers were limited by the Constitution.[85] Moreover, "consolidating" so many powers in the federal government, Madison worried, could enhance the powers of the president and "by degrees transform him into a monarch."[86]

By 1792, the bank bill and Hamilton's "Report on Manufacturing" in particular led Madison to believe that national policies were now being shaped by a minority faction that represented eastern speculators and financiers at the expense of ordinary Americans. Whereas throughout the mid-1780s, Madison had primarily feared the influence of "interested and overbearing" majorities, especially in the states, he now believed the greatest threats to the young republic came from the Federalist cabal that controlled the federal government.[87] Madison's fear of despotic federal power reached its zenith with the passage of the Alien and Sedition Acts in 1798. The Sedition Act was especially alarming because it violated the express provisions of the First Amendment and attacked the "right of freely examining public characters and measures," which was the "only effectual guardian of every other right."[88]

Madison's response to the machinations of the Federalist Party and an untethered, oppressive federal government was to give life to his idea of a "defensive concert . . . against the oppression of those entrusted with the administration."[89] Rousing public opinion became central to this goal. Madison cofounded with Jefferson an opposition newspaper, the *National Gazette*, made numerous contributions to it, worked in Congress to lower the tax on newspapers to increase their circulation, and organized public meetings to protest administration policies.[90] His essays for the *National Gazette* offered a new twist to his earlier understanding of public opinion. As Publius, Madison had observed that citizens' veneration for their government produced political stability.[91] Now he emphasized that veneration for the Constitution required vigilance against an administration that violated it.[92]

As the decade progressed, however, Madison became increasingly dissatisfied with this tactic of using public writings to influence public opinion and turned instead to legislative resolutions, most famously the "Virginia Resolutions" and the more substantive and ambitious "Report of 1800."[93] Such resolutions, he came to believe, were the most effective method for arousing public opinion and opposing federal tyranny. Madison's "Virginia Resolutions" and "Report of 1800" forcefully denounced censorship of speech and press, wherever it occurs, as inherently destructive of republican government. They also declared the Alien and Sedition Acts unconstitutional and argued that, in case of a "deliberate, palpable and dangerous" exercise of power by the federal government, the states—as parties to the constitutional compact—"have the right, and are in duty bound, to interpose for arresting the progress of the evil." This document closed by calling upon the other states to concur in declaring these acts unconstitutional and "cooperating with this State in maintaining unimpaired the authorities, rights, and liberties, reserved to the States respectively, or to the people."[94]

Some of Madison's contemporaries (and many historians) claimed that Madison's "Virginia Resolutions" represented a reversal of his constitutional principles, from nationalism in the 1780s to full embrace of state sovereignty by 1798—from which it would follow that he reversed his principles once again in denouncing nullification three decades later.[95] In fact, however, his words and actions were fundamentally different from Jefferson's and consistent with his writings as Publius. In contrast to Jefferson's draft of the "Kentucky Resolutions," Madison's "Virginia Resolutions" did not assert a right of nullification and did not invoke sovereignty at all, except in the amorphous sense that the American people are the ultimate constitutional authority.[96] Madison invoked the ambiguous and protean idea of interposition, but each time he concretely discussed how the states should interpose, he concluded, as he did in *Federalist* 44 and 46, that the state legislatures would sound the alarm and promote the election of new representatives who would change existing laws. Despite the altered political circumstances, Madison's response to the Sedition Act was also consistent with the "double security" federalism of *Federalist* 51 and with his proposal that the Bill of Rights bind both federal government and states. A vigilant American people, in his view, should be ready to use either state or federal government to defend constitutional rights and liberties against threats from either direction.

Three final incidents from later in Madison's career demonstrate both the continuing evolution and the basic consistency of Madison's postconvention federalism. In 1816, President Madison signed the second Bank of the United States into law. A year later, he vetoed the Bonus Bill, which would have authorized the use of profits from the national bank to fund extensive and much-needed internal improvements such as roads and canals. Finally, in his retirement, he rebuked John C. Calhoun's doctrine of nullification and vehemently denied that he had supported this idea in his 1798 "Virginia Resolutions."

Madison's willingness to approve a second charter for the national bank in 1816 signified an important addition to his doctrine of modified strict construction. In 1791, he had opposed the bank bill because no constitutional language authorized the federal government to exercise such a power. By 1816 he allowed that legislative precedents could establish the constitutionality of an institution such as the bank if those precedents were "deliberate and reiterated," accepted by successive administrations, approved by all three branches of government, and affirmed by the nation at large. Madison here recognized a narrow channel for the people to legitimately expand federal power.[97]

A year later, Madison's veto of the Bonus Bill reaffirmed his commitment to a modified version of strict construction. Madison's veto surprised many, but only those who, in Madison's mind, had not been paying attention. In his veto message, he explained that the power to fund internal improvements could not be found in the enumerated powers of Congress or fair readings of the necessary and proper clause, the commerce clause, or the taxing and spending clause without creating a government and especially a legislature with unbounded powers. Internal improvements, Madison conceded, would advance the general prosperity of the nation, but the power to enact them required a constitutional amendment. For Madison, usefulness was no proof of constitutionality.[98]

In the final years of his life, Madison fought vehemently against the doctrine of nullification, which he believed posed a fundamental threat to the Constitution and Union to which he had devoted his life. Madison's postconvention federalism, as classically formulated in *Federalist* 39, was inherently tension-ridden. These tensions were manageable as long as it was understood that the Constitution's federalism was a new phenomenon on earth, an unprecedented system for which traditional doctrines of sovereignty were out of place.[99] The nullifiers disrupted this complex balancing act by reviving notions of full and inviolable state sovereignty. The arch theorist of nullification, Calhoun, focused directly on *Federalist* 39: "What can be more contradictious," Calhoun asked, than a "government partly federal and partly national?" Sovereignty was all or nothing. "We might just as well speak of half a square, or half of a triangle, as of half a sovereignty." Calhoun argued that every state, as sovereign, had the right to nullify any federal law or act within its own boundaries, including legislation such as the tariff that the Constitution assigned to the federal government. The state's nullification would stand unless and until three-fourths of the states overturned the act with a constitutional amendment.[100]

Madison saw nullification as a perversion of the Constitution. His response was to reaffirm the argument of *Federalist* 39 and emphasize the centrality of the principle of majority rule in republican governments.[101] Though he shared Calhoun's concern with majority tyranny, Madison had always sought a "Republican remedy" for the diseases of republican government.[102] In contrast, nullifiers, Madison observed in an 1830 public letter, "would overturn the first principle of free government" by allowing the minority to rule the majority. In response to the claim that his "Virginia Resolutions" of 1798 supported nullification, Madison argued that those resolutions nowhere authorized "an indiv[idua]l State, to arrest by force the execution of a law of the U.S." but instead urged measures "*concurrently* and cooperatively taken" by the people of the United States. A federal Union in which each state claimed to be final judge of a shared Constitution would invite violent contests and "speedily put an end to the Union itself."[103]

Madison's posthumous "Advice to My Country" urged his fellow Americans "that the Union of the States be cherished and perpetuated" and implicitly warned them that nullification was "the Serpent creeping with his deadly wiles into Paradise."[104] Still, this fell on deaf ears when it came to the nullifiers and their progeny, whose commitment to a regime unabashedly founded on the "positive good" of slavery is described in Peter C. Myers's essay for this volume.[105] The constitutional subtleties and tensions within the constitutional system that Madison had spent a lifetime exploring and defending were now exploited as weaknesses by men who cherished slavery more than the Union.

The Legacies of Madisonian Federalism

We have traced the character and evolution of Madisonian federalism, arguing that the Constitution did not embody several of Madison's constitutional reform proposals but that he nevertheless developed a consistent defense of it after its ratification. We have also indicated that the legacies of Madisonian federalism not only include his *apologia* for the Constitution but also spring from his rejected proposals and his analysis of its flaws.

The most important example of the continuing influence of Madison's rejected proposals is the Fourteenth Amendment to the Constitution. As we have seen, immediately after the Constitutional Convention, Madison predicted that the new experiment in republican government might well fail because the national government lacked a universal power to veto state laws. In the First Congress, he sought to protect the rights of conscience, freedom of the press, and the trial by jury in criminal cases from violations by the states as well as the federal government. This amendment was unsuccessful, but it was inadvertently revived with the passage of the Fourteenth Amendment in 1868 and the subsequent incorporation of the Bill of Rights against the states. Although drafted and ratified under dramatically different political circumstances than the Constitution and the Bill of Rights, the Fourteenth Amendment has become over time a means for completing Madison's vision of national stewardship of fundamental rights against violation by states.

Furthermore, the three postwar amendments—the Thirteenth, Fourteenth, and Fifteenth Amendments—with their accompanying clauses stating that "Congress shall have power to enforce, by appropriate legislation, the provisions of this article"—have cumulatively strengthened Madison's rejection of nullification. The postwar amendments do not negate the constitutional principle that certain powers are reserved to the states. Still, in the aftermath of the Fourteenth Amendment, states cannot plausibly claim to reserve a power to be final judge of the Constitution.[106]

In addition to this legacy of Madison's sponsorship of the universal veto, Madison's objection to the representational distortions of the Senate serves as the foundation of a recurrent criticism of the American political system.[107] Like Madison, commentators on the Constitution continue to bemoan the injustices and deleterious effects of equal representation for all states in the Senate. And, they argue, this problem continues to grow. The ratio of overrepresentation of Wyoming, the least populous state, to California, the most populated, is approximately 70 to 1 today.[108] This proportional gap far exceeds the gap between large and small states in 1787 and continues to expand because of demographic trends. Nevertheless reform is highly improbable. Small states, which are unlikely to favor a more proportional representation in the Senate, control the amendment process; and the Constitution (Article V) provides that no state can be denied equal representation in the Senate without its consent. The Senate's routine resort to the filibuster has added to this obstruction of majority rule by providing the minority a de facto veto on legislation of every kind, further magnifying an inequality that Madison considered a basic violation of republican principle.

Madison's observations about the "double security" features of the American political system serve as yet another broad legacy of his federalism. The course of American history has abundantly demonstrated that Madison was right that both the federal government and the states can threaten fundamental rights and liberties. During the twentieth century, the most persistent violation of constitutional rights—denial of Fourteenth Amendment equal protection and Fifteenth Amendment voting rights to citizens of African descent—was perpetrated by states and only belatedly remedied by the federal judiciary and federal legislation. In their effort to maintain racial segregation, southern states also suppressed freedom of speech and press via the mechanism of libel laws in ways comparable to the Sedition Act (see *New York Times v. Sullivan*, 1964). Rights violations by the federal government include the Palmer Raids after World War I, the arbitrary detention of Japanese American citizens during World War II, and many of the congressional and executive actions taken in the name of the so-called War on Terror after September 11, 2001.

Madison's "double security" thesis holds that when rights are threatened by one level of government, another level can be mobilized as remedy. This feature of federalism has functioned as Madison hoped on some occasions, but American history also reveals discouraging episodes of state complicity in rights violations by the federal government, national complicity in the face of state violations, and indifference by the sovereign people. The internment of Japanese Americans, for example, resulted from explicit federal policy (an executive order), was affirmed by Supreme Court opinions, and was pushed forward by the affected states while most

Americans stood by silently. The unwillingness of any branch or level of government, or the people collectively, to speak on behalf of minorities on such occasions underscores Madison's melancholy reflection that "experience proves the inefficacy of a bill of rights on those occasions when its controul [*sic*] is most needed."[109]

On the positive side, Madison's commitment to the Bill of Rights, which in principle binds all levels of government, has over time become "incorporated with the national sentiment." It is a testament to Madison's prescience that today most college students—indeed most Americans—consider the Bill of Rights the heart and soul of the Constitution. They are surprised to learn that the original Constitution contained no bill of rights and that initially the Bill of Rights did not apply against violations by the states. The Bill of Rights has become deeply embedded in public consciousness as "fundamental maxims of free Government" in a way that Madison anticipated, and today it functions in multiple and ever-evolving ways to support liberty.[110]

The most complicated legacy of Madison's federalism concerns the overall scope of federal authority and the relationship of the states to the federal government. When the Constitutional Convention rejected Madison's universal veto, it ensured that the relationship of the states to the federal government would develop in multiple and sometimes conflicting directions. Madison never claimed the line between federal and state authority would always be clear, though he did insist that some "tribunal" of the federal government, not the states, draw that line.

In disputed cases, Madison himself sometimes argued for cautious expansion of national authority, sometimes for reining it in; he sometimes favored strict construction of constitutional language and sometimes allowed legitimate expansion of federal power via cumulative precedent. He clearly rejected "consolidation" on one side and nullification on the other; but in the complicated middle ranges of state-federal disputes, he can often be plausibly enlisted on either side of the question. This ensures the relevance of his legacy no less than does his sponsorship of the Bill of Rights. When Madison and the framers "split the atom of sovereignty," as Justice Anthony Kennedy put it, and created an unprecedented federal system, they ensured that issues of federalism would remain at the center of the American conversation over liberty and equality.[111]

Separation of Powers

FEDERALIST 47

Having reviewed the general form of the proposed government and the general mass of power allotted to it, I proceed to examine the particular structure of this government, and the distribution of this mass of power among its constituent parts.

One of the principal objections inculcated by the more respectable adversaries to the Constitution, is its supposed violation of the political maxim, that the legislative, executive, and judiciary departments ought to be separate and distinct. In the structure of the federal government, no regard, it is said, seems to have been paid to this essential precaution in favor of liberty. The several departments of power are distributed and blended in such a manner as at once to destroy all symmetry and beauty of form, and to expose some of the essential parts of the edifice to the danger of being crushed by the disproportionate weight of other parts.

No political truth is certainly of greater intrinsic value, or is stamped with the authority of more enlightened patrons of liberty, than that on which the objection is founded. The accumulation of all powers, legislative, executive, and judiciary, in the same hands, whether of one, a few, or many, and whether hereditary, self-appointed, or elective, may justly be pronounced the very definition of tyranny. Were the federal Constitution, therefore, really chargeable with the accumulation of power, or with a mixture of powers, having a dangerous tendency to such an accumulation, no further arguments would be necessary to inspire a universal reprobation of the system. I persuade myself, however, that it will be made apparent to everyone, that the charge cannot be supported, and that the maxim on which it relies has been totally misconceived and misapplied. In order to form correct ideas on this important subject, it will be proper to investigate the sense in which the preservation of liberty requires that the three great departments of power should be separate and distinct.

The oracle who is always consulted and cited on this subject is the celebrated Baron de Montesquieu. If he be not the author of this invaluable precept in the science of politics, he has the merit at least of displaying and recommending it most effectually to the attention of mankind. Let us endeavor, in the first place, to ascertain his meaning on this point.

The British Constitution was to Montesquieu what Homer has been to the didactic writers on epic poetry. As the latter have considered the work of the immortal bard as the perfect model from which the principles and rules of the epic art were to be drawn, and by which all similar works were to be judged, so this great political critic appears to have viewed the Constitution of England as the standard, or to use his own expression, as the mirror of political liberty; and to have delivered, in the form of elementary truths, the several characteristic principles of that particular system. That we may be sure, then, not to mistake his meaning in this case, let us recur to the source from which the maxim was drawn.

On the slightest view of the British Constitution, we must perceive that the legislative, executive, and judiciary departments are by no means totally separate and distinct from each other. The executive magistrate forms an integral part of the legislative authority. He alone has the prerogative of making treaties with foreign sovereigns, which, when made, have, under certain limitations, the force of legislative acts. All the members of the judiciary department are appointed by him, can be removed by him on the address of the two Houses of Parliament, and form, when he pleases to consult them, one of his constitutional councils. One branch of the legislative department forms also a great constitutional council to the executive chief, as, on another hand, it is the sole depositary of judicial power in cases of impeachment, and is invested with the supreme appellate jurisdiction in all other cases. The judges, again, are so far connected with the legislative department as often to attend and participate in its deliberations, though not admitted to a legislative vote.

From these facts, by which Montesquieu was guided, it may clearly be inferred that, in saying "There can be no liberty where the legislative and executive powers are united in the same person, or body of magistrates," or, "if the power of judging be not separated from the legislative and executive powers," he did not mean that these departments ought to have no *partial agency* in, or no *control* over, the acts of each other. His meaning, as his own words import, and still more conclusively as illustrated by the example in his eye, can amount to no more than this, that where the *whole* power of one department is exercised by the same hands which possess the *whole* power of another department, the fundamental principles of a free constitution are subverted. This would have been the case in the constitution examined by him, if the king, who is the sole executive magistrate, had possessed also the complete legislative power, or the supreme administration of justice; or if the entire legislative body had possessed the supreme judiciary, or the supreme executive authority. This, however, is not among the vices of that constitution. The magistrate in whom the whole executive power resides cannot of himself make a law, though he can put a negative on every law; nor administer justice in person, though he has the appointment of those who do administer it. The judges can exercise no executive prerogative, though they are shoots from the executive stock; nor any legislative function, though they may be advised with by the legislative councils. The entire legislature can perform no judiciary act, though by the joint act of two of its branches the judges may be removed from their offices, and though one of its branches is possessed of the judicial power in the last resort. The entire legislature, again, can exercise no executive prerogative, though one of its branches constitutes the supreme executive magistracy, and another, on the impeachment of a third, can try and condemn all the subordinate officers in the executive department.

The reasons on which Montesquieu grounds his maxim are a further demonstration of his meaning. "When the legislative and executive powers are united in the same person or body," says he, "there can be no liberty, because apprehensions may arise lest *the same* monarch or senate should *enact* tyrannical laws to *execute* them in a tyrannical manner." Again: "Were the power of judging joined with the legislative, the life and liberty of the subject would be exposed to arbitrary control, for *the judge* would then be *the legislator*. Were it joined to the executive power, *the judge* might behave with all the violence of *an oppressor*." Some of these reasons are more fully explained in other passages; but briefly stated as they are here, they sufficiently establish the meaning which we have put on this celebrated maxim of this celebrated author.

FEDERALIST 51

To what expedient, then, shall we finally resort, for maintaining in practice the necessary partition of power among the several departments, as laid down in the Constitution? The only answer that can be given is, that as all these exterior provisions are found to be inadequate, the defect must be supplied, by so contriving the interior structure of the government as that its several constituent parts may, by their mutual relations, be the means of keeping each other in their proper places. Without presuming to undertake a full development of this important idea, I will hazard a few general observations, which may perhaps place it in a clearer light, and enable us to form a more correct judgment of the principles and structure of the government planned by the convention.

In order to lay a due foundation for that separate and distinct exercise of the different powers of government, which to a certain extent is admitted on all hands to be essential to the preservation of liberty, it is evident that each department should have a will of its own; and consequently should be so constituted that the members of each should have as little agency as possible in the appointment of the members of the others. Were this principle rigorously adhered to, it would require that all the appointments for the supreme executive, legislative, and judiciary magistracies should be drawn from the same fountain of authority, the people, through channels having no communication whatever with one another. Perhaps such a plan of constructing the several departments would be less difficult in practice than it may in contemplation appear. Some difficulties, however, and some additional expense would attend the execution of it. Some deviations, therefore, from the principle must be admitted. In the constitution of the judiciary department in particular, it might be inexpedient to insist rigorously on the principle: first, because peculiar qualifications being essential in the members, the primary consideration ought to be to select that mode of choice which best secures these qualifications; secondly, because the permanent tenure by which the appointments are held in that department, must soon destroy all sense of dependence on the authority conferring them.

It is equally evident, that the members of each department should be as little dependent as possible on those of the others, for the emoluments annexed to their offices. Were the executive magistrate, or the judges, not independent of the legislature in this particular, their independence in every other would be merely nominal.

But the great security against a gradual concentration of the several powers in the same department, consists in giving to those who administer each department the necessary constitutional means and personal motives to resist encroachments of the others. The provision for defense must in this, as in all other cases, be made commensurate to the danger of attack. Ambition must be made to counteract ambition. The interest of the man must be connected with the constitutional rights of the place. It may be a reflection on human nature, that such devices should be necessary to control the abuses of government. But what is government itself, but the greatest of all reflections on human nature? If men were angels, no government would be necessary. If angels were to govern men, neither external nor internal controls on government would be necessary. In framing a government which is to be administered by men over men, the great difficulty lies in this: you must first enable the government to control the governed; and in the next place oblige it to control itself. A dependence on the people is, no doubt, the primary control on the government; but experience has taught mankind the necessity of auxiliary precautions.

This policy of supplying, by opposite and rival interests, the defect of better motives, might be traced through the whole system of human affairs, private as well as public. We see it particularly displayed in all the subordinate distributions of power, where the constant aim is to divide and arrange the several offices in such a manner as that each may be a check on the other that the private interest of every individual may be a sentinel over the public rights. These inventions of prudence cannot be less requisite in the distribution of the supreme powers of the State.

But it is not possible to give to each department an equal power of self-defense. In republican government, the legislative authority necessarily predominates. The remedy for this inconveniency is to divide the legislature into different branches; and to render them, by different modes of election and different principles of action, as little connected with each other as the nature of their common functions and their common dependence on the society will admit. It may even be necessary to guard against dangerous encroachments by still further precautions. As the weight of the legislative authority requires that it should be thus divided, the weakness of the executive may require, on the other hand, that it should be fortified. An absolute negative on the legislature appears, at first view, to be the natural defense with which the executive magistrate should be armed. But perhaps it would be neither altogether safe nor alone sufficient. On ordinary occasions it might not be exerted with the requisite firmness, and on extraordinary occasions it might be perfidiously abused. May not this defect of an absolute negative be supplied by some qualified connection between this weaker department and the weaker branch of the stronger department, by which the latter may be led to support the constitutional rights of the former, without being too much detached from the rights of its own department?

If the principles on which these observations are founded be just, as I persuade myself they are, and they be applied as a criterion to the several State constitutions, and to the federal Constitution it will be found that if the latter does not perfectly correspond with them, the former are infinitely less able to bear such a test.

There are, moreover, two considerations particularly applicable to the federal system of America, which place that system in a very interesting point of view.

First. In a single republic, all the power surrendered by the people is submitted to the administration of a single government; and the usurpations are guarded against by a division of the government into distinct and separate departments. In the compound republic of America, the power surrendered by the people is first divided between two distinct governments, and then the portion allotted to each subdivided among distinct and separate departments. Hence a double security arises to the rights of the people. The different governments will control each other, at the same time that each will be controlled by itself.

Second. It is of great importance in a republic not only to guard the society against the oppression of its rulers, but to guard one part of the society against the injustice of the other part. Different interests necessarily exist in different classes of citizens. If a majority be united by a common interest, the rights of the minority will be insecure. There are but two methods of providing against this evil: the one by creating a will in the community independent of the majority that is, of the society itself; the other, by comprehending in the society so many separate descriptions of citizens as will render an unjust combination of a majority of the whole very improbable, if not impracticable. The first method prevails in all governments possessing an hereditary or self-appointed authority. This, at best, is but a precarious security; because a power independent of the society may as well espouse the unjust views of the major, as the rightful interests of the minor party, and may possibly be turned against both parties. The second method will be exemplified in the federal republic of the United States. Whilst all authority in it will be derived from and dependent on the society, the society itself will be broken into so many parts, interests, and classes of citizens, that the rights of individuals, or of the minority, will be in little danger from interested combinations of the majority. In a free government the security for civil rights must be the same as that for religious rights. It consists in the one case in the multiplicity of interests, and in the other in the multiplicity of sects.

The degree of security in both cases will depend on the number of interests and sects; and this may be presumed to depend on the extent of country and number of people comprehended under the same government. This view of the subject must particularly recommend a proper federal system to all the sincere and considerate friends of republican government, since it shows that in exact proportion as the territory of the Union may be formed into more circumscribed Confederacies, or States oppressive combinations of a majority will be facilitated: the best security, under the republican forms, for the rights of every class of citizens, will be diminished: and consequently the stability and independence of some member of the government, the only other security, must be proportionately increased. Justice is the end of government. It is the end of civil society. It ever has been and ever will be pursued until it be obtained, or until liberty be lost in the pursuit. In a society under the forms of which the stronger faction can readily unite and oppress the weaker, anarchy may as truly be said to reign as in a state of nature, where the weaker individual is not secured against the violence of the stronger; and as, in the latter state, even the stronger individuals are prompted, by the uncertainty of their condition, to submit to a government which may protect the weak as well as themselves; so, in the former state, will the more powerful factions or parties be gradually induced, by a like motive, to wish for a government which will protect all parties, the weaker as well as the more powerful. It can be little doubted that if the State of Rhode Island was separated from the Confederacy and left to itself, the insecurity of rights under the popular form of government within such narrow limits would be displayed by such reiterated oppressions of factious majorities that some power altogether independent of the people would soon be called for by the voice of the very factions whose misrule had proved the necessity of it. In the extended republic of the United States, and among the great variety of interests, parties, and sects which it embraces, a coalition of a majority of the whole society could seldom take place on any other principles than those of justice and the general good; whilst there being thus less danger to a minor from the will of a major party, there must be less pretext, also, to provide for the security of the former, by introducing into the government a will not dependent on the latter, or, in other words, a will independent of the society itself. It is no less certain than it is important, notwithstanding the contrary opinions which have been entertained, that the larger the society, provided it lie within a practical sphere, the more duly capable it will be of self-government. And happily for the *republican cause*, the practicable sphere may be carried to a very great extent, by a judicious modification and mixture of the *federal principle*.

FEDERALIST 71

Duration in office has been mentioned as the second requisite to the energy of the Executive authority. This has relation to two objects: to the personal firmness of the executive magistrate, in the employment of his constitutional powers; and to the stability of the system of administration which may have been adopted under his auspices. With regard to the first, it must be evident, that the longer the duration in office, the greater will be the probability of obtaining so important an advantage. It is a general principle of human nature, that a man will be interested in whatever he possesses, in proportion to the firmness or precariousness of the tenure by which he holds it; will be less attached to what he holds by a momentary or uncertain title, than to what he enjoys by a durable or certain title; and, of course, will be willing to risk more for the sake of the one, than for the sake of the other. This remark is not less applicable to a political privilege, or honor, or trust, than to any article of ordinary property. The inference from it is, that a man acting in the capacity of chief magistrate, under a consciousness that in a very short time he *must* lay down his office, will be apt to feel himself too little interested in it to hazard any material censure or perplexity, from the independent exertion of his powers, or from encountering the ill-humors, however transient, which may happen to prevail, either in a considerable part of the society itself, or even in a predominant faction in the legislative body. If the case should only be, that he *might* lay it down, unless continued by a new choice, and if he should be desirous of being continued, his wishes, conspiring with his fears, would tend still more powerfully to corrupt his integrity, or debase his fortitude. In either case, feebleness and irresolution must be the characteristics of the station.

There are some who would be inclined to regard the servile pliancy of the Executive to a prevailing current, either in the community or in the legislature, as its best recommendation. But such men entertain very crude notions, as well of the purposes for which government was instituted, as of the true means by which the public happiness may be promoted. The republican principle demands that the deliberate sense of the community should govern the conduct of those to whom they entrust the management of their affairs; but it does not require an unqualified complaisance to every sudden breeze of passion, or to every transient impulse which the people may receive from the arts of men, who flatter their prejudices to betray their interests. It is a just observation, that the people commonly *intend* the *public good*. This often applies to their very errors. But their good sense would despise the adulator who should pretend that they always *reason right* about the *means* of promoting it. They know from experience that they sometimes err; and the wonder is that they so seldom err as they do, beset, as they continually are, by the wiles of parasites and sycophants, by the snares of the ambitious, the avaricious, the desperate, by the artifices of men who possess their confidence more than they deserve it, and of those who seek to possess rather than to deserve it. When occasions present themselves, in which the interests of the people are at variance with their inclinations, it is the duty of the persons whom they have appointed to be the guardians of those interests, to withstand the temporary delusion, in order to give them time and opportunity for more cool and sedate reflection. Instances might be cited in which a conduct of this kind has saved the people from very fatal consequences of their own mistakes, and has procured lasting monuments of their gratitude to the men who had courage and magnanimity enough to serve them at the peril of their displeasure.

But however inclined we might be to insist upon an unbounded complaisance in the Executive to the inclinations of the people, we can with no propriety contend for a like complaisance to the humors of the legislature. The latter may sometimes stand in opposition to the former, and at other times the people may be entirely neutral. In either supposition, it is certainly desirable that the Executive should be in a situation to dare to act his own opinion with vigor and decision.

The same rule which teaches the propriety of a partition between the various branches of power, teaches us likewise that this partition ought to be so contrived as to render the one independent of the other. To what purpose separate the executive or the judiciary from the legislative, if both the executive and the judiciary are so constituted as to be at the absolute devotion of the legislative? Such a separation must be merely nominal, and incapable of producing the ends for which it was established. It is one thing to be subordinate to the laws, and another to be dependent on the legislative body. The first comports with, the last violates, the fundamental principles of good government; and, whatever may be the forms of the Constitution, unites all power in the same hands. The tendency of the legislative authority to absorb every other, has been fully displayed and illustrated by examples in some preceding numbers. In governments purely republican, this tendency is almost irresistible. The representatives of the people, in a popular assembly, seem sometimes to fancy that they are the people themselves, and betray strong symptoms of impatience and disgust at the least sign of opposition from any other quarter; as if the exercise of its rights, by either the executive or judiciary, were a breach of their privilege and an outrage to their dignity. They often appear disposed to exert an imperious control over the other departments; and as they commonly have the people on their side, they always act with such momentum as to make it very difficult for the other members of the government to maintain the balance of the Constitution.

It may perhaps be asked, how the shortness of the duration in office can affect the independence of the Executive on the legislature, unless the one were possessed of the power of appointing or displacing the other. One answer to this inquiry may be drawn from the principle already remarked that is, from the slender interest a man is apt to take in a short-lived advantage, and the little inducement it affords him to expose himself, on account of it, to any considerable inconvenience or hazard. Another answer, perhaps more obvious, though not more conclusive, will result from the consideration of the influence of the legislative body over the people; which might be employed to prevent the re-election of a man who, by an upright resistance to any sinister project of that body, should have made himself obnoxious to its resentment.

It may be asked also, whether a duration of four years would answer the end proposed; and if it would not, whether a less period, which would at least be recommended by greater security against ambitious designs, would not, for that reason, be preferable to a longer period, which was, at the same time, too short for the purpose of inspiring the desired firmness and independence of the magistrate.

It cannot be affirmed, that a duration of four years, or any other limited duration, would completely answer the end proposed; but it would contribute towards it in a degree which would have a material influence upon the spirit and character of the government. Between the commencement and termination of such a period, there would always be a considerable interval, in which the prospect of annihilation would be sufficiently remote, not to have an improper effect upon the conduct of a man endued with a tolerable portion of fortitude; and in which he might reasonably promise himself, that there would be time enough before it arrived, to make the community sensible of the propriety of the measures he might incline to pursue. Though it be probable that, as he approached the moment when the public were, by a new election, to signify their sense of his conduct, his confidence, and with it his firmness, would decline; yet both the one and the other would derive support from the opportunities which his previous continuance in the station had afforded him, of establishing himself in the esteem and good-will of his constituents. He might, then, hazard with safety, in proportion to the proofs he had given of his wisdom and integrity, and to the title he had acquired to the respect and attachment of his fellow-citizens. As, on the one hand, a duration of four years will contribute to the firmness of the Executive in a sufficient degree to render it a very valuable ingredient in the composition; so, on the other, it is not enough to justify any alarm for the public liberty. If a British House of Commons, from the most feeble beginnings, *from the mere power of assenting or disagreeing to the imposition of a new tax*, have, by rapid strides, reduced the prerogatives of the crown and the privileges of the nobility within the limits they conceived to be compatible with the principles of a free government, while they raised themselves to the rank and consequence of a coequal branch of the legislature; if they have been able, in one instance, to abolish both the royalty and the aristocracy, and to overturn all the ancient establishments, as well in the Church as State; if they have been able, on a recent occasion, to make the monarch tremble at the prospect of an innovation attempted by them, what would be to be feared from an elective magistrate of four years' duration, with the confined authorities of a President of the United States? What, but that he might be unequal to the task which the Constitution assigns him? I shall only add, that if his duration be such as to leave a doubt of his firmness, that doubt is inconsistent with a jealousy of his encroachments.

DEMOCRACY IN AMERICA, VOLUME II, PART 2, CHAPTER 8: "HOW THE AMERICANS COMBAT INDIVIDUALISM BY THE DOCTRINE OF INTEREST WELL UNDERSTOOD"

I showed in a preceding chapter how equality of conditions developed among all men the taste for well-being, and directed their minds toward the search for what is useful.

Elsewhere, while talking about individualism, I have just shown how this same equality of conditions broke the artificial bonds that united citizens in aristocratic societies, and led each man to search for what is useful to himself alone.

These various changes in the social constitution and in the tastes of humanity cannot fail to influence singularly the theoretical idea that men form of their duties and their rights.

When the world was led by a small number of powerful and rich individuals, the latter loved to form a sublime idea of the duties of man; they took pleasure in professing that it is glorious to forget self and that it is right to do good without interest, just like God. That was the official doctrine of this time in the matter of morality.

I doubt that men were more virtuous in aristocratic centuries than in others, but it is certain that they then talked constantly about the beauties of virtue; they only studied in secret how it was useful. But as imagination soars less and as each person concentrates on himself, moralists become afraid of this idea of sacrifice, and they no longer dare to offer it to the human mind; so they are reduced to trying to find out if the individual advantage of citizens would not be to work toward the happiness of all, and, when they have discovered one of these points where particular interest meets with general interest and merges with it, they hasten to bring it to light; little by little similar observations multiply. What was only an isolated remark becomes a general doctrine, and you believe finally that you see that man, by serving his fellows, serves himself, and that his particular interest is to do good.

I have already shown, in several places in this work, how the inhabitants of the United States almost always knew how to combine their own well-being with that of their fellow citizens. What I want to note here is the general theory by the aid of which they succeed in doing so.

In the United States, you almost never say that virtue is beautiful. You maintain that it is useful, and you prove it every day. American moralists do not claim that you must sacrifice yourself for your fellows because it is great to do so; but they say boldly that such sacrifices are as necessary to the person who imposes them on himself as to the person who profits from them.

They have noticed that, in their country and time, man was led back toward himself by an irresistible force and, losing hope of stopping him, they have thought only about guiding him.

So they do not deny that each man may follow his interest, but they strive to prove that the interest of each man is to be honest.

Here I do not want to get into the details of their reasons, which would take me away from my subject; it is enough for me to say that they have persuaded their fellow citizens.

A long time ago, Montaigne said: "When I would not follow the right road because of rectitude, I would follow it because I found by experience that in the end it is usually the happiest and most useful path."

So the doctrine of interest well understood is not new; but, among the Americans of today, it has been universally admitted; it has become popular; you find it at the bottom of all actions; it pokes through all discussions. You find it no less in the mouths of the poor than in those of the rich.

In Europe the doctrine of interest is much cruder than in America, but at the same time, it is less widespread and above all less evident, and great devotions that are felt no more are still feigned among us every day.

The Americans, in contrast, take pleasure in explaining almost all the actions of their life with the aid of interest well understood; they show with satisfaction how enlightened love of themselves leads them constantly to help each other and disposes them willingly to sacrifice for the good of the State a portion of their time and their wealth. I think that in this they often do not do themselves justice; for you sometimes see in the United States, as elsewhere, citizens give themselves to the disinterested and unconsidered impulses that are natural to man; but the Americans hardly ever admit that they yield to movements of this type; they prefer to honor their philosophy rather than themselves.

I could stop here and not try to judge what I have just described. The extreme difficulty of the subject would be my excuse. But I do not want to take advantage of it, and I prefer that my readers, clearly seeing my purpose, refuse to follow me rather than remain in suspense.

Interest well understood is a doctrine not very lofty, but clear and sure. It does not try to attain great objectives, but without too much effort it attains all those it targets. Since the doctrine is within reach of all minds, each man grasps it easily and retains it without difficulty. Accommodating itself marvelously to the weaknesses of men, it easily gains great dominion and it is not difficult for it to preserve that dominion, because the doctrine turns personal interest back against itself and, to direct passions, uses the incentive that excites them.

The doctrine of interest well understood does not produce great devotions; but it suggests small sacrifices every day; by itself, it cannot make a man virtuous, but it forms a multitude of steady, temperate, moderate, farsighted citizens who have self-control; and, if it does not lead directly to virtue by will, it imperceptibly draws closer to virtue by habits.

If the doctrine of interest well understood came to dominate the moral world entirely, extraordinary virtues would undoubtedly be rarer. But I also think that then the coarsest depravities would be less common. The doctrine of interest well understood perhaps prevents some men from rising very far above the ordinary level of humanity; but a great number of others who fall below encounter the doctrine and cling to it. Consider a few individuals, it lowers them. Envisage the species, it elevates it.

I will not be afraid to say that the doctrine of interest well understood seems to me, of all philosophical theories, the most appropriate to the needs of the men of our time, and that I see in it the most powerful guarantee remaining to them against themselves. So it is principally toward this doctrine that the mind of the moralists of today should turn. Even if they were to judge it as imperfect, it would still have to be adopted as necessary.

I do not believe, everything considered, that there is more egoism among us than in America; the only difference is that there it is enlightened and here it is not. Each American knows how to sacrifice a portion of his particular interests in order to save the rest. We want to keep everything, and often everything escapes us.

I see around me only men who seem to want to teach their contemporaries, every day by their word and their example, that what is useful is never dishonorable. Will I never finally find some men who undertake to make their contemporaries understand how what is honorable can be useful?

There is no power on earth that can prevent the growing equality of conditions from leading the human mind toward the search for what is useful, and from disposing each citizen to become enclosed within himself.

So you must expect individual interest to become more than ever the principal, if not the sole motivating force of the actions of men; but how each man will understand his individual interest remains to be known.

If citizens, while becoming equal, remained ignorant and coarse, it is difficult to predict to what stupid excess their egoism could be led, and you cannot say in advance into what shameful miseries they would plunge themselves, out of fear of sacrificing something of their well-being to the prosperity of their fellows.

I do not believe that the doctrine of interest, as it is preached in America, is evident in all its parts; but it contains a great number of truths so evident that it is enough to enlighten men in order for them to see them. So enlighten them at all cost, for the century of blind devotions and instinctive virtues is already fleeing far from us, and I see the time drawing near when liberty, the public peace and the social order itself will not be able to do without enlightenment.

SUGGESTED ADDITIONAL READINGS (Freely Available Online)

Federalist 48
Federalist 62
Federalist 70
Federalist 78

THE SEPARATION OF POWERS

Michael P. Zuckert

The twenty-first century has once again thrust the separation of powers into the center of Americans' political consciousness. Perhaps the most striking manifestation of the renewed salience of separation of powers issues was the lawsuit filed by Speaker of the House John Boehner in the summer of 2014 challenging President

Barack Obama's use of executive orders and other "work-arounds" to accomplish political goals the president felt unable to accomplish through Congress.[112] Boehner's threatened suit was met with guffaws from both left and right. Congress is armed, after all, with its legislative power, which, if exercised, could easily thwart the president's executive initiatives. However, Congress cannot act to do this because it has been marked by stalemate during much of the twenty-first century, which prevents significant legislation from passing. The very same stalemate that prevents Boehner from acting through his own branch of government was the original impetus behind the president's resolve to act independently of Congress when he could. As President Obama said in response to news of Boehner's threatened suit, "As long as they're doing nothing, I'm not going to apologize for doing something."[113]

This little episode of the Boehner lawsuit epitomizes almost all the issues that have arisen about the separation of powers in the late twentieth and early twenty-first centuries. The institutional structure when public opinion is divided and control of the branches is in the hands of different parties tends naturally, it is said, toward stalemate. Indeed, as we will see below, it is often thought that such stalemate or checking of power is the main intent of the separation of powers, a thought well captured in the title of a now classic book on the separation of powers, James McGregor Burns's *Deadlock of Democracy*.[114] The "Madisonian system," said Burns, is designed to thwart majority power by separating and deadlocking powers. In response to the deadlock, however, the executive takes the initiative and acts quasi-independently of Congress. For this and other reasons, the bloating of the executive is seen as one of the pathologies of the separation of powers system. In response to perceived executive overreach Boehner threatens a lawsuit, that is, threatens to take the issue to the courts, ultimately the Supreme Court, in order to control the executive. However, when people are not complaining about the growth of the executive they are complaining about the growth of judicial power, a national pastime at least since the Warren Court of the 1950s and 1960s. So Boehner, rather than using the powers of his own office, acts to increase the power of one branch, the judiciary, to counter the growth of power in another branch, the executive. That is all to say that nothing seems quite right about the separation of powers.

The separation of powers is not, however, a merely tangential or peripheral part of the constitutional architecture. It is one of the three chief devices for governance built into the original Constitution by its framers. First there was federalism, the establishment of two sets of governments with two sets of powers dividing up the totality of governing business between the states and the national government. Then there was republicanism, or the political arrangements meant to establish control by the people over their governors. Most important here, of course, are fixed terms of office and elections.[115] Separation of powers is introduced as an "auxiliary" to elections; as James Madison put it in *Federalist* 51: "A dependence on the people is, no doubt, the primary control on the government; but experience has taught mankind the necessity of auxiliary precautions."[116]

The dominant, or what we might call the textbook, version of separation of powers takes its point of departure from the sentence quoted from Madison above and maintains that the "branches of the United States government are kept distinct in order to prevent abuse of power. This . . . form of separation of powers is associated with a system of checks and balances."[117] Thus saith Wikipedia, the authority of our age. Perhaps we could more precisely capture the textbook version in the formula: separation of powers is for the sake of checks and balances. If that indeed is the purpose of separation, then the resultant deadlock ought to be seen as a rational and even desired result of the system as established in the Constitution. The idea behind the textbook version is that dividing power prevents concentration of power in any one set of hands and arms each institution with the power to check others in the system.

So far is the textbook version from the truth about the aims of the separation of powers, however, that the obverse of it is much more nearly the truth: checks and balances are for the sake of the separation of powers. The deficiencies of the textbook-deadlock theory of governance are evident even from the Madisonian text, when read in its context, that is so often used in support of the textbook version. *Federalist* 51 contains this programmatic passage: "In framing a government which is to be administered by men over men, the great difficulty lies in this: *you must first enable the government to control the governed*; and in the next place oblige it to control itself."[118] The first task is to "control the governed," that is, to govern. To govern means to act effectively to accomplish the sorts of goals set forth in the preamble of the Constitution; for example, to "insure domestic Tranquility, provide for the common Defence, promote the general Welfare, and secure the Blessings of Liberty." Accomplishing those large goals requires that the government be able to act. A stalemate system will never do, so that cannot have been the aim of the separation of powers.

As presented in *Federalist* 51, the task facing designers of constitutions is a complex one—they must establish institutions at once strong enough and capable enough to govern effectively but at the same time able to be controlled. The separation of powers is such an important part of the constitutional arrangement because it is one of the chief devices by which both of these nearly contradictory goals can be achieved.

The separation of powers was designed to contribute to the tasks of governance in two major ways, both of which are explained at length in *The Federalist*. The system of separated powers serves, first, by establishing rule of law, and second, by providing the means whereby the several diverse qualities required of governing institutions can be supplied. Let us consider these in turn.

Separation of Powers and Rule of Law

The service of the separated powers to the rule of law is underappreciated because readers (and the authors of textbooks) usually fail to pay sufficient attention to the series of papers of which it is a part. *Federalist* 51 is normally consulted, but its significance is not properly appreciated because it is read in isolation from the series of essays, *Federalist* 47–51, to which it belongs. But part of the blame for the misunderstanding of separated powers lies with the rhetoric of this series of papers as well, for, like much of *The Federalist*, the presentation of the argument in *Federalist* 47–51 is shaped (and partly misshaped) by its address to concerns and criticisms of the proposed Constitution by its anti-Federalist opponents.

Madison's point of departure in *Federalist* 47 is an anti-Federalist criticism to the effect that the proposed Constitution does not keep the institutions or powers sufficiently separated. In order to answer that criticism Madison has to raise the question of what is the point of having separated powers. In light of the answer he must then determine what kind of separation is needed and what the viable means are for maintaining the separation of powers. This question then dominates the discussion in *Federalist* 48–51, deflecting attention from more fundamental issues regarding the purpose and point of the separated powers. Although in this context Madison must address the question of the purpose of the separation of powers, he does not do so at length or with very much analytical force. The reason for his less-than-thorough treatment of this important topic is again related to the polemical context of the entire *Federalist*. Madison and his coauthors were eager to refute the objections raised by the anti-Federalists, and they, with a very few exceptions, did not object to the separation of powers per se. Their complaint was that the powers had not been kept separate enough. For example, the Senate, with its advise and consent power, was to share in the executive powers; the president with his veto power would share in the legislative power. The polemical situation thus did not require of the *Federalist* authors a full-blown defense of the separation of powers, but only a defense of the particular version they were proposing. The overall point of the series of *Federalist* 48–51 is to show that the partial sharing of powers, and thus the provision of checks and balances, was the only effective way to maintain the separation; a demonstration effected by a consideration of alternate ideas for keeping the great departments separate. These other proposals are deftly shown to be inadequate to the task. In *Federalist* 51 Madison answers the anti-Federalists directly: partial sharing of powers is the only effective means to maintain the overall separation.

Although it is one of the relatively neglected papers, *Federalist* 47 is of capital importance for correctly understanding the much-misunderstood system of separation of powers, for it is here that Madison does, rather elliptically, consider the purposes of the separation. According to him, separated powers are a great good.

"No political truth is of greater intrinsic value" than the need to keep the powers separated. "The accumulation of all powers, legislative, executive, and judiciary, in the same hands . . . may justly be pronounced the very definition of tyranny."[119] Unlike the textbook writers of today, however, Madison believed that it is necessary "to investigate the sense in which the preservation of liberty requires that the three great departments of power should be separate and distinct."[120] The answer that comes to our lips so readily—checking and balancing—did not come so readily to his. He seems to have had something else in mind, for it is not separated or fragmented power per se that he pronounced required for the "preservation of liberty," one of the great ends announced in the preamble. Rather it is a particular separation—of the "three great departments of power."

In order to elucidate the liberty-preserving potencies of the separation of powers, Madison turned to the "oracle that is always consulted and cited on this subject, the celebrated Montesquieu." Madison's analysis is often overlooked, I suspect, because he presented it in the laconic phrases of the French philosopher. His point is often lost, also, because he presented the case for the separation of powers in the context of the explicit anti-Federalist critique he is addressing in these *Federalist* essays, the charge that the Constitution improperly blends or mixes powers. That focus deflects from the most significant aspect of Madison's and Montesquieu's theory of separation.

Their chief point can be gleaned well enough if we attend carefully to the most important passages Madison quoted in his text: "The reasons, on which Montesquieu grounds his maxim, are a further demonstration of his meaning. . . . 'Were the powers of judging joined with the legislative, the life and liberty of the subject would be exposed to arbitrary control, for *the judge* would then be *the legislator*. Were it joined to the executive power, *the judge* might behave with all the violence of *an oppressor*.'"[121] On these passages Madison commented, "They sufficiently establish the meaning which we have put on this celebrated maxim of this celebrated author."[122]

It is clear from the passages Madison quoted that it is not mere fragmentation and checking of powers that is important to the "celebrated" Frenchman but the separation of these particular powers or functions. The point of the separation becomes visible when we perceive what these three powers are. These are three stages in the making and implementation of law. The point of the theory of separation is to establish that the stages of law are to be entrusted to different and separate institutions, with each to be constructed so as to best suit that stage of the process and the whole system of separation to guarantee rule of law. The reasoning is this: liberty is being subject to rule of law rather than arbitrary control. To be free, Montesquieu had concluded, is to be able to believe that one is secure in one's life, liberty, and possessions, to know in advance what actions are permissible and what not, to be confident that one will not be liable to the coercive power of government for actions not specified in the law, to be confident that processes are in place to guarantee that government proceeds according to the law. Liberty is not the right to do whatever one pleases—that is license and produces anarchy—but it is the right to treatment by and under a law in which one has oneself or through one's deputies had a hand in making or enforcing.

The best way to think about the theory of separation of powers is in terms of a relay race. The race begins with one body, the legislature, making laws, then passing the baton of the law to the executive, who then passes it to the judiciary. The separation of powers, as explained by Montesquieu and more or less institutionalized in the British Constitution, thus establishes a sequence of actions in which one body, the legislature, exercises will in making laws, but neither does it possess the force of the community, which lies with the executive, nor can it apply the law it makes to individuals, which is the province of the judicial system. Law is to be made by a special kind of body, composed of representatives of the community, drawn from the "great body of the people."[123] Law, a set of general rules and not specific dictates aimed at particular individuals, must apply to the legislators and their connections as well to everyone else. The executive wields the ever-dangerous coercive force of the community but is limited at either end by an inability to make the rules it applies, which must come from the legislature, and by an inability to apply coercion against individuals unless the judiciary concurs. The judiciary is the crucial link between government, with its coercively enforced rules, and the people. As Hamilton said, it has "neither force nor will, but merely judgment."[124] In the Montesquieuean model the core of the judiciary is not the judges but the jury. Like the legislature it is drawn from the "great body of the people." Thus the sense of the community is brought into government both in the making of law and in the application of law to individuals.

For the system to work properly to establish rule of law the powers must be kept separate, that is, the different stages or functions must be exercised by specialized agencies particularly suited to their task. The exercise of more than one of the powers threatens liberty by providing means for evading the rule of law. Thus Madison could affirm that the "accumulation of all powers, legislative, executive, and judiciary, in the same hands, may justly be pronounced the very definition of tyranny," for the one in whose hands all powers lay could act in a perfectly arbitrary manner, leaving citizens perfectly insecure in their rights. Even lesser degrees of shared powers pose serious threats to liberty. So, to take the Montesquieuean examples Madison quoted in his text, let us say the legislative and judicial powers are joined. That means that he who applies the laws to individuals is also the one who makes the rules to be applied. This might look like a particularly effective way to guarantee the application of the law as the legislature meant it. It might seem a particularly effective guard against judicial overreach, or the judiciary substituting its will for the legislature.

Although judicial overreach is a potential problem in a system such as the American one in which judges exercise very extraordinary powers via the institution of judicial review, the theory of separation of powers guards against a far more dangerous possibility in establishing separate institutions for making and applying laws to individuals. The joining of legislative and judicial powers would have foreseeably harmful effects on both the legislative and adjudicating activities. First and in Montesquieu's eyes perhaps foremost, the joining of legislative and judicial powers cancels the most powerful institutional guarantee of legislation that at least seeks, even if it does not always achieve, the public good—namely, that the laws apply equally and uniformly to all, and in particular to the members of the legislature and their families, friends, and favorites. If the legislature were free to apply the law to whom and as it sees fit, this impersonal character of law would be lost, and little could be expected but self-favoring and arbitrary law making.

At the other end, if the legislature also possessed the judicial power and it or its delegates could exercise that power, the excellence of the judiciary that contributes to liberty would be lost. For one, the jury, so much the mainstay of a properly constituted judicial power, would no longer have a place. Because the jury is an ad hoc body with little occasion for the individual jurors to benefit from their decisions and with nothing on which to base their decision but the general rules handed to them from the legislature, the evidence in the case, and the moral predilections of the community as brought by the jurors into the courtroom, the likelihood that the judiciary will serve liberty rather than arbitrariness is high. Moreover, courts normally evolve processes and procedures that work toward a certain fairness in judicial decision making that would be lost if the legislature could both make all the rules and then apply them at will to individuals. As Montesquieu rightly said, "Were the powers of judging joined with the legislative, the life and liberty of the subject would be exposed to arbitrary control, for the *judge* would then be *the legislator*."

Madison also quotes Montesquieu's fears that "were [the judicial power] joined to the executive power, *the judge* might behave with all the violence of an oppressor." That is, if the part of the government possessing the means of coercion were also to have the power to decide on its own to whom coercion may be applied, the result again is destruction of the rule of law and invitation to the wielders of coercion to arbitrariness.

It is thus of great importance to liberty that the powers be kept separate, not so much so they can check each other but so they play their proper role in the relay race of the rule of law. After it is established that the separation of powers is desirable it becomes necessary to find means to keep the institutions separate. Madison agrees with the anti-Federalists on this need, but he disagrees on the means to do so. From *Federalist* 48 to 51 Madison considers a number of schemes designed to maintain the separation. He differs from the critics of the Constitution (and from the drafters of many of the state constitutions) in a general principle related to the establishment in America of republican governments. Most of the "founders of our republic" remained fixed on the idea that the great dangers to liberty and rule of law came "from the overgrown and all-grasping prerogative of an hereditary magistrate, supported and fortified by an hereditary branch of the legislative authority."[125] This is a real danger in a mixed regime such as that of the British Constitution, but in a full republic the real "danger [is] from legislative usurpations, which, by assembling all powers in the same hands, must lead to the same tyranny as is threatened by executive usurpations."

Prior American efforts toward maintaining the separation of powers have thus failed in two separate, though related, ways. On the one side they relied on "parchment barriers," that is, constitutional proclamations that powers of one sort not be exercised by a branch to which they did not rightly belong.[126] Such decrees were of themselves completely ineffective. On the other side, and partly in response to that ineffectuality, some of the states established enforcement mechanisms that were no more effective and in particular were not constructed to protect against the great dangers of the "legislative...vortex" in republican America.[127] Madison cited the examples of the special constitutional commission in Pennsylvania and the special convention proposed by Thomas Jefferson for Virginia for "correcting breaches" of the Constitution.[128] Madison showed, among several other important things, that these special conventions were most likely to fall under the sway of the same majority that dominated the legislature and thus were likely to favor the legislature in case of conflict among the branches; that is, that they would fail to solve the problem of maintaining the separated powers.

The solution hit on in the Constitution is defended by Madison in his famous *Federalist* 51. The end to be achieved, recall, is maintenance of the separation of powers as a means to maintenance of the rule of law; the means to maintenance of separation of powers, in turn, is checks and balances: "The great security against a gradual concentration of the several powers in the same department, consists in giving to those who administer each department, the necessary constitutional means, and personal motives, to resist encroachments of the others."[129] Each branch must be given some authority overlapping with the other branches so that it can check the others in defense of its own prerogatives. In the American republican system this means, for the most part, protecting against and therefore checking the legislature. Thus the central checking device to be exercised on behalf of both executive and judiciary is the presidential veto. Contrary to the sense of many anti-Federalists that the executive should have no part of the legislative power—it seemed to them an antirepublican relic of the monarchical past—Madison argued that it was precisely the republicanism of the American constitutional order that made executive sharing in the legislative power absolutely necessary.[130] The situation to be avoided is one in which "the *whole* power of one department is exercised by the same hands which possess the *whole* power of another department."[131] Sharing of some powers for the sake of introducing separation-maintaining checks does not, therefore, violate the separation of powers but is the only realistic way of maintaining such in the real world of politics.

Madison's very famous statement on the means to provide "security against a gradual concentration of the several powers in the same department" also violates other standard anti-Federalist (and commonsense?) principles. According to Madison, that security arises from "giving to those who administer each department, the necessary constitutional means, and personal motives, to resist encroachments of others. . . . The interest of the man must be connected with the constitutional rights of the place."[132] Madison's point is that the common good, as embodied in the securing of the separation of powers, must be achieved through appeal to the particular goods, or the particular interests, of the officeholders. Anti-Federalist theory, mimicking classical republicanism in this respect, held that political virtue meant suppressing one's private and particular interest for the sake of the public good. Madison's principle of constitutional design is thus somewhat like the use of markets in the economic sphere—the system works via the convergence of private interest and the public good. It differs from markets, however, in that the convergence between public and private good is consciously engineered by the designers of the constitutional institutions.

In the case of the separation of powers, Madison means that offices must be constructed in such a way that officeholders derive private satisfactions from holding them and so will fight to protect the office from encroachments by others. Thus, rather than countering private satisfaction by constructing unrewarding conditions of public service, Madison would heighten the rewards by building attractive offices that promise power and prestige to the officeholders. The attractive offices provide incentives to maintain the prerogatives and independence of the institutions, but to the incentives must be added constitutional powers that can be deployed to protect the office. Again the executive veto is a good example. The president, occupying a powerful office, alone at the summit of the government, has plenty of incentives to protect the office; armed with the veto power he has a constitutional resource to forfend legislative encroachments on his office or on the judiciary. The powers of his office also give him something of an incentive to protect the judiciary as well, for it is with him that the power of appointment lies. He serves the public good by serving his own good—but only if the private and public goods are properly aligned by the designers of the institutions.

The separation of powers exists for the sake of the rule of law, the rule of law is a means to liberty of the citizenry, and checks and balances are the means to maintain the separation.

Separation of Powers and the Necessary Qualities of Governance

The contribution of the separation of powers to governance under the Constitution is not exhausted by its role in furthering the rule of law. It was also seen by the founders of the American republic as the chief means by which the qualities necessary to good governance could be produced.

Ever since the Progressive Era and the political science it spawned, it has been an item in American democratic theory that the chief task of a proper constitution is to provide for the gathering and implementation in policy of popular preferences. This is thought to be what it means for the people to rule. Publius's emphasis is quite elsewhere and a great deal more complex than Progressive democratic theory. He begins with the idea that there are certain things government must do and certain governmental qualities needed to do those things. He emphasizes the latter in *Federalist* 37. It is unclear whether the list of requisite qualities is meant to be exhaustive—most likely not, for some obvious ones such as wisdom or prudence go unmentioned. The listed ones bring out particularly well, however, the problem Publius meant to illustrate. As opposed to many opponents of the proposed Constitution, he emphasized that the needed qualities of government are multiple. Many of the anti-Federalists wrote as if the only serious concern was the provision of devices for ensuring that government would not be oppressive, often called "safety."

Among the multiple requirements of good government, according to Publius, is "energy," for "energy in government is essential to that security against external and internal danger, and to that prompt and salutary execution of the laws, which enter into the very definition of good government."[133] Neither "safety," as the anti-Federalists had it, nor "preference effectuation," as modern democratic theorists have it, is the first requirement of government. If "safety" were the first need, then one could do even better and have no government at all, which even the anti-Federalists did not advocate. Government is the institution in society empowered to make law, that is, rules backed up by coercion, to regulate behavior and provide security to citizens in their lives, liberties, and properties.[134] These may be threatened both internally and externally, so the first requirement of good government is the ability to fend off these threats and provide energy, or the ability to act forcefully and in a timely manner. We may note again what Publius said in *Federalist* 51: "You must first enable the government to control the governed; and in the next place oblige it to control itself."[135]

Governments must also provide stability, for this quality "is essential to national character, and to the advantages annexed to it, as well as to that repose and confidence in the minds of the people, which are among the chief blessings of civil society."[136] He meant by stability a situation marked by regular and immutable legislation,[137] a feature not characterizing the state governments of the day. Such instability as the states experienced was "evil in itself" and "odious to the people."[138]

Fixedness in the laws gives "character" to a society, that is, not only a certain fixedness of disposition or way of acting, but good reputation with others. Stability in government complements energy by giving the people an environment in which they can act with "repose and confidence" based on their ability to know that the legal environment will be much the same tomorrow as it is today. Where energy is an active principle of government, stability is a principle that activates and energizes the people in the sphere of life we have come to call "civil society," that is, the subpolitical sphere of individual and associational action and enterprise. Energy provides for strong government, stability for strong civil society. Liberty, the ability of the people to act on their own without fear or insecurity, partly results from energy and stability, but it is a separate requirement as well. It is separate because liberty also includes what we have referred to as safety, the guarantee of nonoppressive government, which is not automatically supplied by energy and stability.

The plurality of requisite governmental qualities demonstrates that the task of constitutional construction is complex: it is not enough to maximize one desired quality. However, the problem of constitutional design is even more complex, for there is a great "difficulty [in] mingling [the desired qualities] together in their due proportions."[139] The difficulty derives from two facts. The first is that the kinds of political structures that tend to produce one quality are antithetical to those that produce the others. As Publius briefly put it, "Energy . . . requires not only a certain duration of power, but the execution of it by a single hand," whereas stability "requires, that the hands in which power is lodged, should continue for a length of time the same" because "frequent change of men will result from a frequent return of elections, and frequent change of measures, from a frequent change of men."[140] Deeply at odds with both are the apparent structural requirements of "republican liberty." This liberty "seems to demand on one side, . . . that those entrusted with [power] should be kept in dependence on the people, by a short duration of their appointments; and that, even during this short period, the trust should be placed not in a few, but in a number of hands."[141]

Combining the different qualities seems very difficult indeed, but the task is rendered even more difficult in the American context, for the Americans are committed to doing this strictly within the bounds of the "republican form." Publius in *Federalist* 39 gives a relatively stringent definition of the republican form as opposed to both common usage of the time and the tradition of political thought. Regimes like that of Venice, "where absolute power over the great body of the people, is exercised in the most absolute manner, by a small body of hereditary nobles," are generally called republics, and important theorists of republicanism such as Machiavelli and Montesquieu so considered them also.

Publius, however, rejected the idea that Venice or most of the other regimes considered republican in general opinion deserved that title. He substituted a far more democratic definition: "a government which derives all its powers directly or indirectly from the great body of the people; and is administered by persons holding their offices during pleasure, for a limited period, or during good behavior."[142] The decisive feature of this definition is that no officer of government can lay any claim to political power but from an ultimate appointment by the people, who, according to the philosophy of the Declaration of Independence, are the fount of all political power.[143] All officers are also ultimately responsible to, in the sense of removable by, authorities themselves responsible to the people. This definition rejects all heritable or self-perpetuating political power. It does not mandate direct democracy, or even completely directly representative government, for it allows much indirect responsibility to the people, as in, for example, the constitutional provision for the appointment of Supreme Court justices by the conjoint action of the indirectly elected president and the indirectly elected Senate.

The definition of republic Publius invoked complicated the achievement of the mixture of governmental qualities called for in *Federalist* 37, for the typical solution to achieving that mixture in past theory and practice was the mixed regime. That regime, as described by political writers from Polybius in Roman times to Montesquieu in the eighteenth century, involved the mixing of different estates or classes in government, with only one part satisfying the Publian definition of republicanism. As he said of England, Montesquieu's model for such a mixed regime, it "has one republican branch only, combined with [an unacceptable] hereditary aristocracy and monarchy." It is therefore not a genuine republic.[144] In a proper republic all parts of the government must be drawn from the people, and thus it is even more difficult to achieve the various qualities needed for good governance because the qualities a monarch and a House of Lords might bring to governance are unavailable.

So, how to combine these apparently irreconcilable qualities emerged as a very pressing and difficult problem for the designers of the constitutional institutions. In *The Federalist*'s discussion of the institutions of the general government, Publius showed how intelligently structured, wholly republican institutions can mimic the operation of the mixed regime and supply the different qualities needed by all good governments. The separation of powers makes possible the provision of the apparently impossible combination of governmental qualities. Thus, to simplify considerably, Publius demonstrated how the unitary presidency can supply energy, the Senate stability, and the House of Representatives republican liberty. Once again we see that the separated powers are only partly for the sake of the checks and balances with which they are normally identified. More fundamentally, the separated powers, as embodied in the separate institutions, are for the sake of providing the mixture of necessary governmental qualities.

There were two possible basic approaches to building institutions that could supply the requisite governmental qualities. The mixed regime was an example of one approach: let the people make the institution. The idea here is institutions should be constructed so as to draw certain kinds of individuals into the government and have their preexisting qualities shape the character of the institution. Thus, to take the example so often on the minds of the American founders, the British Constitution had the three main institutions of the monarch, the House of Lords, and the House of Commons, in which the two latter institutions drew their character for the most part from the character of the individuals in the social stratum from which they were drawn. The House of Lords contained the wealthy, old, established aristocratic families and operated accordingly. The House of Commons drew from a different social stratum and operated according to the different social bases on which it depended.

There were Americans—John Adams, for example—who sought to build a set of separate and differently empowered institutions on this same principle of "the man makes the institution." Of course this approach ran up against the fact that America did not have the kind of social structure on which the mixed regime had been built. There was no royal family, no aristocracy, only the commons; and a mixed regime could not be built on one social estate only.

Adams countered with his theory of natural aristocracy. Every society, not merely those with formal aristocracies, has an aristocratic element. There was, we can paraphrase Adams as saying, a natural tendency to aristocracy in every society. By this he meant that there is a tendency for natural leaders to arise in every society, individuals who are not strictly speaking the political equals of their fellows. These "natural aristocrats" (a misnomer in some ways) derived more influence over their fellows through any number of qualities—the advantage of being born into a well-known and respected family (think Kennedy), personal wealth, education, intellect, good looks, and an indefinite list of other qualities that tend to encourage human beings to favor and follow others. These "natural aristocrats" were not by any means necessarily the persons of most merit for governing, but they were the ones favored when there was free choice of leaders. They rose to the top in part because they tended also to be the most ambitious, energetic, and capably self-serving individuals in any given population. Adams was convinced they could bring valuable qualities to governing, but he also saw them as potentially dangerous. As much to keep a good eye on them and to control them, Adams proposed that in a bicameral legislature one house be, in effect, set aside for these aristocrats and the other for the more ordinary folk. The character of each of the two houses was to be set by the type of person recruited into it—natural aristocrat or natural commoner.[145]

Of course, it is difficult in a society like that of America, with no officially recognized aristocracy, to establish institutions that can reliably represent the two main types of individuals. Some of the anti-Federalists, especially the very important Melancton Smith, took over the kind of analysis Adams put forward, attached it to a specific critique of the American system, and developed a specific demand for modification of the new Constitution. Smith feared that the small number of seats in the legislature proposed under the Constitution would produce a situation in which both houses of Congress would be filled with the ambitious and therefore "natural aristocrats." His remedy was to call for a much-enlarged legislature in which (as in the states) there would be enough posts to leave room for the "middling sort" to achieve office. A healthy representation of the middling sort, of the "yeomen," would offset the ambitious few and keep the government attuned to the true goals of republican government—liberty, small government, honesty.[146]

However, as Smith rightly discerned, the Constitution was not designed to produce institutions of that sort. The constitutional separation of powers scheme depends instead on a mode of construction we might call institutional republicanism. The principle here is the reverse of that on which the mixed regime model relied: the institution makes the man; or rather, the structure of the institution produces or at least pushes officeholders within it toward the kind of behavior that leads to the desired governmental quality. Roughly speaking, the different institutions of the separated powers scheme are to produce the different and conflicting requirements of governance, with the Senate the chief locus for supplying stability and the unitary executive for supplying energy. The constituting aim in designing the institutions when viewed in this light is not the place in the stages of law the institution fills but rather the particular governmental quality it is to supply. These two different sets of considerations do not necessarily impose conflicting imperatives of institutional design, but they do make the design problem more complex in that more factors are relevant to the proper design of the institution.

The general point of the institutional republican system of separated powers works with the idea that the behavior of the institution can be shaped by its design and features and does not depend on preformed individuals of any particular sort. So the way the Senate is constructed is to produce stability—its long term of office without term limits, its relatively small number, the visibility of its members, its staggered terms of office, its indirect selection by the states. These features of the institution are, as far as possible within republican (nonhereditary, nonlife terms) offices, to work toward stability. The much shorter term of members of the House, the fact that all stand for election at once, the much larger body—these features of the institution lead toward its fulfilling the requirements of republican safety through popular control.

Publius gave one of the best defenses of the founders' ideas about engineering this convergence between structure and behavior when he defended the provisions for indefinite reeligibility for the presidency. This provision ran counter to the political instincts of the nation, where suspicion and distrust of executive power was a very powerful force. "Nothing appears more plausible at first sight, nor more ill-founded upon close inspection," Publius tells us, "than a scheme . . . of continuing the chief magistrate in office for a certain time, and then excluding him from it."[147] The effects of this at first sight "plausible scheme" would be, he warns, "for the most part rather pernicious than salutary."[148] The perniciousness of these arrangements lay in the "diminution of the inducements to good behavior" they would produce. The system requires, especially in the presidency, individuals who seek not only the "negative merit of not doing harm" but also the "positive merit of doing good." This latter, more positive, aim required the same sort of intelligent constitutional design as did the achievement of the more negative aim but required it on a grander and more daring scale. One must enlist or encourage the "love of fame, the ruling passion of the noblest minds." One needs individuals who not only wish to remain in office but who wish for much more; individuals who wish to found a republic, or to save a republic, or to preserve the nation from economic crisis or war, or to establish a new system of health care, and who would thus bring the necessary energy to governing. This love of fame "would prompt a man to plan and undertake extensive and arduous enterprises for the public benefit, requiring considerable time to mature and perfect them." However, there is a necessary interaction between love of fame (and the great actions that love would prompt) and the structure of offices. The lover of fame would be prompted to undertake these enterprises "if he could flatter himself with the prospect of being allowed to finish what he had begun." A short term of office with no possibility of extending his term "would, on the contrary, deter him from the undertaking, when he foresaw that he must quit the scene before he could accomplish the work, and must commit that, together with his own reputation, to hands which might be unequal or unfriendly to the task."[149] Although Publius did not bring out the point in this context, we must mention one other feature implicit in the argument. Long terms and reeligibility not only provide incentives for the lovers of fame to act as Hamilton described but they also conduce to the transformation of the officeholder's psychological motives. Someone who starts off with lesser aims, for example, to merely hold office, might come to higher motives, for example, to seek fame, by virtue of the opportunity the institutional structure provides. The kind of offices the founders designed not only gives scope for action to the lover of fame but also conduces to the emergence of love of fame itself in their holders.

Conclusion

There are a number of lessons in the founders' way of thinking about the separation of powers that we ought to pause to notice. First, contrary to what we learn in the usual textbook, the point of the separation of powers is not merely to supply checks and balances; it does far more than that. Second, we can notice the richness of the founders' political science. It is difficult not to contrast it with the approach typical of contemporary political science, which tends to view political institutions through the lens supplied by a simplistic democratic theory, which sees the point of political institutions as merely to collect and implement popular preferences.

Although contemporary political scientists have many powerful tools for the study of politics that the founding generation lacked, their approach to it is quite impoverished at the more important conceptual level, which sets out the agenda of what to study and why.

To return for a moment to the concerns about the separation of powers with which we began: on the one hand, there is a sense that the separation of powers has failed because of the stalemate that has marked so much of the early twenty-first century. We now see, I should hope, that stalemate or deadlock was no part of the founders' plans for the separated powers system. It is a potentiality of that system when opinion is so divided in the nation that one set of opinions can dominate one of the branches and another set dominate another, but as American history demonstrates, deadlock has not been the universal experience of government under the separation of powers. If nothing else, however, I hope this presentation of the separation of powers inclines us to look elsewhere for a full appreciation of the contribution of this kind of system of divided powers to the great ends of governance. The founders' thinking on the separation of powers ought to focus our attention on the two major areas that system was designed to serve: establishing the rule of law and supplying the otherwise very difficult combination of qualities needed for good republican government. With a clear idea of what the separation of powers system can do, and of what it was supposed to do, we can assess the contemporary performance of these structures according to a richer set of criteria than we are wont to bring to the task.

3 • Liberty, Equality, and Religion

JOHN WINTHROP, "A MODEL OF CHRISTIAN CHARITY"

It rests now to make some application of this discourse, by the present design, which gave the occasion of writing of it. Herein are four things to be propounded; first the persons, secondly, the work, thirdly the end, fourthly the means.

First, for the persons. We are a company professing ourselves fellow members of Christ, in which respect only, though we were absent from each other many miles, and had our employments as far distant, yet we ought to account ourselves knit together by this bond of love and live in the exercise of it, if we would have comfort of our being in Christ. This was notorious in the practice of the Christians in former times; as is testified of the Waldenses, from the mouth of one of the adversaries Aeneas Sylvius "mutuo ament peneantequamnorunt"— they use to love any of their own religion even before they were acquainted with them.

Secondly, for the work we have in hand. It is by a mutual consent, through a special overvaluing providence and a more than ordinary approbation of the churches of Christ, to seek out a place of cohabitation and consortship under a due form of government both civil and ecclesiastical. In such cases as this, the care of the public must oversway all private respects, by which, not only conscience, but mere civil policy, doth bind us. For it is a true rule that particular estates cannot subsist in the ruin of the public.

Thirdly, the end is to improve our lives to do more service to the Lord; the comfort and increase of the body of Christ, whereof we are members, that ourselves and posterity may be the better preserved from the common corruptions of this evil world, to serve the Lord and work out our salvation under the power and purity of his holy ordinances.

Fourthly, for the means whereby this must be effected. They are twofold, a conformity with the work and end we aim at. These we see are extraordinary, therefore we must not content ourselves with usual ordinary means. Whatsoever we did, or ought to have done, when we lived in England, the same must we do, and more also, where we go. That which most in their churches maintain as truth in profession only, we must bring into familiar and constant practice; as in this duty of love, we must love brotherly without dissimulation, we must love one another with a pure heart fervently. We must bear one another's burdens. We must not look only on our own things, but also on the things of our brethren.

Neither must we think that the Lord will bear with such failings at our hands as he doth from those among whom we have lived; and that for these three reasons:

First, in regard of the more near bond of marriage between Him and us, wherein He hath taken us to be His, after a most strict and peculiar manner, which will make Him the more jealous of our love and obedience. So He tells the people of Israel, you only have I known of all the families of the earth, therefore will I punish you for your transgressions.

Secondly, because the Lord will be sanctified in them that come near Him. We know that there were many that corrupted the service of the Lord; some setting up altars before his own; others offering both strange fire and strange sacrifices also; yet there came no fire from heaven, or other sudden judgment upon them, as did upon Nadab and Abihu, whom yet we may think did not sin presumptuously.

Thirdly, when God gives a special commission He looks to have it strictly observed in every article; When He gave Saul a commission to destroy Amaleck, He indented with him upon certain articles, and because he failed in one of the least, and that upon a fair pretense, it lost him the kingdom, which should have been his reward, if he had observed his commission.

Thus stands the cause between God and us. We are entered into covenant with Him for this work. We have taken out a commission. The Lord hath given us leave to draw our own articles. We have professed to enterprise these and those accounts, upon these and those ends. We have hereupon besought Him of favor and blessing. Now if the Lord shall please to hear us, and bring us in peace to the place we desire, then hath He ratified this covenant and sealed our commission, and will expect a strict performance of the articles contained in it; but if we shall neglect the observation of these articles which are the ends we have propounded, and, dissembling with our God, shall fall to embrace this present world and prosecute our carnal intentions, seeking great things for ourselves and our posterity, the Lord will surely break out in wrath against us, and be revenged of such a people, and make us know the price of the breach of such a covenant.

Now the only way to avoid this shipwreck, and to provide for our posterity, is to follow the counsel of Micah, to do justly, to love mercy, to walk humbly with our God. For this end, we must be knit together, in this work, as one man. We must entertain each other in brotherly affection. We must be willing to abridge ourselves of our superfluities, for the supply of others' necessities. We must uphold a familiar commerce together in all meekness, gentleness, patience and liberality. We must delight in each other; make others' conditions our own; rejoice together, mourn together, labor and suffer together, always having before our eyes our commission and community in the work, as members of the same body. So shall we keep the unity of the spirit in the bond of peace. The Lord will be our God, and delight to dwell among us, as His own people, and will command a blessing upon us in all our ways, so that we shall see much more of His wisdom, power, goodness and truth, than formerly we have been acquainted with. We shall find that the God of Israel is among us, when ten of us shall be able to resist a thousand of our enemies; when He shall make us a praise and glory that men shall say of succeeding plantations, "may the Lord make it like that of New England." For we must consider that we shall be as a city upon a hill. The eyes of all people are upon us. So that if we shall deal falsely with our God in this work we have undertaken, and so cause Him to withdraw His present help from us, we shall be made a story and a by-word through the world. We shall open the mouths of enemies to speak evil of the ways of God, and all professors for God's sake. We shall shame the faces of many of God's worthy servants, and cause their prayers to be turned into curses upon us till we be consumed out of the good land whither we are going.

And to shut this discourse with that exhortation of Moses, that faithful servant of the Lord, in his last farewell to Israel, Deut. 30. "Beloved, there is now set before us life and death, good and evil," in that we are commanded this day to love the Lord our God, and to love one another, to walk in his ways and to keep his Commandments and his ordinance and his laws, and the articles of our Covenant with Him, that we may live and be multiplied, and that the Lord our God may bless us in the land whither we go to possess it. But if our hearts shall turn away, so that we will not obey, but shall be seduced, and worship other Gods, our pleasure and profits, and serve them; it is propounded unto us this day, we shall surely perish out of the good land whither we pass over this vast sea to possess it. Therefore let us choose life, that we and our seed may live, by obeying His voice and cleaving to Him, for He is our life and our prosperity.

JAMES MADISON, "MEMORIAL AND REMONSTRANCE AGAINST RELIGIOUS ASSESSMENTS"

We the subscribers, citizens of the said Commonwealth, having taken into serious consideration, a Bill printed by order of the last Session of General Assembly, entitled "A Bill establishing a provision for Teachers of the Christian Religion," and conceiving that the same if finally armed with the sanctions of a law, will be a dangerous abuse of power, are bound as faithful members of a free State to remonstrate against it, and to declare the reasons by which we are determined. We remonstrate against the said Bill,

1. Because we hold it for a fundamental and undeniable truth, "that Religion or the duty which we owe to our Creator and the manner of discharging it, can be directed only by reason and conviction, not by force or violence." The Religion then of every man must be left to the conviction and conscience of every man; and it is the right of every man to exercise it as these may dictate. This right is in its nature an unalienable right. It is unalienable, because the opinions of men, depending only on the evidence contemplated by their own minds cannot follow the dictates of other men: It is unalienable also, because what is here a right towards men, is a duty towards the Creator. It is the duty of every man to render to the Creator such homage and such only as he believes to be acceptable to him. This duty is precedent, both in order of time and in degree of obligation, to the claims of Civil Society. Before any man can be considered as a member of Civil Society, he must be considered as a subject of the Governor of the Universe: And if a member of Civil Society, who enters into any subordinate Association, must always do it with a reservation of his duty to the General Authority; much more must every man who becomes a member of any particular Civil Society, do it with a saving of his allegiance to the Universal Sovereign. We maintain therefore that in matters of Religion, no man's right is abridged by the institution of Civil Society and that Religion is wholly exempt from its cognizance. True it is, that no other rule exists, by which any question which may divide a Society, can be ultimately determined, but the will of the majority; but it is also true that the majority may trespass on the rights of the minority.

2. Because if Religion be exempt from the authority of the Society at large, still less can it be subject to that of the Legislative Body. The latter are but the creatures and vicegerents of the former. Their jurisdiction is both derivative and limited: It is limited with regard to the co-ordinate departments, more necessarily is it limited with regard to the constituents. The preservation of a free Government requires not merely, that the metes and bounds which separate each department of power be invariably maintained; but more especially that neither of them be suffered to overleap the great Barrier which defends the rights of the people. The Rulers who are guilty of such an encroachment, exceed the commission from which they derive their authority, and are Tyrants. The People who submit to it are governed by laws made neither by themselves nor by an authority derived from them, and are slaves.

3. Because it is proper to take alarm at the first experiment on our liberties. We hold this prudent jealousy to be the first duty of Citizens, and one of the noblest characteristics of the late Revolution. The free men of America did not wait till usurped power had strengthened itself by exercise, and entangled the question in precedents. They saw all the consequences in the principle, and they avoided the consequences by denying the principle. We revere this lesson too much soon to forget it. Who does not see that the same authority which can establish Christianity, in exclusion of all other Religions, may establish with the same ease any particular

sect of Christians, in exclusion of all other Sects? that the same authority which can force a citizen to contribute threepence only of his property for the support of any one establishment, may force him to conform to any other establishment in all cases whatsoever?

4. Because the Bill violates that equality which ought to be the basis of every law, and which is more indispensible [*sic*], in proportion as the validity or expediency of any law is more liable to be impeached. If "all men are by nature equally free and independent," all men are to be considered as entering into Society on equal conditions; as relinquishing no more, and therefore retaining no less, one than another, of their natural rights. Above all are they to be considered as retaining an "*equal* title to the free exercise of Religion according to the dictates of Conscience." Whilst we assert for ourselves a freedom to embrace, to profess and to observe the Religion which we believe to be of divine origin, we cannot deny an equal freedom to those whose minds have not yet yielded to the evidence which has convinced us. If this freedom be abused, it is an offence against God, not against man: To God, therefore, not to man, must an account of it be rendered. As the Bill violates equality by subjecting some to peculiar burdens, so it violates the same principle, by granting to others peculiar exemptions. Are the Quakers and Menonists the only sects who think a compulsive support of their Religions unnecessary and unwarrantable? Can their piety alone be entrusted with the care of public worship? Ought their Religions to be endowed above all others with extraordinary privileges by which proselytes may be enticed from all others? We think too favorably of the justice and good sense of these denominations to believe that they either covet pre-eminences over their fellow-citizens or that they will be seduced by them from the common opposition to the measure.

5. Because the Bill implies either that the Civil Magistrate is a competent Judge of Religious Truth; or that he may employ Religion as an engine of Civil policy. The first is an arrogant pretension falsified by the contradictory opinions of Rulers in all ages, and throughout the world: the second an unhallowed perversion of the means of salvation.

6. Because the establishment proposed by the Bill is not requisite for the support of the Christian Religion. To say that it is, is a contradiction to the Christian Religion itself, for every page of it disavows a dependence on the powers of this world: it is a contradiction to fact; for it is known that this Religion both existed and flourished, not only without the support of human laws, but in spite of every opposition from them, and not only during the period of miraculous aid, but long after it had been left to its own evidence and the ordinary care of Providence. Nay, it is a contradiction in terms; for a Religion not invented by human policy, must have pre-existed and been supported, before it was established by human policy. It is moreover to weaken in those who profess this Religion a pious confidence in its innate excellence and the patronage of its Author; and to foster in those who still

reject it, a suspicion that its friends are too conscious of its fallacies to trust it to its own merits.

7. Because experience witnesseth that ecclesiastical establishments, instead of maintaining the purity and efficacy of Religion, have had a contrary operation. During almost fifteen centuries has the legal establishment of Christianity been on trial. What have been its fruits? More or less in all places, pride and indolence in the Clergy, ignorance and servility in the laity, in both, superstition, bigotry and persecution. Enquire of the Teachers of Christianity for the ages in which it appeared in its greatest lustre; those of every sect, point to the ages prior to its incorporation with Civil policy. Propose a restoration of this primitive State in which its Teachers depended on the voluntary rewards of their flocks, many of them predict its downfall. On which Side ought their testimony to have greatest weight, when for or when against their interest?

8. Because the establishment in question is not necessary for the support of Civil Government. If it be urged as necessary for the support of Civil Government only as it is a means of supporting Religion, and it be not necessary for the latter purpose, it cannot be necessary for the former. If Religion be not within the cognizance of Civil Government how can its legal establishment be necessary to Civil Government? What influence in fact have ecclesiastical establishments had on Civil Society? In some instances they have been seen to erect a spiritual tyranny on the ruins of the Civil authority; in many instances they have been seen upholding the thrones of political tyranny: in no instance have they been seen the guardians of the liberties of the people. Rulers who wished to subvert the public liberty, may have found an established Clergy convenient auxiliaries. A just Government instituted to secure & perpetuate it needs them not. Such a Government will be best supported by protecting every Citizen in the enjoyment of his Religion with the same equal hand which protects his person and his property; by neither invading the equal rights of any Sect, nor suffering any Sect to invade those of another.

9. Because the proposed establishment is a departure from that generous policy, which, offering an Asylum to the persecuted and oppressed of every Nation and Religion, promised a luster to our country, and an accession to the number of its citizens. What a melancholy mark is the Bill of sudden degeneracy? Instead of holding forth an Asylum to the persecuted, it is itself a signal of persecution. It degrades from the equal rank of Citizens all those whose opinions in Religion do not bend to those of the Legislative authority. Distant as it may be in its present form from the Inquisition, it differs from it only in degree. The one is the first step, the other the last in the career of intolerance. The magnanimous sufferer under this cruel scourge in foreign Regions, must view the Bill as a Beacon on our Coast, warning him to seek some other haven, where liberty and philanthropy in their due extent, may offer a more certain repose from his Troubles.

10. Because it will have a like tendency to banish our Citizens. The allurements

presented by other situations are every day thinning their number. To spread a fresh motive to emigration by revoking the liberty which they now enjoy, would be the same species of folly which has dishonored and depopulated flourishing kingdoms.

11. Because it will destroy that moderation and harmony which the forbearance of our laws to intermeddle with Religion has produced among its several sects. Torrents of blood have been spilt in the old world, by vain attempts of the secular arm, to extinguish Religious discord, by proscribing all difference in Religious opinion. Time has at length revealed the true remedy. Every relaxation of narrow and rigorous policy, wherever it has been tried, has been found to assuage the disease. The American Theatre has exhibited proofs that equal and complete liberty, if it does not wholly eradicate it, sufficiently destroys its malignant influence on the health and prosperity of the State. If with the salutary effects of this system under our own eyes, we begin to contract the bounds of Religious freedom, we know no name that will too severely reproach our folly. At least let warning be taken at the first fruits of the threatened innovation. The very appearance of the Bill has transformed "that Christian forbearance, love and charity," which of late mutually prevailed, into animosities and jealousies, which may not soon be appeased. What mischiefs may not be dreaded, should this enemy to the public quiet be armed with the force of a law?

12. Because the policy of the Bill is adverse to the diffusion of the light of Christianity. The first wish of those who enjoy this precious gift ought to be that it may be imparted to the whole race of mankind. Compare the number of those who have as yet received it with the number still remaining under the dominion of false Religions; and how small is the former! Does the policy of the Bill tend to lessen the disproportion? No; it at once discourages those who are strangers to the light of revelation from coming into the Region of it; and countenances by example the nations who continue in darkness, in shutting out those who might convey it to them. Instead of Leveling as far as possible, every obstacle to the victorious progress of Truth, the Bill with an ignoble and unchristian timidity would circumscribe it with a wall of defense against the encroachments of error.

13. Because attempts to enforce by legal sanctions, acts obnoxious to so great a proportion of Citizens, tend to enervate the laws in general, and to slacken the bands of Society. If it be difficult to execute any law which is not generally deemed necessary or salutary, what must be the case, where it is deemed invalid and dangerous? And what may be the effect of so striking an example of impotency in the Government, on its general authority?

14. Because a measure of such singular magnitude and delicacy ought not to be imposed, without the clearest evidence that it is called for by a majority of citizens, and no satisfactory method is yet proposed by which the voice of the majority in this case may be determined, or its influence secured. "The people of the respective counties are indeed requested to signify their opinion respecting the adoption of the Bill to the next Session of Assembly." But the representation must be made

equal, before the voice either of the Representatives or of the Counties will be that of the people. Our hope is that neither of the former will, after due consideration, espouse the dangerous principle of the Bill. Should the event disappoint us, it will still leave us in full confidence, that a fair appeal to the latter will reverse the sentence against our liberties.

15. Because finally, "the equal right of every citizen to the free exercise of his Religion according to the dictates of conscience" is held by the same tenure with all our other rights. If we recur to its origin, it is equally the gift of nature; if we weigh its importance, it cannot be less dear to us; if we consult the "Declaration of those rights which pertain to the good people of Virginia, as the basis and foundation of Government," it is enumerated with equal solemnity, or rather studied emphasis. Either then, we must say, that the Will of the Legislature is the only measure of their authority; and that in the plenitude of this authority, they may sweep away all our fundamental rights; or, that they are bound to leave this particular right untouched and sacred: Either we must say, that they may control the freedom of the press, may abolish the Trial by Jury, may swallow up the Executive and Judiciary Powers of the State; nay that they may despoil us of our very right of suffrage, and erect themselves into an independent and hereditary Assembly or, we must say, that they have no authority to enact into law the Bill under consideration. We the Subscribers say, that the General Assembly of this Commonwealth have no such authority: And that no effort may be omitted on our part against so dangerous an usurpation, we oppose to it, this remonstrance; earnestly praying, as we are in duty bound, that the Supreme Lawgiver of the Universe, by illuminating those to whom it is addressed, may on the one hand, turn their Councils from every act which would affront his holy prerogative, or violate the trust committed to them: and on the other, guide them into every measure which may be worthy of his blessing, may redound to their own praise, and may establish more firmly the liberties, the prosperity and the happiness of the Commonwealth.

GEORGE WASHINGTON, LETTER TO THE ANNUAL MEETING OF QUAKERS

Government being, among other purposes, instituted to protect the persons and consciences of men from oppression, it certainly is the duty of rulers, not only to abstain from it themselves, but, according to their stations, to prevent it in others.

The liberty enjoyed by the people of these states of worshiping Almighty God agreeably to their consciences, is not only among the choicest of their *blessings*, but also of their *rights*. While men perform their social duties faithfully, they do all that society or the state can with propriety demand or expect; and remain responsible only to their Maker for their religion, or modes of faith, which they may prefer or profess.

Your principles and conduct are well known to me; and it is doing the people called Quakers no more than justice to say, that (except their declining to share with others the burden of the common defense) there is no denomination among us, who are more exemplary and useful citizens.

I assure you very explicitly, that in my opinion the conscientious scruples of all men should be treated with great delicacy and tenderness; and it is my wish and desire, that the laws may always be as extensively accommodated to them, as a due regard to the protection and essential interests of the nation may justify and permit.

THOMAS JEFFERSON, VIRGINIA STATUTE ON RELIGIOUS FREEDOM

Whereas Almighty God hath created the mind free; that all attempts to influence it by temporal punishments or burdens, or by civil incapacitations, tend only to beget habits of hypocrisy and meanness, and are a departure from the plan of the Holy author of our religion, who being Lord both of body and mind, yet chose not to propagate it by coercions on either, as it was in his Almighty power to do; that the impious presumption of legislators and rulers, civil as well as ecclesiastical, who being themselves but fallible and uninspired men, have assumed dominion over the faith of others, setting up their own opinions and modes of thinking as the only true and infallible, and as such endeavoring to impose them on others, hath established and maintained false religions over the greatest part of the world, and through all time; that to compel a man to furnish contributions of money for the propagation of opinions which he disbelieves, is sinful and tyrannical; that even the forcing him to support this or that teacher of his own religious persuasion, is depriving him of the comfortable liberty of giving his contributions to the particular pastor, whose morals he would make his pattern, and whose powers he feels most persuasive to righteousness, and is withdrawing from the ministry those temporary rewards, which proceeding from an approbation of their personal conduct, are an additional incitement to earnest and unremitting labors for the instruction of mankind; that our civil rights have no dependence on our religious opinions, any more than our opinions in physics or geometry; that therefore the proscribing any citizen as unworthy the public confidence by laying upon him an incapacity of being called to offices of trust and emolument, unless he profess or renounce this or that religious opinion, is depriving him injuriously of those privileges and advantages to which in common with his fellow-citizens he has a natural right; that it tends only to corrupt the principles of that religion it is meant to encourage, by bribing with a monopoly of worldly honors and emoluments, those who will externally profess and conform to it; that though indeed these are criminal who do not withstand such temptation, yet neither are those innocent who lay the bait in their way; that to suffer the civil magistrate to intrude his powers into the field of opinion, and to restrain the profession or propagation of principles on supposition of their ill tendency, is a dangerous fallacy, which at once destroys all religious liberty, because he being of course judge of that tendency will make his opinions the rule of judgment, and approve or condemn the sentiments of others only as they shall square with or differ from his own; that it is time enough for the rightful purposes of civil government, for its officers to interfere when principles break out into overt acts against peace and good order; and finally, that truth is great and will prevail if left to herself, that she is the proper and sufficient antagonist to error, and has nothing to fear from the conflict, unless by human interposition disarmed of her natural weapons, free argument and debate, errors ceasing to be dangerous when it is permitted freely to contradict them:

Be it enacted by the General Assembly, That no man shall be compelled to frequent or support any religious worship, place, or ministry whatsoever, nor shall be enforced, restrained, molested, or burthened in his body or goods, nor shall otherwise suffer on account of his religious opinions or belief; but that all men shall be free to profess, and by argument to maintain, their opinion in matters of religion, and that the same shall in no wise diminish, enlarge, or affect their civil capacities.

And though we well know that this assembly elected by the people for the ordinary purposes of legislation only, have no power to restrain the acts of succeeding assemblies, constituted with powers equal to our own, and that therefore to declare this act to be irrevocable would be of no effect in law; yet we are free to declare, and do declare, that the rights hereby asserted are of the natural rights of mankind, and that if any act shall be hereafter passed to repeal the present, or to narrow its operation, such act shall be an infringement of natural right.

THOMAS JEFFERSON, LETTER TO DANBURY BAPTISTS

The affectionate sentiments of esteem and approbation which you are so good as to express towards me, on behalf of the Danbury Baptist association, give me the highest satisfaction. My duties dictate a faithful and zealous pursuit of the interests of my constituents, & in proportion as they are persuaded of my fidelity to those duties, the discharge of them becomes more and more pleasing.

Believing with you that religion is a matter which lies solely between Man & his God, that he owes account to none other for his faith or his worship, that the legitimate powers of government reach actions only, & not opinions, I contemplate with sovereign reverence that act of the whole American people which declared that their legislature should "make no law respecting an establishment of religion, or prohibiting the free exercise thereof," thus building a wall of separation between Church & State. Adhering to this expression of the supreme will of the nation in behalf of the rights of conscience, I shall see with sincere satisfaction the progress of those sentiments which tend to restore to man all his natural rights, convinced he has no natural right in opposition to his social duties.

I reciprocate your kind prayers for the protection & blessing of the common father and creator of man, and tender you for yourselves & your religious association, assurances of my high respect & esteem.

DEMOCRACY IN AMERICA, VOLUME I, PART 2, CHAPTER 9: "OF THE PRINCIPAL CAUSES THAT TEND TO MAINTAIN THE DEMOCRATIC REPUBLIC IN THE UNITED STATES"

Of the Influence of Mores on Maintaining the Democratic Republic in the United States

I said above that I considered the mores as one of the great general causes to which maintaining the democratic republic in the United States can be attributed.

I understand the expression *mores* here in the sense that the ancients attached to the word *mores;* I apply it not only to mores strictly speaking, which could be called habits of the heart, but to the different notions that men possess, to the diverse opinions that are current among them, and to the ensemble of ideas from which the habits of the mind are formed.

So by this word I understand the whole moral and intellectual state of a people. My goal is not to draw a picture of American mores; I limit myself at this moment to trying to find out what among them is favorable for maintaining the political institutions.

Indirect Influence Exercised by Religious Beliefs on Political Society in the United States

I have just shown what the direct action of religion on politics was in the United States. Its indirect action seems even more powerful to me, and it is when religion is not speaking about liberty that it best teaches the Americans the art of being free.

There is an innumerable multitude of sects in the United States. All differ in the worship that must be given to the Creator, but all agree on the duties of men toward one another. So each sect worships God in its way, but all sects preach the same morality in the name of God. If it is very useful to a man as an individual that his religion be true, it is not the same for society. Society has nothing either to fear or to hope concerning the other life; and what is most important for society is not so much that all citizens profess the true religion but that they profess a religion. All the sects in the United States are, moreover, within the great Christian unity, and the morality of Christianity is the same everywhere.

You are free to think that a certain number of Americans, in the worship they give to God, follow their habits more than their convictions. In the United States, moreover, the sovereign is religious, and consequently hypocrisy must be common; but America is still the place in the world where the Christian religion has most retained true power over souls; and nothing shows better how useful and natural religion is to man, since the country where today it exercises the most dominion is at the same time the most enlightened and most free.

I said that American priests come down in a general way in favor of civil liberty, without excepting even those who do not allow religious liberty; you do not see them lend their support, however, to any political system in particular. They take care to keep out of public affairs and do not get mixed up in the schemes of the parties. So you cannot say that in the United States religion exercises an influence on laws or on the detail of political opinions, but it directs mores, and it is by regulating the family that it works to regulate the State.

I do not doubt for an instant that the great severity of mores that is noticed in the United States has its primary source in beliefs. Religion there is often powerless to restrain the man amid the innumerable temptations presented by fortune. It cannot moderate in him the ardor to grow rich that comes to goad everyone, but it rules with sovereign power over the soul of the woman, and it is the woman who shapes the mores. America is assuredly the country in the world in which the marriage bond is most respected, and in which the highest and most sound idea of conjugal happiness has been conceived.

In Europe, nearly all of the disorders of society are born around the domestic hearth and not far from the marital bed. That is where men conceive scorn for natural bonds and permitted pleasures, taste for disorder, restlessness of heart, instability of desires. Agitated by the tumultuous passions that have often troubled his own dwelling, the European submits only with difficulty to the legislative powers of the State. When, coming from the agitation of the political world, the American returns to the bosom of his family, he immediately encounters the image of order and peace. There, all his pleasures are simple and natural, his joys innocent and tranquil; and as he achieves happiness by the regularity of life, he easily gets used to regulating his opinions as well as his tastes.

While the European seeks to escape his domestic sorrows by troubling society, the American draws from his home the love of order that he then carries into the affairs of the State.

In the United States, religion regulates not only mores; it extends its dominion even to the mind.

Among the Anglo-Americans, some profess Christian dogmas because they believe them; others, because they fear not appearing to believe them. So Christianity rules without obstacles, with the consent of all; as a result, as I have already said elsewhere, everything is certain and fixed in the moral world, while the political world seems abandoned to discussion and to the experiments of men. Thus the human mind never sees a limitless field before it; whatever its audacity, it feels from time to time that it must stop before insurmountable barriers. Before innovating, it is forced to accept certain primary givens, and to subject its boldest conceptions to certain forms that retard and stop it.

So the imagination of the Americans, in its greatest departures, has only a circumspect and uncertain movement; its ways are hampered and its works incomplete. These habits of restraint are found in political society and singularly favor the tranquility of the people, as well as the continued existence of the institutions that the people have given themselves. Nature and circumstances had made out of the inhabitant of the United States an audacious man; it is easy to judge so when you see how he pursues fortune. If the mind of the Americans were free of all hindrances, you would soon find among them the boldest innovators and the most implacable logicians in the world. But the revolutionaries of America are obliged to profess publicly a certain respect for Christian morality and equity that does not allow them to violate laws easily when the laws are opposed to the execution of their designs; and if they could rise above their scruples, they would still feel checked by the scruples of their partisans. Until now no one has been found in the United States who has dared to advance this maxim: that everything is allowed in the interest of society. Impious maxim, that seems to have been invented in a century of liberty in order to legitimate all the tyrants to come.

Therefore, at the same time that the law allows the American people to do everything, religion prevents them from conceiving of everything and forbids them to dare everything.

So religion, which among the Americans never directly takes part in the government of society, must be considered as the first of their political institutions; for if it does not give them the taste for liberty, it singularly facilitates their use of it.

It is also from this point of view that the inhabitants of the United States themselves consider religious beliefs. I do not know if all Americans have faith in their religion, for who can read the recesses of the heart? But I am sure that they believe it necessary for maintaining republican institutions. This opinion does not belong to one class of citizens or to one party, but to the whole nation; you find it among all ranks.

In the United States, when a politician attacks a sect, it is not a reason for even the partisans of that sect not to support him; but if he attacks all sects together, each one flees from him, and he remains alone.

While I was in America, a witness appeared before the assizes of the county of Chester (State of New York) and declared that he did not believe in the existence of God and in the immortality of the soul. The presiding judge refused to admit his oath, given, he said, that the witness had destroyed in advance any faith that could be given to his words. The newspapers reported the fact without comment.

Americans mix Christianity and liberty so completely in their mind that it is nearly impossible to make them conceive one without the other; and, among them, this is not one of those sterile beliefs that the past bequeaths to the present and that seem more to vegetate deep in the soul than to live.

I have seen Americans join together to send priests into the new states of the West and to found schools and churches there; they are afraid that religion may come to be lost in the middle of the woods, and that the people who are arising there may not be as free as those from whom they came. I met rich inhabitants of New England who abandoned the country of their birth with the goal of going to lay the foundations of Christianity and liberty on the banks of the Missouri or on the prairies of Illinois. This is how religious zeal in the United States constantly warms up at the hearth of patriotism. You think that these men act uniquely in consideration of the other life, but you are mistaken: eternity is only one of their concerns. If you question these missionaries of Christian civilization, you will be very surprised to hear them speak so often about the good things of this world and to find politicians where you thought to see only men of religion. "All the American republics stand together one with the others, they will say to you; if the republics of the West fell into anarchy or submitted to the yoke of despotism, the republican institutions that flourish on the shores of the Atlantic Ocean would be in great peril; so we have an interest that these new states are religious, in order that they allow us to remain free."

Such are the opinions of the Americans; but their error is clear. For each day someone proves to me very learnedly that everything is good in America, except precisely this religious spirit that I admire; and I learn that the only thing missing from the liberty and happiness of the human species, on the other side of the Ocean, is to believe with Spinoza in the eternity of the world, and to uphold with Cabanis that the brain secretes thought. To that I have nothing to reply, in truth, if not that those who use this language have not been to America, and have not seen religious peoples any more than free peoples. So I will await their return.

For me, if something could make me despair of the destiny of Europe, it is to see the strange confusion that reigns there in minds. I see pious men who would like to suffocate liberty, as if liberty, this great privilege of man, was not a nearly holy thing. Further along, I see others who think to arrive at being free by attacking all beliefs, but I do not see any who seem to notice the tight and necessary knot that ties religion to liberty.

There are men in France who consider republican institutions as the temporary instrument of their grandeur. They measure with their eyes the immense gap that separates their vices and their miseries from power and riches, and they would like to pile up ruins in this abyss in order to try to fill it. These men are to liberty what the free companies of the Middle Ages were to kings; they make war on their own behalf even when they wear his colors; the republic will always live long enough to pull them out of their present low position. I am not speaking to them. But there are others who see in the republic a permanent and tranquil state, a necessary end toward which ideas and mores lead modern societies each day, and who would sincerely like to prepare men to be free. When these men attack religious beliefs, they follow their passions and not their interests. Despotism can do without faith, but not liberty. Religion is much more necessary in the republic that they advocate than in the monarchy that they attack, and in democratic republics more than in all others. How could society fail to perish if, while the political bond grows loose, the moral bond does not become tighter? And what to do with a people master of itself, if it is not subject to God?

Of the Principal Causes That Make Religion Powerful in America

The philosophers of the 18th century explained the gradual weakening of beliefs in a very simple way. Religious zeal, they said, must fade as liberty and enlightenment increase. It is unfortunate that facts do not agree with this theory.

There is such a European population whose disbelief is equaled only by its brutishness and ignorance, while in America you see one of the most free and most enlightened peoples in the world fulfill with ardor all the external duties of religion.

When I arrived in the United States, it was the religious aspect of the country that first struck my eyes. As I prolonged my journey, I noticed the great political consequences that flowed from these new facts.

I had seen among us the spirit of religion and the spirit of liberty march almost always in opposite directions. Here, I found them intimately joined the one to the other: they reigned together over the same soil.

Each day I felt my desire to know the cause of this phenomenon increase.

To find it out, I asked the faithful of all communions; I sought, above all, the company of priests who are the keepers of the different faiths and who have a personal interest in their continued existence. The religion I profess brought me particularly close to the Catholic clergy, and I did not delay in striking up a sort of intimacy with several of its members. To each of them I expressed my astonishment and revealed my doubts. I found that all of these men differed among themselves only on the details; but all attributed the peaceful dominion that religion exercises in their country principally to the complete separation of Church and State. I am not afraid to assert that, during my visit in America, I did not meet a single man, priest or layman, who did not agree on this point.

This led me to examine more attentively than I had done until then the position that American priests occupy in political society. I realized with surprise that they fill no public position. I did not see a single one of them in the administration, and I discovered that they were not even represented within the assemblies.

This further goes to attribute towards the seperation of church & state.

The law, in several states, had closed a political career to them; opinion, in all the others.

When finally I found out what the mind of the clergy itself was, I noticed that most of its members seemed to remove themselves voluntarily from power, and to take a kind of professional pride in remaining apart from it.

I heard them anathematize ambition and bad faith, whatever the political opinions that ambition and bad faith carefully used to cover themselves. But I learned, by listening to them, that men cannot be blameworthy in the eyes of God because of these very opinions, when the opinions are sincere, and that there is no more sin in being wrong in matters of government than in being mistaken about the way in which your dwelling must be built or your furrow must be plowed.

I saw them separate themselves with care from all parties, and flee contact with all the ardor of personal interest.

These facts succeeded in proving to me that I had been told the truth. Then I wanted to go back from facts to causes. I asked myself how it could happen that by diminishing the apparent strength of a religion, you came to increase its true power, and I believed that it was not impossible to find out.

Never will the short space of sixty years enclose all of the imagination of man; the incomplete joys of this world will never be enough for his heart. Among all beings, man alone shows a natural distaste for existence and an immense desire to exist: he scorns life and fears nothingness. These different instincts constantly push his soul toward the contemplation of another world, and it is religion that leads him there. So religion is only a particular form of hope, and it is as natural to the human heart as hope itself. It is by a type of mental aberration and with the help of a kind of moral violence exercised over their own nature, that men remove themselves from religious beliefs; an irresistible inclination brings them back to beliefs. Unbelief is an accident; faith alone is the permanent state of humanity.

So by considering religion only from a human viewpoint, you can say that all religions draw from man himself an element of strength that they can never lack, because it is due to one of the constituent principles of human nature.

I know that there are times when religion can add to this influence, which is its own, the artificial power of laws and the support of the physical powers that lead society. We have seen religions, intimately united with the governments of the earth, dominate souls by terror and by faith at the same time; but when a religion contracts such an alliance, I am not afraid to say, it acts as a man could: it sacrifices the future with the present in mind, and by obtaining a power that is not its due, it puts its legitimate power at risk.

When a religion seeks to found its dominion only on the desire for immortality that equally torments the hearts of all men, it can aim for universality; but when it comes to unite with a government, it must adopt maxims that are applicable only to certain peoples. Therefore, by allying itself to a political power, religion increases its power over some and loses the hope of reigning over all.

As long as a religion relies only on the sentiments that console all miseries, it can attract the heart of the human species. Mingled with the bitter passions of this world, religion is sometimes constrained to defend allies that have offered interest rather than love; and it must reject as adversaries men who often still love it, even as they fight those men with whom religion is united. So religion cannot share the material strength of those who govern without burdening itself with a portion of the hatreds caused by those who govern.

The political powers that appear most established have as a guarantee of their continued existence only the opinions of a generation, the interests of a century, often the life of a man. A law can modify the social state that seems most definitive and most firm, and with it everything changes.

The powers of society are all more or less fleeting, just as our years upon the earth; they rapidly follow one another, like the various cares of life; and you have never seen a government that relied on an invariable disposition of the human heart and that was able to base itself on an immortal interest.

As long as a religion finds its strength in the sentiments, the instincts, the passions that are reproduced in the same way in all periods of history, it defies the effort of time, or at least it can be destroyed only by another religion. Political powers can do nothing against it. But when religion wants to rely on the interests of this world, it becomes almost as fragile as all the powers of the earth. Alone, religion can hope for immortality; tied to ephemeral powers, it follows their fortune, and often falls with the passions of the day that sustain those powers.

So by uniting with different political powers, religion can only contract an onerous alliance. It does not need their help to live, and by serving them it can die.

The danger that I have just pointed out exists at all times, but it is not always as visible.

There are centuries when governments appear immortal, and others when you would say that the existence of society is more fragile than that of a man.

Certain constitutions keep citizens in a sort of lethargic sleep, and others deliver them to a feverish agitation.

When governments seem so strong and laws so stable, men do not notice the danger that religion can run by uniting with power.

When governments prove to be so weak and laws so changeable, the peril strikes all eyes, but then there is often no more time to escape. So you must learn to see it from afar.

To the extent that a nation assumes a democratic social state and you see societies lean toward the republic, it becomes more and more dangerous to unite religion with authority; for the time is coming when power will pass from hand to hand, when political theories will succeed one another, when men, laws, constitutions themselves will disappear or change each day, and not for a time, but constantly. Agitation and instability stem from the nature of democratic republics, as immobility and sleep form the law of absolute monarchies.

If the Americans, who change the head of State every four years, who every two years choose new legislators, and replace provincial administrators every year; if the Americans, who have delivered the political world to the experiments of innovators, had not placed their religion somewhere outside of the political world, to what could they cling in the ebb and flow of human opinions? Amid the struggle of parties, where would the respect be that religion is due? What would become of its immortality when everything perishes around it?

American priests have seen this truth before anyone else, and they model their conduct on it. They have seen that religious influence had to be renounced, if they wanted to acquire a political power, and they preferred to lose the support of power than to share its vicissitudes.

In America, religion is perhaps less powerful than it has been in certain times and among certain peoples, but its influence is more durable. It has reduced itself to its own forces that no one can take away from it; it acts only within a single circle, but it covers it entirely and predominates within it without effort.

In Europe I hear voices that are raised on all sides; people deplore the absence of beliefs and ask how to give religion something of its former power.

It seems to me that we must first try attentively to find out what should be, today, the *natural state* of men in matters of religion. Then, knowing what we are able to hope and what we have to fear, we will see clearly the goal toward which our efforts must tend.

Two great dangers menace the existence of religions: schisms and indifference.

During centuries of fervor, men sometimes happen to abandon their religion, but they escape its yoke only to submit to the yoke of another religion. Faith changes objects; it does not die. The old religion then excites fervent love or implacable hatred in all hearts; some leave it with anger, others follow it with a new ardor: beliefs differ, irreligion is unknown.

But it is not the same when a religious belief is silently undermined by doctrines that I will call negative, because while asserting the falsity of one religion they establish the truth of no other.

Then prodigious revolutions take place in the human spirit, without man seeming to aid the revolutions with his passions and without suspecting them, so to speak. You see men who allow, as if by forgetfulness, the object of their most cherished hopes to escape. Carried along by an imperceptible current against which they do not have the courage to struggle, but to which they yield with regret, they abandon the faith that they love to follow the doubt that leads them to despair.

During the centuries that we have just described, you abandon your beliefs by coldness rather than by hatred; you do not reject them, they leave you. While ceasing to believe religion true, the unbeliever continues to judge it useful. Considering religious beliefs from a human aspect, he recognizes their dominion over mores, their influence over laws. He understands how they can make men live in peace and gently prepare men for death. So he regrets faith after losing it, and deprived of a good of which he knows the whole value, he is afraid to take it away from those who still possess it.

From his side, the one who continues to believe is not afraid to reveal his faith to all eyes. In those who do not share his hopes, he sees unfortunate men rather than adversaries; he knows that he can gain their esteem without following their example; so he is at war with no one; and not considering the society in which he lives as an arena in which religion must struggle constantly against a thousand fierce enemies, he loves his contemporaries at the same time that he condemns their weaknesses and is distressed by their errors.

Those who do not believe, hiding their unbelief, and those who do believe, showing their faith, create a public opinion in favor of religion; it is loved, it is upheld, it is honored, and you must penetrate to the recesses of souls to discover the wounds that it has received.

The mass of men, whom religious sentiment never abandons, then see nothing that separates them from established beliefs. The instinct of another life leads them without difficulty to the foot of altars and delivers their hearts to the precepts and consolations of faith.

Why does this picture not apply to us?

I notice among us men who have ceased to believe in Christianity without adhering to any religion.

I see others who have halted at doubt, and already pretend to believe no more.

Further along, I meet Christians who still believe and dare not say so.

Amid these lukewarm friends and fiery adversaries, I finally discover a small number of the faithful ready to defy all obstacles and to scorn all dangers for their beliefs. The latter have acted contrary to human weakness in order to rise above common opinion. Carried away by this very effort, they no longer know precisely where they should stop. Since they have seen that, in their country, the first use that man made of independence has been to attack religion, they fear their contemporaries and withdraw with terror from the liberty that the former pursue. Since unbelief appears to them as something new, they include in the same hatred everything that is new. So they are at war with their century and their country, and in each of the opinions that are professed there they see a necessary enemy of faith.

Such should not be today the natural state of man in matters of religion.

An accidental and particular cause is found among us that prevents the human spirit from following its inclination and pushes it beyond the limits at which it should naturally stop.

I am profoundly persuaded that this particular and accidental cause is the intimate union of politics and religion.

Unbelievers in Europe pursue Christians as political enemies, rather than as religious adversaries; they hate faith as the opinion of a party much more than as a mistaken belief; and in the priest they reject the representative of God less than the friend of power.

In Europe, Christianity allowed itself to be intimately united with the powers of the earth. Today these powers are falling and Christianity is as though buried beneath their debris. It is a living thing that someone wanted to bind to the dead: cut the ties that hold it and it will rise again.

I do not know what must be done to give Christianity in Europe the energy of youth. God alone would be able to do so; but at least it depends on men to leave to faith the use of all of the forces that it still retains.

DEMOCRACY IN AMERICA, VOLUME II, PART 2, CHAPTER 15: "HOW FROM TIME TO TIME RELIGIOUS BELIEFS DIVERT THE SOUL OF THE AMERICANS TOWARD NON-MATERIAL ENJOYMENTS"

In the United States, when the seventh day of each week arrives, commercial and industrial life seems suspended; all noise ceases. A profound rest, or rather a kind of solemn recollection follows; the soul, finally, regains self-possession and contemplates itself.

During this day, the places consecrated to commerce and industry are deserted; each citizen, surrounded by his children, goes to church; there strange discourses are held forth that do not seem much made for his ears. He hears about the innumerable evils caused by pride and covetousness. He is told about the necessity to control his desires, about the fine enjoyments attached to virtue alone, and about the true happiness that accompanies it.

Back at home, you do not see him run to his business ledgers. He opens the book of the Holy Scriptures; there he finds sublime or touching portrayals of the grandeur and the goodness of the Creator, of the infinite magnificence of the works of God, of the elevated destiny reserved for men, of their duties and their rights to immortality.

This is how, from time to time, the American escapes in a way from himself, and how, tearing himself away for a moment from the petty passions that agitate his life and from the transitory interests that fill it, he enters suddenly into an ideal world where everything is great, pure, eternal.

In another place in this work, I looked for the causes to which the maintenance of political institutions in America had to be attributed, and religion seemed to me one of the principal ones. Today, when I am concerned with individuals, I find religion again and notice that it is no less useful to each citizen than to the whole State.

The Americans show, by their practice, that they feel the entire necessity of moralizing democracy by religion. What they think in this regard about themselves is a truth that must penetrate every democratic nation.

I do not doubt that the social and political constitution of a people disposes them to certain beliefs and to certain tastes in which they easily abound afterward; while these same causes turn them away from certain opinions and certain tendencies without their working at it themselves, and so to speak without their suspecting it.

All the art of the legislator consists in clearly discerning in advance these natural inclinations of human societies, in order to know where the effort of the citizens must be aided, and where it would instead be necessary to slow it down. For these obligations differ according to the times. Only the end toward which humanity must always head is unchanging; the means to reach that end constantly vary.

There are vices or erroneous opinions that can only be established among a people by struggling against the general current of society. These are not to be feared; they must be considered as unfortunate accidents. But there are others that, having a natural rapport with the very constitution of the people, develop by themselves and effortlessly among the people. Those, however small they may be at their beginning and however rare they seem, deserve to attract the great care of the legislator.

If I were born in an aristocratic century, amid a nation in which the hereditary wealth of some and the irremediable poverty of others diverted men from the idea of the better and, as well, held souls as if benumbed in the contemplation of another world, I would want it to be possible for me to stimulate among such a people the sentiment of needs; I would think about finding more rapid and easier means to satisfy the new desires that I would have brought about, and, diverting the greatest efforts of the human mind toward physical study, I would try to excite the human mind in the pursuit of well-being.

If it happened that some men caught fire thoughtlessly in the pursuit of wealth and exhibited an excessive love for material enjoyments, I would not become alarmed; these particular traits would soon disappear in the common physiognomy.

Legislators of democracies have other concerns.

Give democratic peoples enlightenment and liberty and leave them alone. They will easily succeed in drawing from this world all the material goods that it can offer; they will perfect each one of the useful arts and daily make life more comfortable, easier, sweeter; their social state pushes them naturally in this direction. I am not afraid that they will stop.

But while man takes pleasure in this honest and legitimate pursuit of well-being, it is to be feared that in the end he may lose the use of his most sublime faculties, and that by wanting to improve everything around him, he may in the end degrade himself. The danger is there and nowhere else.

So legislators in democracies and all honest and enlightened men who live in democracies must apply themselves without respite to lifting up souls and keeping them pointed toward heaven. It is necessary that all those who are interested in the future of democratic societies unite, and that all in concert make continual efforts to spread within these societies the taste for the infinite, the sentiment for the grand and the love for non-material pleasures.

If among the opinions of a democratic people there exist a few of these harmful theories that tend to make you believe that everything perishes with the body, consider the men who profess them as the natural enemies of the people.

There are many things that offend me in the materialists. Their doctrines seem pernicious to me, and their pride revolts me. If their system could be of some use to man, it seems that it would be in giving him a modest idea of himself. But they do not show that this is so; and when they believe that they have sufficiently established that men are only brutes, they appear as proud as if they had demonstrated that men were gods.

Materialism is, among all nations, a dangerous sickness of the human mind; but it must be particularly feared among a democratic people, because it combines marvelously with the vice of the heart most familiar to these people.

Democracy favors the taste for material enjoyments. This taste, if it becomes excessive, soon disposes men to believe that everything is only matter; and materialism, in turn, finally carries them with an insane fervor toward these same enjoyments. Such is the fatal circle into which democratic nations are pushed. It is good that they see the danger and restrain themselves.

Most religions are only general, simple and practical means to teach men the immortality of the soul. That is the greatest advantage that a democratic people draws from belief, and what makes these beliefs more necessary for such a people than for all others.

So when no matter which religion has put down deep roots within a democracy, be careful about weakening it; but instead protect it carefully as the most precious heritage of aristocratic centuries; do not try to tear men away from their ancient religious opinions in order to substitute new ones, for fear that, during the transition from one faith to another, when the soul finds itself for one moment devoid of beliefs, love of material enjoyments comes to spread and fill the soul entirely.

I do not believe that all religions are equally true and equally good, but I think that there is none so false or so bad that it would not still be advantageous for a democratic people to profess.

Assuredly, metempsychosis is not more reasonable than materialism; but if it were absolutely necessary for a democracy to make a choice between the two, I would not hesitate, and I would judge that its citizens risk becoming brutalized less by thinking that their soul is going to pass into the body of a pig than by believing that it is nothing.

The belief in a non-material and immortal principle, united for a time to matter, is so necessary for the grandeur of man, that it still produces beautiful effects even when you do not join the opinion of rewards and punishments with it and when you limit yourself to believing that after death the divine principle contained in man is absorbed in God or goes to animate another creature.

Even the latter consider the body as the secondary and inferior portion of our nature; and they scorn it even when they undergo its influence; while they have a natural esteem and secret admiration for the non-material part of man, even though they sometimes refuse to submit themselves to its dominion. This is enough to give a certain elevated turn to their ideas and their tastes, and to make them tend without interest, and as if on their own, toward pure sentiments and great thoughts.

It is not certain that Socrates and his school had well-fixed opinions on what must happen to man in the other life; but the sole belief on which they were settled, that the soul has nothing in common with the body and survives it, was enough to give to platonic philosophy the sort of sublime impulse that distinguishes it.

When you read Plato, you notice that in the times prior to him and in his time, many writers existed who advocated materialism. These writers have not survived to our time or have survived only very incompletely. It has been so in nearly all the centuries; most of the great literary reputations are joined with spiritualism. The instinct and the taste of humanity uphold this doctrine; they often save this doctrine despite the men themselves and make the names of those who are attached to it linger on. So it must not be believed that in any time, and in whatever political state, the passion for material enjoyments and the opinions that are linked with it will be able to suffice for an entire people. The heart of man is more vast than you suppose; it can at the same time enclose the taste for the good things of the earth and the love of the good things of heaven; sometimes the heart seems to give itself madly to one of the two; but it never goes for a long time without thinking of the other.

If it is easy to see that, particularly in times of democracy, it is important to make spiritual opinions reign, it is not easy to say what those who govern democratic peoples must do for those opinions to reign.

I do not believe in the prosperity any more than in the duration of official philosophies, and as for State religions, I have always thought that if sometimes they could temporarily serve the interests of political power, they always sooner or later become fatal to the Church.

Nor am I one of those who judge that in order to raise religion in the eyes of the people, and to honor the spiritualism that religion professes, it is good to grant indirectly to its ministers a political influence that the law refuses to them.

I feel so convinced of the nearly inevitable dangers that beliefs run when their interpreters mingle in public affairs, and I am so persuaded that Christianity must at all cost be maintained within the new democracies, that I would prefer to chain priests within the sanctuary than to allow them out of it.

So what means remain for authority to lead men back toward spiritualistic opinions or keep them in the religion that suggests these opinions?

What I am going to say is going to do me harm in the eyes of politicians. I believe that the only effective means that governments can use to honor the dogma of the immortality of the soul is to act each day as if they believed it themselves; and I think that it is only by conforming scrupulously to religious morality in great affairs that they can claim to teach citizens to know, love and respect religious morality in little affairs.

DEMOCRACY IN AMERICA, VOLUME II, PART 1, CHAPTER 5: "HOW, IN THE UNITED STATES, RELIGION KNOWS HOW TO MAKE USE OF DEMOCRATIC INSTINCTS"

I established in one of the preceding chapters that men cannot do without dogmatic beliefs, and that it was even much to be desired that they had such beliefs. I add here that, among all dogmatic beliefs, the most desirable seem to me to be dogmatic beliefs in the matter of religion; that very clearly follows, even if you want to pay attention only to the interests of this world alone.

There is hardly any human action, no matter how particular you assume it to be, that is not born out of a very general idea that men have conceived of God, of God's relationships with humanity, of the nature of their soul and of their duties toward their fellows. You cannot keep these ideas from being the common source from which all the rest flows.

So men have an immense interest in forming very fixed ideas about God, their soul, their general duties toward their creator and toward their fellows; for doubt about these first points would leave all their actions to chance and would condemn them in a way to disorder and impotence.

So this matter is the one about which it is most important for each one of us to have fixed ideas, and unfortunately it is also the one on which it is most difficult for each person, left to himself and by the sole effort of his reason, to come to fix his ideas.

Only minds very emancipated from the ordinary preoccupations of life, very perceptive, very subtle, very practiced are able with the help of a great deal of time and care to break through to such necessary truths.

Yet we see that these philosophers themselves are almost always surrounded by uncertainties; at each step the natural light that illumines them grows dark and threatens to go out, and despite all their efforts they still have been able to discover only a small number of contradictory notions, in the middle of which the human mind has drifted constantly for thousands of years, unable to grasp the truth firmly or even to find new errors. Such studies are far beyond the average capacity of men, and, even if most men were capable of devoting themselves to such studies, it is clear that they would not have the leisure to do so.

Fixed ideas about God and human nature are indispensable for the daily practice of their life, and this practice prevents them from being able to acquire those ideas.

That seems unique to me. Among the sciences, there are some, useful to the crowd, that are within its grasp; others are only accessible to a few persons and are not cultivated by the majority, which needs only the most remote of their applications. But the daily practice of this science is indispensable to all, even though its study is inaccessible to the greatest number.

General ideas relative to God and to human nature are, therefore, among all ideas, those most suitable to remove from the habitual action of individual reason, and for which there is the most to gain and the least to lose by recognizing an authority.

The first object, and one of the principal advantages of religions, is to provide for each of these primordial questions a clear, precise answer, intelligible to the crowd and very enduring.

There are very false and very absurd religions. You can say however that every religion that remains within the circle that I have just pointed out and that does not claim to go outside of it, as several have tried to do in order to stop the free development of the human mind in all directions, imposes a salutary yoke on the intellect; and it must be recognized that, if religion does not save men in the other world, it is at least very useful to their happiness and to their grandeur in this one.

This is above all true of men who live in free countries.

When religion is destroyed among a people, doubt takes hold of the highest portions of the intellect and half paralyzes all the others. Each person gets accustomed to having only confused and changing notions about the matters that most interest his fellows and himself. You defend your opinions badly or you abandon them, and, since you despair of being able, by yourself, to solve the greatest problems that human destiny presents, you are reduced like a coward to not thinking about them.

Such a state cannot fail to enervate souls; it slackens the motivating forces of will and prepares citizens for servitude.

Then not only does it happen that the latter allow their liberty to be taken, but they often give it up.

When authority no longer exists in religious matters, any more than in political matters, men are soon frightened by the sight of this limitless independence. This perpetual agitation of all things disturbs and exhausts them. Since everything shifts in the intellectual world, they at least want everything to be firm and stable in the material order, and, no longer able to recapture their ancient beliefs, they give themselves a master.

For me, I doubt that man can ever bear complete religious independence and full political liberty at the same time; and I am led to think that, if he does not have faith, he must serve, and, if he is free, he must believe.

I do not know, however, if this great utility of religions is not still more visible among peoples where conditions are equal, than among all others.

It must be recognized that equality, which introduces great advantages into the world, nevertheless suggests, as will be shown below, very dangerous instincts to men; it tends to isolate them from one another and to lead each one of them to be interested only in himself alone.

It opens their souls excessively to love of material enjoyments.

The greatest advantage of religions is to inspire entirely opposite instincts. There is no religion that does not place the object of the desires of men above and beyond the good things of the earth, and that does not naturally elevate his soul toward realms very superior to those of the senses. Nor is there any religion that does not impose on each man some duties toward the human species or in common with it, and that does not in this way drag him, from time to time, out of contemplation of himself. This is found in the most false and most dangerous religions.

So religious peoples are naturally strong precisely in the places where democratic peoples are weak; this makes very clear how important it is for men to keep their religion while becoming equal.

SUGGESTED ADDITIONAL READINGS (Freely Available Online)

Thomas Jefferson, *Notes on Virginia*, "Religion" (http://xroads.virginia.edu/~Hyper/JEFFERSON/ch17.html)

George Washington, Farewell Address (http://teachingamericanhistory.org/library/document/farewell-address/)

Everson v. Board of Education (http://www.law.cornell.edu/supremecourt/text/330/1)

US Conference of Catholic Bishops, "Our First, Most Cherished Liberty" (http://www.usccb.org/issues-and-action/religious-liberty/our-first-most-cherished-liberty.cfm)

ON RELIGIOUS LIBERTY AND ITS SPECIAL STATUS IN AMERICAN LIFE

Wilfred M. McClay

The status of religious liberty seems fated to be one of the central issues of the twenty-first century. This is self-evidently the case in the international arena, where many of the world's bloodiest and most intractable conflicts involve believers of various stripes and the nations, communities, tribes, and enclaves within which their respective faiths are rooted. Such conflicts are taking a particularly heavy toll upon vulnerable religious and ethnic minorities. In Europe, the ability of orthodox Jews to practice their time-honored rite of male circumcision (*brit milah*, or *bris*) has come up against intense legal and political pressure in ways that suggest such strictures may be the entering wedge of a more comprehensive anti-Jewish sentiment, the return of the repressed. In Iraq, Syria, and Egypt, long-established Christian communities that have existed for a thousand or more years are suddenly faced with the prospect of brutal, willful extinction at the hands of Islamist militants. In India, the enduring and often violent enmities between Hindus and Muslims, and the vulnerable status of the latter group, have only been rendered more volatile and dangerous by the political rise of strident Hindu nationalism. In countries such as Turkey and Saudi Arabia, the very idea of official recognition for religious liberty and religious pluralism seems inconceivable. Meanwhile, in some parts of the West, the preaching of traditional Christian moral teachings about human sexuality has been labeled a human rights violation and proscribed by courts.

One could go on at considerable length and cite other examples, but the general pattern is clear. The kind of respectful tolerance needed to underwrite the free, robust, and uncoerced expression of religious belief is becoming a rarer thing in the world. In some places the cause of the trouble is militant religion, in other places aggressive irreligion. Caught between the postreligious secularism of a receding Europe and the virulent sectarianism of much of the rest of the world, the generous ideal of religious freedom, with its emphasis upon the integrity of the individual human conscience, finds itself vulnerable if not altogether abandoned.

Such, though, has been the case for most of human history, which is why the achievement of a high degree of religious liberty in the United States has always been such a cause for celebration and gratitude. Religious liberty is a fragile and exceedingly difficult idea in both theory and practice because it holds in tension two conflicting ideals: the right to order one's life according to the truth as one understands it and the obligation to tolerate those who understand things differently and order their lives differently. It is sometimes thought religious liberty can flourish only where the truth claims of religion are regarded as relatively weak and secondary, and the stakes are correspondingly lowered. In America, however, as Alexis de Tocqueville was among the first to observe, religious belief and practice have generally flourished, in remarkably diverse and inventive forms, precisely because it has not had to rely on the coercions of religious establishment to protect it. Although the American record regarding religious liberty has been far from perfect—the tale includes many exceptions to the general rule, as in the painful experience of Quakers, Catholics, Mormons, Jews, and other religious minorities—the story has on the whole been positive and inspiring, and moreover has unfolded over time as a story of steady expansion and improvement.

It has, however, been a complex, dialectical, and often paradoxical process and has not unfolded neatly or predictably. A reading of John Winthrop's 1630 lay sermon "A Model of Christian Charity," which laid down the social, political, and moral template for Puritan New England, shows how profoundly a deeply Christian and intensely communitarian ethos informed the origins of American life. Although Winthrop's brand of religion did not prevail, it remains the case that for much of the country's history, there was an *informal* establishment of religion, a form of generic Protestant Christianity, that both shaped and delimited the characteristics of American religious liberty.

However, that informal establishment has lost much (though perhaps not all) of its hold over the course of the past century. Beginning in the 1940s, Supreme Court jurisprudence began making greater use of the so-called establishment clause of the Constitution's First Amendment. That clause was initially designed mainly to proscribe the establishment of an Anglican-style church of the United States. But more recently it has been construed to place ever-more-demanding limits on the role of all religion and religious institutions in public life, in ways that have seemed to many observers to ignore or downplay the First Amendment's corresponding and coequal free exercise clause.

The results of this development admit of more than one interpretation. One can plausibly argue that the effect of even such controversial Supreme Court rulings as the 1962 *Engel v. Vitale* decision (which forbade as unconstitutional the use of government-prescribed prayers in public schools) was to enhance rather than diminish religious liberty precisely by diminishing the coercive power of the informal establishment. However, the same developments could also be plausibly interpreted as a movement in the direction of secularism, that is, in the direction of a public life that banishes religious expression altogether and thus marginalizes the principle of free exercise. By the 1980s, in the wake of such still-controversial Court decisions as *Roe v. Wade* (which outraged Catholics and other religious conservatives by enshrining abortion as a privacy right and striking down state laws outlawing it), it began to seem to many observers that the nation was being steered, against its will, precisely toward a religion-free public life: a "naked public square," in the resounding words of Richard John Neuhaus, that would be contrary both to the nation's historical commitments and to its current needs as a pluralistic and heavily religious society.

In this view, the health of American democratic institutions depends as much on the free and vibrant public presence of the nation's religious traditions, and their values-forming influence, as it does on the constraints placed on religions' ability to exercise direct political power or operate as an establishment. Both influences, both forces, are needed, and a healthy balance between them needs to be achieved. Theocracy of any kind violates the principle of religious liberty, but so does the naked public square, a version of public life in which meaningful public religious expression has been completely proscribed. Such a state of affairs would traduce the cause of energetic pluralism by erecting a counterestablishment of public secularism to which every knee must bend, and in the face of which every alternative faith must withdraw into the realm of private predilection. The better way, the achievement of a *civil* public square, would strike the right equilibrium between a healthy and inclusive national ethos and healthy values-forming mediating institutions. In short, Neuhaus argued our choices should not be restricted to either the complete privatization of religion on the one hand or the complete integration of church and state on the other. The separation of church and state is a sound principle, but only if applied in moderation. It is not, and cannot be, absolute, he believed, and it does not, and cannot, require the segregation of religion from public life.

This view seemed triumphant in the ethos of the latter 1980s and 1990s, years far more favorable to the public expression of religion than those that had preceded them. The world-historical importance of the pontificate of John Paul II in the overcoming of Soviet communism surely had something to do with that development, but there were strictly political indices as well. The Bill Clinton administration, along with near unanimity from Democrats and Republicans in Congress, supported the wildly popular Religious Freedom Restoration Act of 1993, a corrective to the 1990 Supreme Court decision in *Employment Division v. Smith*, which had been perceived to be an overstepping move. President Clinton's welfare-reform measures included the principle of "charitable choice," which established a level playing field for faith-based organizations seeking government contracts for the provision of social-welfare programs. No longer would Christian drug-abuse counselors, for example, be denied the right to compete for government contracts, notwithstanding their proven effectiveness in doing the job, simply on account of their religious affiliation.

This balance lasted well into the administration of George W. Bush, who enthusiastically endorsed and expanded what Clinton had begun, establishing an Office of Faith-Based and Community Initiatives in the White House and showing a strikingly religion-friendly disposition in his speeches and policy making. There was every reason to believe Barack Obama would continue in that vein, if one were to base one's belief on his words and conduct during the 2008 presidential campaign, which indicated a serious engagement with religion and a striking deference to people of faith, and in which he openly reached out to evangelical groups such as Sojourners and Call to Renewal.

That expectation was not, however, to be borne out in Obama's presidency. Indeed, his administration has seemed to disrupt the era of balance and to initiate a push toward official secularism that is striking and perhaps unprecedented in its scope and force. As a consequence, the administration has been subjected to strenuous criticism for its perceived hostility, or at best cavalier indifference, to the cause of religious freedom in the United States.

A few examples will have to suffice. One early indication of where things would be going was the president's and his administration's subtle but unmistakable shift toward expressing their commitment to religious liberty in the language of "freedom of worship," a much more restricted right than "freedom of religion," one that serves to narrow religious freedom to include only the protection of a discrete private activity rather than as an all-embracing way of life for its adherents, with both private and public ramifications.

The legal strategy behind this shift of language became evident in the 2012 *Hosanna-Tabor* case, in which government lawyers had sought to deny that a "ministerial exemption" from broad antidiscrimination employment laws could be applied to the staffing of church-run schools, arguing instead that the ministerial exemption should be applied narrowly to ordained clergy employed in worship-related activity. The Supreme Court emphatically dismissed this argument, seeing it as an unacceptable infringement upon religious liberty, and rejected the government's case with nine-to-zero unanimity. Less clear-cut has been the series of still-simmering cases regarding Obama's signature health-care law, the Patient Protection and Affordable Care Act, and in particular the Department of Health and Human Services (HHS) mandate (not itself part of the legislation but the result of an administrative prerogative afforded by the law) that would require all employers including church-run schools, hospitals, and charities to provide their employees health-insurance plans covering contraceptives, abortifacients, and sterilization procedures—a requirement that would necessitate, particularly for the Roman Catholic Church, the violation of some of its core moral teachings. These cases have not all run their course at the time of this writing, but the *Hobby Lobby* decision rendered by the Court in 2014, in which a family-owned corporation was accorded the right to decline to provide its employees certain forms of insurance coverage mandated by the HHS, specifically coverage for abortifacient forms of contraception, made it clear that only a razor-thin majority on the Court was willing to protect the more expansive understanding of religious liberty as applied to business owners.

The HHS mandate was immediately polarizing, and opposition to it was swift and unequivocal. It produced an unprecedented degree of unity among the often fractious American Catholic bishops—who were, ironically, among the biggest supporters of health-care reform along the lines of the ACA—and quickly brought into being a remarkably ecumenical coalition embracing a broad array of evangelical leaders, such as the president of Wheaton College as well as eminent figures from across the full spectrum of American religious communities: Jews, Muslims, Mormons, Sikhs, and so on. Everywhere the rallying cry was directed not to the support of specific Catholic doctrines regarding reproduction and contraception but to the general defense of religious freedom and the right of men and women of faith to shape for themselves and their children a way of life that accorded with the dictates of their religiously formed consciences.

Secular supporters of the Obama administration were equally vehement in their disagreement and seemed both annoyed and mystified by the protests. How, wondered Ed Kilgore, writing in the *Washington Monthly*, did "religious freedom" ever come to mean the "right to have one's particular religious views explicitly reflected in public policy"? What gives Catholic bishops the right to "contend they should be able to operate a wide range of quasi-public services and also enjoy the use of public subsidies, while refusing to comply with laws and regulations that contradict their religious or moral teachings"? Were they not in fact seeking a "sort of unwritten concordat—a broad zone of immunity from laws they choose to regard as offensive"? Were they not seeking "special privileges"?[1]

Kilgore raised important questions that deserve a thoughtful and respectful response. Religious believers need to prepare themselves to hear such questions asked again and again in the years to come and to contemplate how they will answer them. For beneath the controversy about religious liberty is a deeper controversy about the nature and status of religion itself in the American legal and political order. Is religion no different from any other form of personal predilection, to be protected (if at all) only insofar as it is understood as a private right?

That controversy is nothing new, of course. It runs through much of American history, taking on different guises and embracing different antagonists and issues at different times. It figures, for example, in the controversy in early Virginia about the use of public funds to support religious institutions, a debate in which the revolutionary patriot Patrick Henry, who favored such assessments, found himself pitted against James Madison, who vehemently opposed them and whose "Memorial and Remonstrance against Religious Assessments" would subsequently become one of the most important documents of religious freedom in American history.[2] However, it has achieved a unique importance and potency at this historical moment, when we are more intent than ever upon upholding the principle of neutrality in all things. What is so special about religion that it should receive any such "special privileges"? Why should we treat a church or other religious association differently than we treat any other social club or cultural organization, or treat the rights of a religious adherent any differently than we would treat the expressive liberties of any other individual? Why, asks the legal scholar Brian Leiter, taking the question a step further, should we even *tolerate* religion?[3]

The drive to ask such questions is a fairly recent development in our history and perhaps a sign of the growing secularity of so much of our public life. But there is no denying the fact that, in some sense, religion and religious institutions are not treated according to a principle of strict neutrality. To be sure, the recognition and support of religion is something dramatically different from the establishment of a particular religion, a distinction the First Amendment sought to codify with its two religion clauses (and Neuhaus sought to underscore in his understanding of a "civil" public square). The fact remains, though, that something like a generic monotheism enjoys a privileged public status in present-day America, even though many religious believers fail to notice it or complain of its thinness and lack of specificity, whereas many secular Americans find it an intolerable imposition.

Examples abound. One still sees the name of God on the American currency, in the Pledge of Allegiance, in the oaths we take in court, in the concluding words of presidential speeches, and even, it seems, popping up in the 2012 Democratic Party Platform. Chaplains are still employed by the armed services and Congress, and the latter still duly commences its sessions with the invocation of a prayer. The tax exemption of religious institutions remains intact and seemingly impregnable, at least for the moment. Our most solemn observances, such as the National Day of Prayer and Remembrance in the wake of 9/11, are held in the Washington National Cathedral and are conducted in a manner that draws heavily on the liturgical and musical heritage of Western Christianity, particularly Anglicanism, the chief "established" religion in the American heritage. One could compose a long list of similar examples. We are a long way from being an officially secular country, even if we may be tending in that direction. However much we accept, or claim to accept, a principle of church-state separation, a better description of the way we actually have conducted ourselves would be selective interpenetration.

Secular critics worry that privileging religion in any way flies in the face of the principle of separation and represents an illegitimate coercion of conscience. Some religious believers see merit in these contentions, particularly the second one, in a country where the freedom of the individual is so often taken to be the very sum and essence of religious freedom. Georgetown professor Jacques Berlinerblau's lively and valuable book *How to Be Secular* is subtitled *A Call to Arms for Religious Freedom*, reflecting a freewheeling understanding of religious freedom that is as jealously protective of atheism and "freedom from" religion as it is of belief.[4]

In addition, there are respectable *religious* arguments against religion being granted a privileged status. Some of them are reminiscent of the views of Roger Williams, the great American dissenter, and recall one of the central arguments against any establishment of religion: that installation of a state religion inevitably leads, in the long run, to perfunctoriness, place-seeking, faithlessness, coercion, cooptation, atrophy, and spiritual death. In other words, the establishment of religion is bad for religion. When one looks at the sad and irrelevant state of the empty established churches of Europe today, one sees the power of the argument. By contrast, as Tocqueville was able to see as early as the 1830s, the American style of religious freedom, far from diminishing the hold of religion, kept it vital and energetic precisely by making it voluntary. Indeed, many Christians, particularly those drawing on the Anabaptist tradition, would contend that when churches are cut loose from entanglement in the polity and its civil religion, committed only to being a people set apart, they are freed to be more radical, more sacrificial, and more faithful, a living sign of contradiction.

But the example of the HHS mandate shows the limits of this approach, when one is dealing with an act of comprehensive public policy designed to be universal in character. One does not have the option of declaring one's independence from such an all-embracing policy, or opting out of it, for there is nowhere to go and no place to hide. Hence the significance of Kilgore's misunderstanding of the Catholic bishops, who in fact are not seeking to use public policy to bar Americans from using and paying for artificial contraceptives, or even to use the legal system to bar Catholics from using them, but instead are opposing the use of government's coercive power to compel Catholic organizations to pay for their use. This would seem to be a small accommodation to the long-settled and fundamental religious identity of the Catholic Church—an organization that, as I have already pointed out, has a long and consistent record in support of universal health care. Viewed in this way, the bishops' opposition to the HHS mandate was clearly not an insistence that their religious views should dominate public policy.

They *were*, however, insisting upon being dealt with separately, with respect shown for their particular commitments. They, and the religiously devout Green family that owns Hobby Lobby, are doing so in a way that presumes religious freedom means not merely do-what-you-want neutrality but a kind of deference paid to religion per se. That is precisely the point here at issue. What is so special about religion that it should be granted such deferential attention? Can we draw on the American political tradition to produce arguments for that proposition that will be compelling, or at least plausible, in the contemporary context?

I want to offer five such arguments in what follows. These surely do not exhaust all the possibilities but begin to suggest some of the reasons the discussions about religious freedom that we will be having in the years to come should be placed in a larger and richer context than the sterile logic of abstract neutrality can allow. Each of them echoes, in some manner, Tocqueville's contention that religion was the "first" of America's political institutions while pointing, as James Madison did in his "Memorial and Remonstrance against Religious Assessments," to the prepolitical sources of religious obligation.[5]

First there is what I will call the *foundational* argument, which points back to our historical roots in the Western Judeo-Christian tradition and more specifically to the spirit animating the American founders and the constitutional order they devised and instituted. The founders had diverse views about a variety of matters, very much including their own personal religious convictions, but they were in agreement about one thing: the general importance of religion, and of the active encouragement of religious belief, for the success of the American experiment. Examples of this view are plentiful. John Adams insisted that "man is constitutionally, essentially and unchangeably a religious animal. Neither philosophers or politicians can ever govern him any other way."[6] The universally respected George Washington was a particularly eloquent exponent of the view that religion was essential to the maintenance of public morality, without which a republican government could not survive. The familiar words of his Farewell Address in 1796—"of all the dispositions and habits which lead to political prosperity, Religion and morality are indispensable supports"—can be made to stand in for countless others, from John Adams to Benjamin Rush to John Jay and so on, as an indicative example.[7] That this high regard extended to religious institutions as well as individual religious beliefs is made clear by Washington's remark, in 1789, "If I could have entertained the slightest apprehension that the Constitution framed in the Convention, where I had the honor to preside, might possibly endanger the religious rights of any ecclesiastical Society, certainly I would never have placed my signature to it."[8] If we are looking for a plausible grounding for our deference paid to religion, we can begin with the testimony of the founders of the American constitutional order itself.

Very well, you may respond, but that was then, and this is now. Why should we feel bound by the founders' beliefs or their eighteenth-century mentalities? None of the founders could possibly have envisioned the cultural and religious diversity of America in the twenty-first century. Their vision assumed a degree of cultural uniformity that would be beyond our power to restore, even if we wanted to.

True enough, but the very fact of that diversity itself leads to a second argument for deference to religion, a *pluralistic* argument that would seek to protect religion all the more zealously as a source of moral order and social cohesion.

There is a reason accounts of the history of American immigration and of the history of American religion so often end up relating the very same history. From the mid-nineteenth century on, every new wave of immigration to America brought peoples for whom a set of distinctive religious beliefs and practices formed the core of their identity. Some of the worst examples of religious prejudice in our nation's history come out of the cultural clashes and anxieties of these years; but so too did the idea of pluralism as a central feature of American life. As Neuhaus and Berger came to formulate it, "This nation is constituted as an exercise in pluralism, as the *unum* within which myriad *plures* are sustained."[9] In other words, the American national ethos has a powerful but limited scope; it does not seek to produce a pure "national moral community" in which all forms of intermediate association and local affiliation are abolished or neutralized. This is not to say we do not have places of national piety, such as Arlington Cemetery and the Lincoln Memorial, which embody and express the nation's civil religion. However, the persistence of regional, religious, ethnic, and other differences, as long as they are not invidious or destructive in character or dependent upon unjust or illegal segregation or restriction, is something to be desired, because it means that the thick moral communities within which consciences are formed—churches, synagogues, mosques, and the like—remain healthy. Hence in America, the national purpose rightly understood ought to seek not to undermine particular affinities or purposes but to strengthen them. The American civil religion, on this argument, exists to support the strength and freedom of smaller moral communities that stand apart from it.

One consequence of the pluralistic argument is that religious freedom should be understood not only as an individual liberty but also as a *corporate* liberty, a liberty that applies to and inheres in *groups* and defends the integrity and self-governance of such groups. How could it be otherwise, because a religion, like a language, is an inherently social thing, quintessentially an activity of groups rather than the property of isolated individuals? Religious freedom should be understood in this dual aspect, protecting not only the liberty of individuals but also the liberty of churches and other religious institutions and communities; protecting their freedom to define what they are and what they are not, to control the meaning and terms of their membership, to freely exercise their faith by the way they choose to raise their children and order their community life, seeking to embody their religions' moral self-understanding in lived experience.

There are, of course, limits to this autonomy, as there must be to all liberties and all forms of pluralism. Religious liberty is not a carte blanche, or an all-purpose get-out-of-jail card, and its limits cannot be established once and for all by the invocation of some pristine abstract principle. The essential place of religion in the healthy life of the *plures* should, though, ensure for it a high degree of respect and set the bar very high for any government action that would have the effect of burdening its free exercise. That respect and that high bar have, in fact, generally been affirmed by the federal courts and Congress.

A third argument for the special place of religion might be called an *anthropological* one. Human beings are theotropic by their nature, inclined toward religion as a helianthus inclines to the sun and driven to relate their understanding of the highest things to their lives as lived in community together, both metaphysically and morally. As Tocqueville said, "There is hardly any human action, no matter how particular you assume it to be, that is not born out of a very general idea that men have conceived of God, of God's relationships with humanity, of the nature of their soul and of their duties toward their fellows. You cannot keep these ideas from being the common source from which all the rest flows."[10] Whether this characteristic can be attributed to built-in endowment, evolutionary adaptation, deep cultural conditioning, or some other source, it would seem to be a good thing for the secular order to affirm our theotropic impulses rather than seek to proscribe them or inhibit their expression. The vote of public confidence implied by such affirmation naturally engenders a sense of general loyalty to the polity and binds religious believers affectionately to the secular political project far more effectively than would an insistence upon a rigorously secularist public square. Indeed, the latter course would present the very real danger of producing alienated subcultures of religious believers whose sectarian disaffection with the mainstream could become so profound as to represent a threat to the very cohesion of the nation. Secularists who worry about religion taking an outsized role in public life might, then, be better advised to give some strategic ground on that issue and acknowledge the theotropic dimension in our makeup, even if they believe it to be a weakness or debility.

Such acknowledgement has the added benefit of promoting the development of a healthy civil religion, which is nothing more than an expression of our incorrigible need to relate secular things to ultimate purposes in the manner eloquently described by Tocqueville. Civil religion promotes political and social cohesion while serving as a visible embodiment, of sorts, of the generalized thing we call *religion*, but there are better and worse ways of doing this. Civil religion can, of course, be extremely dangerous, a form of playing with fire, and is viewed with understandable suspicion from all quarters. It borrows from the energy of specific faiths but always carries with it the danger of usurping and displacing them and underwriting a pernicious idolatry of the state or the nation. Hence it should be kept relatively "thin" and kept on a short leash.

However, properly understood, the American civil religion also draws upon sources of moral authority that transcend the state and are capable of holding the state accountable to a standard higher than itself. A civil religion can be, as Yale sociologist Philip Gorski has argued, "a mediating tradition that allows room for both religious and political values."[11] The more the activity of specific religions is accorded respect in the public sphere, the less likely a civil religion will succeed in displacing them.

A fourth argument might be called the *meliorist* argument, which would acknowledge the special place of religion in American life because of the extensive social good that religious institutions have done, and continue to do, in the world; and because the doing of such good works is an essential part of the free exercise of religion. This argument follows in the footsteps of the founders' emphasis on moral formation of citizens and embraces the role of religious groups in abolishing slavery, promoting civil rights, running orphanages, caring for the indigent, and the like. It has, though, taken on a weight of its own today, given the vast scale and scope of charitable, medical, and educational activities still undertaken by religious groups today. Let the Catholic Church stand as a powerful example of this. The HHS mandate was so consequential because the Catholic Church is so heavily involved in precisely these three areas, as the operator of nearly 7,500 primary and secondary schools, enrolling 2.5 million students, and more than 600 hospitals (constituting nearly 13 percent of American hospitals and 15 percent of hospital beds), 400 health centers, and 1,500 specialized homes, making it the operator of the largest private educational and health-care systems in the country.[12] In addition, Catholic Charities USA is the seventh-largest charity in the nation (the second largest being the religiously oriented Salvation Army).

Looking at the matter of the life-improving qualities of religion from another angle, one can point to a growing body of social-scientific evidence, appearing in the work of writers as diverse as Byron Johnson, Arthur Brooks, Jonathan Haidt, and Robert Putnam, indicating that religious belief correlates very reliably with the fostering of generosity, law abidingness, helpfulness to others, civic engagement, social trust, and many other traits essential to a peaceful, productive, and harmonious society. One must, of course, stipulate that there will always be hypocrites, charlatans, fakes, and abusers in religious organizations, as in all walks of life. It would appear, however, that far from religion being a poison, as the late Christopher Hitchens liked to argue, it has, at least in America, been an antidote. It seems counterproductive to downplay its many benefits.

Last but not least, there is an argument that I will call *metaphysical.* It is often said that religious freedom is the first freedom because it is grounded in the dignity and integrity of the human person, which requires that each of us be permitted to fulfill our right, and duty, to seek and embrace the truth about our existence, and live out our lives in accordance with our understanding of that truth. This was the central contention of James Madison's great "Memorial and Remonstrance against Religious Assessments" in arguing that it is the "duty of every man to render to the Creator such homage and such only as he believes to be acceptable to him."[13] This is, or should be, a universal freedom, because the great questions of human existence are not the exclusive province of professors and savants, and are not the concern of the state, but belong to us all, individually and in whatever associations we choose to forge with one another. Any good society, committed to the flourishing of its members, should recognize and encourage and support that search; it certainly has no business curtailing it. To acknowledge that fact in a public way, with an explicit recognition of the valuable place of religion, could stand as an important declaration about the value a society places on the spiritual and moral life of its members.

One might argue, moreover, that there is far more to the metaphysical argument than that. Indeed, there is a growing recognition that, in a postmodern world dominated by immense bureaucratic governments and sprawling transnational business corporations, entities that increasingly seem to operate in tandem, behemoths that are neither responsive to the tools of democratic governance nor accountable to national law nor answerable to any well-established code of behavior, religion serves as an indispensable counterweight. It is an essential resource for upholding human dignity and moral order, for speaking truth to power, for giving support to the concept of human rights, and for insisting that a voice of moral urgency—whether celebrating, exhorting, or rebuking—never become banished from the cold logic of instrumental rationality. Only the most hardened enemies of religion can fail to acknowledge that much.

Even a cursory glance at American history reveals that religion has played this role before and done so heroically. Evangelical religious conviction provided the animating force behind what was arguably the greatest reform movement in American history, the nineteenth-century movement to abolish slavery. The moral leadership of Pope John Paul II played a key role in bringing about the end of Soviet tyranny in Eastern Europe. As sociologist Jose Casanova eloquently argued in his 1994 book *Public Religions in the Modern World*, the modern world runs the risk of being "devoured by the inflexible, inhuman logic of its own creations" unless it restores a "creative dialogue" with the very religious traditions it has eviscerated or abandoned.[14] That dialogue will not be fruitful unless religion maintains its distinctive and powerful voice, which is likely in turn to depend upon our sustaining and protecting the special public standing that religion has hitherto enjoyed.

There is an even deeper question here, the question of whether freedom itself, and more generally the liberal individualism we have come to embrace in the modern West, is sustainable absent the Judeo-Christian religious assumptions that have hitherto accompanied and upheld it. Italian writer Marcello Pera, for example, despite being himself an atheist, has argued that it is a dangerous illusion to believe that such ideas as the dignity of the human person can be sustained for long without some ultimate grounding in the deep normative orientation of the Christian faith.[15] In this regard, Pera echoes the earlier perspective of Tocqueville, who doubted "whether man can ever support at the same time complete religious independence and entire public freedom . . . if faith be wanting in him, he must serve; and if he be free, he must believe."[16] Ironically, the very possibility of freedom operating within a "secular" realm of politics, which we embrace in the West as a good thing (and which is the necessary basis for any robust understanding of religious freedom), may depend upon the presence of certain specifically Christian distinctives embodied in culture as much as in doctrine.

This is an assertion that other thoughtful secularists ought to find at least plausible. Indeed, Pera's concerns had been precisely anticipated by one of the most religiously heterodox figures of early American history, Thomas Jefferson, a great favorite of the late Hitchens. On one of the panels decorating the walls of the Jefferson Memorial in Washington appear these searing words: "God who gave us life gave us liberty. Can the liberties of a nation be secure when we have removed a conviction that these liberties are the gift of God? Indeed I tremble for my country when I reflect that God is just, that His justice cannot sleep forever."[17]

Jefferson was speaking in that passage of the moral scourge of slavery and asking, rhetorically, whether there could be any moral justification for the failure to extend the blessings of liberty to all men. But there is a larger implicit point. Jefferson was asking whether the very possibility of human liberty itself, the liberty of each and every man and woman, was dependent upon our prior willingness to understand liberty as a gift of God rather than a dispensation of man. Whatever one may assert about Jefferson's beliefs or nonbeliefs, one cannot escape the fact that the name of God serves as far more than a mere rhetorical device in this context. Even a world-class skeptic such as Jefferson understood that erasing the name of God from the foundations of American public life could lead to fearful consequences, which provides yet another reason why defending the special status of religion in American life is not merely a reasonable and defensible path, but a task of the most fundamental importance.

4 • Liberty, Equality, and Race

ALEXANDER HAMILTON TO JOHN JAY

March 14, 1779

Dear Sir,

Col Laurens, who will have the honor of delivering you this letter, is on his way to South Carolina, on a project, which I think, in the present situation of affairs there, is a very good one and deserves every kind of support and encouragement. This is to raise two three or four battalions of negroes; with the assistance of the government of that state, by contributions from the owners in proportion to the number they possess. If you should think proper to enter upon the subject with him, he will give you a detail of his plan. He wishes to have it recommended by Congress to the state; and, as an inducement, that they would engage to take those battalions into Continental pay.

It appears to me, that an expedient of this kind, in the present state of Southern affairs, is the most rational, that can be adopted, and promises very important advantages. Indeed, I hardly see how a sufficient force can be collected in that quarter without it; and the enemy's operations there are growing infinitely serious and formidable. I have not the least doubt, that the negroes will make very excellent soldiers, with proper management; and I will venture to pronounce, that they cannot be put in better hands than those of Mr. Laurens. He has all the zeal, intelligence, enterprise, and every other qualification requisite to succeed in such an undertaking. It is a maxim with some great military judges, that with sensible officers soldiers can hardly be too stupid; and on this principle it is thought that the Russians would make the best troops in the world, if they were under other officers than their own. The King of Prussia is among the number who maintain this doctrine and has a very emphatical saying on the occasion, which I do not exactly recollect. I mention this, because I frequently hear it objected to the scheme of embodying negroes that they are too stupid to make soldiers. This is so far from appearing to me a valid objection that I think their want of cultivation (for their natural faculties are probably as good as ours) joined to that habit of subordination which they acquire from a life of servitude, will make them sooner become soldiers than our White inhabitants. Let officers be men of sense and sentiment, and the nearer the soldiers approach to machines perhaps the better.

I foresee that this project will have to combat much opposition from prejudice and self-interest. The contempt we have been taught to entertain for the blacks, makes us fancy many things that are founded neither in reason nor experience; and an unwillingness to part with property of so valuable a kind will furnish a thousand arguments to show the impracticability or pernicious tendency of a scheme which requires such a sacrifice. But it should be considered, that if we do not make use of them in this way, the enemy probably will; and that the best way to counteract the temptations they will hold out will be to offer them ourselves. An essential part of the plan is to give them their freedom with their muskets. This will secure their fidelity, animate their courage, and I believe will have a good influence upon those who remain, by opening a door to their emancipation. This circumstance, I confess, has no small weight in inducing me to wish the success of the project; for the dictates of humanity and true policy equally interest me in favor of this unfortunate class of men.

THOMAS JEFFERSON, *NOTES ON THE STATE OF VIRGINIA*

Query XIV: The administration of justice and description of the laws?

The plan of the revisal was this. The common law of England, by which is meant, that part of the English law which was anterior to the date of the oldest statutes extant, is made the basis of the work. It was thought dangerous to attempt to reduce it to a text: it was therefore left to be collected from the usual monuments of it. Necessary alterations in that, and so much of the whole body of the British statutes, and of acts of assembly, as were thought proper to be retained, were digested into 126 new acts, in which simplicity of stile was aimed at, as far as was safe. The following are the most remarkable alterations proposed:

To change the rules of descent, so as that the lands of any person dying intestate shall be divisible equally among all his children, or other representatives, in equal degree.

To make slaves distributable among the next of kin, as other moveables.

To have all public expenses, whether of the general treasury, or of a parish or county, (as for the maintenance of the poor, building bridges, court-houses, &c.) supplied by assessments on the citizens, in proportion to their property.

To hire undertakers for keeping the public roads in repair, and indemnify individuals through whose lands new roads shall be opened.

To define with precision the rules whereby aliens should become citizens, and citizens make themselves aliens.

To establish religious freedom on the broadest bottom.

To emancipate all slaves born after passing the act. The bill reported by the revisors does not itself contain this proposition; but an amendment containing it was prepared, to be offered to the legislature whenever the bill should be taken up, and further directing, that they should continue with their parents to a certain age, then be brought up, at the public expense, to tillage, arts or sciences, according to their geniuses, till the females should be eighteen, and the males twenty-one years of age, when they should be colonized to such place as the circumstances of the time should render most proper, sending them out with arms, implements of household and of the handicraft arts, feeds, pairs of the useful domestic animals, &c. to declare them a free and independent people, and extend to them our alliance and protection, till they shall have acquired strength; and to send vessels at the same time to other parts of the world for an equal number of white inhabitants; to induce whom to migrate hither, proper encouragements were to be proposed.

It will probably be asked, Why not retain and incorporate the blacks into the state, and thus save the expense of supplying, by importation of white settlers, the vacancies they will leave? Deep rooted prejudices entertained by the whites; ten thousand recollections, by the blacks, of the injuries they have sustained; new provocations; the real distinctions which nature has made; and many other circumstances, will divide us into parties, and produce convulsions which will probably never end but in the extermination of the one or the other race.

To these objections, which are political, may be added others, which are physical and moral. The first difference which strikes us is that of color. Whether the black of the negro resides in the reticular membrane between the skin and scarf-skin, or in the scarf-skin itself; whether it proceeds from the color of the blood, the color of the bile, or from that of some other secretion, the difference is fixed in nature, and is as real as if its seat and cause were better known to us. And is this difference of no importance? Is it not the foundation of a greater or less share of beauty in the two races? Are not the fine mixtures of red and white, the expressions of every passion by greater or less suffusions of color in the one, preferable to that eternal monotony, which reigns in the countenances, that immoveable veil of black which covers all the emotions of the other race? Add to these, flowing hair, a more elegant symmetry of form, their own judgment in favor of the whites, declared by their preference of them, as uniformly as is the preference of the Oranootan for the black women over those of his own species. The circumstance of superior beauty, is thought worthy attention in the propagation of our horses, dogs, and other domestic animals; why not in that of man? Besides those of color, figure, and hair, there are other physical distinctions proving a difference of race. They have less hair on the face and body. They secrete less by the kidneys, and more by the glands of the skin, which gives them a very strong and disagreeable odor. This greater degree of transpiration renders them more tolerant of heat, and less so of cold, than the whites. Perhaps too a difference of structure in the pulmonary apparatus, which a late ingenious experimentalist has discovered to be the principal regulator of animal heat, may have disabled them from extricating, in the act of inspiration, so much of that fluid from the outer air, or obliged them in expiration, to part with more of it. They seem to require less sleep. A black, after hard labor through the day, will be induced by the slightest amusements to sit up till midnight, or later, though knowing he must be out with the first dawn of the morning. They are at least as brave, and more adventuresome. But this may perhaps proceed from a want of forethought, which prevents their seeing a danger till it be present. When present, they do not go through it with more coolness or steadiness than the whites. They are more ardent after their female: but love seems with them to be more an eager desire, than a tender delicate mixture of sentiment and sensation. Their griefs are transient. Those numberless afflictions, which render it doubtful whether heaven has given life to us in mercy or in wrath, are less felt, and sooner forgotten with them. In general, their existence appears to participate more of sensation than reflection. To this must be ascribed their disposition to sleep when abstracted from their diversions, and unemployed in labor. An animal whose body is at rest, and who does not reflect, must be disposed to sleep of course. Comparing them by their faculties of memory, reason, and imagination, it appears to me, that in memory they are equal to the whites; in reason much inferior, as I think one could scarcely be found capable of tracing and comprehending the investigations of Euclid; and that in imagination they are dull, tasteless, and anomalous.

It would be unfair to follow them to Africa for this investigation. We will consider them here, on the same stage with the whites, and where the facts are not apocryphal on which a judgment is to be formed. It will be right to make great allowances for the difference of condition, of education, of conversation, of the sphere in which they move. Many millions of them have been brought to, and born in America. Most of them indeed have been confined to tillage, to their own homes, and their own society: yet many have been so situated, that they might have availed themselves of the conversation of their masters; many have been brought up to the handicraft arts, and from that circumstance have always been associated with the whites. Some have been liberally educated, and all have lived in countries where the arts and sciences are cultivated to a considerable degree, and have had before their eyes samples of the best works from abroad. The Indians, with no advantages of this kind, will often carve figures on their pipes not destitute of design and merit. They will crayon out an animal, a plant, or a country, so as to prove the existence of a germ in their minds which only wants cultivation. They astonish you with strokes of the most sublime oratory; such as prove their reason and sentiment strong, their imagination glowing and elevated. But never yet could I find that a black had uttered a thought above the level of plain narration; never see even an elementary trait of painting or sculpture. In music they are more generally gifted than the whites with accurate ears for tune and time, and they have been found capable of imagining a small catch. Whether they will be equal to the composition of a more extensive run of melody, or of complicated harmony, is yet to be proved. Misery is often the parent of the most affecting touches in poetry.—Among the blacks is misery enough, God knows, but no poetry. Love is the peculiar estrum of the poet. Their love is ardent, but it kindles the senses only, not the imagination. Religion indeed has produced a Phyllis Whately [Phillis Wheatley]; but it could not produce a poet. The compositions published under her name are below the dignity of criticism. The heroes of the Dunciad are to her, as Hercules to the author of that poem. Ignatius Sancho has approached nearer to merit in composition; yet his letters do more honor to the heart than the head. They breathe the purest effusions of friendship and general philanthropy, and show how great a degree of the latter may be compounded with strong religious zeal. He is often happy in the turn of his compliments, and his style is easy and familiar, except when he affects a Shandean fabrication of words. But his imagination is wild and extravagant, escapes incessantly from every restraint of reason and taste, and, in the course of its vagaries, leaves a tract of thought as incoherent and eccentric, as is the course of a meteor through the sky. His subjects should often have led him to a process of sober reasoning: yet we find him always substituting sentiment for demonstration. Upon the whole, though we admit him to the first place among those of his own color who have presented themselves to the public judgment, yet when we compare him with the writers of the race among whom he lived, and particularly with the epistolary class, in which he has taken his own stand, we are compelled to enroll him at the bottom of the column. This criticism supposes the letters published under his name to be genuine, and to have received amendment from no other hand; points which would not be of easy investigation. The improvement of the blacks in body and mind, in the first instance of their mixture with the whites, has been observed by everyone, and proves that their inferiority is not the effect merely of their condition of life.

. . . Whether further observation will or will not verify the conjecture, that nature has been less bountiful to them in the endowments of the head, I believe that in those of the heart she will be found to have done them justice. That disposition to theft with which they have been branded, must be ascribed to their situation, and not to any depravity of the moral sense. The man, in whose favor no laws of property exist, probably feels himself less bound to respect those made in favor of others. When arguing for ourselves, we lay it down as a fundamental, that laws, to be just, must give a reciprocation of right: that, without this, they are mere arbitrary rules of conduct, founded in force, and not in conscience: and it is a problem which give to the master to solve, whether the religious precepts against the violation of property were not framed for him as well as his slave? And whether the slave may not as justifiably take a little from one, who has taken all from him, as he may slay one who would slay him? That a change in the relations in which a man is placed should change his ideas of moral right and wrong, is neither new, nor peculiar to the color of the blacks. Homer tells us it was so 2600 years ago: "Jove fix'd it certain, that whatever day/Makes man a slave, takes half his worth away." But the slaves of which Homer speaks were whites. Notwithstanding these considerations which must weaken their respect for the laws of property, we find among them numerous instances of the most rigid integrity, and as many as among their better instructed masters, of benevolence, gratitude, and unshaken fidelity.–The opinion, that they are inferior in the faculties of reason and imagination, must be hazarded with great diffidence. To justify a general conclusion, requires many observations, even where the subject may be submitted to the Anatomical knife, to Optical glasses, to analysis by fire, or by solvents. How much more then where it is a faculty, not a substance, we are examining; where it eludes the research of all the senses; where the conditions of its existence are various and variously combined; where the effects of those which are present or absent bid defiance to calculation; let me add too, as a circumstance of great tenderness, where our conclusion would degrade a whole race of men from the rank in the scale of beings which their Creator may perhaps have given them. To our reproach it must be said, that though for a century and a half we have had under our eyes the races of black and of red men, they have never yet been viewed by us as subjects of natural history. Advance it therefore as a suspicion only, that the blacks, whether originally a distinct race, or made distinct by time and circumstances, are inferior to the whites in the endowments both of body and mind. It is not against experience to suppose, that different species of the same genus, or varieties of the same species, may possess different qualifications. Will not a lover of natural history then, one who views the gradations in all the races of animals with the eye of philosophy, excuse an effort to keep those in the department of man as distinct as nature has formed them? This unfortunate difference of color, and perhaps of faculty, is a powerful obstacle to the emancipation of these people. Many of their advocates, while they wish to vindicate the liberty of human nature, are anxious also to preserve its dignity and beauty. Some of these, embarrassed by the question 'What further is to be done with them?' join themselves in opposition with those who are actuated by sordid avarice only. Among the Romans emancipation required but one effort. The slave, when made free, might mix with, without staining the blood of his master. But with us a second is necessary, unknown to history. When freed, he is to be removed beyond the reach of mixture.

Query XVIII: The particular customs and manners that may happen to be received in that state?

It is difficult to determine on the standard by which the manners of a nation may be tried, whether *catholic*, or *particular*. It is more difficult for a native to bring to that standard the manners of his own nation, familiarized to him by habit. There must doubtless be an unhappy influence on the manners of our people produced by the existence of slavery among us. The whole commerce between master and slave is a perpetual exercise of the most boisterous passions, the most unremitting despotism on the one part, and degrading submissions on the other. Our children see this, and learn to imitate it; for man is an imitative animal. This quality is the germ of all education in him. From his cradle to his grave he is learning to do what he sees others do. If a parent could find no motive either in his philanthropy or his self-love, for restraining the intemperance of passion towards his slave, it should always be a sufficient one that his child is present. But generally it is not sufficient. The parent storms, the child looks on, catches the lineaments of wrath, puts on the same airs in the circle of smaller slaves, gives a loose to his worst of passions, and thus nursed, educated, and daily exercised in tyranny, cannot but be stamped by it with odious peculiarities. The man must be a prodigy who can retain his manners and morals undepraved by such circumstances. And with what execration should the statesman be loaded, who permitting one half the citizens thus to trample on the rights of the other, transforms those into despots, and these into enemies, destroys the morals of the one part, and the *amor patriae* of the other. For if a slave can have a country in this world, it must be any other in preference to that in which he is born to live and labor for another: in which he must lock up the faculties of his nature, contribute as far as depends on his individual endeavors to the evanishment of the human race, or entail his own miserable condition on the endless generations proceeding from him. With the morals of the people, their industry also is destroyed. For in a warm climate, no man will labor for himself who can make another labor for him. This is so true, that of the proprietors of slaves a very small proportion indeed are ever seen to labor. And can the liberties of a nation be thought secure when we have removed their only firm basis, a conviction in the minds of the people that these liberties are of the gift of God? That they are not to be violated but with his wrath? Indeed I tremble for my country when reflect that God is just: that his justice cannot sleep for ever: that considering numbers, nature and natural means only, a revolution of the wheel of fortune, an exchange of situation, is among possible events: that it may become probable by supernatural interference! The Almighty has no attribute which can take side with us in such a contest.—But it is impossible to be temperate and to pursue this subject through the various considerations of policy, of morals, of history natural and civil. We must be contented to hope they will force their way into every one's mind. I think a change already perceptible, since the origin of the present revolution. The spirit of the master is abating, that of the slave rising from the dust, his condition mollifying, the way I hope preparing, under the auspices of heaven, for a total emancipation, and that this is disposed, in the order of events, to be with the consent of the masters, rather than by their extirpation.

Jefferson believes in a more divine & peaceful way of freeing the slaves with the owners' consent.

FEDERALIST 54

The next view which I shall take of the House of Representatives relates to the appointment of its members to the several States which is to be determined by the same rule with that of direct taxes.

It is not contended that the number of people in each State ought not to be the standard for regulating the proportion of those who are to represent the people of each State. The establishment of the same rule for the appointment of taxes, will probably be as little contested; though the rule itself in this case, is by no means founded on the same principle. In the former case, the rule is understood to refer to the personal rights of the people, with which it has a natural and universal connection. In the latter, it has reference to the proportion of wealth, of which it is in no case a precise measure, and in ordinary cases a very unfit one. But notwithstanding the imperfection of the rule as applied to the relative wealth and contributions of the States, it is evidently the least objectionable among the practicable rules, and had too recently obtained the general sanction of America, not to have found a ready preference with the convention.

All this is admitted, it will perhaps be said; but does it follow, from an admission of numbers for the measure of representation, or of slaves combined with free citizens as a ratio of taxation, that slaves ought to be included in the numerical rule of representation? Slaves are considered as property, not as persons. They ought therefore to be comprehended in estimates of taxation which are founded on property, and to be excluded from representation which is regulated by a census of persons. This is the objection, as I understand it, stated in its full force. I shall be equally candid in stating the reasoning which may be offered on the opposite side.

"We subscribe to the doctrine," might one of our Southern brethren observe, "that representation relates more immediately to persons, and taxation more immediately to property, and we join in the application of this distinction to the case of our slaves. But we must deny the fact, that slaves are considered merely as property, and in no respect whatever as persons. The true state of the case is, that they partake of both these qualities: being considered by our laws, in some respects, as persons, and in other respects as property. In being compelled to labor, not for himself, but for a master; in being vendible by one master to another master; and in being subject at all times to be restrained in his liberty and chastised in his body, by the capricious will of another, the slave may appear to be degraded from the human rank, and classed with those irrational animals which fall under the legal denomination of property. In being protected, on the other hand, in his life and in his limbs, against the violence of all others, even the master of his labor and his liberty; and in being punishable himself for all violence committed against others, the slave is no less evidently regarded by the law as a member of the society, not as a part of the irrational creation; as a moral person, not as a mere article of property. The federal Constitution, therefore, decides with great propriety on the case of our slaves, when it views them in the mixed character of persons and of property. This is in fact their true character. It is the character bestowed on them by the laws under which they live; and it will not be denied, that these are the proper criterion; because it is only under the pretext that the laws have transformed the negroes into subjects of property, that a place is disputed them in the computation of numbers; and it is admitted, that if the laws were to restore the rights which have been taken away, the negroes could no longer be refused an equal share of representation with the other inhabitants.

This question may be placed in another light. It is agreed on all sides, that numbers are the best scale of wealth and taxation, as they are the only proper scale of representation. Would the convention have been impartial or consistent, if they had rejected the slaves from the list of inhabitants, when the shares of representation were to be calculated, and inserted them on the lists when the tariff of contributions was to be adjusted? Could it be reasonably expected, that the Southern States would concur in a system, which considered their slaves in some degree as men, when burdens were to be imposed, but refused to consider them in the same light, when advantages were to be conferred? Might not some surprise also be expressed, that those who reproach the Southern States with the barbarous policy of considering as property a part of their human brethren, should themselves contend, that the government to which all the States are to be parties, ought to consider this unfortunate race more completely in the unnatural light of property, than the very laws of which they complain?

It may be replied, perhaps, that slaves are not included in the estimate of representatives in any of the States possessing them. They neither vote themselves nor increase the votes of their masters. Upon what principle, then, ought they to be taken into the federal estimate of representation? In rejecting them altogether, the Constitution would, in this respect, have followed the very laws which have been appealed to as the proper guide.

This objection is repelled by a single observation. It is a fundamental principle of the proposed Constitution, that as the aggregate number of representatives allotted to the several States is to be determined by a federal rule, founded on the aggregate number of inhabitants, so the right of choosing this allotted number in each State is to be exercised by such part of the inhabitants as the State itself may designate. The qualifications on which the right of suffrage depend are not, perhaps, the same in any two States. In some of the States the difference is very material. In every State, a certain proportion of inhabitants are deprived of this right by the constitution of the State, who will be included in the census by which the federal Constitution apportions the representatives. In this point of view the Southern States might retort the complaint, by insisting that the principle laid down by the convention required that no regard should be had to the policy of particular States towards their own inhabitants; and consequently, that the slaves, as inhabitants, should have been admitted into the census according to their full number, in like manner with other inhabitants, who, by the policy of other States, are not admitted to all the rights of citizens. A rigorous adherence, however, to this principle, is waived by those who would be gainers by it. All that they ask is that equal moderation be shown on the other side. Let the case of the slaves be considered, as it is in truth, a peculiar one. Let the compromising expedient of the Constitution be mutually adopted, which regards them as inhabitants, but as debased by servitude below the equal level of free inhabitants, which regards the *slave* as divested of two fifths of the *man*.

After all, may not another ground be taken on which this article of the Constitution will admit of a still more ready defense? We have hitherto proceeded on the idea that representation related to persons only, and not at all to property. But is it a just idea? Government is instituted no less for protection of the property, than of the persons, of individuals. The one as well as the other, therefore, may be considered as represented by those who are charged with the government. Upon this principle it is, that in several of the States, and particularly in the State of New York, one branch of the government is intended more especially to be the guardian of property, and is accordingly elected by that part of the society which is most interested in this object of government. In the federal Constitution, this policy does not prevail. The rights of property are committed into the same hands with the personal rights. Some attention ought, therefore, to be paid to property in the choice of those hands.

For another reason, the votes allowed in the federal legislature to the people of each State, ought to bear some proportion to the comparative wealth of the States. States have not, like individuals, an influence over each other, arising from superior advantages of fortune. If the law allows an opulent citizen but a single vote in the choice of his representative, the respect and consequence which he derives from his fortunate situation very frequently guide the votes of others to the objects of his choice; and through this imperceptible channel the rights of property are conveyed into the public representation. A State possesses no such influence over other States. It is not probable that the richest State in the Confederacy will ever influence the choice of a single representative in any other State. Nor will the representatives of the larger and richer States possess any other advantage in the federal legislature, over the representatives of other States, than what may result from their superior number alone. As far, therefore, as their superior wealth and weight may justly entitle them to any advantage, it ought to be secured to them by a superior share of representation. The new Constitution is, in this respect, materially different from the existing Confederation, as well as from that of the United Netherlands, and other similar confederacies. In each of the latter, the efficacy of the federal resolutions depends on the subsequent and voluntary resolutions of the states composing the union. Hence the states, though possessing an equal vote in the public councils, have an unequal influence, corresponding with the unequal importance of these subsequent and voluntary resolutions. Under the proposed Constitution, the federal acts will take effect without the necessary intervention of the individual States. They will depend merely on the majority of votes in the federal legislature, and consequently each vote, whether proceeding from a larger or smaller State, or a State more or less wealthy or powerful, will have an equal weight and efficacy: in the same manner as the votes individually given in a State legislature, by the representatives of unequal counties or other districts, have each a precise equality of value and effect; or if there be any difference in the case, it proceeds from the difference in the personal character of the individual representative, rather than from any regard to the extent of the district from which he comes."

Such is the reasoning which an advocate for the Southern interests might employ on this subject; and although it may appear to be a little strained in some points, yet, on the whole, I must confess that it fully reconciles me to the scale of representation which the convention have established.

In one respect, the establishment of a common measure for representation and taxation will have a very salutary effect. As the accuracy of the census to be obtained by the Congress will necessarily depend, in a considerable degree on the disposition, if not on the co-operation, of the States, it is of great importance that the States should feel as little bias as possible, to swell or to reduce the amount of their numbers. Were their share of representation alone to be governed by this rule, they would have an interest in exaggerating their inhabitants. Were the rule to decide their share of taxation alone, a contrary temptation would prevail. By extending the rule to both objects, the States will have opposite interests, which will control and balance each other, and produce the requisite impartiality.

JAMES MADISON, MEMORANDUM ON AN AFRICAN COLONY FOR FREED SLAVES

Without enquiring into the practicability or the most proper means of establishing a Settlement of freed blacks on the Coast of Africa, it may be remarked as one motive to the benevolent experiment that if such an asylum was provided, it might prove a great encouragement to manumission in the Southern parts of the U.S. and even afford the best hope yet presented of putting an end to the slavery in which not less than 600,000 unhappy negroes are now involved.

In all the Southern States of N. America, the laws permit masters, under certain precautions to manumit their slaves. But the continuance of such a permission in some of the States is rendered precarious by the ill effects suffered from freedmen who retain the vices and habits of slaves. The same consideration becomes an objection with many humane masters against an exertion of their legal right of freeing their slaves. It is found in fact that neither the good of the Society, nor the happiness of the individuals restored to freedom is promoted by such a change in their condition.

In order to render this change eligible as well to the Society as to the Slaves, it would be necessary that a complete incorporation of the latter into the former should result from the act of manumission. This is rendered impossible by the prejudices of the Whites, prejudices which proceeding principally from the difference of color must be considered as permanent and insuperable.

It only remains then that some proper external receptacle be provided for the slaves who obtain their liberty. The interior wilderness of America, and the Coast of Africa seem to present the most obvious alternative. The former is liable to great if not invincible objections. If the settlement were attempted at a considerable distance from the White frontier, it would be destroyed by the Savages who have a peculiar antipathy to the blacks. If the attempt were made in the neighborhood of the White Settlements, peace would not long be expected to remain between Societies, distinguished by such characteristic marks, and retaining the feelings inspired by their former relation of oppressors & oppressed. The result then is that an experiment for providing such an external establishment for the blacks as might induce the humanity of Masters, and by degrees both the humanity & policy of the Governments, to forward the abolition of slavery in America, ought to be pursued on the Coast of Africa or in some other foreign situation.

DEMOCRACY IN AMERICA, VOLUME I, PART 2, CHAPTER 10: "SOME CONSIDERATIONS ON THE PRESENT STATE AND PROBABLE FUTURE OF THE THREE RACES THAT INHABIT THE TERRITORY OF THE UNITED STATES"

The principal task that I had set for myself has now been fulfilled; I have succeeded, at least as much as I could, in showing what the laws of the American democracy were; I have made its mores known. I could stop here, but the reader would perhaps find that I have not satisfied his expectation.

You encounter in America something more than an immense and complete democracy; the peoples who inhabit the New World can be seen from more than one point of view.

In the course of this work, my subject often led me to speak about Indians and Negroes, but I never had the time to stop to show what position these two races occupy in the midst of the democratic people that I was busy portraying; I said according to what spirit, with the aid of what laws, the Anglo-American confederation had been formed; I could only indicate in passing, and in a very incomplete way, the dangers that menace this confederation, and it was impossible for me to explain in detail what its chances of enduring were, apart from laws and mores. While speaking about the united republics, I hazarded no conjecture about the permanence of republican forms in the New World, and although alluding frequently to the commercial activity that reigns in the Union, I was not able to deal with the future of the Americans as a commercial people.

These topics touch on my subject, but do not enter into it; they are American without being democratic, and above all I wanted to portray democracy. So I had to put them aside at first; but I must return to them as I finish.

The territory occupied today, or claimed by the American Union, extends from the Atlantic Ocean to the shores of the Pacific Ocean. So in the east or in the west, its limits are those of the continent itself; the territory advances in the south to the edge of the Tropics and then goes back up to the middle of the frozen areas of the North.

The men spread throughout this space do not form, as in Europe, so many offshoots of the same family. You discover among them, from the outset, three naturally distinct and, I could almost say, enemy races. Education, laws, origins and even the external form of their features, have raised an almost insurmountable barrier between them; fortune gathered them together on the same soil, but it mixed them together without being able to blend them, and each one pursues its destiny apart.

Among such diverse men, the first who attracts attention, the first in enlightenment, in power, in happiness, is the white man, the European, man *par excellence*; below him appear the Negro and the Indian.

These two unfortunate races have neither birth, nor facial features, nor language, nor mores in common; their misfortunes alone are similar. Both occupy an equally inferior position in the country that they inhabit; both suffer the effects of tyranny; and if their miseries are different, they can blame the same authors for them.

Wouldn't you say, seeing what is happening in the world, that the European is to the men of other races what man himself is to the animals? He makes them serve his purposes, and when he cannot make them bend, he destroys them.

Oppression deprived the descendants of the Africans at a stroke of nearly all the privileges of humanity. The Negro of the United States has lost even the memory of his country; he no longer hears the language spoken by his fathers; he has renounced their religion and forgotten their mores. While thus ceasing to belong to Africa, however, he has acquired no right to the good things of Europe; but he has stopped between the two societies; he has remained isolated between the two peoples; sold by the one and repudiated by the other; finding in the whole world only the home of his master to offer him the incomplete picture of a native land.

The Negro has no family; he cannot see in a woman anything other than the temporary companion of his pleasures and, at birth, his sons are his equals.

Shall I call it a benefit of God or a final curse of His anger, this disposition of the soul that makes man insensible to extreme miseries and often even gives him a kind of depraved taste for the cause of his misfortunes?

Plunged into this abyss of evils, the Negro scarcely feels his misfortune; violence had placed him in slavery; the practice of servitude has given him the thoughts and ambition of a slave; he admires his tyrants even more than he hates them, and finds his joy and his pride in servile imitation of those who oppress him.

His intelligence has fallen to the level of his soul.

The Negro enters into servitude and into life at the same time. What am I saying? Often he is purchased right from the womb of his mother, and so to speak he starts to be a slave before being born.

Without need as without pleasure, useless to himself, he understands, by the first notions that he receives of existence, that he is the property of another, whose interest is to watch over his days; he sees that the care for his own fate has not devolved upon him. The very use of thought seems to him a useless gift from Providence, and he peacefully enjoys all the privileges of his servility.

If he becomes free, independence often then seems to him to be a heavier chain than slavery itself; for in the course of his existence, he has learned to submit to everything, except to reason; and when reason becomes his sole guide, he cannot recognize its voice. A thousand new needs besiege him, and he lacks the knowledge and the energy necessary to resist them. Needs are masters that must be fought, and he has only learned to submit and to obey. So he has reached this depth of misery in which servitude brutalizes him and liberty destroys him.

Oppression has exercised no less influence over the Indian races, but its effects are different.

Before the arrival of whites in the New World, the men who inhabited North America lived tranquilly in the woods. Given over to the ordinary vicissitudes of savage life, they exhibited the vices and virtues of uncivilized peoples. Europeans, after scattering the Indian tribes far into the wilderness, condemned them to a wandering and restless life, full of inexpressible miseries.

Savage nations are governed only by opinions and mores.

By weakening the sentiment of native land among the Indians of North America, by scattering their families, by obscuring their traditions, by interrupting the chain of memory, by changing all their habits, and by increasing their needs inordinately, European tyranny has made them more disorderly and less civilized than they already were. The moral condition and physical state of these peoples did not cease to deteriorate at the same time, and they became more barbaric as they became more unhappy. Nonetheless, Europeans have not been able entirely to modify the character of the Indians, and with the power to destroy them, they have never had that of civilizing and subjugating them.

The Negro is placed at the furthest limits of servitude; the Indian, at the extreme limits of liberty. The effects of slavery on the first are scarcely more harmful than the effects of independence on the second.

The Negro has lost even ownership of his person, and he cannot dispose of his own existence without committing a kind of larceny.

The savage is left to himself as soon as he can act. He has hardly known the authority of family; he has never bent his will to that of his fellows; no one has taught him to distinguish a voluntary obedience from a shameful subjection, and he is unaware of even the name of law. For him, to be free is to escape nearly all the bonds of society. He delights in this barbarous independence, and he would prefer to perish rather than to sacrifice the smallest part of it. Civilization has little hold over such a man.

The Negro makes a thousand hapless efforts in order to enter into a society that pushes him away; he bows to the tastes of his oppressors, adopts their opinions, and aspires, by imitating them, to be mingled with them. He has been told since birth that his race is naturally inferior to that of the whites and he is not far from believing it; so he is ashamed of himself. In each one of his features he finds a mark of slavery and, if he could, he would joyfully consent to repudiate himself completely.

The Indian, in contrast, has an imagination entirely filled with the alleged nobility of his origin. He lives and dies amid these dreams of his pride. Far from wanting to bend his mores to ours, he is attached to barbarism as a distinctive sign of his race, and he rejects civilization perhaps still less out of hatred for it than out of fear of resembling the Europeans.

To the perfection of our arts, he wants to oppose only the resources of the wilderness; to our tactics, only his undisciplined courage; to the depth of our plans, only the spontaneous instincts of his savage nature. He succumbs in this unequal struggle.

The Negro would like to mingle with the European, and he cannot do so. The Indian could, to a certain point, succeed in doing so, but he disdains to try. The servility of the one delivers him to slavery, and the pride of the other, to death.

I remember that traveling through the forests that still cover the state of Alabama, I arrived one day next to the cabin of a pioneer. I did not want to enter the dwelling of the American, but I went to rest for a few moments at the edge of a spring not far from there in the woods. While I was in this place, an Indian woman came (we then were near the territory occupied by the Creek nation); she held the hand of a small girl five or six years old, belonging to the white race, whom I supposed to be the daughter of the pioneer. A Negro woman followed them. A kind of barbaric luxury distinguished the costume of the Indian woman: metal rings were suspended from her nostrils and ears; her hair, mixed with glass beads, fell freely over her shoulders, and I saw that she wasn't married, for she still wore the shell necklace that virgins customarily put down on the nuptial bed. The Negro woman was dressed in European clothes almost in tatters.

All three came to sit down beside the spring, and the young savage, taking the child in her arms, lavished on her caresses that you could have believed were dictated by a mother's heart; on her side, the Negro woman sought by a thousand innocent tricks to attract the attention of the small Creole. The latter showed in her slightest movements a sentiment of superiority that contrasted strangely with her weakness and her age; you would have said that she received the attentions of her companions with a kind of condescension.

Squatting in front of her mistress, watching closely for each of her desires, the Negro woman seemed equally divided between an almost maternal attachment and a servile fear; while a free, proud, and almost fierce air distinguished even the savage woman's effusion of tenderness.

I approached and contemplated this spectacle in silence; my curiosity undoubtedly displeased the Indian woman, for she suddenly arose, pushed the child far away from her with a kind of roughness, and, after giving me an irritated look, plunged into the woods.

I had often happened to see gathered in the same places individuals belonging to the three human races that people North America. I had already recognized by a thousand various effects the preponderance exercised by the whites. But, in the scene that I have just described, there was something particularly touching: a bond of affection united the oppressed to the oppressors here, and nature, by trying hard to bring them together, made still more striking the immense space put between them by prejudice and laws.

Position That the Black Race Occupies in the United States; Dangers to Which Its Presence Exposes the Whites

The Indians will die in isolation as they lived; but the destiny of the Negroes is in a way intertwined with that of the Europeans. Although the two races are bound to each other, they do not blend together. It is as difficult for them to separate completely as to unite.

The most formidable of all the evils that threaten the future of the United States arises from the presence of Blacks on their soil. When you seek the cause of the present troubles and future dangers of the Union, you almost always end up at this first fact, from no matter where you start.

Men generally need to make great and constant efforts to create lasting evils; but there is one evil that enters into the world furtively. At first, you barely notice it amid the usual abuses of power; it begins with an individual whose name is not preserved by history; it is deposited like an accursed seed at some point in the soil; it then feeds on itself, spreads effortlessly, and grows naturally with the society that received it. This evil is slavery.

Christianity had destroyed servitude; the Christians of the sixteenth century reestablished it; but they never allowed it in their social system other than as an exception, and they took care to restrict it to a single one of the human races. They therefore gave humanity a wound not as extensive, but infinitely more difficult to heal.

Two things must be carefully distinguished: slavery in itself and its consequences.

The immediate evils produced by slavery were nearly the same among ancient peoples as they are among modern peoples, but the consequences of these evils were different. Among the ancients the slave belonged to the same race as his master, and often he was superior to him in education and in enlightenment. Liberty alone separated them; once liberty was granted, they easily blended.

So the ancients had a very simple means to rid themselves of slavery and its consequences; this means was emancipation, and as soon as they used it in a general way, they succeeded.

Not that the marks of servitude in antiquity did not still continue to exist for some time after servitude was destroyed.

There is a natural prejudice that leads man to scorn the one who has been his inferior, long after he has become his equal; real inequality produced by fortune or law is always followed by an imaginary inequality that has its roots in mores; but among the ancients this secondary effect of slavery came to an end. The emancipated man so strongly resembled the men who were born free that it soon became impossible to distinguish him from them.

What was more difficult among the ancients was to change the law; what is more difficult among modern peoples is to change mores, and for us the real difficulty begins where in antiquity it ended.

This happens because among modern peoples the non-material and transitory fact of slavery is combined in the most fatal way with the material and permanent fact of the difference of race. The memory of slavery dishonors the race, and race perpetuates the memory of slavery.

There is not an African who came freely to the shores of the New World; from that it follows that all those who are found there today are slaves or emancipated. Thus the Negro, together with life, transmits to all of his descendants the external sign of his shame. Law can destroy servitude; but only God alone can make its mark disappear.

The modern slave differs from the master not only in liberty, but also in origin. You can make the Negro free, but he remains in the position of a stranger vis-à-vis the European.

That is still not all. In this man who is born in lowliness, in this stranger that slavery introduced among us, we scarcely acknowledge the general features of humanity. His face appears hideous to us, his intelligence seems limited to us, his tastes are base; we very nearly take him for an intermediate being between brute and man.

So after abolishing slavery, modern peoples still have to destroy three prejudices much more elusive and more tenacious than slavery: the prejudice of the master, the prejudice of race, and finally the prejudice of the white.

It is very difficult for us, who have had the good fortune to be born among men whom nature made our fellows and the law our equals; it is very difficult for us, I say, to understand what insurmountable distance separates the Negro of America from the European. But we can have a remote idea of it by reasoning by analogy.

We formerly saw among us great inequalities whose principles were only in legislation. What more fictitious than a purely legal inequality! What more contrary to the instinct of man than permanent differences established among men clearly similar! These differences have continued to exist for centuries however; they still continue to exist in a thousand places; everywhere they have left imaginary marks that time can scarcely erase. If the inequality created solely by laws is so difficult to uproot, how to destroy the one that seems to have its immutable foundations in nature itself?

As for me, when I consider what difficulty aristocratic bodies of whatever nature have merging with the mass of the people, and the extreme care that they take to preserve for centuries the imaginary barriers that separate them, I despair of seeing an aristocracy founded on visible and imperishable signs disappear.

So those who hope that one day the Europeans will blend with the Negroes seem to me to entertain a chimera. My reason does not lead me to believe it, and I see nothing in the facts that indicate it.

Until now, wherever whites have been the most powerful, they have held Negroes in degradation or in slavery. Wherever Negroes have been the strongest, they have destroyed whites; it is the only accounting that might ever be possible between the two races.

If I consider the United States of our day, I see clearly that in a certain part of the country the legal barrier that separates the two races is tending to fall, but not that of mores. I see slavery receding; the prejudice to which it gave birth is immovable.

. . . What I limit myself to saying at this moment is this. The Americans are, of all modern peoples, those who have pushed equality and inequality furthest among men. They have combined universal suffrage and servitude. They seem to have wanted to prove in this way the advantages of equality by opposite arguments. It is claimed that the Americans, by establishing universal suffrage and the dogma of sovereignty of the people, have made clear to the world the advantages of equality. As for me, I think that they have above all proved this by establishing servitude, and I find that they establish the advantages of equality much less by democracy than by slavery.

> . . . I met in the South of the Union an old man who formerly had lived in an illegitimate union with one of his Negro women. He had had several children with her, who coming into the world became slaves of their father. Several times the latter had thought to bequeath them at least liberty, but years had gone by before he was able to overcome the obstacles raised to emancipation by the legislator. During this time old age came, and he was about to die. He then imagined his sons led from market to market and passing from paternal authority to the rod of a stranger. These horrible images threw his dying imagination into delirium. I saw him prey to the agonies of despair, and I then understood how nature knew how to avenge the wounds done to it by laws.

These evils are awful, without doubt; but are they not the foreseeable and necessary consequence of the very principle of servitude among modern peoples?

From the moment when Europeans took their slaves from within a race of men different from their own, that many among them considered as inferior to other human races, and with which all envisaged with horror the idea of ever assimilating, they supposed slavery to be eternal; for, between the extreme inequality that servitude creates and the complete equality that independence naturally produces among men, there is no intermediate lasting state. The Europeans vaguely sensed this truth, but without admitting it. Every time it concerned Negroes, you saw the Europeans obey sometimes their interest or their pride, sometimes their pity. Toward the Black they violated all the rights of humanity, and then they instructed him in the value and inviolability of these rights. They opened their ranks to their slaves, and when the latter attempted to enter, they chased them away in disgrace. Wanting servitude, the Europeans allowed themselves to be led despite themselves or without their knowing toward liberty, without having the courage of being either completely iniquitous or entirely just.

If it is impossible to foresee a period when the Americans of the South will mix their blood with that of the Negroes, can they, without exposing themselves to perishing, allow the latter to attain liberty? And if, in order to save their own race, they are obliged to want to keep them in chains, must you not excuse them for taking the most effective means to succeed in doing so?

What is happening in the South of the Union seems to me at the very same time the most horrible and the most natural consequence of slavery. When I see the order of nature overturned, when I hear humanity cry out and struggle in vain under the laws, I admit that I do not find the indignation to condemn the men of today, authors of these outrages; but I summon up all of my hatred against those who after more than a thousand years of equality introduced servitude again into the world.

Whatever the efforts of the Americans of the South to keep slavery, moreover, they will not succeed forever. Slavery, squeezed into a single point of the globe, attacked by Christianity as unjust, by political economy as fatal; slavery, amid the democratic liberty and the enlightenment of our age, is not an institution that can endure. It will end by the deed of the slave or by that of the master. In both cases, great misfortunes must be expected.

WILLIAM LLOYD GARRISON, ON THE CONSTITUTION AND THE UNION

There is much declamation about the sacredness of the compact which was formed between the free and slave states, on the adoption of the Constitution. A sacred compact, forsooth! We pronounce it the most bloody and heaven-daring arrangement ever made by men for the continuance and protection of a system of the most atrocious villainy ever exhibited on earth. Yes—we recognize the compact, but with feelings of shame and indignation; and it will be held in everlasting infamy by the friends of justice and humanity throughout the world. It was a compact formed at the sacrifice of the bodies and souls of millions of our race, for the sake of achieving a political object—an unblushing and monstrous coalition to do evil that good might come. Such a compact was, in the nature of things and according to the law of God, null and void from the beginning. No body of men ever had the right to guarantee the holding of human beings in bondage. Who or what were the framers of our government, that they should dare confirm and authorize such high-handed villainy—such a flagrant robbery of the inalienable rights of man—such a glaring violation of all the precepts and injunctions of the gospel—such a savage war upon a sixth part of our whole population?—They were men, like ourselves—as fallible, as sinful, as weak, as ourselves. By the infamous bargain which they made between themselves, they virtually dethroned the Most High God, and trampled beneath their feet their own solemn and heaven-attested Declaration, that all men are created equal, and endowed by their Creator with certain inalienable rights—among which are life, liberty, and the pursuit of happiness. They had no lawful power to bind themselves, or their posterity, for one hour—for one moment—by such an unholy alliance. It was not valid then—it is not valid now. Still they persisted in maintaining it—and still do their successors, the people of Massachusetts, of New-England, and of the twelve free States, persist in maintaining it. A sacred compact! a sacred compact! What, then, is wicked and ignominious?

This, then, is the relation in which we of New-England stand to the holders of slaves at the south, and this is virtually our language toward them—"Go on, most worthy associates, from day to day, from month to month, from year to year, from generation to generation, plundering two millions of human beings of their liberty and the fruits of their toil—driving them into the fields like cattle—starving and lacerating their bodies—selling the husband from his wife, the wife from her husband, and children from their parents—spilling their blood—withholding the bible from their hands and all knowledge from their minds—and kidnapping annually sixty thousand infants, the offspring of pollution and shame! Go on, in these practices—we do not wish nor mean to interfere, for the rescue of your victims, even by expostulation or warning—we like your company too well to offend you by denouncing your conduct—although we know that by every principle of law which does not utterly disgrace us by assimilating us to pirates, that they have as good and as true a right to the equal protection of the law as we have; and although we ourselves stand prepared to die, rather than submit even to a fragment of the intolerable load of oppression to which we are subjecting them—yet, never mind—let that be—they have grown old in suffering and we iniquity—and we have nothing to do now but to speak *peace, peace,* to one another in our sins. We are too wicked ever to love them as God commands us to do—we are so resolute in our wickedness as not even to desire to do so—and we are so proud in our iniquity that we will hate and revile whoever disturbs us in it. We want, like the devils of old, to be let alone in our sin. We are unalterably determined, and neither God nor man shall move us from this resolution, that our colored fellow subjects never shall be free or happy in their native land. Go on, from bad to worse—add link to link to the chains upon the bodies of your victims—add constantly to the intolerable burdens under which they groan—and if, goaded to desperation by your cruelties; they should rise to assert their rights and redress their wrongs, fear nothing—we are pledged, by a sacred compact, to shoot them like dogs and rescue you from their vengeance! Go on—we never will forsake you, for 'there is honor among thieves'—our swords are ready to leap from their scabbards, and our muskets to pour forth deadly vollies [*sic*], as soon as you are in danger. We pledge you our physical strength, by the sacredness of the national compact—a compact by which we have enabled you already to plunder, persecute and destroy two millions of slaves, who now lie beneath the sod; and by which we now give you the same piratical license to prey upon a much larger number of victims and all their posterity. Go on—and by this sacred instrument, the Constitution of the United States, *dripping as it is with human blood,* we solemnly pledge you our lives, our fortunes, and our sacred honor, that we will stand by you to the last."

People of New-England, and of the free States! is it true that slavery is no concern of yours? Have you no right even to protest against it, or to seek its removal? Are you not the main pillars of its support? How long do you mean to be answerable to God and the world, for spilling the blood of the poor innocents? Be not afraid to look the monster SLAVERY boldly in the face. He is your implacable foe—the vampire who is sucking your life-blood—the ravager of a large portion of your country, and the enemy of God and man. Never hope to be a united, or happy, or prosperous people while he exists. He has an appetite like the grave—a spirit as malignant as that of the bottomless pit—and an influence as dreadful as the corruption of death. Awake to your danger! the struggle is a mighty one—it cannot be avoided—it should not be, if it could.

It is said that if you agitate this question, you will divide the Union. Believe it not; but should disunion follow, the fault will not be yours. You must perform your duty, faithfully, fearlessly and promptly, and leave the consequences to God: that duty clearly is, to cease from giving countenance and protection to southern kidnappers. Let them separate, if they can muster courage enough—and the liberation of their slaves is certain. Be assured that slavery will very speedily destroy this Union, *if it be let alone*; but even if the Union can be preserved by treading upon the necks, spilling the blood, and destroying the souls of millions of your race, we say it is not worth a price like this, and that it is in the highest degree criminal for you to continue the present compact. Let the pillars thereof fall—let the superstructure crumble into dust—if it must be upheld by robbery and oppression.

FREDERICK DOUGLASS, "WHAT TO THE SLAVE IS THE FOURTH OF JULY?"

Fellow-citizens, pardon me, allow me to ask, why am I called upon to speak here to-day? What have I, or those I represent, to do with your national independence? Are the great principles of political freedom and of natural justice, embodied in that Declaration of Independence, extended to us? and am I, therefore, called upon to bring our humble offering to the national altar, and to confess the benefits and express devout gratitude for the blessings resulting from your independence to us?

Would to God, both for your sakes and ours, that an affirmative answer could be truthfully returned to these questions! Then would my task be light, and my burden easy and delightful. For who is there so cold, that a nation's sympathy could not warm him? Who so obdurate and dead to the claims of gratitude, that would not thankfully acknowledge such priceless benefits? Who so stolid and selfish, that would not give his voice to swell the hallelujahs of a nation's jubilee, when the chains of servitude had been torn from his limbs? I am not that man. In a case like that, the dumb might eloquently speak, and the "lame man leap as an hart."

But, such is not the state of the case. I say it with a sad sense of the disparity between us. I am not included within the pale of this glorious anniversary! Your high independence only reveals the immeasurable distance between us. The blessings in which you, this day, rejoice, are not enjoyed in common. The rich inheritance of justice, liberty, prosperity and independence, bequeathed by your fathers, is shared by you, not by me. The sunlight that brought life and healing to you, has brought stripes and death to me. This Fourth of July is *yours*, not *mine*. *You* may rejoice, *I* must mourn. To drag a man in fetters into the grand illuminated temple of liberty, and call upon him to join you in joyous anthems, were inhuman mockery and sacrilegious irony. Do you mean, citizens, to mock me, by asking me to speak to-day? If so, there is a parallel to your conduct. And let me warn you that it is dangerous to copy the example of a nation whose crimes, lowering up to heaven, were thrown down by the breath of the Almighty, burying that nation in irrecoverable ruin! I can to-day take up the plaintive lament of a peeled and woe-smitten people!

. . . Fellow-citizens; above your national, tumultuous joy, I hear the mournful wail of millions! whose chains, heavy and grievous yesterday, are, to-day, rendered more intolerable by the jubilee shouts that reach them. If I do forget, if I do not faithfully remember those bleeding children of sorrow this day, "may my right hand forget her cunning, and may my tongue cleave to the roof of my mouth!" To forget them, to pass lightly over their wrongs, and to chime in with the popular theme, would be treason most scandalous and shocking, and would make me a reproach before God and the world. My subject, then fellow-citizens, is AMERICAN SLAVERY. I shall see, this day, and its popular characteristics, from the slave's point of view. Standing, there, identified with the American bondman, making his wrongs mine, I do not hesitate to declare, with all my soul, that the character and conduct of this nation never looked blacker to me than on this 4th of July! Whether we turn to the declarations of the past, or to the professions of the present, the conduct of the nation seems equally hideous and revolting. America is false to the past, false to the present, and solemnly binds herself to be false to the future. Standing with God and the crushed and bleeding slave on this occasion, I will, in the name of humanity which is outraged, in the name of liberty which is fettered, in the name of the constitution and the Bible, which are disregarded and trampled upon, dare to call in question and to denounce, with all the emphasis I can command, everything that serves to perpetuate slavery—the great sin and shame of America! "I will not equivocate; I will not excuse;" I will use the severest language I can command; and yet not one word shall escape me that any man, whose judgment is not blinded by prejudice, or who is not at heart a slaveholder, shall not confess to be right and just.

But I fancy I hear some one of my audience say, it is just in this circumstance that you and your brother abolitionists fail to make a favorable impression on the public mind. Would you argue more, and denounce less, would you persuade more, and rebuke less, your cause would be much more likely to succeed. But, I submit, where all is plain there is nothing to be argued. What point in the anti-slavery creed would you have me argue? On what branch of the subject do the people of this country need light? Must I undertake to prove that the slave is a man? That point is conceded already. Nobody doubts it. The slaveholders themselves acknowledge it in the enactment of laws for their government. They acknowledge it when they punish disobedience on the part of the slave. There are seventy-two crimes in the State of Virginia, which, if committed by a black man (no matter how ignorant he be), subject him to the punishment of death; while only two of the same crimes will subject a white man to the like punishment. What is this but the acknowledgement that the slave is a moral, intellectual and responsible being? The manhood of the slave is conceded. It is admitted in the fact that Southern statute books are covered with enactments forbidding, under severe fines and penalties, the teaching of the slave to read or to write. When you can point to any such laws, in reference to the beasts of the field, then I may consent to argue the manhood of the slave. When the dogs in your streets, when the fowls of the air, when the cattle on your hills, when the fish of the sea, and the reptiles that crawl, shall be unable to distinguish the slave from a brute, *then* will I argue with you that the slave is a man!

For the present, it is enough to affirm the equal manhood of the Negro race. Is it not astonishing that, while we are ploughing, planting and reaping, using all kinds of mechanical tools, erecting houses, constructing bridges, building ships, working in metals of brass, iron, copper, silver and gold; that, while we are reading, writing and ciphering, acting as clerks, merchants and secretaries, having among us lawyers, doctors, ministers, poets, authors, editors, orators and teachers; that, while we are engaged in all manner of enterprises common to other men, digging gold in California, capturing the whale in the Pacific, feeding sheep and cattle on the hill-side, living, moving, acting, thinking, planning, living in families as husbands, wives and children, and, above all, confessing and worshipping the Christian's God, and looking hopefully for life and immortality beyond the grave, we are called upon to prove that we are men!

Would you have me argue that man is entitled to liberty? that he is the rightful owner of his own body? You have already declared it. Must I argue the wrongfulness of slavery? Is that a question for Republicans? Is it to be settled by the rules of logic and argumentation, as a matter beset with great difficulty, involving a doubtful application of the principle of justice, hard to be understood? How should I look to-day, in the presence of Americans, dividing, and subdividing a discourse, to show that men have a natural right to freedom? speaking of it relatively, and positively, negatively, and affirmatively. To do so, would be to make myself ridiculous, and to offer an insult to your understanding. There is not a man beneath the canopy of heaven, that does not know that slavery is wrong *for him*.

What, am I to argue that it is wrong to make men brutes, to rob them of their liberty, to work them without wages, to keep them ignorant of their relations to their fellow men, to beat them with sticks, to flay their flesh with the lash, to load their limbs with irons, to hunt them with dogs, to sell them at auction, to sunder their families, to knock out their teeth, to bum their flesh, to starve them into obedience and submission to their masters? Must I argue that a system thus marked with blood, and stained with pollution, is *wrong*? No! I will not. I have better employments for my time and strength than such arguments would imply.

What, then, remains to be argued? Is it that slavery is not divine; that God did not establish it; that our doctors of divinity are mistaken? There is blasphemy in the thought. That which is inhuman, cannot be divine! Who can reason on such a proposition? They that can, may; I cannot. The time for such argument is passed.

At a time like this, scorching irony, not convincing argument, is needed. O! had I the ability, and could I reach the nation's ear, I would, today, pour out a fiery stream of biting ridicule, blasting reproach, withering sarcasm, and stern rebuke. For it is not light that is needed, but fire; it is not the gentle shower, but thunder. We need the storm, the whirlwind, and the earthquake. The feeling of the nation must be quickened; the conscience of the nation must be roused; the propriety of the nation must be startled; the hypocrisy of the nation must be exposed; and its crimes against God and man must be proclaimed and denounced.

What, to the American slave, is your 4th of July? I answer: a day that reveals to him, more than all other days in the year, the gross injustice and cruelty to which he is the constant victim. To him, your celebration is a sham; your boasted liberty, an unholy license; your national greatness, swelling vanity; your sounds of rejoicing are empty and heartless; your denunciations of tyrants, brass fronted impudence; your shouts of liberty and equality, hollow mockery; your prayers and hymns, your sermons and thanksgivings, with all your religious parade, and solemnity, are, to him, mere bombast, fraud, deception, impiety, and hypocrisy—a thin veil to cover up crimes which would disgrace a nation of savages. There is not a nation on the earth guilty of practices, more shocking and bloody, than are the people of these United States, at this very hour.

Go where you may, search where you will, roam through all the monarchies and despotisms of the old world, travel through South America, search out every abuse, and when you have found the last, lay your facts by the side of the everyday practices of this nation, and you will say with me, that, for revolting barbarity and shameless hypocrisy, America reigns without a rival.

Take the American slave-trade, which, we are told by the papers, is especially prosperous just now. Ex-Senator Benton tells us that the price of men was never higher than now. He mentions the fact to show that slavery is in no danger. This trade is one of the peculiarities of American institutions. It is carried on in all the large towns and cities in one-half of this confederacy; and millions are pocketed every year, by dealers in this horrid traffic. In several states, this trade is a chief source of wealth. It is called (in contradistinction to the foreign slave-trade) "*the internal slave trade.*" It is, probably, called so, too, in order to divert from it the horror with which the foreign slave-trade is contemplated. That trade has long since been denounced by this government, as piracy. It has been denounced with burning words, from the high places of the nation, as an execrable traffic. To arrest it, to put an end to it, this nation keeps a squadron, at immense cost, on the coast of Africa. Everywhere, in this country, it is safe to speak of this foreign slave-trade, as a most inhuman traffic, opposed alike to the laws of God and of man. The duty to extirpate and destroy it, is admitted even by our DOCTORS OF DIVINITY. In order to put an end to it, some of these last have consented that their colored brethren (nominally free) should leave this country, and establish themselves on the western coast of Africa! It is, however, a notable fact that, while so much execration is poured out by Americans upon those engaged in the foreign slave-trade, the men engaged in the slave-trade between the states pass without condemnation, and their business is deemed honorable.

Behold the practical operation of this internal slave-trade, the American slave-trade, sustained by American politics and American religion. Here you will see men and women reared like swine for the market. You know what is a swine-drover? I will show you a man-drover. They inhabit all our Southern States. They perambulate the country, and crowd the highways of the nation, with droves of human stock. You will see one of these human flesh-jobbers, armed with pistol, whip and bowie-knife, driving a company of a hundred men, women, and children, from the Potomac to the slave market at New Orleans. These wretched people are to be sold singly, or in lots, to suit purchasers. They are food for the cotton-field, and the deadly sugar-mill. Mark the sad procession, as it moves wearily along, and the inhuman wretch who drives them. Hear his savage yells and his blood-chilling oaths, as he hurries on his affrighted captives! There, see the old man, with locks thinned and gray. Cast one glance, if you please, upon that young mother, whose shoulders are bare to the scorching sun, her briny tears falling on the brow of the babe in her arms. See, too, that girl of thirteen, weeping, *yes*! weeping, as she thinks of the mother from whom she has been torn! The drove moves tardily. Heat and sorrow have nearly consumed their strength; suddenly you hear a quick snap, like the discharge of a rifle; the fetters clank, and the chain rattles simultaneously; your ears are saluted with a scream, that seems to have torn its way to the center of your soul! The crack you heard, was the sound of the slave-whip; the scream you heard, was from the woman you saw with the babe. Her speed had faltered under the weight of her child and her chains! that gash on her shoulder tells her to move on. Follow the drove to New Orleans. Attend the auction; see men examined like horses; see the forms of women rudely and brutally exposed to the shocking gaze of American slave-buyers. See this drove sold and separated forever; and never forget the deep, sad sobs that arose from that scattered multitude. Tell me citizens, WHERE, under the sun, you can witness a spectacle more fiendish and shocking. Yet this is but a glance at the American slave-trade, as it exists, at this moment, in the ruling part of the United States.

I was born amid such sights and scenes. To me the American slave-trade is a terrible reality. When a child, my soul was often pierced with a sense of its horrors. I lived on Philpot Street, Fell's Point, Baltimore, and have watched from the wharves, the slave ships in the Basin, anchored from the shore, with their cargoes of human flesh, waiting for favorable winds to waft them down the Chesapeake. There was, at that time, a grand slave mart kept at the head of Pratt Street, by Austin Woldfolk. His agents were sent into every town and county in Maryland, announcing their arrival, through the papers, and on flaming "*hand-bills*," headed CASH FOR NEGROES. These men were generally well dressed men, and very captivating in their manners. Ever ready to drink, to treat, and to gamble. The fate of many a slave has depended upon the turn of a single card; and many a child has been snatched from the arms of its mother by bargains arranged in a state of brutal drunkenness.

The flesh-mongers gather up their victims by dozens, and drive them, chained, to the general depot at Baltimore. When a sufficient number have been collected here, a ship is chartered, for the purpose of conveying the forlorn crew to Mobile, or to New Orleans. From the slave prison to the ship, they are usually driven in the darkness of night; for since the antislavery agitation, a certain caution is observed.

In the deep still darkness of midnight, I have been often aroused by the dead heavy footsteps, and the piteous cries of the chained gangs that passed our door. The anguish of my boyish heart was intense; and I was often consoled, when speaking to my mistress in the morning, to hear her say that the custom was very wicked; that she hated to hear the rattle of the chains, and the heart-rending cries. I was glad to find one who sympathized with me in my horror.

Fellow-citizens, this murderous traffic is, to-day, in active operation in this boasted republic. In the solitude of my spirit, I see clouds of dust raised on the highways of the South; I see the bleeding footsteps; I hear the doleful wail of fettered humanity, on the way to the slave-markets, where the victims are to be sold like *horses*, *sheep*, and *swine*, knocked off to the highest bidder. There I see the tenderest ties ruthlessly broken, to gratify the lust, caprice and rapacity of the buyers and sellers of men. My soul sickens at the sight.

Is this the land your Fathers loved,
The freedom which they toiled to win?
Is this the earth whereon they moved?
Are these the graves they slumber in?

But a still more inhuman, disgraceful, and scandalous state of things remains to be presented. By an act of the American Congress, not yet two years old, slavery has been nationalized in its most horrible and revolting form. By that act, Mason and Dixon's line has been obliterated; New York has become as Virginia; and the power to hold, hunt, and sell men, women, and children as slaves remains no longer a mere state institution, but is now an institution of the whole United States. The power is co-extensive with the Star-Spangled Banner and American Christianity. Where these go, may also go the merciless slave-hunter. Where these are, man is not sacred. He is a bird for the sportsman's gun. By that most foul and fiendish of all human decrees, the liberty and person of every man are put in peril. Your broad republican domain is hunting ground for *men*. Not for thieves and robbers, enemies of society, merely, but for men guilty of no crime. Your lawmakers have commanded all good citizens to engage in this hellish sport. Your President, your Secretary of State, our *lords*, *nobles*, and ecclesiastics, enforce, as a duty you owe to your free and glorious country, and to your God, that you do this accursed thing. Not fewer than forty Americans have, within the past two years, been hunted down and, without a moment's warning, hurried away in chains, and consigned to slavery and excruciating torture. Some of these have had wives and children, dependent on them for bread; but of this, no account was made. The right of the hunter to his prey stands superior to the right of marriage, and to *all* rights in this republic, the rights of God included! For black men there are neither law, justice, humanity, nor religion. The Fugitive Slave *Law* makes mercy to them a crime; and bribes the judge who tries them. An American judge gets ten dollars for every victim he consigns to slavery, and five, when he fails to do so. The oath of any two villains is sufficient, under this hell-black enactment, to send the most pious and exemplary black man into the remorseless jaws of slavery! His own testimony is nothing. He can bring no witnesses for himself. The minister of American justice is bound by the law to hear but *one* side; and *that* side, is the side of the oppressor. Let this damning fact be perpetually told. Let it be thundered around the world, that, in tyrant-killing, king-hating, people-loving, democratic, Christian America, the seats of justice are filled with judges, who hold their offices under an open and palpable *bribe*, and are bound, in deciding in the case of a man's liberty, *hear only his accusers*!

In glaring violation of justice, in shameless disregard of the forms of administering law, in cunning arrangement to entrap the defenseless, and in diabolical intent, this Fugitive Slave Law stands alone in the annals of tyrannical legislation. I doubt if there be another nation on the globe, having the brass and the baseness to put such a law on the statute-book. If any man in this assembly thinks differently from me in this matter, and feels able to disprove my statements, I will gladly confront him at any suitable time and place he may select.

I take this law to be one of the grossest infringements of Christian Liberty, and, if the churches and ministers of our country were not stupidly blind, or most wickedly indifferent, they, too, would so regard it.

At the very moment that they are thanking God for the enjoyment of civil and religious liberty, and for the right to worship God according to the dictates of their own consciences, they are utterly silent in respect to a law which robs religion of its chief significance, and makes it utterly worthless to a world lying in wickedness. Did this law concern the "*mint, anise, and cumin*"—abridge the right to sing psalms, to partake of the sacrament, or to engage in any of the ceremonies of religion, it would be smitten by the thunder of a thousand pulpits. A general shout would go up from the church, demanding *repeal, repeal, instant repeal*!—And it would go hard with that politician who presumed to solicit the votes of the people without inscribing this motto on his banner. Further, if this demand were not complied with, another Scotland would be added to the history of religious liberty, and the stern old Covenanters would be thrown into the shade. A John Knox would be seen at every church door, and heard from every pulpit, and Fillmore would have no more quarter than was shown by Knox, to the beautiful, but treacherous queen Mary of Scotland. The fact that the church of our country, (with fractional exceptions), does not esteem "the Fugitive Slave Law" as a declaration of war against religious liberty, implies that that church regards religion simply as a form of worship, an empty ceremony, and *not* a vital principle, requiring active benevolence, justice, love and good will towards man. It esteems sacrifice above mercy; psalm-singing above right doing; solemn meetings above practical righteousness. A worship that can be conducted by persons who refuse to give shelter to the houseless, to give bread to the hungry, clothing to the naked, and who enjoin obedience to a law forbidding these acts of mercy, is a curse, not a blessing to mankind. The Bible addresses all such persons as "scribes, Pharisees, hypocrites, who pay tithe of *mint, anise*, and *cumin*, and have omitted the weightier matters of the law, judgment, mercy and faith."

. . . One is struck with the difference between the attitude of the American church towards the anti-slavery movement, and that occupied by the churches in England towards a similar movement in that country. There, the church, true to its mission of ameliorating, elevating, and improving the condition of mankind, came forward promptly, bound up the wounds of the West Indian slave, and restored him to his liberty. There, the question of emancipation was a high religious question. It was demanded, in the name of humanity, and according to the law of the living God. The Sharps, the Clarksons, the Wilberforces, the Buxtons, and Burchells and the Knibbs, were alike famous for their piety, and for their philanthropy. The anti-slavery movement *there* was not an anti-church movement, for the reason that the church took its full share in prosecuting that movement: and the anti-slavery movement in this country will cease to be an anti-church movement, when the church of this country shall assume a favorable, instead of a hostile position towards that movement. Americans! your republican politics, not less than your republican religion, are flagrantly inconsistent. You boast of your love of liberty, your superior civilization, and your pure Christianity, while the whole political power of the nation (as embodied in the two great political parties), is solemnly pledged to support and perpetuate the enslavement of three millions of your countrymen. You hurl your anathemas at the crowned headed tyrants of Russia and Austria, and pride yourselves on your Democratic institutions, while you yourselves consent to be the mere *tools* and *body-guards* of the tyrants of Virginia and Carolina. You invite to your shores fugitives of oppression from abroad, honor them with banquets, greet them with ovations, cheer them, toast them, salute them, protect them, and pour out your money to them like water; but the fugitives from your own land you advertise, hunt, arrest, shoot and kill. You glory in your refinement and your universal education yet you maintain a system as barbarous and dreadful as ever stained the character of a nation—a system begun in avarice, supported in pride, and perpetuated in cruelty. You shed tears over fallen Hungary, and make the sad story of her wrongs the theme of your poets, statesmen and orators, till your gallant sons are ready to fly to arms to vindicate her cause against her oppressors; but, in regard to the ten thousand wrongs of the American slave, you would enforce the strictest silence, and would hail him as an enemy of the nation who dares to make those wrongs the subject of public discourse! You are all on fire at the mention of liberty for France or for Ireland; but are as cold as an iceberg at the thought of liberty for the enslaved of America. You discourse eloquently on the dignity of labor; yet, you sustain a system which, in its very essence, casts a stigma upon labor. You can bare your bosom to the storm of British artillery to throw off a three-penny tax on tea; and yet wring the last hard-earned farthing from the grasp of the black laborers of your country. You profess to believe "that, of one blood, God made all nations of men to dwell on the face of all the earth," and hath commanded all men, everywhere to love one another; yet you notoriously hate (and glory in your hatred), all men whose skins are not colored like your own. You declare, before the world, and are understood by the world to declare, that you "*hold these truths to be self-evident, that all men are created equal; and are endowed by their Creator with certain unalienable rights; and that, among these are, life, liberty, and the pursuit of happiness*;" and yet, you hold securely, in a bondage which, according to your own Thomas Jefferson, "*is worse than ages of that which your fathers rose in rebellion to oppose*," a *seventh part* of the inhabitants of your country.

Fellow-citizens! I will not enlarge further on your national inconsistencies. The existence of slavery in this country brands your republicanism as a sham, your humanity as a base pretence, and your Christianity as a lie. It destroys your moral power abroad; it corrupts your politicians at home. It saps the foundation of religion; it makes your name a hissing, and a bye-word to a mocking earth. It is the antagonistic force in your government, the only thing that seriously disturbs and endangers your *Union*. It fetters your progress; it is the enemy of improvement, the deadly foe of education; it fosters pride; it breeds insolence; it promotes vice; it shelters crime; it is a curse to the earth that supports it; and yet, you cling to it, as if it were the sheet anchor of all your hopes. Oh! be warned! be warned! a horrible reptile is coiled up in your nation's bosom; the venomous creature is nursing at the tender breast of your youthful republic; *for the love of God*, tear away, and fling from you the hideous monster, and *let the weight of twenty millions crush and destroy it forever*!

But it is answered in reply to all this, that precisely what I have now denounced is, in fact, guaranteed and sanctioned by the Constitution of the United States; that the right to hold and to hunt slaves is a part of that Constitution framed by the illustrious Fathers of this Republic.

. . . Now, take the Constitution according to its plain reading, and I defy the presentation of a single pro-slavery clause in it. On the other hand it will be found to contain principles and purposes, entirely hostile to the existence of slavery.

I have detained my audience entirely too long already. At some future period I will gladly avail myself of an opportunity to give this subject a full and fair discussion.

Allow me to say, in conclusion, notwithstanding the dark picture I have this day presented of the state of the nation, I do not despair of this country. There are forces in operation, which must inevitably work the downfall of slavery. "The arm of the Lord is not shortened," and the doom of slavery is certain. I, therefore, leave off where I began, with hope. While drawing encouragement from the Declaration of Independence, the great principles it contains, and the genius of American Institutions, my spirit is also cheered by the obvious tendencies of the age. Nations do not now stand in the same relation to each other that they did ages ago. No nation can now shut itself up from the surrounding world, and trot round in the same old path of its fathers without interference. The time was when such could be done. Long established customs of hurtful character could formerly fence themselves in, and do their evil work with social impunity. Knowledge was then confined and enjoyed by the privileged few, and the multitude walked on in mental darkness. But a change has now come over the affairs of mankind. Walled cities and empires have become unfashionable. The arm of commerce has borne away the gates of the strong city. Intelligence is penetrating the darkest corners of the globe. It makes its pathway over and under the sea, as well as on the earth. Wind, steam, and lightning are its chartered agents. Oceans no longer divide, but link nations together. From Boston to London is now a holiday excursion. Space is comparatively annihilated. Thoughts expressed on one side of the Atlantic, are distinctly heard on the other. The far off and almost fabulous Pacific rolls in grandeur at our feet. The Celestial Empire, the mystery of ages, is being solved. The fiat of the Almighty, "Let there be Light," has not yet spent its force. No abuse, no outrage whether in taste, sport or avarice, can now hide itself from the all-pervading light.

SEVENTH LINCOLN-DOUGLAS DEBATE: ALTON, ILLINOIS

Mr. Lincoln's Speech

On being introduced to the audience, after the cheering had subsided Mr. Lincoln said:

. . . So far as Judge Douglas addressed his speech to me, or so far as it was about me, it is my business to pay some attention to it. I have heard the Judge state two or three times what he has stated to-day—that in a speech which I made at Springfield, Illinois, I had in a very especial manner complained that the Supreme Court in the Dred Scott case had decided that a negro could never be a citizen of the United States. I have omitted by some accident heretofore to analyze this statement, and it is required of me to notice it now. In point of fact it is *untrue*. I never have complained *especially* of the Dred Scott decision because it held that a negro could not be a citizen, and the Judge is always wrong when he says I ever did so complain of it. I have the speech here, and I will thank him or any of his friends to show where I said that a negro should be a citizen, and complained especially of the Dred Scott decision because it declared he could not be one. I have done no such thing, and Judge Douglas so persistently insisting that I have done so, has strongly impressed me with the belief of a predetermination on his part to misrepresent me. He could not get his foundation for insisting that I was in favor of this negro equality anywhere else as well he could by assuming that untrue proposition. Let me tell this audience what is true in regard to that matter; and the means by which they may correct me if I do not tell them truly is by a recurrence to the speech itself. I spoke of the Dred Scott decision in my Springfield speech, and I was then endeavoring to prove that the Dred Scott decision was a portion of a system or scheme to make slavery national in this country. I pointed out what things had been decided by the court. I mentioned as a fact that they had decided that a negro could not be a citizen—that they had done so, as I supposed, to deprive the negro, under all circumstances, of the remotest possibility of ever becoming a citizen and claiming the rights of a citizen of the United States under a certain clause of the Constitution. I stated that, without making any complaint of it at all. I then went on and stated the other points decided in the case, namely: that the bringing of a negro into the State of Illinois and holding him in slavery for two years here was a matter in regard to which they would not decide whether it would make him free or not; that they decided the further point that taking him into a United States Territory where slavery was prohibited by act of Congress, did not make him free, because that act of Congress, as they held, was unconstitutional. I mentioned these three things as making up the points decided in that case. I mentioned them in a lump taken in connection with the introduction of the Nebraska bill, and the amendment of Chase, offered at the time, declaratory of the right of the people of the Territories to *exclude slavery*, which was voted down by the friends of the bill. I mentioned all these things together, as evidence tending to prove a combination and conspiracy to make the institution of slavery national. In that connection and in that way I mentioned the decision on the point that a negro could not be a citizen, and in no other connection.

Out of this, Judge Douglas builds up his beautiful fabrication—of my purpose to introduce a perfect, social, and political equality between the white and black races. His assertion that I made an "especial objection" (that is his exact language) to the decision on this account, is untrue in point of fact.

Now, while I am upon this subject, and as Henry Clay has been alluded to, I desire to place myself, in connection with Mr. Clay, as nearly right before this people as may be. I am quite aware what the Judge's object is here by all these allusions. He knows that we are before an audience, having strong sympathies southward by relationship, place of birth, and so on. He desires to place me in an extremely Abolition attitude. He read upon a former occasion, and alludes without reading today, to a portion of a speech which I delivered in Chicago. In his quotations from that speech, as he has made them upon former occasions, the extracts were taken in such a way as, I suppose, brings them within the definition of what is called *garbling*—taking portions of a speech which, when taken by themselves, do not present the entire sense of the speaker as expressed at the time. I propose, therefore, out of that same speech, to show how one portion of it which he skipped over (taking an extract before and an extract after) will give a different idea, and the true idea I intended to convey. It will take me some little time to read it, but I believe I will occupy the time that way.

You have heard him frequently allude to my controversy with him in regard to the Declaration of Independence. I confess that I have had a struggle with Judge Douglas on that matter, and I will try briefly to place myself right in regard to it on this occasion. I said—and it is between the extracts Judge Douglas has taken from this speech, and put in his published speeches:

> It may be argued that there are certain conditions that make necessities and impose them upon us, and to the extent that a necessity is imposed upon a man he must submit to it. I think that was the condition in which we found ourselves when we established this Government. We had slaves among us, we could not get our Constitution unless we permitted them to remain in slavery, we could not secure the good we did secure if we grasped for more; and having by necessity submitted to that much, it does not destroy the principle that is the charter of our liberties. Let the charter remain as our standard.

Now I have upon all occasions declared as strongly as Judge Douglas against the disposition to interfere with the existing institution of slavery. You hear me read it from the same speech from which he takes garbled extracts for the purpose of proving upon me a disposition to interfere with the institution of slavery, and establish a perfect social and political equality between negroes and white people.

Allow me while upon this subject briefly to present one other extract from a speech of mine, more than a year ago, at Springfield, in discussing this very same question, soon after Judge Douglas took his ground that negroes were not included in the Declaration of Independence:

> I think the authors of that notable instrument intended to include *all* men, but they did not mean to declare all men equal *in all respects*. They did not mean to say all men were equal in color, size, intellect, moral development or social capacity. They defined with tolerable distinctness in what they did consider all men created equal—equal in certain inalienable rights, among which are life, liberty, and the pursuit of happiness. This they said, and this they meant. They did not mean to assert the obvious untruth, that all were then actually enjoying that equality, or yet, that they were about to confer it immediately upon them. In fact they had no power to confer such a boon. They meant simply to declare the *right*, so that the *enforcement* of it might follow as fast as circumstances should permit.

> They meant to set up a standard maxim for free society which should be familiar to all: constantly looked to, constantly labored for, and even, though never perfectly attained, constantly approximated, and thereby constantly spreading and deepening its influence and augmenting the happiness and value of life to all people, of all colors, everywhere.

There again are the sentiments I have expressed in regard to the Declaration of Independence upon a former occasion—sentiments which have been put in print and read wherever anybody cared to know what so humble an individual as myself chose to say in regard to it.

At Galesburgh the other day, I said in answer to Judge Douglas, that three years ago there never had been a man, so far as I knew or believed, in the whole world, who had said that the Declaration of Independence did not include negroes in the term "all men." I reassert it to-day. I assert that Judge Douglas and all his friends may search the whole records of the country, and it will be a matter of great astonishment to me if they shall be able to find that one human being three years ago had ever uttered the astounding sentiment that the term "all men" in the Declaration did not include the negro. Do not let me be misunderstood. I know that more than three years ago there were men who, finding this assertion constantly in the way of their schemes to bring about the ascendancy and perpetuation of slavery, *denied the truth of it.* I know that Mr. Calhoun and all the politicians of his school denied the truth of the Declaration. I know that it ran along in the mouth of some Southern men for a period of years, ending at last in that shameful though rather forcible declaration of Pettit of Indiana, upon the floor of the United States Senate, that the Declaration of Independence was in that respect "a self-evident lie," rather than a self-evident truth. But I say, with a perfect knowledge of all this hawking at the Declaration without directly attacking it, that three years ago there never had lived a man who had ventured to assail it in the sneaking way of pretending to believe it and then asserting it did not include the negro. I believe the first man who ever said it was Chief Justice Taney in the Dred Scott case, and the next to him was our friend, Stephen A. Douglas. And now it has become the catch-word of the entire party. I would like to call upon his friends everywhere to consider how they have come in so short a time to view this matter in a way so entirely different from their former belief? to ask whether they are not being borne along by an irresistible current—whither, they know not?

. . . And when this new principle—this new proposition that no human being ever thought of three years ago—is brought forward, I *combat* it as having an evil tendency, if not an evil design. I combat it as having a tendency to dehumanize the negro—to take away from him the right of ever striving to be a man. I combat it as being one of the thousand things constantly done in these days to prepare the public mind to make property, and nothing but property, of the *negro in all the States of this Union.*

But there is a point that I wish, before leaving this part of the discussion, to ask attention to. I have read and I repeat the words of Henry Clay:

> I desire no concealment of my opinions in regard to the institution of slavery. I look upon it as a great evil, and deeply lament that we have derived it from the parental Government, and from our ancestors. I wish every slave in the United States was in the country of his ancestors. But here they are; the question is how they can best be dealt with? If a state of nature existed, and we were about to lay the foundations of society, no man would be more strongly opposed than I should be, to incorporate the institution of slavery among its elements.

The principle upon which I have insisted in this canvass, is in relation to laying the foundations of new societies. I have never sought to apply these principles to the old States for the purpose of abolishing slavery in those States. It is nothing but a miserable perversion of what I *have* said, to assume that I have declared Missouri, or any other slave State, shall emancipate her slaves. I have proposed no such thing. But when Mr. Clay says that in laying the foundations of societies in our Territories where it does not exist, he would be opposed to the introduction of slavery as an element, I insist that we have *his warrant*—his license for insisting upon the exclusion of that element which he declared in such strong and emphatic language *was most hateful to him.*

Judge Douglas has again referred to a Springfield speech in which I said "a house divided against itself cannot stand." The Judge has so often made the entire quotation from that speech that I can make it from memory. I used this language:

> We are now far into the fifth year, since a policy was initiated with the avowed object and confident promise of putting an end to the slavery agitation. Under the operation of this policy, that agitation has not only not ceased, but has constantly augmented. In my opinion it will not cease until a crisis shall have been reached and passed. "A house divided against itself cannot stand." I believe this Government cannot endure permanently half slave and half free. I do not expect the house to fall—but I do expect it will cease to be divided. It will become all one thing, or all the other. Either the opponents of slavery will arrest the further spread of it, and place it where the public mind shall rest in the belief that it is in the course of ultimate extinction, or its advocates will push it forward till it shall become alike lawful in all the States—old as well as new, North as well as South.

That extract and the sentiments expressed in it, have been extremely offensive to Judge Douglas. He has warred upon them as Satan wars upon the Bible. His perversions upon it are endless. Here now are my views upon it in brief.

I said we were now far into the fifth year, since a policy was initiated with the avowed object and confident promise of putting an end to the slavery agitation. Is it not so? When that Nebraska bill was brought forward four years ago last January, was it not for the "avowed object" of putting an end to the slavery agitation? We were to have no more agitation in Congress, it was all to be banished to the Territories. By the way, I will remark here that, as Judge Douglas is very fond of complimenting Mr. Crittenden in these days, Mr. Crittenden has said there was a falsehood in that whole business, for there was *no slavery agitation at that time to allay*. We were for a little while *quiet* on the troublesome thing, and that very allaying plaster of Judge Douglas's stirred it up again. But was it not understood or intimated with the "confident promise" of putting an end to the slavery agitation? Surely it was. In every speech you heard Judge Douglas make, until he got into this "imbroglio," as they call it, with the Administration about the Lecompton Constitution, every speech on that Nebraska bill was full of his felicitations that we were *just at the end* of the slavery agitation. The last tip of the last joint of the old serpent's tail was just drawing out of view. But has it proved so? I have asserted that under that policy that agitation "has not only not ceased, but has constantly augmented." When was there ever a greater agitation in Congress than last winter? When was it as great in the country as to-day?

There was a collateral object in the introduction of that Nebraska policy which was to clothe the people of the Territories with a superior degree of self-government, beyond what they had ever had before. The first object and the main one of conferring upon the people a higher degree of "self-government," is a question of fact to be determined by you in answer to a single question. Have you ever heard or known of a people anywhere on earth who had as little to do, as, in the first instance of its use, the people of Kansas had with this same right of "self-government"? In its main policy and in its collateral object, *it has been nothing but a living, creeping lie from the time of its introduction till to-day*.

I have intimated that I thought the agitation would not cease until a crisis should have been reached and passed. I have stated in what way I thought it would be reached and passed. I have said that it might go one way or the other. We might, by arresting the further spread of it, and placing it where the fathers originally placed it, put it where the public mind should rest in the belief that it was in the course of ultimate extinction. Thus the agitation may cease. It may be pushed forward until it shall become alike lawful in all the States, old as well as new, North as well as South. I have said, and I repeat, my wish is that the further spread of it may be arrested, and that it may be placed where the public mind shall rest in the belief that it is in the course of ultimate extinction. I have expressed that as my wish. I entertain the opinion upon evidence sufficient to my mind, that the fathers of this Government placed that institution where the public mind *did* rest in the belief that it was in the course of ultimate extinction. Let me ask why they made provision that the source of slavery—the African slave-trade—should be cut off at the end of twenty years? Why did they make provision that in all the new territory we owned at that time, slavery should be forever inhibited? Why stop its spread in one direction and cut off its source in another, if they did not look to its being placed in the course of ultimate extinction?

Again; the institution of slavery is only mentioned in the Constitution of the United States two or three times, and in neither of these cases does the word "slavery" or "negro race" occur; but covert language is used each time, and for a purpose full of significance. What is the language in regard to the prohibition of the African slave-trade? It runs in about this way: "The migration or importation of such persons as any of the States now existing shall think proper to admit, shall not be prohibited by the Congress prior to the year one thousand eight hundred and eight."

The next allusion in the Constitution to the question of slavery and the black race, is on the subject of the basis of representation, and there the language used is, "Representatives and direct taxes shall be apportioned among the several States which may be included within this Union, according to their respective numbers, which shall be determined by adding to the whole number of free persons, including those bound to service for a term of years, and excluding Indians not taxed-three-fifths of all other persons."

It says "persons," not slaves, not negroes; but this "three-fifths" can be applied to no other class among us than the negroes.

Lastly, in the provision for the reclamation of fugitive slaves, it is said: "No person held to service or labor in one State, under the laws thereof, escaping into another, shall in consequence of any law or regulation therein, be discharged from such service or labor, but shall be delivered up, on claim of the party to whom such service or labor may be due." There again there is no mention of the word "negro" or of slavery. In all three of these places, being the only allusions to slavery in the instrument, covert language is used. Language is used not suggesting that slavery existed or that the black race were among us. And I understand the contemporaneous history of those times to be that covert language was used with a purpose, and that purpose was that in our Constitution, which it was hoped and is still hoped will endure forever—when it should be read by intelligent and patriotic men, after the institution of slavery had passed from among us—there should be nothing on the face of the great charter of liberty suggesting that such a thing as negro slavery had ever existed among us. This is part of the evidence that the fathers of the Government expected and intended the institution of slavery to come to an end. They expected and intended that it should be in the course of ultimate extinction. And when I say that I desire to see the further spread of it arrested, I only say I desire to see that done which the fathers have first done. When I say I desire to see it placed where the public mind will rest in the belief that it is in the course of ultimate extinction, I only say I desire to see it placed where they placed it. It is not true that

So it was long expected that slavery would end and just so they could be safe from accusations they did not use the terms "slavery" or "negro", how clever.

our fathers, as Judge Douglas assumes, made this Government part slave and part free. Understand the sense in which he puts it. He assumes that slavery is a rightful thing within itself—was introduced by the framers of the Constitution. The exact truth is, that they found the institution existing among us, and they left it as they found it. But in making the Government they left this institution with many clear marks of disapprobation upon it. They found slavery among them, and they left it among them because of the difficulty—the absolute impossibility of its immediate removal. And when Judge Douglas asks me why we cannot let it remain part slave and part free, as the fathers of the Government made it, he asks a question based upon an assumption which is itself a falsehood; and I turn upon him and ask him the question, when the policy that the fathers of the Government had adopted in relation to this element among us was the best policy in the world—the only wise policy—the only policy that we can ever safely continue upon—that will ever give us peace unless this dangerous element masters us all and becomes a national institution—*I turn upon him and ask him why he could not let it alone*. I turn and ask him why he was driven to the necessity of introducing a *new policy* in regard to it? He has himself said he introduced a new policy. He said so in his speech on the 22d of March of the present year, 1858. I ask him why he could not let it remain where our fathers placed it? I ask too of Judge Douglas and his friends why we shall not again place this institution upon the basis on which the fathers left it? I ask you, when he infers that I am in favor of setting the free and slave States at war, when the institution was placed in that attitude by those who made the constitution, *did they make any war*? If we had no war out of it when thus placed, wherein is the ground of belief that we shall have war out of it if we return to that policy? Have we had any peace upon this matter springing from any other basis? I maintain that we have not. I have proposed nothing more than a return to the policy of the fathers.

I confess, when I propose a certain measure of policy, it is not enough for me that I do not intend anything evil in the result, but it is incumbent on me to show that it has not a *tendency* to that result. I have met Judge Douglas in that point of view. I have not only made the declaration that I do not *mean* to produce a conflict between the States, but I have tried to show by fair reasoning, and I think I have shown to the minds of fair men, that I propose nothing but what has a most peaceful tendency. The quotation that I happened to make in that Springfield speech, that "a house divided against itself cannot stand," and which has proved so offensive to the Judge, was part and parcel of the same thing. He tries to show that variety in the domestic institutions of the different States is necessary and indispensable. I do not dispute it. I have no controversy with Judge Douglas about that. I shall very readily agree with him that it would be foolish for us to insist upon having a cranberry law here, in Illinois, where we have no cranberries, because they have a cranberry law in Indiana, where they have cranberries. I should insist that it would be exceedingly wrong in us to deny to Virginia the right to enact oyster laws where they have oysters, because we want no such laws here. I understand, I hope, quite as well as Judge Douglas or anybody else, that the variety in the soil and climate and face of the country, and consequent variety in the industrial pursuits and productions of a country, require systems of law conforming to this variety in the natural features of the country. I understand quite as well as Judge Douglas, that if we here raise a barrel of flour more than we want, and the Louisianians raise a barrel of sugar more than they want, it is of mutual advantage to exchange. That produces commerce, brings us together, and makes us better friends. We like one another the more for it. And I understand as well as Judge Douglas, or anybody else, that these mutual accommodations are the cements which bind together the different parts of this Union—that instead of being a thing to "divide the house"—figuratively expressing the Union—they tend to sustain it; they are the props of the house tending always to hold it up.

But when I have admitted all this, I ask if there is any parallel between these things and this institution of slavery? I do not see that there is any parallel at all between them. Consider it. When have we had any difficulty or quarrel amongst ourselves about the cranberry laws of Indiana, or the oyster laws of Virginia, or the pine lumber laws of Maine, or the fact that Louisiana produces sugar, and Illinois flour? When have we had any quarrels over these things? When have we had perfect peace in regard to this thing which I say is an element of discord in this Union? We have sometimes had peace, but when was it? It was when the institution of slavery remained quiet where it was. We have had difficulty and turmoil whenever it has made a struggle to spread itself where it was not. I ask, then, if experience does not speak in thunder-tones, telling us that the policy which has given peace to the country heretofore, being returned to, gives the greatest promise of peace again. You may say, and Judge Douglas has intimated the same thing, that all this difficulty in regard to the institution of slavery is the mere agitation of office seekers and ambitious Northern politicians. He thinks we want to get "his place," I suppose. I agree that there are office seekers amongst us. The Bible says somewhere that we are desperately selfish. I think we would have discovered that fact without the Bible. I do not claim that I am any less so than the average of men, but I do claim that I am not more selfish than Judge Douglas.

But is it true that all the difficulty and agitation we have in regard to this institution of slavery springs from office seeking—from the mere ambition of politicians? Is that the truth? How many times have we had danger from this question? Go back to the day of the Missouri Compromise. Go back to the Nullification question, at the bottom of which lay this same slavery question. Go back to the time of the Annexation of Texas. Go back to the troubles that led to the Compromise of 1850. You will find that every time, with the single exception of the Nullification question, they sprung from an endeavor to spread this institution. There never was a party in the history of this country, and there probably never will be, of sufficient strength to disturb the general peace of the country. Parties themselves may be divided and quarrel on minor questions, yet it extends not beyond the parties themselves. But does *not* this question make a disturbance outside of political circles? Does it not enter into the churches and rend them asunder? What divided the great Methodist Church into two parts, North and South? What has raised this constant disturbance in every Presbyterian General Assembly that meets? What disturbed the Unitarian Church in this very city two years ago? What has jarred and shaken the great American Tract Society recently, not yet splitting it, but sure to divide it in the end? Is it not this same mighty, deep-seated power that somehow operates on the minds of men, exciting and stirring them up in every avenue of society—in politics, in religion, in literature, in morals, in all the manifold relations of life? Is this the work of politicians? Is that irresistible power which for fifty years has shaken the Government and agitated the people to be stilled and subdued by pretending that it is an exceedingly simple thing, and we ought not to talk about it? If you will get everybody else to stop talking about it, I assure you I will quit before they have half done so. But where is the philosophy or statesmanship which assumes that you can quiet that disturbing element in our society which has disturbed us for more than half a century, which has been the only serious danger that has threatened our institutions—I say, where is the philosophy or the statesmanship based on the assumption that we are to quit talking about it, and that the public mind is all at once to cease being agitated by it? Yet this is the policy here in the north that Douglas is advocating—that we are to care nothing about it! I ask you if it is not a false philosophy? Is it not a false statesmanship that undertakes to build up a system of policy upon the basis of caring nothing about *the very thing that everybody does care the most about?*—a thing which all experience has shown we care a very great deal about?

The Judge alludes very often in the course of his remarks to the exclusive right which the States have to decide the whole thing for themselves. I agree with him very readily that the different States have that right. He is but fighting a man of straw when he assumes that I am contending against the right of the States to do as they please about it. Our controversy with him is in regard to the new Territories. We agree that when the States come in as States they have the right and the power to do as they please. We have no power as citizens of the free States or in our federal capacity as members of the Federal Union through the General Government, to disturb slavery in the States where it exists. We profess constantly that we have no more inclination than belief in the power of the Government to disturb it; yet we are driven constantly to defend ourselves from the assumption that we are warring upon the rights of the *States*. What I insist upon is, that the new Territories shall be kept free from it while in the Territorial condition. Judge Douglas assumes that we have no interest in them—that we have no right whatever to interfere. I think we have some interest. I think that as white men we have. Do we not wish for an outlet for our surplus population, if I may so express myself? Do we not feel an interest in getting to that outlet with such institutions as we would like to have prevail there? If *you* go to the Territory opposed to slavery and another man comes upon the same ground with his slave, upon the assumption that the things are equal, it turns out that he has the equal right all his way and you have no part of it your way. If he goes in and makes it a slave Territory, and by consequence a slave State, is it not time that those who desire to have it a free State were on equal ground? Let me suggest it in a different way. How many Democrats are there about here [voice in the crowd: "a thousand"] who have left slave States and come into the free State of Illinois to get rid of the institution of slavery? [another voice in the crowd: "a thousand and one"] I reckon there are a thousand and one. [laughter] I will ask you, if the policy you are now advocating had prevailed when this country was in a Territorial condition, where would you have gone to get rid of it? Where would you have found your free State or Territory to go to? And when hereafter, for any cause, the people in this place shall desire to find new homes, if they wish to be rid of the institution, where will they find the place to go to?

Now irrespective of the moral aspect of this question as to whether there is a right or wrong in enslaving a negro, I am still in favor of our new Territories being in such a condition that white men may find a home—may find some spot where they can better their condition—where they can settle upon new soil and better their condition in life. I am in favor of this not merely (I must say it here as I have elsewhere) for our own people who are born amongst us, but as an outlet for *free white people everywhere*, the world over—in which Hans and Baptiste and Patrick, and all other men from all the world, may find new homes and better their conditions in life.

I have stated upon former occasions, and I may as well state again, what I understand to be the real issue in this controversy between Judge Douglas and myself. On the point of my wanting to make war between the free and the slave States, there has been no issue between us. So, too, when he assumes that I am in favor of introducing a perfect social and political equality between the white and black races. These are false issues, upon which Judge Douglas has tried to force the controversy. There is no foundation in truth for the charge that I maintain either of these propositions. The real issue in this controversy—the one pressing upon every mind—is the sentiment on the part of one class that looks upon the institution of slavery *as a wrong*, and of another class that *does not* look upon it as a wrong. The sentiment that contemplates the institution of slavery in this country as a wrong is the sentiment of the Republican party. It is the sentiment around which all their actions—all their arguments circle—from which all their propositions radiate. They look upon it as being a moral, social and political wrong; and while they contemplate it as such, they nevertheless have due regard for its actual existence among us, and the difficulties of getting rid of it in any satisfactory way and to all the constitutional obligations thrown about it. Yet having a due regard for these, they desire a policy in regard to it that looks to its not creating any more danger. They insist that it should as far as may be, *be treated* as a wrong, and one of the methods of treating it as a wrong is to *make provision that it shall grow no larger*. They also desire a policy that looks to a peaceful end of slavery at some time, as being wrong. These are the views they entertain in regard to it as I understand them; and all their sentiments—all their arguments and propositions are brought within this range. I have said and I repeat it here, that if there be a man amongst us who does not think that the institution of slavery is wrong in any one of the aspects of which I have spoken, he is misplaced and ought not to be with us. And if there be a man amongst us who is so impatient of it as a wrong as to disregard its actual presence among us and the difficulty of getting rid of it suddenly in a satisfactory way, and to disregard the constitutional obligations thrown about it, that man is misplaced if he is on our platform. We disclaim sympathy with him in practical action. He is not placed properly with us.

On this subject of treating it as a wrong, and limiting its spread, let me say a word. Has anything ever threatened the existence of this Union save and except this very institution of Slavery? What is it that we hold most dear amongst us? Our own liberty and prosperity. What has ever threatened our liberty and prosperity save and except this institution of Slavery? If this is true, how do you propose to improve the condition of things by enlarging Slavery—by spreading it out and making it bigger? You may have a wen or cancer upon your person and not be able to cut it out lest you bleed to death; but surely it is no way to cure it, to engraft it and spread it over your whole body. That is no proper way of treating what you regard a wrong. You see this peaceful way of dealing with it as a wrong—restricting the spread of it, and not allowing it to go into new countries where it has not already existed. That is the peaceful way, the old-fashioned way, the way in which the fathers themselves set us the example.

On the other hand, I have said there is a sentiment which treats it as *not* being wrong. That is the Democratic sentiment of this day. I do not mean to say that every man who stands within that range positively asserts that it is right. That class will include all who positively assert that it is right, and all who like Judge Douglas treat it as indifferent and do not say it is either right or wrong. These two classes of men fall within the general class of those who do not look upon it as a wrong. And if there be among you anybody who supposes that he, as a Democrat can consider himself "as much opposed to slavery as anybody," I would like to reason with him. You never treat it as a wrong. What other thing that you consider as a wrong, do you deal with as you deal with that? Perhaps you *say* it is wrong, *but your leader never does, and you quarrel with anybody who says it is wrong*. Although you pretend to say so yourself you can find no fit place to deal with it as a wrong. You must not say anything about it in the free States, *because it is not here*. You must not say anything about it in the slave States, *because it is there*. You must not say anything about it in the pulpit, because that is religion and has nothing to do with it. You must not say anything about it in politics, *because that will disturb the security of "my place."* There is no place to talk about it as being a wrong, although you say yourself it *is* a wrong. But finally you will screw yourself up to the belief that if the people of the slave States should adopt a system of gradual emancipation on the slavery question, you would be in favor of it. You would be in favor of it. You say that is getting it in the right place, and you would be glad to see it succeed. But you are deceiving yourself. You all know that Frank Blair and Gratz Brown, down there in St. Louis, undertook to introduce that system in Missouri. They fought as valiantly as they could for the system of gradual emancipation which you pretend you would be glad to see succeed. Now I will bring you to the test. After a hard fight they were beaten, and when the news came over here you threw up your hats and *hurraed for Democracy*. More than that, take all the argument made in favor of the system you have proposed, and it carefully excludes the idea that there is anything wrong in the institution of slavery. The arguments to sustain that policy carefully excluded it. Even here to-day you heard Judge Douglas quarrel with me because I uttered a wish that it might sometime come to an end. Although Henry Clay could say he wished every slave in the United States was in the country of his ancestors, I am denounced by those pretending to respect Henry Clay for uttering a wish that it might sometime, in some peaceful way, come to an end. The Democratic policy in regard to that institution will not tolerate the merest breath, the slightest hint, of the least degree of wrong about it. Try it by some of Judge Douglas's arguments. He says he "don't care whether it is voted up or voted down" in the Territories. I do not care myself in dealing with that expression, whether it is intended to be expressive of his individual sentiments on the subject, or only of the national policy he desires to have established. It is alike valuable for my purpose. Any man can say that who does not see anything wrong in slavery, but no man can logically say it who does see a wrong in it; because no man can logically say he don't care whether a wrong is voted up or voted down. He may say he don't care whether an indifferent thing is voted up or down, but he must logically have a choice between a right thing and a wrong thing. He contends that whatever community wants slaves has a right to have them. So they have if it is not a wrong. But if it is a wrong, he cannot say people have a right to do wrong. He says that upon the score of equality, slaves should be allowed to go in a new Territory, like other property. This is strictly logical if there is no difference between it and other property. If it and other property are equal, his argument is entirely logical. But if you insist that one is wrong and the other right, there is no use to institute a comparison between right and wrong. You may turn over everything in the Democratic policy from beginning to end, whether in the shape it takes on the statute book, in the shape it takes in the Dred Scott decision, in the shape it takes in conversation, or the shape it takes in short maxim-like arguments—it everywhere carefully excludes the idea that there is anything wrong in it.

That is the real issue. That is the issue that will continue in this country when these poor tongues of Judge Douglas and myself shall be silent. It is the eternal struggle between these two principles—right and wrong—throughout the world. They are the two principles that have stood face to face from the beginning of time; and will ever continue to struggle. The one is the common right of humanity and the other the divine right of kings. It is the same principle in whatever shape it develops itself. It is the same spirit that says, "You work and toil and earn bread, and I'll eat it." No matter in what shape it comes, whether from the mouth of a king who seeks to bestride the people of his own nation and live by the fruit of their labor, or from one race of men as an apology for enslaving another race, it is the same tyrannical principle. I was glad to express my gratitude at Quincy, and I re-express it here to Judge Douglas—*that he looks to no end of the institution of slavery*. That will help the people to see where the struggle really is. It will hereafter place with us all men who really do wish the wrong may have an end. And whenever we can get rid of the fog which obscures the real question—when we can get Judge Douglas and his friends to avow a policy looking to its perpetuation—we can get out from among that class of men and bring them to the side of those who treat it as a wrong. Then there will soon be an end of it, and that end will be its "ultimate extinction." Whenever the issue can be distinctly made, and all extraneous matter thrown out so that men can fairly see the real difference between the parties, this controversy will soon be settled, and it will be done peaceably too. There will be no war, no violence. It will be placed again where the wisest and best men of the world placed it. Brooks of South Carolina once declared that when this Constitution was framed, its framers did not look to the institution existing until this day. When he said this, I think he stated a fact that is fully borne out by the history of the times. But he also said they were better and wiser men than the men of these days; yet the men of these days had experience which they had not, and by the invention of the cotton-gin it became a necessity in this country that slavery should be perpetual. I now say that, willingly or unwillingly, purposely or without purpose, Judge Douglas has been the most prominent instrument in changing the position of the institution of slavery which the fathers of the Government expected to come to an end ere this—*and putting it upon Brooks's cotton-gin basis*—placing it where he openly confesses he has no desire there shall ever be an end of it.

I understand I have ten minutes yet. I will employ it in saying something about this argument Judge Douglas uses, while he sustains the Dred Scott decision, that the people of the Territories can still somehow exclude slavery. The first thing I ask attention to is the fact that Judge Douglas constantly said, before the decision, that whether they could or not, *was a question for the Supreme Court*. But after the court has made the decision he virtually says it is *not* a question for the Supreme Court, but for the people. And how is it he tells us they can exclude it? He says it needs "police regulations," and that admits of "unfriendly legislation." Although it is a right established by the Constitution of the United States to take a slave into a Territory of the United States and hold him as property, yet unless the Territorial Legislature will give friendly legislation, and, more especially, if they adopt unfriendly legislation, they can practically exclude him. Now, without meeting this proposition as a matter of fact, I pass to consider the real Constitutional obligation. Let me take the gentleman who looks me in the face before me, and let us suppose that he is a member of the Territorial Legislature. The first thing he will do will be to swear that he will support the Constitution of the United States. His neighbor by his side in the Territory has slaves and needs Territorial legislation to enable him to enjoy that Constitutional right. Can he withhold the legislation which his neighbor needs for the enjoyment of a right which is fixed in his favor in the Constitution of the United States which he has sworn to support? Can he withhold it without violating his oath? And more especially, can he pass unfriendly legislation to violate his oath? Why, this is a *monstrous* sort of talk about the Constitution of the United States! *There has never been as outlandish or lawless a doctrine from the mouth of any respectable man on earth.* I do not believe it is a Constitutional right to hold slaves in a Territory of the United States. I believe the decision was improperly made and I go for reversing it. Judge Douglas is furious against those who go for reversing a decision. But he is for legislating it out of all force while the law itself stands. I repeat that there has never been so monstrous a doctrine uttered from the mouth of a respectable man..

I suppose most of us (I know it of myself) believe that the people of the Southern States are entitled to a Congressional Fugitive Slave law—that is a right fixed in the Constitution. But it cannot be made available to them without Congressional legislation. In the Judge's language, it is a "barren right" which needs legislation before it can become efficient and valuable to the persons to whom it is guaranteed. And as the right is Constitutional I agree that the legislation shall be granted to it—and that not that we like the institution of slavery. We profess to have no taste for running and catching niggers—at least I profess no taste for that job at all. Why then do I yield support to a Fugitive Slave law? Because I do not understand that the Constitution, which guaranties that right, can be supported without it. And if I believed that the right to hold a slave in a Territory was equally fixed in the Constitution with the right to reclaim fugitives, I should be bound to give it the legislation necessary to support it. I say that no man can deny his obligation to give the necessary legislation to support slavery in a Territory, who believes it is a Constitutional right to have it there. No man can, who does not give the Abolitionists an argument to deny the obligation enjoined by the Constitution to enact a Fugitive Slave law. Try it now. It is the strongest Abolition argument ever made. I say if that Dred Scott decision is correct, then the right to hold slaves in a Territory is equally a Constitutional right with the right of a slaveholder to have his runaway returned. No one can show the distinction between them. The one is express, so that we cannot deny it. The other is construed to be in the Constitution, so that he who believes the decision to be correct believes in the right. And the man who argues that by unfriendly legislation, in spite of that Constitutional right, slavery may be driven from the Territories, cannot avoid furnishing an argument by which Abolitionists may deny the obligation to return fugitives, and claim the power to pass laws unfriendly to the right of the slaveholder to reclaim his fugitive. I do not know how such an argument may strike a popular assembly like this, but I defy anybody to go before a body of men whose minds are educated to estimating evidence and reasoning, and show that there is an iota of difference between the Constitutional right to reclaim a fugitive, and the Constitutional right to hold a slave, in a Territory, provided this Dred Scott decision is correct. I defy any man to make an argument that will justify unfriendly legislation to deprive a slaveholder of his right to hold his slave in a Territory, that will not equally, in all its length, breadth and thickness, furnish an argument for nullifying the Fugitive Slave law. Why, there is not such an Abolitionist in the nation as Douglas, after all. [Loud and enthusiastic applause.]

Mr. Douglas's Reply

Mr. Lincoln tries to avoid the main issue by attacking the truth of my proposition, that our fathers made this Government divided into free and slave States, recognizing the right of each to decide all its local questions for itself. Did they not thus make it? It is true that they did not establish slavery in any of the States, or abolish it in any of them; but finding thirteen States, twelve of which were slave and one free, they agreed to form a government uniting them together, as they stood divided into free and slave States, and to guaranty [*sic*] forever to each State the right to do as it pleased on the slavery question. Having thus made the government, and conferred this right upon each State forever, I assert that this Government can exist as they made it, divided into free and slave States, if any one State chooses to retain slavery. He says that he looks forward to a time when slavery shall be abolished everywhere. I look forward to a time when each State shall be allowed to do as it pleases. If it chooses to keep slavery forever, it is not my business, but its own; if it chooses to abolish slavery, it is its own business—not mine. I care more for the great principle of self-government, the right of the people to rule, than I do for all the negroes in Christendom. I would not endanger the perpetuity of this Union, I would not blot out the great inalienable rights of the white men for all the negroes that ever existed. Hence, I say, let us maintain this Government on the principles that our fathers made it, recognizing the right of each State to keep slavery as long as its people determine, or to abolish it when they please. But Mr. Lincoln says that when our fathers made this Government they did not look forward to the state of things now existing, and therefore he thinks the doctrine was wrong; and he quotes Brooks, of South Carolina, to prove that our fathers then thought that probably slavery would be abolished by each State acting for itself before this time. Suppose they did; suppose they did not foresee what has occurred,—does that change the principles of our Government? They did not probably foresee the telegraph that transmits intelligence by lightning, nor did they foresee the railroads that now form the bonds of union between the different States, or the thousand mechanical inventions that have elevated mankind. But do these things change the principles of the Government? Our fathers, I say, made this Government on the principle of the right of each State to do as it pleases in its own domestic affairs, subject to the Constitution, and allowed the people of each to apply to every new change of circumstances such remedy as they may see fit to improve their condition. This right they have for all time to come.

Mr. Lincoln went on to tell you that he does not at all desire to interfere with slavery in the States where it exists, nor does his party. I expected him to say that down here. Let me ask him then how he expects to put slavery in the course of ultimate extinction everywhere, if he does not intend to interfere with it in the States where it exists? He says that he will prohibit it in all Territories, and the inference is, then, that unless they make free States out of them he will keep them out of the Union; for, mark you, he did not say whether or not he would vote to admit Kansas with slavery or not, as her people might apply (he forgot that as usual); he did not say whether or not he was in favor of bringing the Territories now in existence into the Union on the principle of Clay's Compromise measures on the slavery question. I told you that he would not. His idea is that he will prohibit slavery in all the Territories and thus force them all to become free States, surrounding the slave States with a cordon of free States and hemming them in, keeping the slaves confined to their present limits whilst they go on multiplying until the soil on which they live will no longer feed them, and he will thus be able to put slavery in a course of ultimate extinction by starvation. He will extinguish slavery in the Southern States as the French general exterminated the Algerines when he smoked them out. He is going to extinguish slavery by surrounding the slave States, hemming in the slaves and starving them out of existence, as you smoke a fox out of his hole. He intends to do that in the name of humanity and Christianity, in order that we may get rid of the terrible crime and sin entailed upon our fathers of holding slaves. Mr. Lincoln makes out that line of policy, and appeals to the moral sense of justice and to the Christian feeling of the community to sustain him. He says that any man who holds to the contrary doctrine is in the position of the king who claimed to govern by Divine right. Let us examine for a moment and see what principle it was that overthrew the Divine right of George the Third to govern us. Did not these colonies rebel because the British parliament had no right to pass laws concerning our property and domestic and private institutions without our consent? We demanded that the British Government should not pass such laws unless they gave us representation in the body passing them . . . we went to war, on the principle that the Home Government should not control and govern distant colonies without giving them a representation. Now, Mr. Lincoln proposes to govern the Territories without giving them a representation, and calls on Congress to pass laws controlling their property and domestic concerns without their consent and against their will. Thus, he asserts for his party the identical principle asserted by George III and the Tories of the Revolution.

I ask you to look into these things, and then tell me whether the Democracy or the Abolitionists are right. I hold that the people of a Territory, like those of a State (I use the language of Mr. Buchanan in his letter of acceptance) have the right to decide for themselves whether slavery shall or shall not exist within their limits. The point upon which Chief Justice Taney expresses his opinion is simply this, that slaves being property, stand on an equal footing with other property, and consequently that the owner has the same right to carry that property into a Territory that he has any other, subject to the same conditions. Suppose that one of your merchants was to take fifty or one hundred thousand dollars' worth of liquors to Kansas. He has a right to go there under that decision, but when he gets there he finds the Maine liquor law in force, and what can he do with his property after he gets it there? He cannot sell it, he cannot use it, it is subject to the local law, and that law is against him, and the best thing he can do with it is to bring it back into Missouri or Illinois and sell it. If you take negroes to Kansas, as Col. Jeff. Davis said in his Bangor speech, from which I have quoted to-day, you must take them there subject to the local law. If the people want the institution of slavery they will protect and encourage it; but if they do not want it they will withhold that protection, and the absence of local legislation protecting slavery excludes it as completely as a positive prohibition. You slaveholders of Missouri might as well understand what you know practically, that you cannot carry slavery where the people do not want it. All you have a right to ask is that the people shall do as they please; if they want slavery let them have it; if they do not want it, allow them to refuse to encourage it.

My friends, if, as I have said before, we will only live up to this great fundamental principle, there will be peace between the North and the South. Mr. Lincoln admits that under the Constitution on all domestic questions, except slavery, we ought not to interfere with the people of each State. What right have we to interfere with slavery any more than we have to interfere with any other question? He says that this slavery question is now the bone of contention. Why? Simply because agitators have combined in all the free States to make war upon it. Suppose the agitators in the States should combine in one-half of the Union to make war upon the railroad system of the other half? They would thus be driven to the same sectional strife. Suppose one section makes war upon any other peculiar institution of the opposite section, and the same strife is produced. The only remedy and safety is that we shall stand by the Constitution as our fathers made it, obey the laws as they are passed, while they stand the proper test and sustain the decisions of the Supreme Court and the constituted authorities.

How are these arguments being supported? aren't slaves 3/5ths representation meaning they are not completely property.

SUGGESTED ADDITIONAL READINGS (Freely Available Online)

Northwest Ordinance (http://teachingamericanhistory.org/library/document/northwest-ordinance/)
Dred Scott v. Sandford (http://teachingamericanhistory.org/library/document/dred-scott-v-sandford/)
Abraham Lincoln, Speech on the *Dred Scott* Decision (http://teachingamericanhistory.org/library/document/speech-on-the-dred-scott-decision/)
Frederick Douglass, Speech on the *Dred Scott* Decision (http://teachingamericanhistory.org/library/document/speech-on-the-dred-scott-decision-2/)
Alexander Stephens, Cornerstone Speech (http://teachingamericanhistory.org/library/document/cornerstone-speech/)
W. E. B. DuBois, Niagara Movement Speech (http://teachingamericanhistory.org/library/document/niagara-movement-speech/)
Brown v. Board of Education (http://www.law.cornell.edu/supremecourt/text/347/483)
Martin Luther King Jr., "I Have a Dream" (http://www.archives.gov/press/exhibits/dream-speech.pdf)
Martin Luther King Jr., "Letter from a Birmingham City Jail" (http://teachingamericanhistory.org/library/document/letter-from-birmingham-city-jail-excerpts/)
Thurgood Marshall, "Reflections on the Bicentennial of the U.S. Constitution" (http://teachingamericanhistory.org/library/document/reflections-on-the-bicentennial-of-the-united-states-constitution/)
Barack Obama, "A More Perfect Union" (http://my.barackobama.com/page/content/hisownwords/)

LIBERTY, EQUALITY, AND RACE IN AMERICA'S REPUBLICAN EXPERIMENT

Peter C. Myers

For a reflection on liberty, equality, and race in the forging of American political philosophy, a useful starting point is Abraham Lincoln's Gettysburg Address. "Four score and seven years ago," Lincoln began, "our fathers brought forth on this continent, a new nation, conceived in Liberty, and dedicated to the proposition that all men are created equal. Now we are engaged in a great civil war, testing whether that nation, or any nation so conceived and so dedicated, can long endure." In those brief words, Lincoln makes clear that in calling his listeners to consider anew the principled foundations of the American republic, he calls them—us—to reconsider some of the deepest questions of modern political philosophy.

In Lincoln's framing of it, the specific question of whether *that* nation, America, could long endure is the signal application of the general question of whether *any* nation so conceived and dedicated—any nation founded on the principles of liberty and equality and any government "of the people, by the people, and for the people"—can long endure. The question of whether a nation dedicated to the principles of liberty and equality can long endure is the question of whether republican government, informed by modern political philosophy, is a viable political order.[1] Can a viable political society be *both* conceived in liberty and dedicated to human equality? Calling the United States a "new nation," Lincoln highlights the novelty, hence the questionableness, of the founders' enterprise: in the course of human events, had ever a nation so conceived and so dedicated existed, previous to this one? If not, why not? What causes had prevented the creation and maintenance of such a society hitherto, and how had America's founders proposed to overcome or evade them? Had they done so, in fact? Was America really so new, really so exceptional among the nations of the world as Lincoln's words suggest?

For America's founders—its on-site founders, so to speak, along with its philosophical founders, among whom John Locke and the Baron de Montesquieu stand preeminent—the fundamental question of political life is the question of natural equality or inequality, of natural liberty or subjection. It is the question of whether any human being can rightfully claim a natural title of political rule over another. They agreed that reason supplies a clear answer, which would receive its most memorable formulation in the Declaration of Independence: all human beings are created equal as bearers of natural, inalienable rights, and governments derive their just powers from the consent of those they govern. The American founders agreed further that just government so understood was republican government. Yet they, like Lincoln, were proudly and painfully aware of the novelty and the problematic character of their enterprise.

For James Madison, writing as Publius in *The Federalist*, an extensive review of the pertinent history taught that the general cause of the notorious instability and propensity to injustice of republics was the spirit of faction—of partiality in one form or another adverse to the public good or private rights. The spirit of faction is inherent in human nature, Madison observed, or at least in human nature in a condition of political freedom, and therein lies the core of the problem. The truth in the observation that "liberty is to faction, what air is to fire" might easily be taken to justify attempts to solve the problem of faction "by destroying the liberty which is essential to its existence." The fact that any such attempt would be itself factious, as Madison hastened to add,[2] did not diminish the enduring power of illiberal, antirepublican sentiments in the human mind. Such sentiments had received formidable philosophical endorsement in the work of Thomas Hobbes, who blamed doctrines of republican liberty for the "effusion of so much blood" in "these Western parts" of the world.[3] Even the great friend of liberty Montesquieu acknowledged that despotism, a thoroughly odious type of government, is the most prevalent because in some sense the most natural to human beings.[4]

Despite the founders' cautious hopefulness that they had found a remedy in the modern science of politics,[5] the idea that the Declaration of Independence was meant to inter would prove a tenaciously powerful source of faction. It is a sobering fact that within a generation or two after the heroic revolt against British monarchy, a variant of the idea of natural and even hereditary rulers of human beings would gain the endorsement of professedly republican majorities in America.

"The great division of interests in the United States," Madison told his fellow delegates at Philadelphia in 1787, lay not between large and small states but rather "between the Northern & Southern," with those states divided most materially by "their having or not having slaves."[6] With how much justice, then, could Lincoln characterize as "conceived in liberty" a nation in much of which the institution of chattel slavery was already firmly entrenched? A few years prior to Gettysburg, Lincoln observed that the notion of superior and inferior races that his adversary Senator Stephen Douglas ascribed to the Declaration—the notion that served as the ultimate rationale for slavery in America—is essentially the same claim "that kings have made for enslaving the people in all ages of the world. . . . [It] is the same old serpent that says you work and I eat, you toil and I will enjoy the fruits of it. Turn it whatever way you will—whether it come from the mouth of a King, an excuse for enslaving the people of his country, or from the mouth of men of one race as a reason for enslaving the men of another race, it is all the same old serpent."[7]

It was the same old serpent, but with a particular modification that lent special potency to the poison with which it infected the American republic. The propensity to factious oppression was common to all republics, Madison observed, yet in the new world and modern America, it took a special form: "We have seen the mere distinction of colour made in the most enlightened period of time, the ground of the most oppressive dominion ever exercised by man over man."[8] The aristocracy based on this "mere distinction" of color, Alexis de Tocqueville predicted, would sustain the most deeply cherished, most firmly entrenched, most long-lived and life-threatening danger to the cause of liberty, equality, and republican government in America.[9]

The long struggle to vindicate American republicanism against its greatest domestic challenge divides into three stages, corresponding to the three main sections of this essay. The first section addresses the seminal controversy over slavery, and the second and third treat questions concerning integration that arise in the postemancipation era of American history. The second section addresses disputes over *whether* such integration is possible or desirable at all, whereas the third considers post–civil rights controversies concerning *how* or in what mode it may be best achieved. The aim throughout is to consider on the planes of political philosophy and historical American political thought the challenges our controversies over race and color have posed to the causes of liberty, equality, and republican government in America.

The Problem of Slavery

THE FOUNDING GENERATION

At the level of first principles the founders' opinions about slavery are relatively clear and unproblematic. In the speech and writing of the elite founders one finds abundant expressions of antislavery sentiment and almost no sympathy for the proposition that slavery is intrinsically good or naturally right.

"There is not a man living," wrote George Washington in 1786, "who wishes more sincerely than I do, to see the abolition of it." We have noted Madison's characterization of modern slavery as the "most oppressive dominion ever exercised by man over man." In his draft of the Declaration of Independence, Thomas Jefferson called slavery a "cruel war against human nature itself, violating its most sacred rights of life and liberty."[10] Such statements resound as declarations of the fundamental injustice of slavery, made by the men whom posterity acclaims respectively as the Father of the Country, the Father of the Constitution, and the principal author of the most important political document ever produced. The sentiment they expressed was widely shared among prominent members of the founding generation.[11]

For the founders in general, the challenging philosophical question concerned not the justice or injustice of slavery but instead the practical efficacy, in America and elsewhere, of the natural law principles that condemned it. On that question they fatefully disagreed. At the level of practice, they agreed only that no immediate, general emancipation was possible. Abolition would be deferred to some indefinite point or points, with the decision delegated to the individual states. The concrete product of their limited antislavery consensus was a federal Constitution that one could fairly describe as antislavery in spirit, yet marked by several significant accommodations to the existing institution. In *Federalist* 54, Madison captured the Constitution's ambiguity on slavery via the voice of "one of our Southern brethren," observing that it "views [slaves] in the mixed character of persons and of property."[12]

As to their rationale for temporizing with slavery, some founders expressed confidence in the impending abolition of slavery. Mindful of the post-Revolution wave of abolition under way in the northern states, Connecticut's Roger Sherman opined that "the abolition of slavery seemed to be going on in the U.S. & . . . the good sense of the several States would probably by degrees compleat [*sic*] it." Why should delegates have added another divisive controversy to the vexing difficulties already confronting them if they could affirm, with Sherman's Connecticut colleague Oliver Ellsworth, "Slavery in time will not be a speck in our Country"?[13]

Among some of the more philosophically oriented founders, the expectation of the coming abolition of slavery reflects a deeper optimism about the progress and eventual triumph of the natural rights idea throughout the world. "Government founded . . . *on the indefeasible hereditary Rights of Man*," Thomas Paine proclaimed in 1792, "is now revolving from west to east by a stronger impulse than the Government of the sword revolved from east to west."[14] At times Jefferson seemed to take a similar view. In his valedictory word to the country, he offered his prayer and conviction that the principles of the Declaration would spread their liberating influence over the globe: "All eyes are opened, or opening, to the rights of man." The principles that inspired America's revolutionary fathers, he expected, would no less surely supply "grounds of hope for others."[15]

Such generalized optimism coexisted uneasily, however, with indications of doubt and even foreboding in regard to the fate of slavery and of the republic joined to it at birth. The specific indications (in addition to the general doubts concerning faction noted above) begin with the argument that compromise with slavery was necessary to secure the membership in the Union of those states most deeply involved in slavery. Is this not to argue that the temporizing policy was necessitated by the strength of the attachment to slavery in those states? At the Constitutional Convention, that attachment appeared in repeated threats by deep South delegates that failure to protect slavery would result in the dissolution of the fledgling Union. Most ominously, after Virginian George Mason's forceful indictment of the institution, South Carolinian Charles Pinckney ventured perilously close to the affirmative defenses that would arise in the succeeding generation's public debates. "If slavery be wrong," he asserted, "it is justified by the example of all the world." South Carolinian John Rutledge similarly defended the slave trade protection: "Religion & humanity [have] nothing to do with this question.—Interest alone is the governing principle with Nations."[16]

Already deep in 1787, the division would grow dangerously deeper in the ensuing decades. Even amid Jefferson's seemingly uplifting valedictory words, one may detect a note of civic piety, masking a deep foreboding. Those words appear to contain more prayer than conviction when read in the light of earlier, more private communications in which Jefferson expresses far less confidence in any foreseeable victory of the principles of the Declaration over slavery in the United States. Most troubled and troubling among those is his 1820 letter to John Holmes, despairing that Congress's enactment of the Missouri Compromise (formalizing a sharp division, as Jefferson viewed it, between proslavery and antislavery sections of the Louisiana Territory) signaled the "knell of the Union." Believing the law to be the work of self-serving partisans, he added, "I regret that I am now to die in the belief, that the useless sacrifice of themselves by the generation of 1776 . . . is to be thrown away by the unwise and unworthy passions of their sons."[17]

THE ANTEBELLUM PERIOD

America's founders had entered the world stage in the audacity of youth, spearheading a revolutionary movement in which the principles of liberty, equality, and natural human rights seemed to advance in step with one another. They exited it, however, in the exhaustion and resignation of age, with their hopes for the republic they had founded dependent on unknown future events and on the uncertain virtues of successor generations. They exited it, too, amid accumulating evidence that fortune would not prove kind to their hopes for a republic promptly and peacefully purified of slavery.

Two developments in the near aftermath of the founding powerfully strengthened the hold slavery had on the country. One was the revolution in Haiti (1791–1804), which began as a slave revolt and resulted in the deaths of a majority of the members of the erstwhile master class. "The recent scenes transacted in the French colonies in the West Indies are enough to make one shudder," remarked Virginian St. George Tucker, "with the apprehension of realizing similar calamities in this country." The event seemed to confirm some constitutional framers' warnings of the dangers slavery posed to national security,[18] but its deeper, enduring effect was to affix in the minds of American slaveholders a frightful vision of the likely effects of emancipation. Jefferson conceived of it as a conflict between equally indefeasible natural rights. "We have the wolf by the ears," he wrote to Holmes, "and we can neither hold him, nor safely let him go."[19]

Such fears play a substantial part in explaining the long-standing conviction, held by many white (and a minority of black) Americans from the founding era to the onset of the Civil War, that abolition must be conjoined to a policy of "colonization"—of emigration or expatriation—of those newly emancipated. "Why not retain and incorporate the blacks?" Jefferson had asked in his *Notes on the State of Virginia* (1782). Various considerations, including "ten thousand recollections, by the blacks, of the injuries they have sustained," convinced him that "when freed, [the slave] is to be removed beyond the reach of mixture."[20] Madison, too, promoted the colonization idea. An African colony, he wrote in 1789, "might prove a great encouragement to manumission . . . and even afford the best hope yet presented of putting an end to the slavery in which not less than 600,000 unhappy negroes are now involved."[21]

The prospects for any such scheme, however, were gravely doubtful. In his troubling chapter on race in *Democracy in America*, Tocqueville reported, "In twelve years, the Society for the Colonization of Blacks [*sic*] has transported two thousand five hundred Negroes to Africa. During the same space of time, around seven hundred thousand of them were born in the United States." Fearing, like Jefferson, the "most horrible of all civil wars"—a war between the two racial groups—Tocqueville drew the unavoidable conclusion from Jefferson's and other southerners' "wolf-by-the-ears" reasoning. Faced with the impossibility of colonization and regarding racial integration as both impossible and undesirable, they left themselves no alternative but to perpetuate slavery. "Not wanting to mingle with the Negroes, they do not want to set them free."[22]

Nor is it clear that the slaveholding South would have agreed even on a practicable scheme of colonization. The second event in the 1790s that greatly strengthened the attachment to slavery, the invention of the cotton gin, did so via material interest rather than fear. To proceed with colonization would have meant sending away a huge, highly profitable laboring class and an enormous investment of capital. A nearly incredulous James Henry Hammond, South Carolina governor and prominent slaveholding apologist, scoffed at abolitionists' proclaimed strategy of "moral suasion": "Consider: were ever any people civilized or savage persuaded by any argument, human or divine, to surrender voluntarily two thousand millions of dollars?"[23]

In the decades succeeding the founding, then, the power of the slaveholding interest both over the South and over the country as a whole grew steadily, and the dispute over slavery intensified accordingly. A preview of what was to come appeared in 1819–1820 over a proposal in Congress that Missouri commit itself to abolition as a condition of admission to the Union.[24] Barely a decade later arose a new and unprecedentedly militant abolition movement led by a young Massachusetts newspaper editor, William Lloyd Garrison. Garrison's movement was in important respects a precursor of the twentieth-century "Freedom Now!" movement for equal civil rights. Zealously rejecting what had prevailed as conventional antislavery wisdom since the founding, Garrisonians held that abolition must be immediate, not gradual; must include no compensation to slaveholders for their losses; and must issue not in expatriation but in a racially integrated regime of full and equal civil and political rights for all.[25]

To this new, militant abolitionism the slaveholding South reacted with an unprecedentedly militant defense of slavery. The preeminent figure in that reaction was South Carolina senator John C. Calhoun, who asserted in an infamous 1837 speech that it was an error in tactics and in principle to defend slavery only as a necessary evil. "I take higher ground," he told his fellow senators. "I hold that in the present state of civilization . . . the relation now existing in the slaveholding States between the two [races], is, instead of an evil, a good—a positive good."[26]

Calhoun's proposition that American slavery was a positive good signified a root-and-branch rejection of the natural rights argument summarized in the Declaration of Independence. That argument's core premise, that human beings are naturally free and equal, he held to be the "most false and dangerous of all political errors."[27] Against the Lockean principles that inspired the revolutionaries' and the abolitionists' protests against political and domestic slavery, Calhoun contrived an alternative account of the theoretical architecture of a free society, elements of which he may have drawn from his reading of Aristotle and Edmund Burke.[28] The classical liberal idea of the state of nature was to him a pernicious abstraction; the "*real* rights of men," as Burke put it, were only those proper to membership in civil society. Like Burke again, along with Aristotle, Calhoun held that the true, defining purpose of political society is not to secure its members' preservation or their liberty to pursue subjective happiness but rather to promote the perfection of their moral and intellectual faculties.[29]

From some such premises, Calhoun inferred that liberty and generalized human equality are radically in conflict with each other. Genuine liberty and high civilization rest on political and social inequality. Liberty is no common human birthright but instead the "noble and highest reward bestowed on mental and moral development, combined with favorable circumstances." Those more advanced in the attainments of civilization are the rightful rulers of those less so. "[In] proportion as a people are ignorant, stupid, debased, corrupt," he stated bluntly, the power necessary for their governance increases and the liberty afforded them decreases "until the lowest condition is reached, when absolute and despotic power becomes necessary . . . and individual liberty extinct."[30]

Viewed in the abstract, Calhoun's doctrine may appear to be an argument for the primacy of culture or civilizational attainment relative to common human nature as a measure of a given group's qualification for rights. Viewed, however, in the light of actual conditions in the South, it appears as a decorous apology for a regime of subordination founded in fact on a presumption of natural, not merely cultural, racial inequality. "With us," he acknowledged, "the two great divisions of society are not the rich and poor, but white and black," and whereas all whites "belong to the upper class," blacks are "utterly unqualified to possess liberty."[31] In his infamous "Cornerstone" speech, Alexander H. Stephens, newly designated vice president of the Confederate States of America, was even more forthright: "Our new government is founded," Stephens declared, "upon the great truth that the Negro is not equal to the white man; that slavery—subordination to the superior race—is his natural and normal condition."[32]

Yet, despite his opinion of blacks' abject inferiority, Calhoun presented white slave masters' dominion over them as an instance of paternal, not despotic power—a "simple, patriarchal" mode of rule, marked by the "kind, superintending care of . . . master and mistress," serving its subjects in tutelary as well as providential functions. "The Central African race," he claimed in the 1837 speech, "had never existed in so comfortable, so respectable, or so civilized a condition, as that which it now enjoyed in the Southern States." Slavery improved the master class, too, in Calhoun's argument, supplying the leisure and the sense of honor or distinctiveness requisite to republican virtue in its classic form. "The defence of human liberty," he asserted, "had been always the most efficient in States where domestic slavery was found to prevail."[33]

To those and like arguments abolitionists were quick to respond. How, they demanded, could one classify as *paternal*, ordered toward the care and improvement of the ruled, a form of rule whose subjects were addressed throughout their lives as children; who were commonly provided only the barest of material necessities; who were beaten regularly and on occasion murdered with impunity by masters or overseers; who were denied the opportunity to acquire any elements of the education proper to free people; who were likewise denied the opportunity to form legally protected marriages and families; and who were forced, through it all, to labor for others' ease and profit, with no opportunity to earn their own freedom and no hope that their own sacrifices would prepare a better life for their children?[34]

Such a mode of rule could be properly exercised only over beasts, not over human beings. The decisive question, whether slaveholders would admit it or not, was simply whether those enslaved were human beings. Thus Frederick Douglass, in what is often considered the greatest of all abolitionist speeches, asked: "Is it not astonishing that . . . while we are engaged in all manner of enterprises common to other men . . . living, moving, acting, thinking, planning, living in families as husbands, wives and children, and, above all, confessing and worshipping the Christian's God, and looking hopefully for life and immortality beyond the grave, we are called upon to prove that we are men!" And if the humanity of those enslaved be granted, Douglass continued, then so must the atrocity of slavery. "There is not a man beneath the canopy of heaven, that does not know that slavery is wrong *for him*."[35] Lincoln, for his part, addressed the "positive good" school with characteristic dispatch: "Nonsense! Wolves devouring lambs, not because it is good for their own greedy maws, but because it is good for the lambs!!!"[36]

Garrisonian abolitionists and proslavery partisans were images of one another in one crucial respect. Both viewed the founding as incoherent, perceiving a disjunction in principle between the Declaration of Independence and the Constitution—Garrisonians rejecting the Constitution as a betrayal of the natural rights principles of the Declaration, and advocates of slavery rejecting the Declaration and affirming a Constitution purged of its influence. Both therefore rejected the constitutional Union in which the Declaration and Constitution were understood to be in accord, and both rejected any constitutional Union that included the other. "Henceforth," Garrison thundered, "the watchword . . . of every friend of God and liberty, must be . . . 'NO UNION WITH SLAVEHOLDERS!'" Likewise Calhoun: "Abolition and the Union cannot co-exist."[37]

Not all abolitionists shared Garrison's scorn for the Constitution as a "covenant with death."[38] Douglass, himself an ex-Garrisonian, in his famous Fourth of July oration rebuked his erstwhile mentor by declaring, "The Constitution is a GLORIOUS LIBERTY DOCUMENT . . . entirely hostile to the existence of slavery." For Douglass, the Constitution accorded the American government both the power and the duty to abolish slavery instantly and everywhere in the country.[39]

Lincoln had substantial disagreements with both abolitionist schools. Holding the Constitution to be in principle antislavery, he disagreed with Garrison, and holding that the Constitution did not permit, let alone require, the federal government to mandate emancipation in any circumstance short of actual rebellion, he differed with Douglass. He disagreed with both on the prudence of demands for immediate abolition. For Lincoln as for the abolitionists, however, the Declaration contains the "father of all moral principle," and the crucial first step toward abolition was to cleanse the public mind of any notion that slavery was either a positive good or a matter of moral indifference.[40]

Just here, Lincoln observed, was the real issue dividing the country: one side "believes slavery is right, and ought to be extended, while the other believes it is wrong, and ought not to be extended." But "if slavery is not wrong," he argued, "nothing is wrong." Provisional compromise may have been conceivable and desirable, insofar as it restored the founders' policy (as Lincoln interpreted it) of placing slavery "where the public mind will rest in the belief that it is in the course of ultimate extinction." At the level of first principles, however, the conflict was irrepressible. The house was divided and could not so stand forever. There could be no resolution short of abolition and, after slaveholding states rebelled against the election of an antislavery president, no abolition without war. So the war came.[41]

The Question of Integration

The end of the long and desolating war brought also the end of chattel slavery in America, but it did not dispel popular fears and prejudices concerning the consequences of the Emancipation Proclamation. "Everybody has asked the question," Douglass observed in early 1865, "and they learned to ask it early of the abolitionists: 'What shall we do with the negro?'"[42] The question for the Reconstruction era was the question of racial integration.

POSTWAR ACTION AND REACTION: THE RECONSTRUCTION AND JIM CROW ERAS

The question was not yet *how* to integrate but *whether* to do so. Considered in light of the liberal political philosophy that pro-Union Americans generally affirmed, the question might seem relatively simple. Those enslaved in America had been brought here originally "by special invitation," as Booker T. Washington would gently remark, and forced to labor for the profit of their captors.[43] Their captivity estranged them and their descendants from their ancestral cultures and exacted from them a very substantial contribution to this country's material development. Those facts negated any argument for forced or induced expatriation, which depended upon severing the freedpeople's natural right to liberty from their claims to civil and political liberty in America. Does white Americans' natural right of association comprehend a right to compel others, previously uprooted from their homes and societies, to associate with them on grossly exploitive terms for many generations, and after that exploitation is prohibited, to uproot their captives' descendants again from the only homes they had known, the homes they had made in the captors' society, and expel them at the very moment at which their labors in that society might begin to bear real fruit? If it does not, then the newly freedpeople in 1865 had an insuperable natural justice claim to full integration into American society.

Douglass affirmed that argument to its fullest extent. The Civil War drew its meaning and justification from the cause of emancipation, he contended, and the Emancipation Proclamation entailed much more than the prohibition of chattel slavery. President Lincoln's momentous proclamation, he declared in 1862, "contemplates one glorious homogeneous people."[44] In his important 1869 speech "Our Composite Nationality," he maintained that America's true mission is to supply the most "perfect national illustration of the unity and dignity of the human family that the world has ever seen." Around the same time, he teasingly comforted his "Democratic [Party] friends" that the real author of the Fourteenth Amendment was their own Jefferson—meaning that despite Jefferson's doubts about racial integration, the logic of the Declaration of Independence yielded a promise that natural human rights could be secured, as the Fourteenth Amendment now provided, within a universally inclusive society. This, for Douglass, was republican government in the full and proper sense.[45]

Douglass saw clearly the magnitude and difficulty of the task. The endeavor to establish a country where "all nations, kindred, tongues, and peoples" could live together harmoniously, he remarked, constituted a "new experiment."[46] Disagreeing with Jefferson and Madison, who thought white Americans' antiblack prejudice so powerful that it "must be considered as permanent and insuperable,"[47] he yet agreed with Tocqueville that prejudice would intensify after Emancipation Day, both as a result of emancipation itself and also of the manner in which it was accomplished. Events in the postwar years confirmed that expectation, as he wrote in his final autobiography:

> History does not furnish an example of emancipation under conditions less friendly to the emancipated class, than this American example. . . . Liberty came to the freedmen of the United States, not in mercy but in wrath; not by moral choice but by military necessity; not by the generous action of the people among whom they were to live, and whose goodwill was essential to the success of the measure, but by strangers, foreigners, invaders, trespassers, aliens, and enemies. . . . [H]e is a poor student of the human heart who does not see that the old master class would naturally employ every power and means in their

> reach to make the great measure of emancipation unsuccessful and utterly odious.[48]

The postwar reaction Douglass feared commenced promptly during the Reconstruction era and intensified greatly after Union troops were withdrawn from the ex-rebel states in 1877. In a now-familiar story, northern whites and their elected representatives declined to enforce the Reconstruction amendments and the federal legislation they authorized. Blacks' rights, in particular the all-important rights to vote, to acquire property, and to receive due process in the courts, came under sustained assault by a combination of evasive manipulations of law and outright intimidation. Racially motivated lynchings multiplied, with the perpetrators generally left unpunished. What became a pervasive regime of segregation by race—in effect a domestic variant of expatriation—arose in the 1890s. The Supreme Court abetted the reaction in a series of rulings drastically narrowing congressional enforcement powers under the amendments. Entering the final year of his life, Douglass ruefully summarized: "The cause lost in the war is the cause regained in peace, and the cause gained in war is the cause lost in peace."[49]

Beyond the immediate problem of persisting antiblack prejudice lay a deeper problem inherent in republican government and ultimately in human nature itself. "Republics have proverbially short memories," Douglass observed in an impromptu eulogy of Lincoln. Americans after the Civil War, as with the Revolutionary War, would need to be movingly reminded of the principles for which it had been fought. "I am not here to fan the flames of sectional animosity," Douglass told a Decoration Day (later renamed Memorial Day) audience in 1878, but it must never be forgotten that the war was a war over first principles: "a war . . . between a government based upon the broadest and grandest declaration of human rights the world ever heard or read, and another pretended government, based upon an open, bold, and shocking denial of all rights, except the right of the strongest." In his last great protest speech, he called once more for Americans to remember the "advent of a nation, based upon human brotherhood and the self-evident truths of liberty and equality." He concluded: "Put away your race prejudice. Banish the idea that one class must rule over another," and "your Republic will stand and flourish forever."[50]

In the half century following his death, Douglass's legacy of agitation was carried forward most forcefully by the activist intellectual W. E. B. Du Bois, the Harvard-educated author of one of the most influential expressions of black American thought in the entire twentieth century, *The Souls of Black Folk* (1903). The statement of principles he composed for the Niagara Movement, a precursor to the National Association for the Advancement of Colored People (NAACP), which he would help organize a few years later, is animated by the same spirit of indignation, the same relish for battle, and the same demand that the country honor the founding principles that animated Garrison and Douglass and other great agitators in the antebellum and postwar periods. Presenting those principles in a 1906 address, Du Bois decried the disfranchisement, discrimination, and sheer intimidation that blacks were suffering all over the old South: "Against this the Niagara Movement eternally protests. . . . The battle we wage is not for ourselves alone but for all true Americans. It is a fight for ideals."[51]

Given the dominant state of mind among southern whites in the postwar and post-Reconstruction eras, Du Bois's campaign of agitation, like Douglass's, was destined for near-term failure. In a best-selling novel of the latter period Albion Tourgée, a prominent judge, equal rights activist, and a man intimately familiar with prevailing southern sentiments, has his protagonist address to an eminent northern-state senator this incisive commentary on the magnitude of the difficulty in the attempt to build a truly republican society out of a militarily vanquished regime of aristocratic or oligarchic injustice:

> You wise men who concocted these [Reconstruction] measures do not seem to have comprehended the fact that the brain and heart of the South . . . cast in their lot with the late Confederacy with all the self-abandonment and devotion of a people who fought for what they believed to be right. You do not realize that this feeling was intensified a thousand-fold by a prolonged and desperate struggle, and final defeat. You do not seem to appreciate the fact . . . that there is no feeling in the human breast more blind and desperate in its manifestations, or so intense and ineradicable in its nature, as the bitter scorn of a long dominant race for one they have held in bondage. . . . Hate is a sentiment mild and trivial in comparison with it. . . . [It is] a feeling more fatal to any thing [*sic*] like democratic recognition of their rights as citizens than the most undying hate could be.[52]

That witches' brew of antiegalitarian sentiment, as Tourgée and Douglass predicted, would take generations to dissipate. But as the early decades of the twentieth century unfolded, signs of renewed hope appeared, some from an unexpected source.

THE CIVIL RIGHTS ERA

The judicial department in a republic, Alexander Hamilton as Publius argued, stands as an "excellent barrier to the encroachments and oppressions of the representative body."[53] Yet in the infamous *Dred Scott v. Sandford* and in its restrictive readings of the Fourteenth Amendment, the Supreme Court seemed to act instead as a barrier to republican liberty. Those restrictive rulings culminated in *Plessy v. Ferguson* (1896), affirming the constitutionality, under the Fourteenth Amendment, of a Louisiana statute mandating separate train cars for passengers legally classified as black and those classified as white. The lone dissenter in the ruling, Justice John

Marshall Harlan, delivered an ominous prediction and perhaps also a veiled warning to his brethren on the Court: "In my opinion, the judgment this day rendered will, in time, prove to be quite as pernicious as the decision made by this tribunal in the *Dred Scott* case."[54]

With respect to the reputation the *Plessy* ruling would ultimately garner in legal and public opinion, Harlan's prediction proved prescient. It proved surprisingly erroneous, however, with respect to the career of the ruling as a judicial precedent. In a series of rulings in the first half of the twentieth century, the Court invoked *Plessy*'s "separate but equal" doctrine to invalidate state statutes providing for racially separate facilities, not to justify them.[55]

The culmination came, of course, in *Brown v. Board of Education*, in which the separate-but-equal rule in public schools was directly challenged, and the Court held that racially "separate educational facilities are inherently unequal."[56] The Court's conclusion in *Brown* is now almost universally approved, but in its near aftermath the ruling met with determined resistance by a southern racial oligarchy directly descended from the one that largely succeeded in nullifying emancipation. In that resistance, as in much of the history of the slavery and Jim Crow eras, we can see an illustration of a Lockean argument: whatever the commands of formal law, the rights of minorities are likely to remain insecure until a societal majority is moved to see and feel their violation.[57]

That Lockean insight held a place of primacy in the strategic vision of Martin Luther King Jr., leader of the civil rights movement, which commanded the nation's attention in the years immediately following the *Brown* ruling. King and his fellow activists knew that without the support of electoral majorities at the federal level, no victories won in court would stand. Their strategy of nonviolent, direct-action protest, invoking the moral universalism of the Christian religion along with that of the nation's founding principles, was designed to elicit the active sympathy of a majority acting through their elected representatives. It was in this important respect a Madisonian strategy, seeking a republican remedy for the disease most incident to republican government in America.[58]

Unlike their predecessors in the Reconstruction and post-Reconstruction eras, King and his colleagues succeeded in effecting a profound and remarkably rapid reform of American public opinion. This achievement would seem to vindicate the long-standing arguments by civil-rights advocates that race or color prejudice is not natural in the sense of being permanent and ineradicable. Further, by making such prejudice broadly disreputable among white Americans for the first time in American history, the civil rights movement seems to have settled the question that troubled the entire Reconstruction and Jim Crow eras—the question of whether America would be the cosmopolitan republic Douglass envisioned, securing equal rights for all, regardless of race, color, or national origin.

Yet, the settlement of the great question of *whether* to integrate did not mean a settlement of the subsidiary question of *how* integration would be enacted. The latter question has been at the center of race-related controversies in the United States for the past half century.

The Post–Civil Rights Era: The Ways and Means of Integration

The period commonly termed the *post–civil rights era* begins with the achievement of the greatest victories of the civil rights movement. In 1964 and 1965, Congress passed into law the most significant federal equal rights measures in American history, the Civil Rights Act and the Voting Rights Act, respectively. Yet for King and many sympathizers of the movement, those momentous victories did not complete the struggle. As President Lyndon Johnson expressed it in a landmark 1965 speech, "Freedom is not enough."[59]

The Civil Rights and Voting Rights Acts as originally framed embody a classical liberal conception of rights, in which rights signify properties of presumptively free, equal, self-owning persons or citizens,[60] and the proper practical effect of rights is to secure only opportunities to exercise various freedoms, not necessarily to achieve specific, substantive outcomes. For King, the enactment of those laws marked the end only of the movement's first phase; the work of the second phase was to establish a more expansive idea of rights, in which rights are properly secured or possessed only when their exercise bears fruit in satisfactory distributive outcomes. "Of what advantage is it," he asked, "that [the Negro] can be served in integrated restaurants, or accommodated in integrated hotels, if he is bound to . . . financial servitude?"[61] From 1963 onward, he urged Congress to enact a "broad-based and gigantic Bill of Rights for the Disadvantaged" designed to "guarantee a job for all who are able and willing to work" and an "income for all who are not able to work."

Tending to explain race- and class-specific socioeconomic disparities as effects of injustice, King considered such proposals requisites of reparative as well as distributive justice. "No amount of gold could provide an adequate compensation for the exploitation and humiliation of the Negro in America down through the centuries." Programs according "special treatment" for blacks are justified in principle, he argued, even as justice also demands compensatory measures for other and broader classes of the disadvantaged.[62]

Here arise the main controversies that roil the post–civil rights era. The aims of phase one, though achieved only after sustained protest amid much violence by defenders of the old order, became in a relatively brief period objects of a broad national consensus. The aims of phase two did not. In the wake of the civil rights movement, Americans in large majorities have come to affirm the principle of equal rights for all and thus to reject ideas of white supremacy and of any other form of racial or ethnic subordination. We continue to divide, however, over the nature of rights in general and over the use of race-specific measures as means for achieving full civil and political equality. I call the two main partisan camps in this dispute the antiracist Left and the antiracist Right.

The positions of the antiracist Left are, in its mainstream, the second-phase positions of King: rights are conceived in the social democratic mode as guarantees of substantive outcomes, and classifications by race, color, or ethnicity are permissible and even necessary as remedial and preventive antidiscrimination measures. For the antiracist Right, rights are properly conceived in the classical liberal mode, and distinctions among individuals by social identifications such as race, color, ethnic background, or national origin are presumed arbitrary and irrelevant in the assignment of rights and responsibilities. Justice in race relations, in this perspective, is best achieved by enacting the principle of "color-blind" or race-neutral equality under law. "Our Constitution is color-blind," Justice Harlan proclaimed in his famous *Plessy* dissent, and today's antiracist Right enthusiastically agrees.[63]

Each of the main parties in this dispute poses challenging questions for the other. Surveying their counterparts' positions, constituents of the antiracist Left ask: is it not cause for suspicion that the color blindness principle now commands the support of majorities of white Americans, at precisely the historical moment at which it serves their interest to affirm that principle—the moment at which race classifications are employed to elevate rather than to subordinate black Americans? In view of our long history of race-based injustice, is it not reasonable to institute strong, protective, preventive measures against persistent or resurgent racial discrimination? Is there not likewise a strong, principled case for remedial, reparative measures for the victims of slavery and post–Emancipation Proclamation racial injustice? Even if we grant the arbitrariness in principle of using race or color to distribute rights, benefits, and burdens, is there not a Lincolnian prudence in the use of such classifications as temporary, remedial measures?

Surveying the Left's positions, constituents of the antiracist Right no less challengingly ask: if we admire King above all for imploring us to judge others not "by the color of their skin but by the content of their character," then is there not a strong presumption that, in our public and private capacities, we are also not to *render unto* others by color? Would not the Left's advocacy of a temporary and remedial regime of race preferences inevitably evolve into a demand for such measures in perpetuity? Is it not doing so in fact? Would not the institutionalizing of group classifications tend to intensify intergroup grievances and animosities? Is not that approach to reform, bearing such consequences, clearly antithetical to the ideal of a color-blind America? Is not the insistence on color blindness or race neutrality in law and policy therefore a dictate of Lincolnian principle *and* prudence?

This very incomplete sketch of the challenges each side poses to the other may suffice to indicate the depth of the disagreement and the difficulty of the issues presently in dispute. Within the confines of the present essay, no thorough assessment of the dispute is possible, although the present discussion might help prepare such an assessment by inducing heightened self-scrutiny on both or all sides. In this vein, partisans of divergent viewpoints might find a measure of discomforting self-awareness in another acute observation by Tocqueville. "Every time that it has been a question of Negroes," the great French political philosopher noted, white Americans "have been seen to obey sometimes their interest or pride, sometimes their pity"[64]—implying that at *no* point had they been actuated, at least as local or national majorities, by any genuinely egalitarian sentiment.

Can we today say that we are so actuated? Tocqueville's pessimism notwithstanding, in the formation of the particular divisions representative of the post–civil rights era, the friends of equal liberty for all may find cause for hope.

The first two sections of this essay described an America riven by radically antagonistic principles: natural inequality versus natural equality, aristocracy versus democracy. By contrast, the central controversy over race in recent decades appears as a partisan dispute amid a broader consensus on equality and integration. Both parties venerate Martin Luther King Jr. and both claim to advance the fundamental principles to which he dedicated his life. At least by intention, in the post–civil rights era, to adapt Jefferson, we are all antiracists; we are, in the broad sense of the term, democrats. Fragile and incomplete as it may be, this is a remarkable accomplishment. To a degree not envisioned by the founders themselves, it is an impressive vindication of the country's pathbreaking experiment in republican government.

Conclusion

Recent interpretations of the history of race in America range between polar extremes. At one extreme is the view epitomized by King's remark (drawn from the abolitionist minister Theodore Parker) that "the arc of the moral universe is long, but it bends toward justice"[65]—charting the story of race as a grand, progressive trajectory moving from slavery to emancipation to securing equal civil and political rights and, one may hope, to fuller, more substantial equality and liberty in years to come. At the opposite extreme is the "permanence of racism" thesis,[66] yielding a nightmarish Afro-American vision of eternal recurrence—a litany of hope-swelling promises followed by protracted deferrals and even betrayals. Though the evidence weighs in favor of the more hopeful reading, in both these positions there is a useful lesson.

Considering the problem on the plane of political philosophy, the most thoughtful political leaders and reformers in our tradition disagree as to whether race, or racial division or subordination, is natural or historical, permanent or ephemeral. For Jefferson and Madison, racial differences or opinions about such differences run so deep as to be effectively natural. For Douglass, "Races and varieties of the human family appear and disappear" like the waves of the sea, "but humanity remains and will remain forever."[67] Humanity remains, one may add, in its unity and in its dividedness. All could agree with Madison that faction is the bane of republican government; that a propensity to faction is natural to humankind; and that race, the "mere distinction of colour," is somehow the most powerful source of faction among Americans.

America could serve as the world's crucial testing ground for republican government in part because of the uniquely propitious opportunity presented here, but also because of the unique challenge race has posed. America could glorify itself as the world's exemplary natural rights republic,[68] could fulfill its distinctive national mission as its later reformers conceived it, only by overcoming the singular shame of its career as the world's preeminent slaveholding and white supremacist republic. It could do this, its greatest political leaders and reformers agreed, only by rededicating itself to its first principles, the principles of natural, civil, and political liberty and equality upon which it was founded.

Yet, as we are prone by nature to factious division, so too we are prone to forgetfulness of our first principles. We are prone to forget the principles themselves and also the dangers that once fastened us, or our forebears, to them. For the philosophical fathers of liberalism, constant mindfulness of those dangers is a vital requisite for the achievement of such security and liberty as our nature permits. "Man is then most troublesome," observes that great deflator of human self-satisfaction Hobbes, "when he is most at ease."[69] We are most forgetful of the salutary admonitions of the state of nature when we are most at ease in our security or, perhaps worse, in the sense of our wisdom or righteousness. For all concerned to advance the cause of equal rights and free government, Locke adds, it is of the utmost importance to distinguish properly political power from both despotic and paternal power. To remain properly mindful of the state of nature, we must remember that its ills arise both from our despotic urge to vex and oppress and from our similarly natural and powerful urge to be godlike, paternalistic rulers providing for the needs of grateful subjects.[70]

The proneness of his fellow Americans to forget our first principles—our history along with our rights-bearing, rights-violating nature—was the careerlong concern of Lincoln. It was the concern of Douglass, too, who in his greatest speech excoriated the postfounding generations for betraying the revolutionary fathers and who, in the aftermath of emancipation, implored the lovers of liberty among his fellow citizens to remain ever watchful of "what new skin this old snake" of slavery or white supremacy might yet don.[71]

That new skin might be beguilingly race-neutral or egalitarian or benevolent skin. Americans of various, divergent persuasions have long been bold to claim "Washington to our father," as Douglass put it, or to believe ourselves distinctively faithful and favored children of Abraham.[72] Let us strive to make it so, he advised, but as we so strive let us beware of blinding, destructive self-satisfactions, whether born of interest, pride, pity, or zeal. In America's struggles against racial injustice there is genuine, heroic greatness, but the greatness is measurable only in proportion to the injustice. Our history with race teaches with distinctive clarity that we are capable of greatness and of great evil—and at times, of great self-delusion in confusing the two. Americans who sincerely claimed Washington to be their father were ready to destroy the republic to perpetuate slavery, and other Americans sincere in the same claim were ready to destroy the republic to provide liberty and equality for those specially aggrieved. As we labor to complete our predecessors' momentous achievements, we would do well to remember these things.

About the Contributors

PETER S. ONUF is senior research fellow at the Robert H. Smith International Center for Jefferson Studies at Monticello and Thomas Jefferson Foundation professor emeritus at the University of Virginia. He is the author of many works on the history of the early republic, including *Jefferson's Empire: The Language of American Nationhood* (2000), *The Mind of Thomas Jefferson* (2007), and *Most Blessed of Patriarchs: The Worlds Jefferson Made* (with Annette Gordon-Reed, forthcoming).

RALPH KETCHAM is Maxwell Professor of Citizenship and Public Affairs emeritus at Syracuse University. He is the author of many books, including *James Madison* (1971 and 1991), *The Madisons at Montpelier* (2009), and *The Idea of Democracy in the Modern Era* (2004). He is editor of *The Antifederalist Papers and Debates of the Constitutional Convention* (1986 and 2003), *The Political Thought of Benjamin Franklin* (2003), and *The Selected Writings of James Madison* (2006).

ALAN GIBSON is professor of political science at California State University–Chico. He is the author of *Interpreting the Founding: Guide to the Enduring Debates over the Origins and Foundations of the American Republic*, 2nd ed. (2010) and *Understanding the Founding: The Crucial Questions* (2007). He is currently working on a study of the political thought of James Madison, tentatively titled *James Madison and the Creation of an Impartial Republic.*

JAMES H. READ is professor of political science at the College of St. Benedict and St. John's University of Minnesota. He is the author of *Power versus Liberty: Madison, Hamilton, Wilson, and Jefferson* (2000) and *Majority Rule versus Consensus: The Political Thought of John C. Calhoun* (2009) as well as several journal articles and book chapters in the field of American political thought.

MICHAEL P. ZUCKERT is Nancy R. Dreux Professor of political science at the University of Notre Dame. He has published extensively on the American founding era.

WILFRED M. MCCLAY is the G. T. and Libby Blankenship Chair in the history of liberty, and director of the Center for the History of Liberty, at the University of

Oklahoma. He also holds positions as a senior scholar at the Woodrow Wilson International Center for Scholars in Washington, DC; senior fellow at the Ethics and Public Policy Center in Washington, DC; and senior fellow of the Trinity Forum. His book *The Masterless: Self and Society in Modern America* won the 1995 Merle Curti Award of the Organization of American Historians for the best book in American intellectual history. Among his other books are *The Student's Guide to U.S. History, Religion Returns to the Public Square: Faith and Policy in America, Figures in the Carpet: Finding the Human Person in the American Past*, and *Why Place Matters: Geography, Identity, and Public Life in Modern America.*

PETER C. MYERS is professor of political science, specializing in political philosophy and American constitutional law, at the University of Wisconsin–Eau Claire. He is the author of two books: *Our Only Star and Compass: Locke on the Struggle for Political Rationality* (1998) and *Frederick Douglass: Race and the Rebirth of American Liberalism* (2008). He is currently researching a book on the idea of color blindness in American political thought.

Notes

Introduction

1. Rogers Smith, "Ideas and the Spiral of Politics: The Place of American Political Thought in American Political Development," *American Political Thought* 3, no. 1 (Spring 2014): 126–136.

2. Of course there are two conspicuous caveats to this account, both of which are recognized by Tocqueville as important exceptions to his analysis in *Democracy in America*: the presence of the Native Americans and the early introduction of slavery. See pages 228–236 in this volume.

3. See page 43–44.

4. See the recent symposium on "American Exceptionalism" in the inaugural issue of *American Political Thought.*

5. The "c" is purposely lowercase here, referring to "constitution" in the broad sense as including both the political constitution as well as the society and its "mores."

6. This is not, however, to imply that the intended relevance of *The Federalist* consisted only in its application to this immediate context.

7. For an interesting discussion of this general point, see the recent symposium "American Political Thought and American Political Development: A Symposium," *American Political Thought* 3, no. 1 (Spring 2014): 114–176.

8. See Ralph Ketcham's essay in this volume (pages 95–111).

9. Although Locke had said "property" instead of Jefferson's "pursuit of happiness," Jefferson's more mellifluous phrase has a clearly Lockean pedigree.

10. See page 234. See also Peter C. Myers's essay in this volume (pages 265–283).

Chapter 1. Liberty and Equality

1. Thomas Jefferson to Roger Weightman, June 24, 1826, in Merrill D. Peterson, ed., *Thomas Jefferson Writings* (New York: Library of America, 1984), 1516–1517.

2. Thomas Jefferson to William Short, January 3, 1793, *Papers of Thomas Jefferson Digital Edition*, ed. Barbara B. Oberg and J. Jefferson Looney (Charlottesville: University of Virginia Press, Rotunda, 2008). http://rotunda.upress.virginia.edu/founders/TSJN.html.

3. Alexis de Tocqueville, *Democracy in America: Historical-Critical Edition of De la démocratie en Amérique,* 4 vols., ed. Eduardo Nolla, trans. James T. Schleifer (Indianapolis, IN: Liberty Fund, 2010). http://oll.libertyfund.org/titles/2285.

4. Ibid., 6, 10, 13 (see pages 13, 16, 17 in this volume).

5. Ibid., 875, 879 (see pages 31, 33).

6. Ibid., 873 (see page 30).

7. Ibid., 26–27, 77–78, 322 (see page 21).

8. Ibid., 22, 24, 75.

9. Ibid., 24 (see page 20).

10. Ibid., 26 (see page 21).

11. Ibid., 877 (see page 32).

12. Ibid., 26 (see page 21).

13. Ibid., 16 (see page 16).

14. Ibid., 19 (see page 17).

15. Ibid., 19, my emphasis (see page 18).

16. Ibid., 878 (see page 33).

17. Ibid., 20 (see page 18).

18. Ibid.

19. Thomas Jefferson to Henry Lee, May 8, 1825, in *Thomas Jefferson Writings*, 1501.

20. Tocqueville, *Democracy*, 75, 77.

21. Ibid., 6, 7, 9–10 (see pages 14–15).

22. Thomas Jefferson, Draft of the Declaration of Independence, in *Thomas Jefferson Writings*, 423.

23. Ibid., 424.

24. Tocqueville, *Democracy*, 6 (see page 13).

25. Jefferson, in *Thomas Jefferson Writings*, 1516 (see page 12).

26. Sam W. Haynes, *Unfinished Revolution: The Early American Republic in a British World* (Charlottesville: University Press of Virginia, 2010).

27. Tocqueville, *Democracy*, 74, my emphasis.

28. George Washington to Henry Lee Jr., April 28, 1788, in *Papers of George Washington Digital Edition*, ed. Theodore J. Crackel et al. (Charlottesville: University Press of Virginia, Rotunda, 2008). http://rotunda.upress.virginia.edu.proxy.its.virginia.edu/founders/GEWN-04-06-02-0469.

29. Minutes of the Board of Visitors, University of Virginia, March 4, 1825, in *Thomas Jefferson Writings*, 479.

30. Jefferson, Draft of Declaration of Independence, 423–424.

31. Tocqueville, *Democracy*, 187, 189.

32. Josiah Tucker, quoted in Peter Onuf and Nicholas Onuf, *Federal Union, Modern World, 1776–1814* (Madison: University of Wisconsin Press, 1993), 130–131.

33. Jefferson, Draft of Declaration of Independence, 427.

34. Thomas Jefferson, Draft of Instructions to the Virginia Delegates (manuscript text of *A Summary View*, July 1774), *Papers of Jefferson Digital Edition*. http://rotunda.upress.virginia.edu.proxy.its.virginia.edu/founders/TSJN-01-01-02-0090.

35. Jefferson, Draft of Declaration of Independence, 426.

36. Jefferson, Draft of Instructions to the Virginia Delegates.

37. Jefferson, Draft of Declaration of Independence, 431, 432.

38. Ibid., 424.

39. Thomas Jefferson to Edmund Randolph, August 18, 1799, *Papers of Thomas Jefferson Digital Edition*. http://rotunda.upress.virginia.edu.proxy.its.virginia.edu/founders/TSJN-01-31-02-0142.

40. Tocqueville, *Democracy*, 81.

41. Ibid., 9.

42. Ibid., 14, 15.

43. See page 25.

44. Ibid.

45. Thomas Jefferson, *Autobiography* (January–July 1821), in *Thomas Jefferson Writings*, 44.

46. See Tocqueville, *Democracy*, 81 (see page 26).

47. Ibid., 79 (see page 25).

48. Thomas Jefferson, Inaugural Address, March 4, 1801, *Papers of Thomas Jefferson Digital Edition*. http://rotunda.upress.virginia.edu.proxy.its.virginia.edu/founders/TSJN-01-33-02-0116-0004.

49. Tocqueville, *Democracy*, 1191–1192.

50. Ibid., 1193.

51. Ibid., 21, 22, 31–32 (see pages 18–19).

52. A Bill for the More General Diffusion of Knowledge, June 14, 1779, *Papers of Thomas Jefferson Digital Edition*. http://rotunda.upress.virginia.edu.proxy.its.virginia.edu/founders/TSJN-01-02-02-0132-0004-0079.

53. A Bill for Establishing Religious Freedom, June 18, 1779, *Papers of Thomas Jefferson Digital Edition*. http://rotunda.upress.virginia.edu/founders/default.xqy?keys=TSJN-print-01-02-02-0132-0004-0082.

54. Thomas Jefferson to Samuel Kercheval, July 12, 1816, in *Thomas Jefferson Writings*, 1402.

55. Thomas Jefferson to James Madison, September 6, 1789, *Papers of Thomas Jefferson Digital Edition*. http://rotunda.upress.virginia.edu.proxy.its.virginia.edu/founders/TSJN-01-15-02-0375-0003.

56. Jefferson, Draft of the Declaration of Independence, 423.

57. Tocqueville, *Democracy*, 876.

58. Thomas Jefferson to Joseph Cabell, February 2, 1816, in *Thomas Jefferson Writings*, 1380.

59. James Madison to Thomas Jefferson, February 4, 1790, *Papers of Thomas Jefferson Digital Edition*. http://rotunda.upress.virginia.edu.proxy.its.virginia.edu/founders/TSJN-01-16-02-0082.

60. See page 266.

61. Thomas Jefferson to John Holmes, April 22, 1820, in *Thomas Jefferson Writings*, 1434–1435.

62. Ibid., 1434.

Chapter 2. Liberty, Equality, and Constitutional Principles

1. Thomas Jefferson to Henry Lee, letter, May 8, 1825.

2. Aristotle, *Politics*, 1252b 30.

3. See page 165 in this volume.

4. Merrill Jensen, ed., *The Tracts of the American Revolution; 1763–1776* (Indianapolis, IN: Hackett, 1965), 402.

5. Recall Winston Churchill's famous observation that the American colonies had no philosophy of self-government except that of the country against which they rebelled. See Winston Churchill, *A History of the English-Speaking Peoples*, vol. 3: *The Age of Revolution* (London: Cassell and Company Ltd., 1956).

6. See page 38.

7. Jefferson to Henry Lee, letter, May 8, 1825; Thomas Jefferson, "Notes on Virginia," 1782, in Adrienne Koch and William Harwood Peden, eds., *Selected Writings of Jefferson* (New York: Random House, 1993), 204, 656–657.

8. John Adams, "Letter to Hezekiah Niles on the American Revolution," February 13, 1818.

9. John Marshall to John Quincy Adams, August 9th, 1831, in Charles F. Hobson and Joan S. Lovelace, eds., *The Papers of John Marshall*, vol. 12 (Chapel Hill: University of North Carolina Press, 2006), 96; John Marshall to John Quincy Adams, October 6th, 1831, in Charles F. Hobson and Joan S. Lovelace, eds., *The Papers of John Marshall*, vol. 12 (Chapel Hill: University of North Carolina Press, 2006), 97.

10. Ralph Ketcham, ed., *Political Thought of Franklin* (Indianapolis, IN: Hackett, 2003), 336–346; 387–403.

11. Note that those not considered for suffrage in 1787—women, slaves, blacks, and eighteen-year-olds, for example—were left out because they were regarded, anthropologically, as lacking the intelligence, moral capacity, political astuteness, and so forth required for public-spirited participation. All those groups would be included, under the political philosophy of the American Revolution, when perceptions of those alleged "disqualifications" finally dissipated.

12. Reinhold Niebuhr's more modern version of the same point is that "man's capacity for justice makes democracy possible; but man's inclination to injustice makes democracy necessary." See Niebuhr, *The Children of Light and the Children of Darkness* (Chicago: University of Chicago Press, 1944), xiii.

13. Melancton Smith, "New York Ratification Convention Debates," June 20, 1788.

14. Alexander Hamilton, "First Speech of June 21," New York Ratification Convention, June 21, 1788.

15. Smith, "New York Ratification Convention Debates."

16. Ralph Ketcham, *The Anti-Federalist Papers and the Constitutional Convention Debates* (New York: Signet, 1986), 336–357; Morton J. Frisch, ed., *The Selected Writings of Hamilton* (Washington, DC: American Enterprise Institute, 1985), 196–246.

17. James Madison, "Proposed Amendments to the Constitution, June 8, 1789," in Ralph Ketcham, ed., *Papers of Madison* (Indianapolis, IN: Hackett, 2006), 201.

18. James D. Richardson, ed., *A Compilation of Messages and Papers of the Presidents*, vol. 1, pt. 1 (Washington, DC: US Government Printing Office, 1897), 205–216.

19. Edmund Burke, *The Writings and Speeches of Burke*, vol. 2 (Boston: Little, Brown, 1901), 96.

20. Edmund Burke, *Thoughts on the Cause of the Present Discontents* (1770), in Burke, *The Writings and Speeches of Burke*, vol. 1 (Boston: Little, Brown, 1901), 524–525.

21. Jason Madison, "A Candid State of the Parties," *National Gazette*, December 22, 1792.

22. Ibid.

23. Koch and Peden, *Selected Writings of Jefferson*, 301–306.

24. Ibid., 259.

25. Ibid.

26. John Adams to Thomas Jefferson, September 2, 1813, in Lester J. Cappon, ed., *The Adams-Jefferson Letter: The Complete Correspondence between Thomas Jefferson and Abigail and John Adams* (Chapel Hill: University of North Carolina Press, 1987), 371–372; Thomas Jefferson to John Adams, October 28, 1813, in Cappon, ed., *The Adams-Jefferson Letter*, 387–391.

27. Thomas Jefferson to William C. Jarvis, letter, September 28, 1820, in Thomas Jefferson, *The Works of Thomas Jefferson, Federal Edition*, vol. 12. (New York: Putnam, 1904–1905). http://oll.libertyfund.org/titles/808#lf0054-12_head_066.

28. See "Preface to Debates in the Convention: A Sketch Never Finished nor Applied," in Adrienne Koch, ed., *Notes of Debates in the Federal Convention of 1787 Reported by James Madison* (New York: Norton, 1987), 3.

29. For the imperial origins of Madisonian federalism, see Allison La Croix, *The Ideological Origins of American Federalism* (Cambridge, MA: Harvard University Press, 2010), especially 132–174. Quote is from Madison to Washington, April 16, 1787, in William T. Hutchinson et al., eds., *The Papers of James Madison*, vol. 9 (Chicago and Charlottesville: University of Chicago Press and University Press of Virginia, 1962), 383. Hereafter cited as *PJM*.

30. James Madison, *Federalist* 51, in Alexander Hamilton, James Madison, and John Jay, *The Federalist*, ed. Jacob E. Cooke (Middletown, CT: Wesleyan University Press, 1961), 351. Madison later used the term "double security" in arguing for a bill of rights that would bind both federal government and states.

31. On the Fourteenth Amendment as the fulfillment of Madison's constitutional vision, see Michael Zuckert, "Completing the Constitution: The Fourteenth Amendment and Constitutional Rights," *Publius* 22 (Spring 1992): 69–91.

32. Articles of Confederation, Article V.

33. See James Madison, "Vices of the Political System of the United States," *PJM*, vol. 9, 351–352, in which Madison maintains that the federal system under the Articles of Confederation is best thought of as a treaty between independent states because it lacks sanction and coercion—the "vital principles" of a true "political constitution" or government.

34. Articles of Confederation, Article V.

35. Akhil Reed Amar, *America's Constitution: A Biography* (New York: Random House, 2005), 528n16.

36. Ibid., 58.

37. Madison, "Vices of the Political System of the United States," 348–349.

38. Ibid., 349–350.

39. "Memorial and Remonstrance against Religious Assessments," June 20, 1785, *PJM*, vol. 8, 295–306.

40. Madison, *Federalist* 18, 114.

41. Madison, "Vices of the Political System of the United States," 351–352.

42. James Madison to Thomas Jefferson, October 24, 1787, *PJM*, vol. 10, 209.

43. Madison, *Federalist* 18, 117.

44. James Madison to Thomas Jefferson, March 19, 1787, *PJM*, vol. 9, 318–319; James Madison to Edmund Randolph, April 8, 1787, *PJM*, vol. 9, 369–370; James Madison to George Washington, April 16, 1787, *PJM*, vol. 9, 383–385. Quotes are from the Washington letter at 383.

45. Madison to Randolph, April 8, 1787, 369–370; Madison to Washington, April 16, 1787, 383–385. See also the discussion in Lance Banning, *The Sacred Fire of Liberty: James Madison and the Founding of the Federal Republic* (Ithaca, NY: Cornell University Press, 1995), 125–126.

46. Madison to Randolph, April 8, 1787, 369–370.

47. For quote, see "Speech of 6 June: Popular Election of the First Branch of the Legislature," *PJM*, vol. 10, 32; "Speech of 7 June: Election of the Senate," *PJM*, vol. 10, 40; "Speech of 12 June: Salaries for Members of the First Branch of the Legislature," *PJM*, vol. 10, 49–50.

48. Madison to Washington, April 16, 1787, 383–385.

49. Ibid., 384.

50. Madison to Jefferson, October 24, 1787, 212.

51. Ibid., 214; Madison, *Federalist* 14, 83; Madison, *Federalist* 51, 353.

52. Madison to Randolph, April 8, 1787, 369–370. See also Madison, *Federalist* 14, 86.

53. See Michael Zuckert, "Federalism and the Founding: Toward a Reinterpretation of the Constitutional Convention," *Review of Politics* 48 (Spring 1968): 166–210, especially 194–196; Banning, *Sacred Fire of Liberty*, especially 164–166.

54. Zuckert, "Federalism and the Founding"; Michael Zuckert, "A System without Precedent: Federalism in the American Constitution," in Leonard Levy and Dennis Mahoney, eds., *The Framing and Ratification of the Constitution* (New York: Macmillan, 1987), 145.

55. See Madison, "Speech of 8 June," *PJM*, vol. 10, 41–42; "Speech of 28 June," *PJM*, vol. 10, 42–43; "Speech of 17 July," *PJM*, vol. 10, 80; "Speech of 28 August," *PJM*, vol. 10, 102–103; Koch, *Notes of Debates*, 542; see generally Charles Hobson, "The Negative on State Laws: James Madison, the Constitution, and the Crisis of Republican Government," *William and Mary Quarterly* 36 (April 1979): 215–235.

56. Madison to Jefferson, October 24, 1787, 211.

57. Ibid., 212; James Madison to Thomas Jefferson, September 6, 1787, *PJM*, vol. 10, 163–164. Italicized words are those written in the code that Madison and Jefferson developed to communicate confidentially.

58. See especially Madison, "Speech of June 30 at the Constitutional Convention," in Koch, *Notes of Debates*, 223–225.

59. Madison, *Federalist* 62, 416–417.

60. Madison to Jefferson, October 24, 1787, 210–211.

61. Ibid., 210.

62. Madison, *Federalist* 39, 254.

63. Ibid.

64. Ibid., 257.

65. At the Virginia Ratification Convention, Patrick Henry quipped that he was amused by Madison's "treatise of political anatomy." "In the brain," Henry continued sarcastically, "it is national: the stamina are federal—some limbs are federal—others national." Quoted in Jack Rakove, *Original Meanings: Politics and Ideas in the Making of the Constitution* (New York: Knopf, 1996), 162. See also the comments by John C. Calhoun later in this section.

66. Madison, *Federalist* 39, 256.

67. Madison, *Federalist* 44, 305.

68. Madison, *Federalist* 46, 320.

69. Madison, *Federalist* 51, 351.

70. See in particular Madison's late life restatement of *Federalist* 39 in James Madison to

Edward Everett, August 28, 1830, in Jack Rakove, ed., *James Madison: Writings* (New York: Library of America, 1999), 842–852.

71. Rakove, *Original Meanings*, 162.

72. Madison to Jefferson, October 17, 1788, *PJM*, vol. 11, 298–299. See generally James Read, *Power versus Liberty: Madison, Hamilton, Wilson, and Jefferson* (Charlottesville: University Press of Virginia, 2000), 25–53.

73. Madison, "Speech of 24 June: Ratification without Amendments," *PJM*, vol. 11, 176.

74. Madison to Jefferson, October 17, 1788, 297.

75. Madison, "Speech of 8 June: Amendments to the Constitution," *PJM*, vol. 12, 198–199.

76. In his famous exchange with Madison on the necessity of the Bill of Rights, Jefferson argued that written declarations of rights would put a "legal check" in the hands of the judiciary. Madison integrated this suggestion into his speech in Congress in favor of the Bill of Rights. See Jefferson to Madison, March 15, 1789, *PJM*, vol. 12, 13; Madison, "Speech of 8 June: Amendments to the Constitution," 207.

77. Madison, "Speech of 8 June: Amendments to the Constitution," 207.

78. Madison to Jefferson, October 17, 1788, 298–299; Madison, "Speech of 8 June: Amendments to the Constitution," 204–205.

79. Madison, "Speech of 8 June: Amendments to the Constitution," 209.

80. Madison, "Speech of 18 August: Amendments to the Constitution," *PJM*, vol. 12, 346.

81. Madison, "Speech of 17 August: Amendments to the Constitution," *PJM*, vol. 12, 344; Madison, "Speech of 8 June: Amendments to the Constitution," 202.

82. Madison to Jefferson, October 24, 1787, 212.

83. Madison, "Speech of 8 June: Amendments to the Constitution," 208.

84. The US Supreme Court affirmed this position in *Barron v. Baltimore*, 32 U.S. 243 (1833).

85. Madison, "The Bank Bill," 2 February, 1791, *PJM*, vol. 13, 372–382. Quote from 378.

86. Madison, "Consolidation," *National Gazette*, December 5, 1791, *PJM*, vol. 14, 137–139.

87. Madison, *Federalist* 10, 57.

88. Madison, "Virginia Resolutions," December 21, 1798, *PJM*, vol. 17, 188–190. Quotes on 189–190.

89. Madison to Jefferson, October 24, 1787, 214.

90. Madison, "The Origins of Freneau's *National Gazette*," July 25, 1791, *PJM*, vol. 14, 56–57; Madison, "Low Postage for Newspapers," January 9, 1791, *PJM*, vol. 14, 186; Madison, "Resolutions on Franco-American Relations," *PJM*, vol. 15, 76–80; "Madison's 'Helvidius' Essays, August 24–September 18, 1793," *PJM*, vol. 15, 64–74, 80–87, 95–103, 106–110, 113–120; Madison, "Political Observations," *PJM*, vol. 15, 511–534.

91. Madison, *Federalist* 49, 340.

92. See especially Madison, "Charters," *PJM*, vol. 14, 191–192. See generally Alan Gibson, "Veneration and Vigilance: James Madison and Public Opinion, 1785–1800," *Review of Politics* 67 (Winter 2005): 5–35.

93. Madison, "The Report of 1800," *PJM*, vol. 17, 303–351.

94. Madison, "Virginia Resolutions," 185–191. Quotes on 189–190.

95. The most forceful, recent restatement of this position is Kevin Gutzman, "A Trou-

blesome Legacy: James Madison and 'The Principles of 98,'" *Journal of the Early Republic* 15 (Winter 1995): 569–589.

96. Jefferson asserts the sovereign right of each state to declare federal laws "unauthoritative, void, and of no force." He also claims the right of each state to judge for itself "how far the licentiousness of speech and of the press may be abridged without lessening their useful freedom." "Jefferson's Draft of the Kentucky Resolutions," in Julian P. Boyd et al., *The Papers of Thomas Jefferson*, vol. 30 (Princeton, NJ: Princeton University Press, 1950), 536–543. Quotes are on 536–537.

97. James Madison to Jared Ingersoll, June 25, 1831 in Marvin Meyers, ed., *Mind of the Founder: Sources of the Political Thought of James Madison* (Hanover, NH: University Press of New England for Brandeis University Press, 1981), 389–393. See also Gary Rosen, *American Compact: James Madison and the Problem of Founding* (Lawrence: University Press of Kansas, 1999), 171–174.

98. Madison's veto message can be found in Meyers, ed., *Mind of the Founder*, 306–309.

99. Michael Zuckert, "System without Precedent," 132–150.

100. James Read, *Majority Rule versus Consensus: The Political Thought of John C. Calhoun* (Lawrence: University Press of Kansas, 2009), 23–52. Quote is on 47.

101. James Madison to Edward Everett, August 28, 1830, 842–852.

102. Madison, *Federalist* 10, 65.

103. Madison to Edward Everett, August 28, 1830. Quotes are on 849, 852, 851, and 844, respectively.

104. Madison, "Advice to My Country," in Meyers, ed., *Mind of the Founder*, 443.

105. See page 271.

106. James H. Read and Neal Allen, "Living, Dead, and Undead: Nullification Past and Present," *American Political Thought* 1, no. 2 (Fall 2012): 267–297.

107. See, for example, Robert Dahl, *How Democratic Is the American Constitution?* (New Haven, CT: Yale University Press, 2001), 17–18, 48–50, 141–145.

108. Ibid., 50.

109. Quotes are from Madison to Jefferson, October 17, 1788, 297.

110. Quotes are from ibid., 298–299.

111. *U.S. Term Limits*, Inc. *v.* Thornton, 514 *U.S.* 779 (1995).

112. Ashley Parker, "Boehner to Seek Bill to Sue Obama over Executive Actions," *New York Times*, June 25, 2014. http://www.nytimes.com/2014/06/26/us/politics/boehner-to-seek-bill-to-sue-obama-over-executive-actions.html.

113. Julie Hirschfeld Davis, "Obama Urges Congress to Fund Infrastructure Projects," *New York Times*, July 1, 2014. http://www.nytimes.com/2014/07/02/us/obama-urges-funding-for-infrastructure-projects.html.

114. James MacGregor Burns, *The Deadlock of Democracy: Four-Party Politics in America* (Englewood Cliffs, NJ: Prentice Hall, 1963).

115. See pages 57–151.

116. Alexander Hamilton, John Jay, and James Madison, *The Federalist*, ed. George W. Carey and James McClellan (Indianapolis, IN: Liberty Fund, 2001), 269.

117. Wikipedia, "Separation of Powers under the United States Constitution." http://en.wikipedia.org/wiki/Separation_of_powers_under_the_United_States_Constitution.

118. Madison, *Federalist* 51, 269 (emphasis added).

119. Madison, *Federalist* 47, 249.

120. Ibid., 250.
121. Ibid., 251–252 (emphasis in original).
122. Ibid., 252.
123. Madison, *Federalist* 39, 194.
124. Hamilton, *Federalist* 78, 402.
125. Madison, *Federalist* 48, 257.
126. Ibid., 256.
127. Ibid., 256–257.
128. Madison, *Federalist* 49, 261.
129. Madison, *Federalist* 51, 268.
130. See page 153.
131. Madison, *Federalist* 47, 251.
132. Madison, *Federalist* 51, 268.
133. Madison, *Federalist* 37, 181.
134. See Madison, *Federalist* 15.
135. Madison, *Federalist* 51, 269.
136. Madison, *Federalist* 37, 181.
137. Ibid.
138. Ibid.
139. Ibid.
140. Madison, *Federalist* 37, 181–182.
141. Ibid., 37, 181.
142. Madison, *Federalist* 39, 194.
143. See page 9.
144. See page 63.
145. See pages 108–109.
146. See page 102.
147. Madison, *Federalist* 72, 375.
148. Ibid.
149. Ibid.

Chapter 3. Liberty, Equality, and Religion

1. Ed Kilgore, "The Strange New Meaning of 'Religious Freedom,'" *Washington Monthly* (March 27, 2012). http://www.washingtonmonthly.com/political-animal-a/2012_03/the_strange_new_meaning_of_rel036324.php.
2. See page 181 in this volume.
3. Brian Leiter, *Why Tolerate Religion?* (Princeton, NJ: Princeton University Press, 2012).
4. Jacques Berlinerblau, *How to Be Secular: A Call to Arms for Religious Freedom* (New York: Mariner, 2012).
5. See page 182.
6. John Adams to Francis van de Kemp, October 2, 1818.
7. George Washington, Farewell Address, September 19, 1796.
8. George Washington to United Baptist Churches in Virginia, letter.
9. Richard John Neuhaus and Peter Berger, *To Empower People: From State to Civil Society* (Washington: American Enterprise Institute, 1996).

10. See page 202.

11. Philip Gorski, "Breaching the Wall of Separation between Church and State," *Chronicle of Higher Education* (July 30, 2012). http://chronicle.com/article/Breaching-the-Wall-of/133123/?key=QD91dQRoYXdAZX41Pj1BYjtcPSFrMB4nZXgcOil0blFREA==.

12. Statistics from Catholic Health Association of the United States. http://www.chausa.org/about/about/facts-statistics.

13. William T. Hutchinson et al., eds., *The Papers of James Madison*, vol. 8 (Chicago and Charlottesville: University of Chicago Press and University Press of Virginia, 1962), 298–304. http://press-pubs.uchicago.edu/founders/documents/amendI_religions43.html.

14. Jose Casanova, *Public Religions in the Modern World* (Chicago: University of Chicago Press, 1994), 4.

15. Marcello Pera, *Why We Should Call Ourselves Christians: The Religious Roots of Free Societies* (New York: Encounter, 2011).

16. Alexis de Tocqueville, *Democracy in America, Historical-Critical Edition of De la démocratie en Amérique*, vol. 2, ed. Eduardo Nolla, trans. James T. Schleifer (Indianapolis, IN: Liberty Fund, 2010), i, 5. http://oll.libertyfund.org/titles/2285.

17. "Quotations on the Jefferson Memorial." http://www.monticello.org/site/jefferson/quotations-jefferson-memorial.

Chapter 4. Liberty, Equality, and Race

1. Abraham Lincoln, "Address Delivered at the Dedication of the Cemetery at Gettysburg," November 19, 1863, in *Abraham Lincoln: His Speeches and Writings*, ed. Roy P. Basler (Cambridge, MA: DaCapo, 2001), 734. See also Lincoln, "Message to Congress in Special Session," July 4, 1861, in *Abraham Lincoln*, 607.

2. In Alexander Hamilton, James Madison, and John Jay, *The Federalist Papers*, ed. Clinton Rossiter (New York: Mentor, 1961), 77–79.

3. Thomas Hobbes, *Leviathan*, ed. C. B. MacPherson (London: Penguin, 1968), 267–268.

4. Baron de Montesquieu, *The Spirit of the Laws*, Book 5, ed. Anne Cohler, Basia Miller, and Harold Stone (Cambridge, UK: Cambridge University Press, 1989), chps. 13–14. See also John Locke, *Two Treatises of Government*, vol. 2, ed. Peter Laslett (Cambridge, UK: Cambridge University Press, 1988), 105–112, 175.

5. Madison, *Federalist* 9, 72–73; Madison, *Federalist* 10, 84.

6. James Madison, "Speech at the Federal Convention," June 30, 1787, in *Records of the Federal Convention of 1787*, vol. 1, ed. Max Farrand (New Haven, CT: Yale University Press, 1911), 486.

7. Abraham Lincoln, "Speech at Chicago," July 10, 1858, in *Abraham Lincoln*, 402.

8. Madison, "Speech at the Federal Convention," June 6, 1787, in *Records of the Federal Convention of 1787*, vol. 1, 135.

9. Alexis de Tocqueville, *Democracy in America*, vol. 1, pt. 2, ed. Harvey C. Mansfield and Delba Winthrop (Chicago: University of Chicago Press, 2000), ch. 10, 328.

10. George Washington to Robert Morris, April 12, 1786, in *George Washington: A Collection*, ed. W. B. Allen (Indianapolis, IN: Liberty Fund, 1988), 319; Madison, "Speech at the Federal Convention," June 6, 1787; Thomas Jefferson, "A Declaration by the Representatives of the United States of America, in General Congress Assembled," in *The Essential Jefferson*, ed. Jean M. Yarbrough (Indianapolis, IN: Hackett, 2006), 20.

11. See Philip B. Kurland and Ralph Lerner, eds., *The Founders' Constitution*, vol. 1 (Indianapolis, IN: Liberty Fund, 1987), ch. 15.

12. Madison, *Federalist* 54, 337.

13. Sherman and Ellsworth in *Records of the Federal Convention of 1787*, vol. 2, 369–371.

14. Thomas Paine, *The Rights of Man*, in *The Essential Thomas Paine*, pt. 2 (New York: New American Library, 1969), 227 (emphasis in original).

15. Thomas Jefferson to Roger Weightman, June 24, 1826, in *The Essential Jefferson*, 277.

16. For threats of disunion, see *Records of the Federal Convention of 1787*, vol. 1, 593; *Records of the Federal Convention of 1787*, vol. 2, 364, 373, 378; Pinckney, in *Records of the Federal Convention of 1787*, vol. 2, 371; Rutledge, in *Records of the Federal Convention of 1787*, vol. 2, 364.

17. Thomas Jefferson to John Holmes, April 22, 1820, in *The Essential Jefferson*, 254–255. See also Jefferson to Edward Coles, August 25, 1814. http://teachingamericanhistory.org/library/document/letter-to-edward-coles/.

18. See remarks by Rufus King, Gouverneur Morris, Luther Martin, and George Mason, in *Records of the Federal Convention of 1787*, vol. 2, 220, 222–223, 364, 370, respectively.

19. Tucker, "A Dissertation on Slavery," in *The Founders' Constitution*, vol. 1, 564; Jefferson to Holmes, April 22, 1820, 254.

20. Thomas Jefferson, *Notes on the State of Virginia*, Query XIV, in *The Essential Jefferson*, 114, 120.

21. James Madison, "Memorandum on an African Colony for Freed Slaves," October 20, 1789, in *The Founders' Constitution*, vol. 1, 552. See also Madison to Robert Evans, June 15, 1819, in *Madison: Writings* (New York: Library of America, 1999), 728–733.

22. Tocqueville, *Democracy in America*, vol. 1, pt. 2, ch. 10, 345–346.

23. Hammond, "Letter to an English Abolitionist," in *The Ideology of Slavery: Proslavery Thought in the Antebellum South, 1830–1860*, ed. Drew Gilpin Faust (Baton Rouge: Louisiana State University Press, 1981), 198.

24. See James Tallmadge, "Speech of February 16, 1819," in *Annals of Congress*, vol. 33, House of Representatives, 15th Congress, 2nd sess., 1204, responding to threats from the proposal's southern opponents: "Sir, if a dissolution of the Union must take place, let it be so! If civil war, which gentlemen so much threaten, must come, I can only say, let it come!"

25. William Lloyd Garrison, "Declaration of Sentiments of the American Anti-Slavery Convention," in *Selections from the Writings and Speeches of William Lloyd Garrison* (Boston: Wallcut, 1852), 66–69. See also Madison to Evans, June 15, 1819, 728–731.

26. John C. Calhoun, "Speech on the Reception of Abolition Petitions," February 6, 1837, in *Union and Liberty: The Political Philosophy of John C. Calhoun*, ed. Ross M. Lence (Indianapolis, IN: Liberty Fund, 1992), 474.

27. John C. Calhoun, "Speech on the Oregon Bill," June 27, 1848, in *Union and Liberty*, 565–566.

28. See James Read, *Majority Rule versus Consensus: The Political Thought of John C. Calhoun* (Lawrence: University Press of Kansas, 2009), 25, 243n5.

29. Edmund Burke, *Reflection on the Revolution in France*, ed. J. G. A. Pocock (Indianapolis, IN: Hackett, 1987), 7, 51–52, 67, 84–85; John C. Calhoun, "Disquisition on Government" in *Union and Liberty*, 5–6; Calhoun, "Speech on the Oregon Bill," *Union and Liberty*, 567–569. See also Aristotle, *The Politics*, Book 1, ed. Carnes Lord (Chicago: University of Chicago Press, 1984), ch. 2.

30. Calhoun, "Speech on the Oregon Bill," 568–569.

31. Ibid., 564, 569.

32. Alexander H. Stephens, "Cornerstone Speech," March 21, 1861. http://teachingamericanhistory.org/library/document/cornerstone-speech/.

33. Calhoun, "Speech on the Reception of Abolition Petitions," 474, 467, 468.

34. See especially Frederick Douglass, *My Bondage and My Freedom*, in *Douglass: Autobiographies* (New York: Library of America, 1994).

35. Frederick Douglass, "What to the Slave Is the Fourth of July?" July 5, 1852, in *The Frederick Douglass Papers*, Series 1: *Speeches, Debates, and Interviews*, vol. 2: 1847–1854, ed. John W. Blassingame and John R. McKivigan (New Haven, CT: Yale University Press, 1979–1992), 369–370 (emphasis in original).

36. Abraham Lincoln, "Fragment: On Slavery," (October 1, 1858?), in *Abraham Lincoln*, 478.

37. William Lloyd Garrison, "The American Union," in *Selections from the Writings and Speeches of William Lloyd Garrison*, 119; Calhoun, "Speech on the Reception of Abolition Petitions," 472.

38. Garrison, "American Union," 118.

39. Douglass, "What to the Slave Is the Fourth of July?" 385–386; Frederick Douglass, "The American Constitution and the Slave," March 1860, in *Douglass Papers*, Series 1, vol. 3, 340–366.

40. Abraham Lincoln, "The *Dred Scott* Decision," June 26, 1857, in *Abraham Lincoln*, 361; Lincoln, "Speech at Chicago," in *Abraham Lincoln*, 401.

41. Abraham Lincoln, "First Inaugural Address," March 4, 1861, in *Abraham Lincoln*, 586; Lincoln to Albert Hodges, April 4, 1864, in *The Political Thought of Abraham Lincoln*, ed. Richard Current (Indianapolis, IN: Bobbs-Merrill, 1967), 297–298; Lincoln, "Debate at Alton: Lincoln's Reply," in *The Complete Lincoln-Douglas Debates*, ed. Paul M. Angle (Chicago: University of Chicago Press, 1991 [1958]), 385.

42. Douglass, "What the Black Man Wants," January 26, 1865, in *Douglass Papers*, Series 1, vol. 4, 68.

43. Booker T. Washington, "Our New Citizen," January 31, 1896, in *African-American Social and Political Thought, 1850–1920*, 2nd ed., ed. Howard Brotz (New Brunswick, NJ: Transaction, 1992 [1966]), 359.

44. Frederick Douglass, "Emancipation Proclaimed," October 1862, in *Life and Writings*, vol. 3, 274; Douglass to Gerrit Smith, July 3, 1874, in *Life and Writings*, vol. 4, 306. See also *Douglass Papers*, vol. 5, 400.

45. Frederick Douglass, "Our Composite Nationality," December 7, 1869; Douglass, "At Last, at Last, the Black Man Has a Future," April 22, 1870, in *Douglass Papers*, Series 1, vol. 4, 253, 271–272; Douglass, "The Work of the Future," November 1862, in *Life and Writings*, Series 1, vol. 3, 292.

46. *Douglass Papers*, Series 1, vol. 4, 282–283.

47. Madison, "Memorandum on an African Colony for Freed Slaves," 552; Jefferson, *Notes on the State of Virginia*, Query XIV, 114.

48. Frederick Douglass, *Life and Times of Frederick Douglass*, in *The Frederick Douglass Papers*, Series 2: *Autobiographical Writings*, vol. 3, ed. John R. McKivigan (New Haven, CT: Yale University Press, 2012), 477.

49. Frederick Douglass, "Why Is the Negro Lynched?" January 1894, in *Life and Writings*, vol. 4, 511.

50. Frederick Douglass, "Our Martyred President," April 15, 1865, in *Douglass Papers,* Series 1, vol. 4, 76; Douglass, "There Was a Right Side in the Late War," May 30, 1878, in *Douglass Papers,* Series 1, vol. 4, 90; Douglass, "Lessons of the Hour," January 9, 1894, in *Douglass Papers,* Series 1, vol. 5, 607.

51. W. E. B. Du Bois, "The Niagara Movement: Address to the Country," in *W. E. B. Du Bois: A Reader,* ed. David Levering Lewis (New York: Holt, 1995), 367.

52. Albion Tourgée, *A Fool's Errand: By One of the Fools* (New York: Fords, Howard, and Hulburt, 1879), 148.

53. Hamilton, *Federalist* 78, 465.

54. *Plessy v. Ferguson,* 163 U.S. 537 (1896), at 559.

55. Andrew Kull, *The Color-Blind Constitution* (Cambridge, MA: Harvard University Press, 1992), 132–133, 143.

56. *Brown v. Board of Education,* 347 U.S. 483, at 495.

57. John Locke, *Two Treatises of Government,* vol. 2, 208–209.

58. Madison, *Federalist* 10, 84; Martin Luther King Jr., *Why We Can't Wait* (New York: New American Library, 1963), 15, 25, 33–40.

59. Lyndon B. Johnson, "To Fulfill These Rights: Commencement Address at Howard University," June 4, 1965. http://teachingamericanhistory.org/library/document/commencement-address-at-howard-university-to-fulfill-these-rights/.

60. Locke, *Two Treatises of Government,* vol. 2, 4, 6, 7, 27, 44, 123.

61. King, *Why We Can't Wait,* 135–136.

62. Ibid., 136–141; Martin Luther King Jr., *A Testament of Hope* (New York: HarperCollins, 1968), 158–159, 367–369; King, *Where Do We Go from Here?* (Boston: Beacon, 1968), 95.

63. *Plessy v. Ferguson,* at 559.

64. Tocqueville, *Democracy in America,* vol. 1, pt. 2, ch. 10, 348.

65. King, *Testament of Hope,* 252, 277; Theodore Parker, "Of Justice and the Conscience," in *The Collected Works of Theodore Parker,* vol. 2, ed. Francis Power Cobbe (London: Trübner, 1879), 48.

66. Derrick Bell, *Faces at the Bottom of the Well: The Permanence of Racism* (New York: BasicBooks, 1992).

67. Frederick Douglass, "The Future of the Colored Race," May 1866, in *Life and Writings,* vol. 4, 196; Douglass, "A Sentimental Visit to England," September 22, 1887, in *Douglass Papers,* Series 1, vol. 5, 267.

68. Michael P. Zuckert, *The Natural Rights Republic: Studies in the Foundation of the American Political Tradition* (Notre Dame, IN: University of Notre Dame Press, 1996).

69. Hobbes, *Leviathan,* 226.

70. Locke, *Two Treatises of Government,* vol. 2, 53, 92–94, 166.

71. Douglass, "What to the Slave Is the Fourth of July?" 366–369; Douglass, "In What New Skin Will the Old Snake Come Forth?" May 10, 1865, in *Douglass Papers,* Series 1, vol. 4, 85.

72. Douglass, "What to the Slave Is the Fourth of July?" 366–367.

Index